The
Berlin
Airlift

Also by Ann and John Tusa

THE NUREMBERG TRIAL

and

by Ann Tusa

THE LAST DIVISION – A HISTORY OF BERLIN 1945–1989

The
Berlin
Airlift

by

Ann and John Tusa

SARPEDON
New York

Published in the United States by
SARPEDON

Copyright © Ann and John Tusa 1988, 1998

Originally published in the USA by Atheneum, New York in 1988

This edition published in the UK in 1998 by
Spellmount Limited
The Old Rectory, Staplehurst, Kent TN12 0AZ

Library of Congress Cataloging-in-Publication Data available

USA ISBN 1-885119-56-9

Manufactured in Great Britain

10 9 8 7 6 5 4 3 2 1

Contents

List of Plates

All photographs courtesy of Landesbildstelle

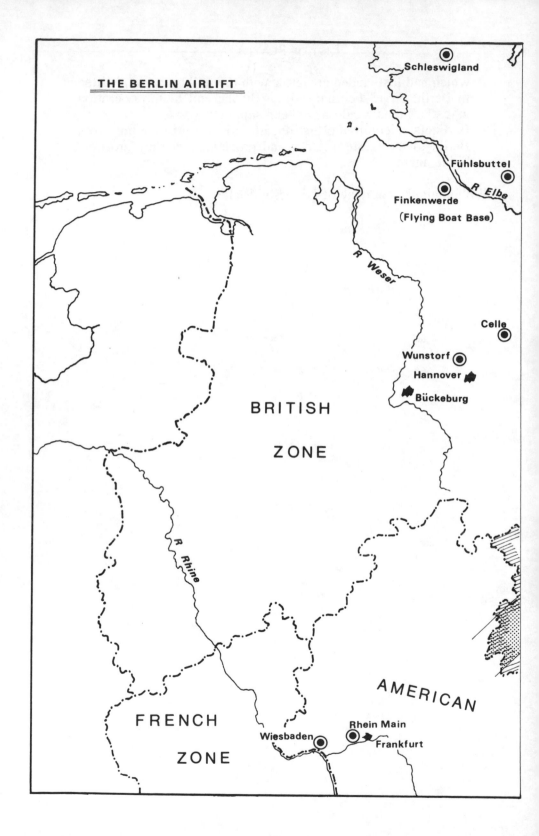

THE BERLIN AIRLIFT

Schleswigland

Fühlsbuttel

Finkenwerde
(Flying Boat Base)

R Elbe

R Weser

Celle

Wunstorf

Hannover

Bückeburg

BRITISH

ZONE

R Rhine

AMERICAN

FRENCH

ZONE

Wiesbaden

Rhein Main

Frankfurt

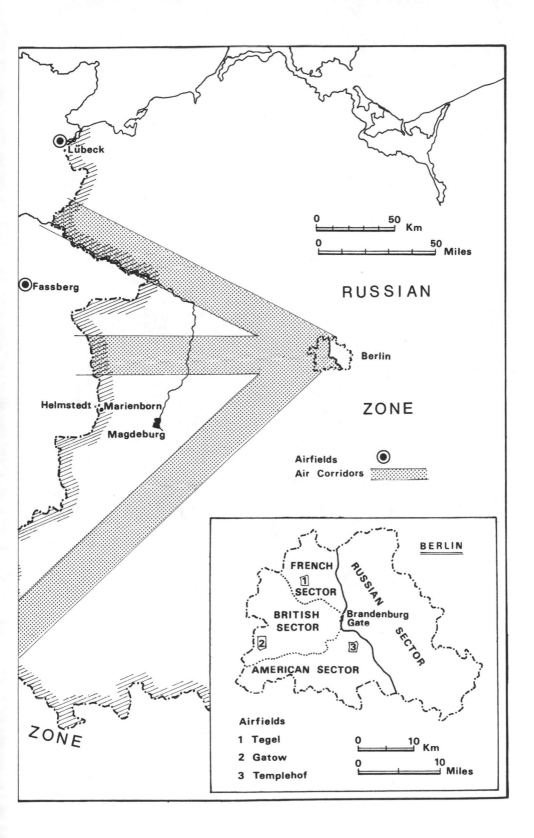

0   50   Km
0   50   Miles

RUSSIAN

Lübeck

Fassberg

Berlin

ZONE

Helmstedt   Marienborn
Magdeburg

Airfields   ◉
Air Corridors ▨

ZONE

BERLIN

FRENCH
SECTOR
1

RUSSIAN

BRITISH
SECTOR
Brandenburg
Gate

SECTOR

2

3

AMERICAN SECTOR

Airfields
1 Tegel
2 Gatow
3 Templehof

0   10   Km
0   10   Miles

Foreword

We are often asked how two people write a book together. The natural reply is that it is very hard to see how one person does it alone. J. B. Priestley said that though many people wanted to write a book, in practice very few had the discipline to stay in a room with themselves for hours at a time to produce it. Writing is solitary, taxing and isolating; it is far easier if two people share the problems of devising, researching and compiling – but only if they are of one mind about the subject and the approach. Fortunately we have never quarrelled about these essentials. During the four years taken to write *The Berlin Airlift*, holidays have been devoted to the travel that was needed; and while Ann worked on the book full time, John gave all the hours not spent at the BBC to his share of the work and took a three-month leave from television for uninterrupted research. Finally we understood why we can work together on a book with no more than the usual marital arguments: we take notes in an identical way so that either of us can gut a document and record its relevant points as if the other had done it, we have common historical values and the same black-humoured response to the material. This made the job a shared experience. Yet credit where credit is due. John wishes to record that the first name on the jacket is that of the principal author. Ann is satisfied that the second name has more than earned its right to be there.

A four-year journey into and through an historical event leaves the travellers with a happy burden of gratitude to discharge. In 1985 Dr. Alice Prohaska, then at the Public Records Office in

Kew, drew our attention to the fact that the British papers of the Allied Control Council had recently been catalogued and were for the first time available for study. We worked through them with growing admiration for the expertise and perseverance with which Dr. Prohaska had brought order to their chaos and made the researcher's task a light one. In West Berlin Maria Calder pored tirelessly and skilfully over the city newspapers and the records of the Magistrat for 1948 and 1949. Her local knowledge and efficiency made our final visit to Berlin particularly fruitful and comfortable. Berliners are exceptionally welcoming and helpful: we would especially like to thank the Senat and the Press Club for assistance and hospitality. The commanders of RAF Gatow and USAF Tempelhof were kind enough to allow us to visit these two key airlift fields and the British Commission arranged a tour of the old Allied Control Council building for us.

At the end of the book we list the many individuals who gave us their time, memories and often their own papers, and who went to enormous trouble to recreate their experiences to give us a better understanding of an event which took place fifty years ago. We hope that, at the end of it all, the account they read strikes them as accurate, but also includes details that enlighten or surprise. Very many more people responded to our requests for eye-witnesses to the airlift than we ever found time to see. We give them our thanks and apologies; by failing to take up the offers we and our readers undoubtedly have missed valuable insights.

Two minor points about the text. The spelling of German place names is inconsistent – "Hannover" but "Cologne," for instance – but was standard usage in English-language documents at the time of the blockade. The numbers splattered over every page refer to the sources of quotations or details which are listed at the back of the book. A few people may find these references of interest, a few others may even find them useful. Most readers would be well advised to ignore them and get on with the story.

This book was first published in 1988. In May 1989 we flew around the West Berlin boundary in a British military helicopter. The pilot showed us sections of Wall being replaced by link fencing. "It's cheaper than concrete" he said "and it will last longer". During the entire course of writing the book, no one suggested the Wall would come down almost before the ink was dry. The Berlin Airlift stands as a turning point in Cold War History. Its success in 1949 ensured that Berlin would ultimately find its freedom.

Introduction

On 31 March 1948 General Lucius D. Clay, the Military Governor of the American zone of occupation in Germany, sent a telegram from Berlin to General Omar Bradley, Chief of Staff of the US Army in Washington:

> Have received a peremptory letter from Soviet Deputy Commander requiring on 24 hours notice that our military and civilian employees proceeding thru Soviet Zone to Berlin will submit to individual documentation and also will submit their personal belongings for Soviet inspection.
>
> Likewise a permit is required from Soviet Commander for all freight brought into Berlin by military trains for the use of our occupation forces.
>
> Obviously these conditions would make impossible travel between Berlin and our zone by American personnel except by air. Moreover, it is undoubtedly the first of a series of restrictive measures designed to drive us from Berlin....
>
> ... it is my intent to instruct our guards to open fire if Soviet soldiers attempt to enter our trains. Obviously the full consequences of this action must be understood. Unless we take a strong stand now, our life in Berlin will become impossible. A retreat from Berlin at this moment would, in my opinion, have serious if not disastrous political consequences in Europe. I do not believe that the Soviets mean war now. However, if they do,

it seems to me that we might as well find out now as later. We cannot afford to be bluffed.

This message was not unexpected. It was frightening nevertheless. It announced a grave crisis in the relations between the four Powers – the United States, the Soviet Union, Britain and France – whose alliance had defeated Germany in 1945 and whose forces had occupied and run the country ever since.

The confrontation between the Soviet Union and the western allies continued for over a year. Clay was right: the Russians did, indeed, take a series of measures to drive the Americans, British and French from Berlin. By June 1948 the city was blockaded, and it seemed likely that two-and-a-half million Berliners would starve to death or be forced to accept Soviet domination. For a year the western Powers too faced a grim choice: either to surrender Berlin, and with it plans for European reconstruction, or to prepare for another tragic war on the Continent. Politicians and diplomats conducted dangerous manœuvres to avoid either terrible possibility. In that time they created a different Germany, formed new alliances in Europe and built up two opposed political and economic systems. From spring 1948 to midsummer 1949 Berlin was the hub of a European emergency and of European change.

The time to avert disaster and create security was found in an element which Clay had mentioned but whose potency no one yet understood: the air. In the air the western allies created what Berliners called a Luftbrücke, an airbridge, which carried food, coal, medicines and raw materials to beleaguered Berlin. This airlift brought more than supplies; it gave hope to the city and to much of Europe.

How the time was used, how Berlin endured the siege is the story of most of this book. To understand why the time was needed it is necessary to go back – to see why the four Powers were in Berlin and why the city was so vital to them all; why the western allies were so vulnerable to Soviet pressure; why some would countenance another world war to retain Berlin; why the West struggled to keep alive those who had so recently been their enemies; why Berliners would risk death rather than their independence.

The
Berlin
Airlift

Fumbling the Peace

From summer 1945 Germany was occupied by the four armies which had done most to defeat her in the Second World War – the Russian, American, British and French. For administrative convenience they divided the country into four zones and split the city of Berlin into four sectors – one zone and one sector for each victorious Power. Berlin remained the capital of Germany, but there was no German government; the country was controlled and run by the military government of the four Powers. In so far as they had common policies, these were drawn up in Berlin by the Allied Control Council, made up of the four Military Governors of the zones.

This much, but little else, had been agreed during the war. The allies who fought Hitler had seldom considered what they would do if they won. As the American Senator Arthur H. Vandenberg put it in February 1943: "We must not fumble the peace . . . but there are very definite limits beyond which post-war planning cannot yet go."[1] The British Prime Minister, Winston Churchill, speaking to a Joint Session of Congress a few months later, gave one reason for this reluctance to look ahead: "We must beware of every topic, however attractive, and every tendency, however natural, which diverts our minds or energies from the supreme objective of the general victory of the United Nations."[2] That victory was far from certain.

It is easy now for historians and armchair generals to spot decisive battles and to identify strategic turning-points when victory was ensured. It was not possible then. No one could feel confident of beating Hitler until his armed forces finally surrendered. Up to the last moment, every effort and resource had to be directed to one goal: winning the war. Decisions on what to do with the peace had to wait.

The four Powers had general aims in the European war, of course. France, like other countries conquered by Hitler, sought liberation, reparation for the degradation and pillage she had suffered, and adjustment of frontiers to give her greater security in the future. The British fought at first to avoid invasion and then to overturn Nazi domination of the Continent. The Americans were fighting to stop fighting. They wanted to end their involvement in yet another quarrel which was of European not American making and which consumed vast American subsidies. They wanted to go home as soon as possible and stay there. Their visions of the future remained broad and idealistic: a world won for democracy and liberal capitalism, which would flourish under a new world organisation created to settle disputes and prevent war ever again. The Secretary of State, Cordell Hull, promised Congress in 1943: "There will no longer be need for spheres of influence, for alliances, for balance of power or any other of the special arrangements through which, in the unhappy past, the nations strove to safeguard their security or to promote their interests."[3] The Soviet Union, by contrast, was often specific and practical. Joseph Stalin, the Soviet Generalissimo, made clear to the British Foreign Secretary, Anthony Eden, in December 1941 that he wanted recognition of all the gains the Red Army had made since 1939 – the Baltic States and part of Poland, for example.[4] His price for entry into the war against Japan in 1945 was to move into Manchuria, North Korea and Sakhalin.

Underlying their aims, the three great Powers – Britain, the United States and the Soviet Union – had interests which would prove incompatible. Britain was concerned with the defence of her Empire, the maintenance of preferential trading agreements with it, and her traditional search for a balance of power in Europe. The United States opposed imperialism, supported a free market, and saw old European diplomatic concepts as indefensible morally and a failure in practice. Yet Britain and the United States had agreed on a set of principles for the post-war world, the 1941 Atlantic Charter: no territorial aggrandisement by the victors and recognition of the right of liberated peoples to choose their own governments. That agreement, however, conflicted sharply with the ambitions of the Soviet Union, whose leader, Stalin, had neither negotiated nor signed it. As the war ended Soviet armies marched into Rumania, Bulgaria, Poland, Hungary and Czechoslovakia. In autumn 1944 Stalin explained to the Yugoslav communist, Milovan Djilas, the political consequences of such military deployment: "whoever occupies a country also imposes on it his own social system. Everyone imposes his own system as far as his army has power to do so. It cannot be otherwise."[5]

Though few were privileged with so clear a statement of Stalin's intentions, many suspected them. But there could be no confrontation with him while the war lasted. The alliance had to be preserved if the war were to be won. Could Stalin be persuaded to change his policies once it ended? Churchill increasingly thought not: Stalin might be bullied but not persuaded. President Roosevelt was more confident: "I can handle Stalin," he often said.[6] And he believed that an alliance with Stalin was essential in the post-war period. If a world organisation were to preserve peace, then the Soviet Union must be a full member of it. If Europe were to be stabilised and rebuilt, the acceptance and assistance of Russia were essential. If Germany's defeat were to be permanent, her military potential must be destroyed once and for all, and the Russians would have to be party to occupation until a new order had been imposed. Stalin appreciated all of this and was ready to play his part where it suited Soviet interests – in security above all. He prophesied to Djilas in 1944: "Germany will recover, and very quickly. It is a highly developed and industrial country with an extremely skilled and numerous working class and technical intelligentsia. Give them twelve to fifteen years and they'll be on their feet again."[7] But not marching, if Stalin could help it.

On one aim at least the three Powers could agree: their coalition would fight until it received Nazi Germany's unconditional surrender. President Roosevelt had been the first to call for it – in 1943, at Casablanca. His fellow leaders responded enthusiastically. All of them had lived with the consequences of Germany's surrender in 1918: the myth that the German politicians had stabbed the military in the back when victory was within sight; the constant danger that Germany would wreck the peace negotiations by refusing to accept their terms; the tragic process through which the Versailles peace settlement was turned into a pretext for Nazi power and renewed war. This time, said the allies, German surrender must be total. The victors would hold the country until it was fit for re-entry into the community of nations.

*   *   *

The allied leaders, however, were unwilling to consider in detail how Germany's institutions should be redesigned for that purpose. Subordinates in London and Washington struggled to draw attention to the need for long-term policies, but they were waved aside. Churchill, in the assessment of one Foreign Office official, was "quite allergic to any proposals for post-war action which he had not himself engendered, or at least discussed personally with the President of the United States."[8] There would have been little point in discussing Germany with Roosevelt. The President told his Secretary of State Cordell Hull in October 1944: "I dislike making detailed plans for a country which we do not yet occupy."[9] Stalin might have had plans, but he did not discuss them with Churchill or Roosevelt.

Yet there was one possibility which the Big Three did discuss during the war: the total dismemberment of Germany. The logic was simple: the unification of Germany by Prussia in the nineteenth century had involved two major wars (with Austria and France) and the ambitions of the new state in the twentieth century had led to two world wars. Never mind the scruples of historians and a few politicians: leaders and public alike during the Second World War blamed Germany for causing it. She must be rendered impotent and broken up.

The suggestion of dismemberment was floated by Stalin as early as December 1941, in his talks with Eden. Stalin wanted to rip out Germany's vital organs, all of which were Prussian and were tainted in the popular imagination with militarism. The Rhineland could be made independent (though areas might be given to France to provide her with a long-sought Rhine frontier); East Prussia could go to Poland and part of Silesia too (Czechoslovakia could take the rest); and with Germany more or less dead, there would be no reason why Bavaria should not be chopped off and become a separate state.[10]

Alternative schemes of dismemberment were considered in Britain and in the United States. According to a folk story, diplomats in London plucked out faded old German princedoms from the *Almanach de Gotha* in case they could be transplanted to a recultivated Holy Roman Empire. One policy committee recommended the creation of at least eight states. In the end the Foreign Office decided to decide nothing and to wait and see if spontaneous separatist tendencies emerged. Many officials in London, however, preferred unity. They feared that the Russians might cut off their own occupied area of Germany from the rest of the country, that the remnants would turn to the West and friction would be created between the allied powers. All too accurately some Foreign Office memos were warning by 1945 that the anti-Nazi alliance must devise common policies for Germany as a whole or else there would be a de facto division of the country, and perhaps even two opposed blocs in Europe.[11]

In Washington an Advisory Committee of Experts, set up by the Secretary of State Cordell Hull in 1942, advised against dismemberment on the grounds that forcible division would encourage German nationalism and aggression. That did not deter the State Department from continued musing on the subject. Should Germany be broken up permanently or only for a punitive period? How many states should there be – three, five, seven? Should the Ruhr, the heart of German coal and steel production and the centre of the armaments industry, be included or put under international control? By the beginning of 1943 the State Department was tentatively considering the creation of three German states, though it was still apprehensive that this might stir up aggressive nationalism. The Department produced a policy paper in July 1943, "H-24 – Germany – Partition," which presented all the arguments for and against. Hull decided against dismemberment.[12] For the time being, so did President Roosevelt. He merely recommended to Eden in March 1943 that "we should encourage the difference and diversities that will spring up within Germany for a separatist movement and, in effect, approve a division which represents German public opinion."[13] One wonders where some British and Americans got the idea that there might be such "separatist tendencies." Was there any evidence that Bavaria or Württemberg had stronger local patriotism than, say, Wales or Texas?

By the end of the war, however, Roosevelt had changed his mind. At the Teheran Conference (from 28 November to 1 December 1943) he talked of splitting Germany into five states and of putting the Ruhr and the Saar, as well as Hamburg with the Kiel Canal, under the United Nations or some other international body. Churchill preferred dividing most of Germany into five, then forming a confederation of the four states which met on the Danube. Stalin remained silent. The matter was dropped. The leaders gave up the leasurable diversion of drawing and colouring in fantasy maps and got on with the serious matter of winning the war.

* * *

5

Though the ultimate shape of Germany had not been decided and no long-term policies for governing the country had been agreed, the United States, Britain and the Soviet Union realised that a few basic arrangements for administration must be made before the end of the war. In Moscow in 1943 Anthony Eden proposed to his fellow Foreign Ministers that they should set up a clearing-house for all European problems connected with the war and its aftermath. The Soviet Foreign Minister, Vyacheslav Mikhailovich Molotov, and Hull, however, preferred to limit its brief: the European Advisory Commission (the EAC) was to stick to planning the terms of German surrender, the nature of the occupation regime, the instruments of control by the allies and the arrangements for the administration of Berlin – a challenging enough task.

The Commission was established in London at Lancaster House. It held its first meeting on 13 December 1943, then a series of formal sessions from 14 January 1944. There were three members – American, Russian and British. Perhaps there should have been a fourth. The British wanted a French representative and the Free French under General de Gaulle put in a request to join. They were blackballed by the Americans and Russians. Stalin was unwilling ever to concede any role to France. He had once suggested to Roosevelt that the victors should be a club of those who had contributed five million men to the war. ("Three million," Churchill had put in sharply.)[14] Stalin despised the French: they had "opened the gates to the enemy," and Pétain, not de Gaulle, was their true representative. Roosevelt, though less scathing about the nation as a whole, did have a strong antipathy to de Gaulle, and the United States did not recognise the French Provisional Government de jure until 24 October 1944. Only then was a French representative invited to join the European Advisory Commission. René Massigli arrived at Lancaster House in November bringing, thought Sir William Strang of the Foreign Office, "a welcome professional touch."[15] It came rather late to be of much use: most of the agreements of the Commission were already drawn up and Massigli could only witness them.

The American member of the European Advisory Commission, the ambassador to Britain John Winant, was remembered by Sir John Colville, Churchill's Private Secretary, as a "gentle, dreamy idealist, whom most men and all women loved."[16] He was a close friend of the Churchill family and enjoyed the full confidence of Roosevelt, though in his EAC role, as will be seen, he was not able to take much advantage of it. An acquaintance reckoned that

Winant was "hopeful and confident of post-war collaboration" with the Soviet Union, "though sometimes rather bewildered by the attitude of his Soviet colleague," F. T. Gusev, the Russian Ambassador in London. However, since Winant was a nice man, he "attributed Soviet intransigence to lack of familiarity" with Americans and worked hard to overcome suspicions.[17] Russian intransigence was familiar to Sir William Strang, the British representative on the EAC, from other dealings with Soviet diplomats including a pre-war mission in Moscow. He was less prepared for Gusev's insistence on keeping everything in his head rather than available on paper. He learned to live with Gusev's typical Russian habit of sticking out for a point for weeks or months then suddenly saying, "I have no objection," without giving any explanation.[18] Strang himself, soon to become Permanent Under-Secretary at the Foreign Office, was a professional diplomat of long experience in German affairs. He had been at Chamberlain's meeting with Hitler in Bad Godesberg in 1939 and head of the Central (European) Department of the Foreign Office with Germany as his main concern.

Strang was the only one of the three who could devote much time to the Commission's work – Winant and Gusev had their ambassadorial duties. He was also the only one who could act quickly – his superiors were on the spot for consultation. Gusev, on the other hand, had to refer every jot and tittle to Moscow, and there were long delays before he received instructions. Moscow was never famous for speedy dispatch of business, but in this matter Gusev's colleagues suspected that the Soviet government was delaying on purpose: hoping their bargaining position would improve as their armies advanced.[19] Winant was kept on a similarly short leash by Washington and responses were equally slow, but for different reasons.

Policy in Washington was confused and authority was divided. Throughout the war the State Department's activities had been restricted to limited matters such as economic warfare and post-war problems such as food, relief and monetary arrangements.[20] Roosevelt had virtually excluded his Secretary of State Hull from high policy decisions and from negotiations with his allies. The President kept these to himself or delegated them to the Department of War, which did not now relish the prospect of losing any of its authority. As a result the State Department did not have sole control of Winant's activities, for all he was an ambassador and engaged in diplomatic negotiation. They had to play second fiddle

7

to the War Department in a special liaison committee created to draw up Winant's instructions. Within this committee the Civil Affairs Division of the War Department (the CAD) acted, in the opinion of a close observer, like lawyers protecting their client's interests rather than as partners in a common purpose, and insisted that topics on the European Advisory Commission's agenda, such as the future zones of occupation, were a purely military matter to be decided not in London by diplomats, but "at the proper time ... at the military level."[21] In his negotiations in London Winant was that most hapless of functionaries, a servant with two masters, one of which – the CAD – did not want him. Because his masters, War and State, could not agree, he was often left without any proper briefing or instructions.

Strang, on the other hand, was fully backed by the Cabinet and Foreign Office and was well-prepared. At the very first meeting of the European Advisory Commission he put on the table a draft document for German surrender and detailed provisions for the boundaries of the future zones of allied occupation. Winant had been given no proposals of his own and no guidelines for discussing anyone else's. He had to refer to Washington. He got no reply. Gusev, however, was relatively quick off the mark. In four days he was ready to suggest alternative surrender terms and to accept almost all the British ideas for zonal boundaries. Gusev was so quick, indeed, that the American team wondered if the British and Russians had been getting together behind the scenes. No one had thought to mention to Winant or the State Department that this was an old territorial proposal, first put to Roosevelt by Britain in November 1943 and discussed with his Chiefs of Staff.[22] In early March Washington sent only an alternative draft of the surrender document, but without explanation or guidance. Winant had to wait until 8 March before getting any directive – and a brief one at that – on drawing the zonal boundaries. He would probably have preferred to do without it.

It was based on a small-scale map shown to the State Department by their rivals in Civil Affairs Division of the War Department the previous month. "Map" was hardly the word; it was more of a sketch of Germany with pencilled lines cutting the country into three segments. Once compared with a full-scale map, it was clear that the United States had been given 51 per cent of the population and 46 per cent of the territory, while the Russians got only 22 per cent of the area, population and resources. The lines slashed through existing administrative boundaries and communications.[23] The

8

border marked for the American zone stopped short of the Czech frontier.[24] In spite of protests, the CAD stubbornly refused to make any adjustments. This division, they said, "represented President Roosevelt's instructions" and was the settlement Winant must press for. The State Department was appalled, but after ten days of argument the proposal was forwarded to London.[25]

Winant was aghast. He sent members of his team back to Washington for clarification, and one of them, George F. Kennan, went to see the President. Roosevelt was not very interested; he was more concerned about who got which zone than where they were. When questioned, he remarked casually that the sketch was "something I once drew on the back of an envelope."[26] (Kennan was later told by an officer who went with Roosevelt to Teheran at the end of 1943 that the President had done just such a sketch to illustrate some general point he was making.) It took much argument and many cables before Washington finally agreed on 1 May that Winant could approve the British zonal proposals first put forward four and a half months before.

The European Advisory Commission now agreed that Germany was to be divided into three zones for military occupation by the United States, the Soviet Union and Britain. As far as possible the zonal lines would be drawn to give rough equality of population, area and resources, and to follow existing administrative boundaries. The members had discarded the British idea of leaving the country intact but interleaving the three armies and exercising joint control: the EAC foresaw inevitable clashes between military authorities, and confusion of supplies and communications.

The occupation zones were carved out within Germany's 1937 frontiers. The eastern zone (Mecklenburg, Pomerania, Brandenburg, Saxony-Anhalt, Thuringia and areas to the east) was to go to the Russians. The south-western zone was made up of the Saar, Hesse-Darmstadt, Württemberg, Baden, Bavaria and areas west of the Rhine – all the best scenery, the Americans were to say. The remaining zone (Brunswick, Hesse-Nassau, the Rhine provinces including the Ruhr, and everything to the north) had all the best industry.

This was the zone the Americans would have liked, but the British were determined to get it. Its attractions were obvious: easy access to vast resources which could regenerate impoverished, exhausted Britain. It could be argued, however, that the British failed to realise that such resources needed financial investment, management skill and technical expertise if they were to be exploited. Britain had

9

little of these; what she had would be stretched thin coping with her own post-war economy and the legacy of a run-down, nineteenth-century industry. But the dazzle of the Ruhr blinded her to these possible drawbacks and to the advantages of using American skill and capital to fuel a quick German recovery in the interests of all Europe, Britain included. Given this struggle between the Americans and the British over possession of the Ruhr, the allocation of the south-west and north-west zones was not decided in the European Advisory Commission but between Roosevelt and Churchill at the Quebec Conference in 1944, when the President accepted the land-locked south-western zone on condition that the Americans were given Bremen and Bremerhaven as supply ports for their occupation troops.

Within these three zones of occupation the EAC intended that the allied forces would exercise wide powers – wider than usually acceptable under international law. Having forced the surrender of the Nazi government, the occupation forces would take full authority over the state and use it to enforce disarmament, the demilitarisation of the economy, the denazification of institutions and the reconstruction of the country along peaceful, democratic lines. Arguments began over whether the Commission should go beyond these broad intentions and specify how they should be carried out. The British, on the one hand, produced a draft surrender document of length and complexity: seventy of its articles dealt with political and economic provisions for the future of Germany. The Americans preferred their own draft of thirteen short articles, all expressed in very general terms. This represented Roosevelt's view that it was better to wait and see Germany's condition before settling details of policy. The Russian draft had twenty-one sections, which revealed their own priorities. Only one article was concerned with how allied power was to be used in occupied Germany: it simply stated that the Germans must accept unconditionally whatever demands the allies might make. The rest were military provisions.[27] For the Russians the stress was always on military victory; its consequences would be beyond dispute.

Unable to reconcile such diverse approaches, the Commission took refuge in the rationalisation that vagueness about occupation policy would stop the Germans fighting on to avoid a harsh settlement. The Germans might well have taken the opposite view: better the devilish terms you know than the devilish possibilities you can only imagine. In any case, the insistence on unconditional surrender, first formulated by Roosevelt and Churchill at Casablanca in 1943, had already inspired a fight to the last.

The surrender terms finally drawn up by the EAC were, therefore, left short and vague. The German government and High Command should acknowledge their defeat and announce unconditional surrender. They must then accept a brief series of military provisions on ending hostilities and disarmament. Thereafter, the three Powers had supreme authority and could present their requirements in proclamations which must be carried out without question. (As it turned out there was no German government by the end of the war and the German army surrendered piecemeal; Supreme Headquarters of the Allied Expeditionary Forces [SHAEF] forgot they had a copy of the EAC's surrender terms so invented their own.)[28]

When the EAC came to discuss the means by which the occupation zones would be controlled both Strang and Gusev had drafts prepared, but Strang acknowledged that the Russian version was noticeably "simple and well-conceived and was the model on which the final text was framed."[29] The Commission's "Agreement on Control Machinery" was to establish Military Governors with full power in their respective zones. Gusev would have preferred to stress this zonal responsibility of the Military Governors. The final "Agreement," however, emphasised that their primary duty was to act collectively in the Allied Control Council and to reach common policies on such matters as the disbanding of the German armed services, disarmament, the eradication of Nazism, the return to a peacetime economy, and preparations for German government and administration based on democratic principles. Yet any chance of Germany being run as a single unit was wrecked by the Commission's proposal that all decisions in the ACC must be unanimous. The EAC seems to have agreed this with little hesitation. Perhaps reasonable prudence had been swept away by the atmosphere of the discussions on the "Agreement," which Strang described as "the most agreeable of the whole series," conducted "without acrimony and in a constructive spirit." By putting "unanimity" on paper the EAC did not create it. The Commission gave each Power in the Allied Control Council a veto, a destructive weapon whose use would prevent the formulation of common policies and bring fatal discord into four-Power government.

The EAC's blueprint for administering Berlin was equally doomed. Berlin had been the capital of Germany since unification in 1871. It was, therefore, the prime political target for the allies and, since it was long assumed that the city would be the heart of Nazi resistance to the invaders, it was also their main strategic aim.

The EAC's drawing of the zonal boundaries had left Berlin deep inside the designated Russian zone. The Commission had toyed briefly with a British speculation that the lines of occupation might converge on an alternative city – Leipzig, for example – so that a central military government could be set up in Tom Tiddler's ground.[30] But Berlin's symbolic and bureaucratic dominance was too strong. The Commission decided that the city must be the seat of the Allied Control Council and that it would have to be divided between the three occupation Powers into three sectors. It was proposed, however, that it would be administered as one unit by a Kommandatura of the three Military Commandants. Yet, as in the ACC, all Kommandatura decisions must be unanimous. Each Commandant had a veto. Deadlock had been built into the system – and, in due course, would wreck it.

How would the British and Americans get to their sectors of Berlin, maintain their garrisons and keep contact with their zones? The EAC did no more than sketch a few hazy lines of communication with the city by road and rail. A much more precise plan had been urged on the State Department by Philip E. Moseley, Winant's adviser. As he explained later: "I believed that the dignity and security of the American authorities to be installed eventually in Berlin required that provision be made in advance for free and direct territorial access to Berlin from the West."[31] He wanted a wide corridor under the control of the Americans and British through the Russian zone to Berlin. But his idea was never taken up in Washington. In Moseley's opinion, it was blocked by malign and short-sighted interference by the Civil Affairs Division of the War Department, ever anxious to keep civilians out of military preserves. Winant himself returned to Washington in May 1944 and raised the problems of access with the CAD. He had been constantly reassured by Gusev that there would be "no difficulty"; "of course" Anglo-American presence in Berlin automatically carried with it the right of access. Even so, Winant thought it might be better to get something in writing. No, said the CAD, nothing specific; how could anyone foresee what American military requirements might be? Who knew what roads would be convenient or even undestroyed? This, they insisted, was another "purely military matter" to be left to the soldiers on the spot.[32]

Winant had shown that he recognised the importance of the matter, but he had been overruled by the CAD; perhaps he felt he could do no more, given their attitude. He was certainly anxious to keep Russian co-operation and finish the work of the EAC; probably he decided to avoid a show-down over access. But his reaction whenever the matter was raised suggests he was ill at ease. Robert Murphy, Eisenhower's Political Adviser on German Affairs, was told in September by a State Department colleague, James Riddleberger, that when he put to Winant the idea of avoiding the access problem by redrawing the zonal lines as slices of a pie converging on Berlin, the Ambassador slapped him down. They had further clashes, during one of which, said Riddleberger, "Winant accused me of not having any faith in Soviet intentions and I replied that on this he was exactly right." Many of Winant's other assistants in London also tried to explain their anxieties about access. They always got the same reply: "The Ambassador does not wish to press the matter now." When finally in September Murphy insisted that a written access agreement was vital, Winant was decidedly tetchy. "You have no right to come along at this late date and make such a proposal just after we have agreed on a draft," he snapped. He told Murphy that this draft had only been possible because "he had established a personal relationship with Ambassador Gusev, after months of patient effort, and had gained the Soviet envoy's confidence." Winant would not hazard that relationship now and damage the chances of future agreements. He assured Murphy that the right of free access to Berlin was implicit and warned that the Russians "were inclined to suspect our motives anyway and if we insisted on this technicality we would intensify their distrust. He would not do it."[33]

Murphy would probably have got the same response from Strang, who also saw the maintenance of co-operation with the Russians as essential. Strang had been given no instructions on the question of access and had decided that the allies would get Russian permission to enter Vienna only if they wore kid gloves over Berlin. When he came to write his memoirs, with all the benefits of hindsight Sir William still reckoned that Gusev would have fended off requests for written guarantees of access to Berlin by claiming that this was a small matter for the military commanders to adjust at their own convenience. Furthermore, he argued that a written agreement on specific routes could have been interpreted as a denial of rights over any and all routes. But in spite of his explanations, the brutal fact remains that at this crucial stage the British and Americans did not take the opportunity to insist on guarantees of free access, for which they had a perfect right and every need. Even Strang was to concede that "the possibility of such an agreement did exist then, and perhaps only then."[34] Britain and the United States gambled on

Russian verbal assurances and continued co-operation – and they lost.

By an appalling irony, the British and Americans, who cheerfully trusted the Russians, did not have such confidence in each other and they conducted a long dispute in the European Advisory Commission about a different access question: how the Americans would get to Bremen and Bremerhaven through the British zone. In this case the United States insisted that they must have specified road and rail links and total control over them; the British put their foot down and refused any such guarantees. Echoing Gusev and the CAD, the British promised that there would be no difficulty over transit to the ports and that everything could be settled by the military on the spot.[35] Their verbal undertaking and allied goodwill proved entirely adequate. The British and American armies came to satisfactory arrangements and kept to them.

The military, however, made no attempt to reach an early settlement of the Berlin access question, though some individuals, having failed with the politicians, kept trying to convince the soldiers of the need for one. When Murphy raised the matter at allied headquarters, neither General Eisenhower nor his staff was interested. The war still had to be won and in its final months, in Murphy's judgment, Eisenhower "consistently differentiated between decisions which had to be made before the surrender – which he regarded as military matters which directly concerned him – and decisions which were to go into effect after the surrender – primarily political and diplomatic business."[36] The General was acting on a sound liberal military principle: fighting is for soldiers, policy is for politicians. The politicians had so far shirked too many of the decisions needed for coping with the consequences of eventual German surrender.

The Big Three – Roosevelt, Stalin and Churchill – failed yet again to address adequately many fundamental German problems when they met in full conference with their diplomatic staffs and Foreign Ministers at Yalta in the Crimea from 4 to 11 February 1945.

The old leaders of the wartime alliance were coming together for the last time. President Roosevelt would be dead in two months. He was already clearly ill. The official explanation was that the President was suffering from a bad cold and infected sinuses, but many people suspected his condition was more grave. It was noticeable that he had been too unwell to do much preparation for the conference.[37] Churchill would be replaced as Prime Minister later in the year after losing a general election. Only Stalin would survive to loom over the peace of Europe. Here, at the conference, he seemed to have the greatest natural authority of the three, for all that he said little and waited until discussions were nearly over before putting forward quiet, seemingly reasonable suggestions.[38]

Roosevelt had come to Yalta with two aims: to get the Soviet Union's help in the war against Japan and its acceptance of his proposals for the structure of the United Nations. He got both, a result he saw as a diplomatic triumph and a sign of Russian goodwill. He now had renewed confidence that by maintaining partnership with the Russians in peace as well as in war, there would be ample opportunity to influence and restrain them. Roosevelt certainly sensed the range of Soviet ambition and foresaw that Russian armies would attempt to impose Soviet domination over the countries through which they advanced to Germany. But he told Hull there was no point in protesting at this stage: the western Powers could do nothing to contain the Soviet Union as yet, and preservation of the alliance was paramount.[39] Instead of confronting the Russians at Yalta, he encouraged Stalin to join him in sniping at Churchill over British imperialism.

This must have been galling for Churchill. He was deeply anxious about the rapidity of Russian military advance and filled with forebodings about Stalin's own imperialistic intentions. He had no faith in Roosevelt's cherished United Nations as a World Instrument for Peace, nor any hope for European peace if Nazi hegemony were replaced by Soviet domination. He knew that the smaller states were powerless and Britain alone was too weak to check Russian expansion. That needed American force. He soon learned it would not be available. Roosevelt announced at Yalta that his troops would stay in Europe for no more than two years after victory.

What delightful news this must have been for Stalin. He certainly wanted an American presence for a while to smash German military might and to force the delivery of reparations to his devastated country. Thereafter, he would welcome American departure. The Soviet Union would then be the only Power in Europe, finding security in a bastion of satellites, consolidating her gains and perhaps adding to them.

Though the views of the three leaders at Yalta diverged, they preserved an image of unity by imposing on themselves a punishing discipline of public smiles, backslapping and feasting. Russian hospitality was lavish, but demanding. There were thirty-eight standing toasts at one dinner (the worldly-wise who watered their vodka presumably still found it hard to stand by the end). Even sitting was not very comfortable – mosquitoes attacked the ankles.[40] It was some help to the head and liver that the daily plenary sessions did not start until 4 p.m.

The talks ranged over a wide area of European problems. As far as Germany was concerned, the Big Three could at least agree to destroy militarism and Nazism. Their final communiqué stressed that it "is not our purpose to destroy the people of Germany," but that "only when Nazism and militarism have been extirpated will there be hope for a decent life for Germans and a place for them in the comity of nations." As a German nation state?

The proposal of dismemberment was revived by Stalin on 5 February; Roosevelt agreed that it was desirable, but one observer thought he was "just giving lip service to a dying idea."[41] Later the President told officials to "study and postpone" a final decision. During the talks Churchill seemed to agree to the principle of breaking up Germany, but in fact he was coming to believe that a united country might be needed by western Europe as a buffer against the Soviet Union. Six weeks after Yalta he was to say: "I hardly like to consider dismemberment until my doubts about Russian intentions have been cleared away."[42] Though Stalin himself had raised the topic, he too must already have been abandoning the idea. On 9 May, without consulting his allies, he issued a message to the German people: "the Soviet Union has no intention of dismembering or destroying Germany."

A strong motive for the Russians' interest in German unity was surely their wish for reparations. They might calculate that the Soviet Union could feed better on the milk from a large cow than on a butchered carcase. At Yalta Stalin asked for $10 billion worth of reparations out of a total of $20 billion. The British wanted reparations too, though they accepted that they deserved less than the Soviet Union, because they had made a smaller contribution to the war and had suffered less destruction in the process. Churchill and Roosevelt, however, preferred not to fix any sums until the capacity of German industry was examined, and the Americans were anxious to avoid a repetition of the reparations farce after the last war when the United States had poured loans into Germany so that others could siphon off their dues. Even so, a secret protocol was agreed: reparations would be paid to those who had carried "the main burden of the war" and "suffered the heaviest losses." These reparations would be in three categories: for two years the allies would remove industrial equipment, machine-tools, ships, rolling-stock, foreign investments and shares in German industrial and transport enterprises and, in so doing, destroy war potential; every year for an unspecified period they would take deliveries from current production; for another undefined period they would use German labour in reconstruction. The protocol did not give any figures or sum total: a committee must first study Germany's ability to pay. However, Roosevelt had unguardedly suggested that it might take Stalin's figures of $20 billion as "a basis for discussion." Stalin took the figure as much more: a promise, and a promise he intended to have honoured.

The three leaders ratified the European Advisory Commission's drafts on occupation zones, the Allied Control Council and the sectors of Berlin, seemingly without alarm at their inadequacies and dangers. They did, however, stumble on a new difficulty: should France be invited to share in the occupation of Germany? Stalin thought not, for all his usual reasons. Roosevelt was reluctant to add another Power in case all the lesser allies then demanded a share too. Churchill, on the other hand, pressed hard for the inclusion of France. The British had always wanted to spread the burden of occupation. Now that the United States threatened to leave Europe within two years, it seemed that there would be no Power on the Continent to balance the Soviet Union; Churchill was, therefore, anxious to bolster Britain's position with French support. He at last persuaded his colleagues to give France a zone. Even so, Stalin resolutely refused to allow her any of the territory earmarked for the Soviet Union. The French zone would have to be carved out of the American and British areas by the EAC. Though Stalin and Roosevelt both conceded the French a role in occupation, they held out against France joining the Allied Control Council. It took an alliance of Churchill and Harry Hopkins (the presidential adviser) to convince Roosevelt that this was illogical. Once the President capitulated, Stalin simply raised his arms in the air: "I surrender."[43]

The gift of a zone drew no thanks from the French. General de Gaulle was already sulking – resentful of his country's lack of influence in the councils of war, sour at not being invited to Yalta and hurt that Roosevelt had not visited him on the way there. The gift only made him sulk the more: he had not been consulted about it. He now refused to play any part while the European Advisory Commission drew the boundaries of the French zone.[44] This might seem like taking a slice off his nose to spite his face, but de Gaulle had a very long and very proud nose. His pride and complexes were shared by his compatriots. The other leaders would rue the day they had offended France; the other Military Governors of Germany would lament that France had ever been asked to share the occupation.

The decisions on Germany taken at Yalta were not happy; many of them created more problems than they solved. Too many aspects of long-term policy for governing occupied Germany had been brushed under the carpet; all contentious matters had been avoided for fear of damaging the alliance. Significantly, the question of Anglo-American access to Berlin had not even been mentioned. Given the failures of the politicians, the realities of post-war Germany were in fact settled by the armies advancing across Germany's frontiers. Crucial among them was the fate of Berlin.

2

Who Is Going to Take Berlin?

Germany's frontiers were first breached in the east, in the second week of January 1945, by the Red Army. Marshal Koniev fought through the gap and on to German soil. By the end of the month another deep salient, established by Marshal Zhukov, brought the Russians to within forty-eight miles of Berlin. Sheer momentum, Zhukov thought, might now carry him to the city. But the speed of the thrust seems to have taken Stalin by surprise; perhaps, suspicious as ever, he could not believe his luck. He did not give the order to advance. Instead, he claimed that the German army was not as vulnerable as it appeared, insisted on building up his own forces and turned the main attack to Upper Silesia and the Baltic. While Zhukov champed at the bit and Stalin preached caution, German reinforcements arrived on the eastern front and strengthened the defences of Berlin.

In the west the allies had lagged behind. They had been held up and badly mauled by a daring German counter-offensive in the Ardennes in December 1944. Though the German army then dug in on its last major defensive line, the steep east bank of the Rhine, an American patrol on 7 March found one bridge intact at Remagen. Within eighteen days the entire Allied Expeditionary Force had crossed the river. It advanced against weakened opposition and enveloped the Ruhr. German troops began to surrender in their thousands – knowing the war was over and preferring a western prisoner-of-war camp to transfer to the Russian front. By the end of March 1945 the western allies were 200 miles from Berlin, but their way was open; the Russians were only thirty-five miles away, but they were being hammered by ferocious German resistance – and Stalin had still not ordered a full assault on the German capital.

Field Marshal Montgomery on the allied northern flank wanted to push on to Berlin. He was convinced he could get there; others were not. At Supreme Headquarters of the Allied Expeditionary Forces there was some appreciation of his great military talents, but there was also a feeling that "if anything was to be done quickly, don't give it to Monty ... Monty would have needed at least six months to prepare an attack on Berlin."[1] Eisenhower's respect for Montgomery was balanced by his irritation at the Field Marshal's prima donna behaviour and arrogance towards American generals; he would not have been pleased to see Berlin fall to Monty. Real strategic considerations rather than personal pique, however, governed Eisenhower's decision on where his next move should be. SHAEF estimated, perhaps wrongly, that the capture of Berlin would cost up to 100,000 casualties. Given the confirmation at Yalta of the future Soviet zone of occupation, such losses were, as General Bradley argued, a "pretty stiff price to pay for a prestige objective, especially when we've got to fall back and let the other fellow take over."[2] Eisenhower agreed with him: "Why should we endanger the life of a single American or British soldier to capture areas we soon will be handing over to the Russians?" he kept saying at staff meetings.[3] And he ceased to see Berlin as his major strategic target. He came to believe intelligence reports that Hitler would order a last stand in the southern mountains round Berchtesgaden; it might be better to direct the bulk of allied forces there. Either way – Berlin or Berchtesgaden – it made sense to meet the Red Army as soon as possible and to forge an axis on which they could all turn north or south as required. The shortest line to meet the Russians ended at Dresden, which faced Eisenhower's centre under the command of the estimable, dependable General Omar Bradley. The centre must make the main thrust.

On 28 March General Eisenhower, without thinking it necessary to consult his allies or Washington, sent a telegram to Stalin suggesting that their armies meet at Dresden. One can only suppose that he thought contact with a self-styled Generalissimo was a purely military matter. Eisenhower, the non-political soldier, seemed unaware that he was making a fundamentally political approach to a man for whom everything was political. Stalin's response was warm, approving and mendacious: Dresden was an excellent meeting-place, he replied, and Berlin had indeed lost its former strategic importance – which was why the Red Army was allocating only secondary forces to it.[4]

When the British learned of Eisenhower's telegram, they were outraged. They protested to General George C. Marshall, the American Chief of Staff, about the disregard for Berlin and Eisenhower's unilateral negotiation with Stalin. On 31 March Churchill urged Eisenhower to advance as far east as possible lest the Russians capture both Berlin and Vienna: "If we deliberately leave Berlin to them ... the double event may strengthen their conviction, already apparent, that they have done everything" to beat Hitler. British complaints, however, served only to stoke American determination. Washington was fully persuaded by Eisenhower's strategic reasoning and resented criticism of their outstandingly successful commander. Churchill was sensitive to this reaction and concerned not to damage the alliance at such a crucial moment. He wrote a paean of praise of Eisenhower to President Roosevelt (copy to the General), but even so repeated: "I deem it highly important that we should shake hands with the Russians as far to the east as possible."

This political crisis between the allies was clearly distressing to Eisenhower. He wrote to Marshall on 7 April insisting that his decision to leave Berlin and concentrate on Dresden was made on purely military grounds and for the best of military reasons. "I am the first to admit that war is waged in pursuance of political aims," he told Marshall, "and if the combined Chiefs of Staff should decide that the Allied effort to take Berlin outweighs purely military considerations in this theatre, I would cheerfully readjust my plans and my thinking so as to carry out such an operation." But the Combined Chiefs did not make that decision; no new directive was sent to Eisenhower. The order to attack Berlin was given by Stalin to the Red Army.

Patently Stalin had already decided on it when he gave his baited answer to Eisenhower on 28 March. On 1 April he held a conference in Moscow with Marshals Koniev and Zhukov and his military advisers. In spite of what Eisenhower had revealed of SHAEF thinking, this conference was solemnly assured that the Anglo-American forces were about to mount an offensive on Berlin and that Montgomery was taking command. Stalin, having goaded his men, gave the last touch of the spur. "Well now," he asked, "who is going to take Berlin? Will we or the Allies?"[5] His question was the signal for a race to Berlin – not between the western allies and the Red Army, as Stalin implied, but between Zhukov and Koniev, the track cleared for them by Eisenhower.

To attack Berlin the Russians assembled two-and-a-half million men, 7,560 aircraft, 6,250 tanks and 41,600 artillery pieces: only just enough given the resistance they met. To the natural defences of the city – rivers, marshes, the Seelow Heights in the east – the Germans had added five defence lines for the outer approaches, three defence belts for the city itself. These gun emplacements, bomb-proof bunkers and walls of rubble were manned by seasoned fighters who expected no mercy from the Red Army. Would they have fought with such passion to the bitter end if the assault had been made by the western allies and not the dreaded Russians?

While the Red Army moved up its men and matériel by dark or under camouflage, the western forces in all ignorance continued to bomb Berlin for them. The US cavalry raced east and, on 11 April, the first American tanks reached the Elbe. A combat group forced the passage of the river and, by the evening of 12 April, three battalions had crossed and were digging in while more crossings were made above and below them. On 14 April these advance units were stunned to learn they were forbidden to go on. General Eisenhower was sending the bulk of his forces either up to Denmark or down the Danube valley to link up with the Red Army; there would be no move on Berlin. Bradley had pleaded with Eisenhower, and General Patton had gasped: "I don't see how you figure that one. We had better take Berlin and quick."[6] Ike would not budge. He had only 50,000 men over the Elbe and they were way ahead of support troops or fighter cover. Since the British still urged him to press on to Berlin, Eisenhower flew to London on 17 April to convince Churchill that the city must be left to the Russians: the Red Army had more men, he argued; they must be denied Denmark and the North Sea; and if the western allies pushed down south of Stuttgart, they could capture German atomic research facilities and the (imaginary) Redoubt.

By that date it was, in fact, too late for Eisenhower to change his mind. On 16 April, while it was still dark, three red flares went up on Zhukov's front line signalling the start of a grim and bloody battle. Given the intensity of German resistance, the Russians had to make horrific sacrifices to advance a mere eighteen miles in four days. But by the evening of 20 April, the first Red Army combat units had reached the outskirts of Berlin. Thousands of Berliners hid in cellars, U-bahn (underground railway) stations and railway tunnels, while crack troops, old men and boys fought street by street, building by building, floor by floor against Russian artillery and tanks; pockets of German defence were cleaned out with grenades and flame-throwers. On 22 April Berliners began to hang out sheets in surrender or to wave red strips torn from Nazi banners to appease the invaders. The SS went round and shot them. Though Koniev had penetrated to within 150 yards of the Reichstag (the home of the old German parliament), Stalin decided to award that prize to Zhukov. He had to fight for three more days before he could take it. On 25 April, as the last link between the Russian fronts was snapped shut round Berlin, the first Russian and American patrols met on the Elbe. On the 29th Hitler at last glimpsed the reality of defeat and, too late to save the lives of hundreds of thousands of Berliners and fighting men, took his own. That evening a Red Victory Banner fluttered from the roof of the Reichstag, though on lower floors defenders still fought on with machine-guns.

At last at 6 a.m. on 2 May 1945 the Red Army accepted the surrender of the city and Soviet guns ceased fire. By Russian calculation the epic defence of Berlin had cost the Germans 480,000 captured men, but no one knew how many dead. In the final three weeks 304,887 Russians had been killed, wounded or declared missing. Neither side had spared civilians: 100,000 Berliners had perished. Their city was now 25 million cubic metres of rubble, pierced in places with jagged fingers of blackened masonry. There was no electricity, no transport except by boat along the flooded lines of the underground railway, little drinking water and even less food. A few people scavenged in the ruins; many still lay in the fetid cellars, afraid. Their fear now was not of artillery or flame-throwers but of bayonets and rape.

The first Red Army troops into Berlin had been disciplined, tidily uniformed, even shaven. The second wave was a horde. These men raped. Having raped, they sometimes offered the woman bread or patted the cheek of a child who had looked on; at other times they kicked the child, stabbed her protesting mother. And they looted. Alcohol first, then anything they could lay their hands on: watches, bicycles, curtains, boots, half a piano. What they could not carry away, they smashed. Looting was not just carried out by individuals on the rampage but officially as policy. Factories were stripped and the contents taken away on Red Army lorries. Such was the greed that machinery was thrown from windows or hacked to pieces to get it through doors. Anything was pillaged, even light fittings, technical drawings, telephones and correspondence.

It could be argued, and with truth, that the Russians had suffered all this and worse when the Nazis invaded the Soviet Union; that they had experienced murder and wholesale robbery, extermination squads, gas vans and all the bestialities of the SS. Perhaps it might be thought natural that they should now want revenge as well as victory. Yet they raped and looted too in the countries they claimed to liberate. Milovan Djilas had protested against the outrages of the Red Army in Yugoslavia in autumn 1944. Stalin had wept, but only at the insult to his army. Could Djilas not understand, he sobbed, "if a soldier who has crossed thousands of kilometres through blood and fire and earth has fun with a woman or takes some trifles?"[7] So in the name of what Stalin called "fun" Berlin women of all ages were raped, often repeatedly; they sought treatment for revolting injuries at hospitals with no medical supplies, they bore unwanted babies and endured syphilis when there was no penicillin. What was left of Berlin homes was pillaged and burnt; precious family belongings were danced on by drunken soldiers, priceless national treasures were crushed. The military authorities did nothing to stem the violence. Soviet political commissars could only look on. But one of them warned: "This will cost us a million roubles a day – political roubles."[8]

He was right. Dreadful though the military assault on Berlin had been, it was the violation that followed which left ineradicable bitterness in Berliners and hardened their view of Russians for ever after. The Soviet authorities planned to follow the actual siege of the city with a metaphorical political investment. Though superficially this campaign seemed successful for a time, severe limits had been set to its effectiveness by the barbarity of the troops in those horrible early days. The Red Army lost Berlin politically at the moment it captured it militarily.

To carry out the political conquest of Berlin, the Red Army had brought with them SMERSH (counter-intelligence), political commissars and the NKVD (later the KGB). In addition, a cadre of ten Moscow-trained German communists was to establish communist institutions and an administration designed not just for the future Soviet sector but for the whole city. Their leader was Walter Ulbricht, a man in his early fifties and a full-time German Communist Party official since the 1920s. He had been trained at the Lenin School in Moscow, worked at Comintern headquarters for three years then, unable to return home while Hitler was in power, fought in the Spanish Civil War before moving back to Moscow to plan the future of Germany. Some members of Ulbricht's team were still in the dark about what their duties in Berlin were to be. The youngest of them, Wolfgang Leonhard, had merely been exhorted in the most general terms to eradicate Fascism and transform Germany into a democracy.[9] Ulbricht, however, knew exactly what must be done. He explained in an interview many years later: "We had worked out all the details from the setting up of the administration to the organisation of culture. We also had a list of opponents of Hitler whom we assumed lived in Berlin.... Thus prepared we arrived in Germany on 30 April, and on 1 May we reached Berlin and began work immediately."[10]

The city, to Leonhard's eyes, was "like a picture of Hell; flaking ruins and starving people shambling about in tattered clothing"; dazed German soldiers, drunk Red Army troops; long queues with buckets at stand-pipes; "all of them looking terribly tired, hungry, tense and demoralised."[11] The Moscow cadre soon made contact with a self-help group, busy distributing food, clearing rubble and repairing water supplies. All such teams were broken up; every activity must be directed by Ulbricht and his Central Committee. From mid-May he held regular Sunday morning meetings with 80 to 100 communists from every part of Berlin to get an overall picture and co-ordinate their work. These men then took control of local groups formed to restore order in their neighbourhoods.

Meanwhile the Moscow comrades raced round the city with their lists of "anti-Fascists" and made lists of their own: of communist sympathisers, suitable people for administrative jobs, empty buildings, stores, vehicles, repair materials. Working through the Red Army the Moscow group got small shops reopened, guards posted on food depots and supplies sent to hospitals. The Army struggled to restore electricity, gas, water and transport. People's committees of old left-wing party workers and Russian appointees chose local men to carry out orders from Ulbricht and the Soviet commanders and to distribute food. By 15 May there were ration cards for allocation. To supervise the rations and to run restored services a city administration was needed – known in Berlin as the Magistrat. An acceptable figurehead was found for Mayor: on 17 May the Soviet military authorities appointed Dr. Werner, a decent, rather colourless non-party man. The key figure, however, in the city government was his deputy Karl Maron, a communist émigré trained in the Soviet Union since the 1930s and part of the Moscow group. Seven of the sixteen departmental chiefs were communists; the heads of personnel and of education were also members of the

25

Moscow cadre; another Deputy Mayor was flown in from the Soviet Union; Ottomar Geschke and Hans Jendretzky (labour and social welfare) were plucked from concentration camps; the heads of information and communications had both been at the Anti-Fascist School in the Soviet Union. This political pattern for the central city administration was then set for local governments in the twenty Bezirke (boroughs) of Berlin. Here again the mayors were not communist: in working-class districts they were usually old Social Democrats; in the middle-class areas they came more often from the conservative parties. Thereafter, at least half the specialist posts such as health, transport and finance went to experts or Social Democrats; But the senior deputy mayor who ran the personnel department, and the heads of education and the police, were always communists. As Ulbricht cynically put it: "it's got to look democratic but we must have everything in our control."[12] Particular care was taken in choosing officials for the Bezirke in the sectors to be taken over by the western forces. Key posts still went to communists, but no more than a third of them in any administration in the hope that the allies would scarcely notice and confirm the appointments en bloc.

While the new machinery of local government was put in place, the Red Army tackled other aspects of city life. In the name of denazification, all "Fascist" shopkeepers had their trading licences withdrawn; all business associations and professional organisations were disbanded, then recreated under the supervision of the Magistrat and given "political tasks." Every bank was closed except the Berliner Stadtbank, whose headquarters was set up in the Soviet zone. There too social insurance was restarted. The judiciary was purged: educated and experienced lawyers were replaced with Party nominees or, on one occasion, by the first man a Russian officer met in the street. Newspapers were closed and new ones founded – first the *Tägliche Rundschau* on 15 May, a German-language paper published by the Red Army, next the *Berliner Zeitung*, an organ of the city government. Papers then allowed to reopen were obliged to print in the Soviet sector under supervision. Radio Berlin was licensed to broadcast, but its staff worked with Russian officers breathing down their necks and every word to be spoken was censored. A new police force was created. Many of its members were old employees, but its chief was Colonel Paul Markgraf, a former prisoner of war in the Soviet Union and a graduate of communist training.

The Russians were not content with laying the foundations of a new communist order in Berlin. They set about installing a system through which they could control their entire zone, with institutions which could be extended throughout Germany. On 9 June a proclamation, Order No. 1, established the Soviet Military Administration (SMA) for the Russian zone. It controlled military administrations in each Land (province), openly issued instructions to them on political, economic, social and cultural matters, and covertly supervised their members. The SMA reported directly to Stalin – a clear indication of the importance he attached to Germany.

Other Russian moves to control their zone and beyond were hidden in democratic camouflage. Trades unions were allowed to re-form in June and to set up an all-party committee to foster amalgamation. From the beginning this committee was strongly influenced by its communist members. The SMA's Order No. 2 permitted the creation of "anti-Fascist" political parties, not just in the Soviet sector and zone but the whole of Germany. First into the field came the KPD (the German Communist Party), all prepared on 11 June with a leader, Wilhelm Pieck from the Moscow group, and with a programme. Its manifesto was an unpleasant surprise for loyal old communists: Marx and Engels were not mentioned, the word "socialism" was never used, and the Soviet system was said not to "correspond to present-day conditions of development in Germany." The new party was told to work for "a democratic anti-Fascist regime, a parliamentary democratic republic with full democratic rights and liberties for the people," and – of all Marxist nightmares – to encourage "complete and unrestricted development of free commerce and private enterprise on the basis of private property." In other words, the new party claimed to be interested in a bourgeois liberal state, not a proletarian Marxist revolution. In fact, its programme was a carefully calculated cover for real communist intentions. When the manifesto was read aloud, one bemused listener asked how it differed from that of any other party. "You'll soon see, Comrade," promised Ulbricht. "Just wait a bit."[13]

There were only a few days to wait for a full-blooded socialist programme, conceived without guidance from Moscow – that of the new SPD (Social Democratic Party). This rousingly promised co-operative agriculture and the nationalisation of all banks, insurance, mining, raw materials and energy. It called for the "organisational unity of the working class," and some of the members of the central committee of the SPD did, indeed, hope to merge with the KPD. They were rebuffed, however, by Ulbricht on

19 June with a warning against "premature fusion." Ulbricht was, in fact, waiting for a much bigger grouping through which all parts of the political spectrum could be manipulated. Necessary elements for it appeared in the following month. A new party was formed, the CDU (Christian Democratic Union), consisting of old conservatives expressing their religious beliefs in a commitment to the fair use of labour and resources. And the LPD (Liberal Party) was revived. Now Ulbricht was ready to encourage the creation of a bloc of the "anti-Fascist democratic" parties with a committee of five nominated members from each to decide policy. By this time the western allies had at last got into Berlin.

They had been an unconscionable time arriving. The Americans had, in fact, been nearly there: they had penetrated the Russian-designated zone on a 400-mile front, in some places to a depth of 120 miles, and occupied Saxony and Thuringia. The US Army was within an hour or two's drive of the city, but the Soviet Union had kept them out. The Russians, having made sure that they and they alone took Berlin, then held it for two whole months and, while claiming to "restore order" or "clear mines," they constructed a political booby-trap for the allies. A few outsiders guessed what was going on. George Kennan, for instance, wrote to Washington on 19 May from the American embassy in Moscow pointing out that the Soviet regime itself had been "forged in the chaotic aftermath of the last war" and the Russians well knew that in the confusion following a military conflict lines are drawn "which congeal into permanency and determine the overall pattern of the future." Kennan warned that the Soviet leaders "attach even greater importance to the decisions of the next few weeks than to the decisions of possible future peace conferences." Such decisions would be seen by them as "largely the products of the actual blows that will have been struck while the iron was hot."[14]

Such Cassandra cries fell on deaf presidential ears. Roosevelt would probably have ignored them, given his anxiety to keep the Russian alliance, but he had died on 12 April. His successor, Harry S. Truman, was not ready to listen. Having unexpectedly taken office, he had inherited other men's words and promises and felt obliged to honour them. He became impatient with those who tried to make him alter policies. From the day he became President, Truman was inundated with messages from Churchill recommending him to press for a summit meeting with Stalin and warning against withdrawal from Saxony and Thuringia until a satisfactory settlement was reached over Soviet policy in Germany and eastern Europe. Truman was determined to stick to the European Advisory Commission's agreement on German occupation zones. Furthermore, he shared Roosevelt's belief that one could do business with Stalin – and Truman's style of business was frank and man to man. While some of his advisers (Averell Harriman, James Forrestal, Admiral William Leahy among them) argued for a show-down with the Soviet Union before any troop withdrawal, while Churchill cabled on 12 May that "an iron curtain is drawn down" on areas held by the Red Army, Truman sent Harry Hopkins to Moscow to announce that the United States had no ambitions in eastern Europe: "Our only interests concern world peace."[15] Hopkins came back "bubbling with enthusiasm" about Soviet friendliness and assured everyone "Stalin will co-operate."[16] Truman felt he must nurture that friendliness. Any outstanding worries could be soothed away at a forthcoming peace conference. The United States, with two million armed men in Europe and Saxony and Thuringia occupied, could have driven a hard bargain with the Soviet Union at this stage. Neither the politicians nor the military thought it right to do so. The priority was still preservation of the Russian alliance; the prevailing mood was one of confidence in ultimate reason and mutual help. The western armies would wait to enter Berlin until it was convenient for the Red Army to allow them in.

At least Eisenhower himself managed to pay a brief visit to the city on 5 June – a month after Zhukov had installed himself. He went with the British and French Commanders-in-Chief, Montgomery and Jean de Lattre de Tassigny, to meet Marshal Zhukov at his headquarters. The four had unfinished business: the European Advisory Commission documents on assumption of supreme power; the zones and sectors and the Allied Control Council so painstakingly prepared months ago had not even been signed let alone put into effect. The circumstances of this meeting were grotesque. Under allied agreement in the EAC and at Yalta the western Powers had every right to be in occupation of the city from the moment of its surrender and should have immediately established the Military Government for Germany. Instead they were now in Berlin as guests of Zhukov, and he refused point-blank to set up the Allied Control Council. As the American report of the meeting put it: "Zhukov made it clear that he was willing to meet periodically to discuss matters not relating to governing Germany as a whole, but that any steps to set up control machinery must await withdrawal into the agreed zones."[17] Nor would the Marshal make any other concessions until that time. Eisenhower asked if he might leave a staff to arrange American entry into Berlin. No, said Zhukov, not until all troops were in their prescribed areas.[18] The western commanders weakly marked their displeasure by refusing a Russian invitation to dinner, but that was the limit of their protest. In their anxiety not to give offence, they had given irrevocable advantages to the Russians at a time when they still held bargaining counters. They meekly left Berlin – abandoning it to the Russians for another few weeks.

While the US Army began to plan withdrawal from Saxony and Thuringia, Churchill pleaded for them to stay put. He had warned Truman on 4 June that he viewed "with profound misgivings the retreat of the American Army to our own line of occupation ... bringing Soviet power into the heart of Western Europe," and again talked in terms of "the descent of an iron curtain between us and everything to the eastward."[19] Churchill kept up the attack until, on 11 June, Truman silenced him by pointing out sharply that the occupation zones had been agreed by the British themselves "after long and detailed discussion" in the EAC and at Yalta. In addition, the President enclosed a message he had drafted to Stalin suggesting 21 June as the date for American withdrawal. Churchill gave up. For Admiral Leahy, at least, this was a sign of the Prime Minister's increasing ill-health and weariness.[20]

Truman sent his message to Stalin on 14 June. Two days later Stalin replied that since Berlin was not yet cleared of "mines," entry of the allied troops would have to be delayed until 1 July. Truman had also asked for free access by road, rail and air for US forces. Stalin's reply did not mention it. Nor did another to Churchill on 17 June, though he too had specifically requested freedom of transit.[21] Neither western leader pressed the point. Both missed an excellent opportunity to define their rights of access to the city. When General Marshall, US Chief of Staff, sent a draft directive to Germany on 25 June for troop transfers, he added a note that transit rights had not been mentioned: "In accordance with the President's message to Stalin [on 14 June] these should be arranged with Russian commanders concerned simultaneously with arrangements for other adjustments."[22] For Washington, access to Berlin was still a "military matter" to be sorted out on the spot.

How should it be done? There were two schools of thought at SHAEF as there had been in Washington. On the one hand, lawyers wanted written agreements from the Russians on free access before any orders were given for redeployment of troops. Philip Moseley had proposed to a SHAEF official that the US Army should choose two railways and two roads for their sole use, carry out all necessary repairs and maintenance on them, and be guaranteed alternatives should they prove unserviceable for any reason. The man only nodded and withdrew. Moseley heard nothing more.[23] On the other hand, the military at headquarters thought "an old-boy agreement with the Soviet commanders would suffice," as a Foreign Office lawyer at SHAEF recollected.[24] The soldiers triumphed over the lawyers; no written agreement was asked for.

In its absence and without Zhukov's permission, an American reconnaissance team tried to get into Berlin on 17 June. It was made up of 500 men, all armed, in about 120 vehicles, some of them tracked. It was commanded by Colonel Frank Howley, one day to be the Commandant of the city's American sector. Once over the American bridge at Dessau the party was stopped by Russian guards on the grounds that "an agreement" allowed transit for only thirty-seven officers, 175 men and fifty vehicles; no half-tracks or machine-guns. In spite of doughty argument by Howley, only this remnant of the party finally proceeded. It was not permitted by the Russians to use the autobahn, so had to bounce along a parallel cobbled road. Before reaching Berlin the party was deflected to Babelsberg, a suburb near Potsdam which was ten miles from its objective. Here the Americans were more or less fenced in until they agreed to leave the Berlin area.[25] Their fruitless journey was perhaps marginally less uncomfortable and humiliating than that of an RAF advance party sent to Gatow airfield in Berlin. This group was slapped by the Russians into Hangar No. 1 for twenty-four hours; the would-be RAF commander of the station was kept under lock and key for two days.[26]

Clearly some better arrangement had to be made if the western troops were to have a trouble-free entry into Berlin on 1 July, let alone proper access thereafter. The British and Americans sent their requirements to Marshal Zhukov, then took up the matter with him when Generals Lucius D. Clay and Sir Ronald Weeks (deputies to Eisenhower and Montgomery) visited Soviet headquarters on 29 June. The Marshal looked at their request: four rail links, two each for the Americans and British to connect with their zones; two roads, one to Frankfurt and the American zone, the other to Brunswick for the British; and air-lanes to Bremen and Frankfurt. These communications, he observed, as if suddenly struck by a startling realisation, ran across the Russian zone; they would have to be protected, and so "an extremely difficult administrative problem"

31

arose. Surely, the Marshal suggested, in his silky, reasonable manner, one railway and one highway would be enough to feed and supply two small western garrisons of barely 50,000 men. They could both pass through Magdeburg – very "convenient" and "economical." And undoubtedly, purred Zhukov, one air-lane over most of the Soviet zone would be adequate: American aircraft from Frankfurt and British from Hannover could meet and be channelled through Magdeburg too. Yes, he acknowledged, this would add fifty kilometres to the route, but "that isn't too much flying," he suggested. General Clay tried to defend his original requests and stressed that he must have freedom of access and full rights over all roads and lines from the west. Yes indeed, Zhukov replied; he was not questioning such rights, just offering the most convenient routes. Of course, he pointed out, Clay could reopen the whole question of access once the Allied Control Council began work.[27] Zhukov did not remind anyone that in the ACC he had a veto.

Clay and Weeks settled for what Zhukov offered. It was less than they had asked for, far less than they knew they needed, but they wanted to be sure they got their men into Berlin on 1 July as agreed. Both men seem to have swallowed Zhukov's eloquent explanations about difficulties of transport given the terrible havoc in the area, shortage of repair equipment and so on. Indeed, they were positively sympathetic: Zhukov was persuaded to accept the offer of American machinery to rebuild the autobahn bridge near Magdeburg. Clay was actually relieved not to have to sign any agreement on specified routes which might be interpreted later as a denial of rights over all routes. He noted with satisfaction Zhukov's guarantee that allied traffic would be free from border search and controls by customs or military officials. He was most reassured by the promise that the ACC could adjust the transit arrangements at any time.[28] He reported to Robert Murphy, who had become the US Military Government Political Adviser, that Zhukov was so reasonable it was safe to assume that there would soon be unlimited access to Berlin. The previously wary Murphy now agreed with Clay's prognosis and informed Washington to that effect.[29] In fact, as Clay argued later, "we were sitting over there with the greatest army that had ever been seen; nobody was concerned about anybody blocking us on roads and railways."[30] The verbal agreement of 29 June seemed so temporary that the Americans did not send their minutes of the meeting to Washington until April 1948.[31] Montgomery was perfectly happy with it. As he recalled afterwards, he felt they had "a sort of friendly agreement, rather loosely defined. It was accepted that we would all do our stuff, and that no one would abuse this gentlemen's agreement."[32] The British and Americans continued to believe that Zhukov, like the Prince of Darkness, was a gentleman, in spite of alarming evidence to the contrary they now received.

Major-General L. O. Lyne, trying to move into Berlin to prepare for the arrival of the British garrison, was told he must take a circuitous route from the west: the autobahn bridge over the Elbe near Magdeburg was "impassable," said the Russians. Lyne refused to accept the excuse, went straight to Zhukov and protested. The Marshal admitted that British troops had a right to free access to the city; "the only question, he explained, was the route to be followed."[33] The British took the side route. Another advance party under Colonel Howley was constantly held up by Russian searches, regardless of Zhukov's promise two days earlier that there would be none. (Howley reckoned the Russians were only after loot and could not comprehend that Americans might leave Saxony and Thuringia without wagon-loads of it.) His party took twenty-four hours to reach the American sector. There they got a message from Zhukov forbidding them to occupy it until the military Kommandatura for the city was set up. Howley took no notice.[34]

Once the allies were in Berlin in the first week of July, Zhukov steamrollered them. On 7 July he told the American and British commanders that though the French might attend the allied Kommandatura, their sector would not be given any Russian territory. (Finally the French got their sector from the British, who were then compensated by the Americans.) Next Zhukov laid down that the city would be governed as a single unit and that no unilateral decisions would be taken in the sectors. The western commanders agreed since they had been given no briefing on the matter. (It is odd that they did not ask for one before agreeing.) Furthermore, Zhukov announced that the western sectors would not be fed from the Russian zone. This statement was breathtaking. Berlin had always been supplied from the surrounding areas, now all in Russian hands. If the western Powers took responsibility for their own sectors, food would have to be transported from their zones along the one crammed autobahn and the single laden railway. Zhukov played for sympathy: the old supply areas had been devastated by the recent fighting, the Red Army was nobly sacrificing its own stocks to keep Berlin alive, the Russian people who had suffered so much could hardly provide food from their own miserable rations. Clay was impressed. He reported to the War Department in Washington: "We must accept [Zhukov's] statements as correct in the absence of confirming information"; there was no choice but to provide food for Berlin.[35] This might well have to come from the United States and Britain as the zones were desperately short.

Not content with gaining an enormous advantage over food supply, Zhukov also insisted that the western Powers must supply their sectors with coal too. By western estimate the public utilities alone consumed about 6,000 tons of hard coal a day, which was obtainable only in the Ruhr and Silesia. There would be no Silesian supply, Zhukov announced: Silesia was now under Polish control (the first anyone had heard of it; no official announcement seems to have been made for another month). The Soviet Union had no powers there, he argued; she could only buy the fuel – and why should she, for western needs? Yet again, the British and Americans found Zhukov's attitude reasonable. They agreed to bring in coal from the Ruhr, on condition the Russians provided 1,500 tons a day of lignite for domestic use. Clay, however, reassured Washington that both the food and the coal commitment must be seen as "an interim measure, until the Allied Control Council machinery had a further opportunity to investigate."[36]

But no ACC existed as yet. In spite of the EAC agreement signed by the Commanders-in-Chief, Zhukov was still not prepared to set it up. At the next meeting, on 10 July, he produced some skimpy arguments about wanting to refer to Moscow and the convenience of waiting until the political leaders had held a conference. The western commanders put up no resistance; they humbly agreed to wait. Clay could see no alternative but continuing to work for four-Power harmony.[37] In the attempt to get it, Clay and the British had made Berlin dependent on Russian goodwill. They had got no written guarantee of access; the minimal routes they were allowed to use were now the essential arteries for the survival of two-thirds of the city.

As if all this were not bad enough, the western Powers blundered further and allowed Berlin to be run on Russian terms. On 11 July, when the four commanders set up the Allied Kommandatura to run the city, they signed a decree drafted by the Russians: "Until specific notice all existing regulations and ordinances issued by the Commander of the Soviet Army garrison and Military Commandant of the city of Berlin and by the German administration under Allied control regulating the order and conduct of the population of Berlin . . . shall remain in force." There could be no comfort in the phrase "until specific notice"; the western commanders might hope it meant "until we decide on changes," but given a Russian veto in the Kommandatura, changes were unlikely. What had happened was that the West had given backdated sanction to all the actions taken in Berlin by the Red Army and the Moscow group since 1 May; they had accepted the financial, social and political structures designed in the Soviet Union and would now have to work within them.

The armies, as Kennan had warned, indeed drew the lines for post-war Berlin and Germany, and for Europe as a whole. But it was the Red Army which had largely determined where those lines would be. When the leaders of the three great allied Powers met at Potsdam outside Berlin from 17 July to 2 August 1945, they found that Stalin had pre-empted many of the decisions which should have been taken by the conference and had unilaterally imposed a settlement on eastern Europe. And he had redrawn the map of Germany: without mentioning anything to his allies, he had signed an agreement with the Poles on 21 April, entrusting them with the administration of German land east of the rivers Oder and Neisse. This included the rich industrial area of Silesia and added up to 21 per cent of the total of pre-war German territory. The Russians themselves had then absorbed a further 3,500 square miles of East Prussia. All in all, Stalin had redistributed a quarter of Germany without a word or a by-your-leave. It was a very different form of dismemberment from any of the plans formerly discussed. At Potsdam he announced these bare facts without blush or apology. His allies protested, of course; but they were not prepared to put real force, military force, behind their words. They appeared ready to pay any political price to maintain wartime co-operation; they dreaded a resumption of fighting, this time with the Soviet Union. So they merely drafted a feeble acknowledgment that the Poles might continue to run the areas they had taken until a "final settlement."

The two western leaders were in no condition to stand up to Stalin. This was Truman's first international conference and he did not feel ready for it. His chief anxieties were over what contribution the Soviet Union would make to the United Nations and the Japanese war (just like Roosevelt at Yalta). His attitude to eastern Europe had already been made clear by Hopkins: he would not intervene. Truman was also impressed by Stalin and disarmed by his affability. Churchill, who had seen through it long since, was tired and disheartened. An American observer was shocked to see how ill-prepared the Prime Minister was and how often he showed no grasp of subjects under discussion.[38] Churchill did not stay at Potsdam long. Much to his surprise the British general election replaced his Conservative government with a Labour administration. His successor, Clement Attlee, and the future Foreign Secretary, Ernest Bevin, had been brought to Potsdam for politeness's sake, but they took over the negotiations from 20 July when Churchill and Eden went home to the back-benches.

The Americans were greatly impressed by the smoothness of the transfer of power and the continuity of British policy. They were less impressed by the new men. Attlee sat silent; he was modest. (Churchill used to sneer that he had a lot to be modest about.) Stalin was rather delighted by him. "He does not look a greedy man," he said with satisfaction.[39] Attlee, though, was much sharper than anyone gave him credit for. He summed up Stalin in no time, and in typical clipped manner: "Reminded me of the Renaissance despots – no principles, any methods, but no flowery language – always Yes or No, though you could only count on him if it was No."[40] Attlee had decided within days of arriving at Potsdam that there was no possibility of real co-operation with the Soviet Union. While he sat quietly and watched, Ernest Bevin was in and out of every assembly, constantly muscling in at meetings of the Foreign Ministers; he was an instantly recognisable fixer and shrewd horsetrader bred of long experience in the trades union movement. It was Bevin who made the biggest explosion over the Polish administration of east German territory. "His manner was so aggressive," complained James Byrnes, the American Secretary of State, "that both the President and I wondered how we would get along with this new Foreign Minister." (In the event, Byrnes never did.) For the moment, however, Bevin's explosions were all noise and no impact; without American backing they had no weight.

On the whole, the Potsdam Conference maintained a veneer of friendliness over growing mistrust. The setting was pleasant enough: the plenary sessions took place in the Cecilienhof Palace of the former Crown Prince ("Stock Exchange Gothic," Attlee called it), a two-storey brown-stone pile set in woodland, with a newly planted twenty-four-foot red star of geraniums at the entrance and gardens stretching to Lake Griebnitz. The three leaders and their advisers sat round a table in the ballroom, cast wistful glances through the great windows at the gardens, and shunted their problems to daily meetings of the military and Foreign Ministers. ("Soon we shall have nothing to do," mused Stalin.)[41] Truman, for one, was glad to get rid of the insoluble. "I have come here to discuss matters upon which we three Chiefs of Government can agree," he explained.[42]

So issues were dodged. They stopped talking about Poland; accepted that German populations in eastern Europe would have to be deported, but imagined this could be done "in an orderly and humane manner," as their final communique put it. They issued a Declaration on Liberated Europe full of fine phrases about "restoration of sovereign rights and self-government," "free elections" and "democratic means" for all that during the drafting of the Declaration Stalin had shown what he meant by "democratic": "If the government is not Fascist, the government is democratic."[43]

It was easy enough for the leaders to declare a common aim to demilitarise and denazify Germany – they were only repeating old slogans, not saying how they could do it all. It was not too difficult for them to announce their intention "that the German people be given the opportunity to prepare for the eventual reconstruction of their life on a democratic and peaceful basis" – they did not specify when, what they meant by "democratic" or what the nature of the "opportunity" would be. The allies could also talk of reorganising the judicial system, decentralising the political structure to develop more local responsibility and breaking up concentrations of economic power found "excessive" (whatever that meant) – they did not spell out how. When they promised Germany freedom of speech, press and religion, they hedged that freedom by subjecting it to undefined "security requirements."

Vague and inadequate as all this may have been, the way in which the leaders addressed the basic matter of Germany's administration was to make bad worse. They aborted any hope of maintaining a united Germany or even a vestige of allied co-operation. Their Protocol spoke of uniform treatment of all areas of Germany, of a single economic unit with common policies and central administrative agencies in which Germans would work under allied supervision. Yet at the same time the Powers divided the country into four separate occupation zones, left full authority in them to the individual Military Governors and gave each a veto in the ACC. They ignored the fact that on 27 July the Soviet authorities had already ordered the creation of eleven central German agencies to start work in the Soviet zone but to develop as an all-German bureaucratic structure. They chose to overlook too the fundamental differences of economic and political principle between the West and the Soviet Union, and the actions already taken in the Soviet zone which would make harmonisation of policies in a united Germany almost impossible, except on Russian terms.

37

A blind eye was also turned at Potsdam to nearly all the problems of reparations. The western leaders forbore to point out how much the Soviet Union had already stripped from its zone in advance of any agreement and did not even enquire if an account was being kept. The American delegation had particular cause to be aware of the thoroughness of Russian seizures: all the fittings in their bathrooms had been taken, though makeshift replacements had been found. The allied Reparations Commission, set up at Yalta in 1944, had met in Moscow thirty-seven times and achieved little except to suggest that there was no basis for the repeated Russian claim to $10 billion. In that time the allied armies had discovered the extent of the damage to German industry and infrastructure, and the British and Americans had decided that the demand for reparations was less important than giving the Germans the means to feed and support themselves. They inserted that principle into their final communique together with a stipulation that exports from current production should "be available in the first place" to pay for essential imports. Time would show that this was a paper agreement only; it failed to bind the Soviet Union. No decision could be reached at Potsdam on the total sum or nature of reparations. A delay of six months was given to calculate the value of capital equipment, assess German needs and investigate the capacity of the economy.

Stalin, however, wanted some specific promise on the proportion the Soviet Union would finally get. Bevin saw this as a splendid opportunity to trade for Russian concessions on the Polish frontier and the nature of the Polish regime. Not so Byrnes. He wanted compromise and Russian co-operation on other matters. Not surprisingly Molotov grabbed his offer of 10 per cent of the industrial equipment to be stripped from the western zones and a further 15 per cent to be exchanged for Russian food, coal, potash, zinc, clay and petroleum products. Molotov had made sure of a tidy sum and given nothing in return.

With so much gained Stalin could afford a small gesture of generosity. It was, however, with predictable reluctance that he agreed that France should now be represented on the Reparations Commission. As from Yalta, so from Potsdam such tardy and minor concessions gave no satisfaction to the French. France had again been deemed unworthy of an invitation to the conference. Like the Fairy Carabosse who was not invited to the princess's christening, France was rancorous. More importantly, having been left out of the decisions at Yalta and Potsdam, the French did not feel bound by them. Having suffered occupation and a Nazi economic policy which amounted to pillage, they felt justified in stripping any German resource; they were horrified by the suggestion of central German administrative departments and the possibility of a new strong state; above all they feared German military revival and wanted a settlement which gave France a secure frontier and deprived Germany of the Rhineland and the Ruhr.

Britain and the United States had no cause for satisfaction with the Potsdam Conference either. It had offered them a chance to dig in their heels, to use their military might and strategic position to challenge the Soviet position in Berlin and eastern Europe. At Potsdam, Truman had announced the test of the American atom bomb; that news alone could have driven the Soviet Union into compliance. Instead, the western leaders had continued to hope against hope that their own willingness to compromise would eventually be met with Russian goodwill and collaboration. Their preparedness to go halfway must have been encouragement to the Soviet Union to go on tugging. There had been few genuine Potsdam agreements; the hazy language of the final communique only just concealed the numerous disagreements between the wartime allies which time would magnify.

The codename Churchill had picked for the Potsdam Conference was "Terminal." The meeting should, indeed, have rounded off the war and ended uncertainties and arguments about the peace. It had the opposite effect. Potsdam was the starting-point for new conflict and anxiety. Significantly, the word "terminal" is often associated with disease. Post-war Germany was sick from the earliest days. Potsdam made her sicker.

3

Doctors or Heirs?

In the nineteenth century when the decaying Turkish Empire was described as the Sick Man of Europe, the Hapsburg Chancellor Metternich put a fundamental question to the other Continental leaders: are we the doctors or the heirs? Much the same alternatives faced the occupation Powers in Germany in 1945. Did they want to restore the country to full vitality? Would they prefer a languishing cripple or invalid? Should they deliver a mortal blow and enjoy the German inheritance of land and industrial wealth?

The temptation for the allies to destroy or at least cripple Germany was strong indeed. The war against Hitler had reduced Europe to indigence. The hostility felt to Germans while the fighting and Nazi occupation continued was intensified by the evidence from the liberated concentration camps, slave labourers, witnesses to SS extermination squads and the victims of Gestapo torture. As the picture of wartime atrocity emerged, few people made any distinction between Nazis and Germans: all were held equally responsible for the monstrous scale of bestiality and for the suffering and devastation the war had brought. Fifty-five million people had died since 1939; millions more were bereaved, orphaned or maimed. Prisoners of war once held by the Germans went home to countries despoiled by the Nazis of industrial machinery, livestock, transport and art treasures; they returned to unemployment and hunger. Surely, it could be argued, Germans deserved to suffer as others suffered. If there were any resources left in Germany they should be given as compensation to the victims. Indeed, why leave Germany in existence and risk this havoc again?

An opinion poll conducted in France in August 1945 recorded that 78 per cent of Frenchmen wanted Germany permanently divided; 71 per cent thought the country should be reduced to a purely agricultural state.[1] During the war the American Secretary to the Treasury, Henry Morgenthau, had thought much the same. His plan, produced in 1943 and long acceptable to President Roosevelt, would have given East Prussia and much of Silesia to Poland, the Saar and adjacent territory to France. The Ruhr would have been gutted: all industrial plant and mining equipment dismantled within six months of Germany's defeat and distributed among the allied nations. Thereafter, preached Morgenthau, "Germany's road to peace leads to the farm." The country must be split into small units and pastoralised. Only a little light industry would be left for the manufacture of agricultural machinery or the processing of food. The population must barely subsist on its own produce and be unable to trade with the rest of the world. Germany would be isolated, impoverished and impotent.

But could Germany be looked at in isolation as a sick man whose death could only benefit everyone? There was a different metaphor: Europe itself was sick and its recovery depended on that of its vital organ, Germany. Without the German economy what would happen to a country like Holland, which before the war had traded up to 30 per cent of its imports and as much as 20 per cent of its exports with Germany, not to mention handling a large proportion of the transit traffic on the Rhine? If German mines were closed down, how would France survive? French industry needed about 70 million tons of coal annually; in mid-1945 national production was no more than 30 million tons. Britain too needed German coal and trade. The United States was eager for markets. American capital, machine-tools, managerial and marketing expertise all awaited the revival of European production and trade. That would not come without German coal and industrial output. The initial Russian instinct was to pillage Germany in retaliation for the hideous destruction and loss of life the Soviet Union had suffered during the war. Prisoners of war were kept for labour, skilled German workers in the eastern zone were kidnapped and deported to Russia, whole factories were loaded on to trains for the Soviet Union. When the western allies entered Berlin, they found that 70 per cent of the industrial equipment of their sectors had already been stripped by the Russians. The very railway tracks on which it had been carried had gone too: by the end of 1945 most of eastern

Germany's lines were single track. Yet the Russians had to ask whether, in the long run, they could ever ransack enough in Germany to make up for their own industrial backwardness and ruin. Might it not be better to leave resources for German skill and labour to provide for Russian needs?

The four victors faced political questions too. All feared the rebirth of an aggressive state, but they had different ideas on how to prevent it. Both the United States and Great Britain favoured transplanting their own democratic institutions, then nursing Germany through a period of military occupation to be sure they were not rejected. The French, on the other hand, believed that their security depended on radical surgery to Germany – the left bank of the Rhine put under permanent military occupation, the Saar integrated with France, the Ruhr separated and perhaps put under international control. To keep Germany cowed and to prevent attempts to win back lost territory, there must be no strong German government nor any effective central administration.

The Soviet Union's political prescription was probably influenced by the fact that Russian fear of Germany had not been allayed by creating a defensive arc of satellites from the Baltic to the Black Sea. These states themselves needed military protection and occupation, and shielding against the attractions of a prosperous, peaceful, democratic Germany, especially if under western patronage. So Germany must be occupied until all resources for revival were destroyed, the satellites were digested and the Soviet Union's own damage repaired. But in contrast to these defensive aims was the expansionist force always present in Soviet policy, the messianic urge to spread Marxist-Leninism. The Russian zone could be developed as a socialist society and used as a base from which to direct revolutionary activity throughout the country. If Germany were won for Marxist socialism not only would the satellite states be more secure, but the Soviet Union could range further afield in its revolutionary ambitions – to unstable states like France or Italy, for example. This offensive strategy, however, would entail some restraint in handling Germany, some effort to show that the Soviet system brought benefits. Given these contradictions the best approach for the Soviet Union may well have seemed to be to leave as many options as possible open. Not for the first time the Soviet government would show itself capable of a high degree of opportunism.

Yet such speculations by the four Powers about ultimate economic and political aims in Germany could be nothing but academic in 1945. The country's immediate problems were overwhelming and demanded instant first aid.

The devastation which the conquering armies found in Germany was beyond any expectation. It was so appalling that many Americans and British, at least, had no desire to triumph in their victory; instead they felt stunned, then almost ashamed. It had been one thing to pick bombing targets on maps or to bombard positions with long-range artillery. It was quite another to come face to face with the results. They could not glory in what they had done.

Off the main roads villages might still be intact, but most big towns were shattered, unrecognisable as centres of work and habitation. Dortmund was almost entirely in ruins; Dresden and Stuttgart little more than ashes after the fire storms created by allied bombing; Hannover and Nuremberg, Münster and Osnabrück were half or three-quarters demolished; Cologne had lost half its houses and the glorious cathedral was a shell. In the Ruhr it was reckoned that there was one "dwelling unit" to every three or four families. This meant about four-and-a-half square yards per person – rather less than the accommodation in most German prisons. Public services everywhere were smashed. There was little communication between wrecked cities: no mail service (and, indeed, local officials in Cologne did not even have paper to write to the occupation authorities), no telephone exchanges or lines. Twelve thousand kilometres of railway in north-western Germany alone were out of action; so were half the locomotives. Seventy-seven per cent of all bridges in west Germany were unusable; all those over the Rhine were totally destroyed. The river itself was so choked with wreckage that this great European waterway was unnavigable.

Something like six million Germans had died during the war; 400,000 of them had been civilians. Up to three million members of the armed services had been declared "missing"; some families would never know if or how they had died. There were two million Germans in prisoner-of-war camps and those in Russian hands would be lucky to survive conditions in the coming winter. Germany was now a country predominantly of the old, the very young and women. There were two million orphans and one-and-a-half million cripples. A generation of young men and education had been lost. The homeless trudged the roads pushing bundles of belongings on carts made from planks and old wheels – "the post-war Volkswagen" they called them.

Everyone was hungry. Even if there had been spare food in the countryside it would have been difficult to move it to towns, given

43

the collapse of transport. But there was all too little. Germany had had to import up to 30 per cent of her food in peacetime. During the war the land had rarely been fertilised, labour was scarce, the horses on which most farmers depended had been taken by the Wehrmacht; the country had eaten what it looted from occupied Europe. Since the end of the war the Poles had taken the agricultural regions in the east. And now Germany suddenly had new mouths to feed – eventually up to twelve million of them. First refugees from the eastern front, then German-speakers expelled from eastern Europe under the Potsdam agreement. The occupation authorities had to take responsibility for them, and they simply did not have enough food. By United Nations calculation the average ration for an adult should be 2,650 calories a day. In the western zones the best that could be promised was 1,500, and this could not always be met. That was why Sir William Strang on a tour of the British Zone soon after the end of the war noticed that Germans working for the Control Commission showed frayed nerves: they were hungry. Workers repairing administrative buildings in the American zone fell off the scaffolding: they were starving. The official ration could not sustain normal health or energy, let alone heavy labour. Small wonder, then, that miners in the Ruhr, who had each produced 1,547 kilos of coal a shift in 1938, could only manage an average of 711 at the end of 1945. They would have to be fed if Europe wanted more coal.

Germany itself certainly needed coal. Industry was at a standstill. It had suffered less from the bombing and fighting than might be imagined, thanks to effective camouflage and dispersal into the countryside. Up to 15 per cent of all chemical plant and 15–20 per cent of engineering capacity had been destroyed, but what had survived could not restart without coal. Thereafter, to keep going it had to have transport, communications, markets and workers with food in their bellies and some incentive to earn. None of these conditions existed. All human energy went into a struggle to survive: to find a few potatoes, a bucket of water, some sticks to light a brief fire. Konrad Adenauer, once Mayor of Cologne and one day to be Chancellor of Germany, summed up the mood in late 1945: "Taking all in all, the present in Germany was hardly bearable and the future looked hopeless."[2]

If anything, things looked even bleaker in Berlin. General Clay found it like "the city of the dead" when he first went there in June 1945.[3] The population had been 4.3 million before the war; fighting and flight had reduced it to just over three million. The people who remained lived in cellars or in the corners of ruins sheltered with strips of lath or flapping curtains. Some 20 per cent of buildings had been totally destroyed; a further 50 per cent were virtually uninhabitable. Stooped over the rubble, old women – *"Trummerfrauen,"* women of the ruins – sifted and scraped old bricks hoping to find some fit for use. Few others had work. There was no longer a German government so no need for civil servants. Forty-eight per cent of Berliners had been employed in industry – mechanical and electrical engineering, chemicals and clothing. There was no industry now: the Russians had taken so much machinery and there was no coal. So days were spent queuing for rations, wandering into the country to forage for food, bartering a few possessions for black-market provisions. A little traffic moved along tracks cleared in the rubble but it had to dodge pedestrians who blundered across, too dazed and slow from hunger to get out of the way.

Berliners had been happy and expectant when the western allies arrived in the city in July 1945. They had given the troops a warm welcome – the war was over and there would be protection from the Red Army. That mood did not last long. Berliners were upset at being treated as "the enemy." They saw the Russians as the common enemy and were horrified that the western allies should co-operate with them. They resented being regarded as Nazis. They thought of themselves as staunch opponents of Hitler. (Where else in Germany in the mid-1930s could a popular cabaret artist come on the stage, raise his arm in the Nazi salute and say "Heil ... What is his name?") They were contemptuous that the western Powers should not stand up to the Soviet Military Administration: that for days all clocks in the western sectors stayed at Moscow time where the Red Army had set them; that Russian guards remained on all public utilities and main buildings throughout the city. They were angry that Russian violations remained unchecked. For the entry of the western troops did not immediately stop the looting and the rapes. Still it was *"Uhre, Uhre"* ("watch") and *"Frau komm"* ("Woman come"). One hospital in the American sector treated 250 rape cases in one day. Every night there were burglaries by Russian troops throughout the city. The western authorities made protests, of course. The Russians gave a standard reply: the criminals were Germans in stolen Red Army uniforms. The civilian police were powerless to cope with the situation; they had to have military help. The Americans finally gave them cards listing basic English vocabulary ("murder," "rape," "robbery") and instructions to call army patrols. Military intervention provoked fights on occasion. If Russians pulled guns, the Americans sometimes shot them. The British, Colonel Howley noticed, "simply preferred beating hell out of them."[4] That suited the Red Army – they got back a chastened live soldier.

Grave though Berlin's problems were, there was a body intended to solve them – the Allied Kommandatura. Regular meetings and an orderly routine gave a superficial impression that the Kommandatura was functioning. The four city Commandants met several times a week in a grey sandstone building in the American sector which had once housed the Nazi Labour Front. In an oak-panelled conference-room on the first floor which overlooked the beflagged entrance and the leafy Dahlem street, they sat round a table so tenderly polished that secretaries were instructed to join staples for documents on the top lest the precious surface be scratched. Each Commandant took the chair for a month at a time and played host at lunch. French food was surprisingly poor. British food was stodgily national, but could be helped down with white wine. Americans provided ample native fare (Virginia ham, corn and carrots, Mocha squares at one typical meal), but only fruit juice and coffee. The Russians were lavish: wild boar on some days, always beer and vodka, sometimes caviar and champagne.[5] Between meals there was argument and frustration.

The Russian Commandant vetoed most western suggestions and prevented the development of real four-Power government or any long-term policies for effective management of the city. Instead, problems had to be tackled by individual Powers in the separate sectors or through a series of working arrangements at a low level. (For instance, the Americans and British finally got rid of Russian guards on buildings in their sectors by surrounding them with troops and glaring until they went away.) For the rest, the western Commandants thought it better to keep talking to the Russians rather than force a show-down and risk losing what little they had gained. They referred their disagreements upwards to the next level of authority, the Allied Control Council. Here the western allies proved equally reluctant to press their case, even over something which should have been clear-cut from the start: their guarantee of access to Berlin where they had every right to be as victors and every need to be as members of a quadripartite government.

At the meeting on 29 June Marshal Zhukov had conceded one road for the western forces to transport their men and supplies through the Soviet zone to Berlin. What had been presumed to be a temporary facility became a permanent inconvenience. No additional roads were made available. The one pre-war autobahn left the west at Helmstedt in the British zone. Travellers might stop for a bit of cheer at the NAAFI before crossing the few hundred yards to barriers at Marienborn, which marked the Soviet zone. Here allied personnel could sit in their vehicles while their papers were checked. German drivers (nearly all lorry drivers since there were virtually no private cars) had to go and queue in an office until their documents were stamped. From Marienborn the road went straight as an arrow for the hundred odd miles to Berlin, first through wooded hills with scattered clearings where buzzards quartered, then across the fertile levels round Magdeburg. There were few settlements, few signs of life. Travellers might pass the occasional German family on foot (some of them would slip off the road and creep through woods to the British zone). Woe betide anyone who broke down on the Helmstedt autobahn. Passing Russian patrols would pick up anyone they found and detain them for hours. There were no garages. The only available help came from a British post forty miles from Helmstedt or an American post forty miles short of Berlin, which had been set up by Soviet permission and provided a few emergency repairs or a bit of warmth and a brew up.

At least the road was less vital and less jammed than the single railway allowed for allied transit. Not only personnel but much of the food and coal for the western sectors had to be brought to Berlin by rail. At the fifth meeting of the ACC on 10 September 1945 the Russians agreed to permit ten allied trains a day to cross their zone; on 3 October 1947 the number was increased to sixteen.[6] There was nothing really free about the passage. Within days of the September agreement, Russian guards tried to enter American trains to check the identities of passengers. The infuriated American Deputy Military Governor, General Clay, threatened the SMA that in future he would put armed guards on his trains.[7] It looked as if he had frightened the Russians off: they made no further attempt to board until 1948. Until then identity papers and travel permits were collected from passengers by an allied officer and handed over at the Marienborn checkpoint. The Russians had, however, made significant gains from their action. They had not formally waived their claim to inspect rail passengers as well as their documents; and to keep Russians off the trains the western allies had promised that only their German employees would travel on them and be

47

confined in sealed coaches. (Others must apply for quadripartite travel documents and use civilian trains.)

The road and rail agreements were purely verbal. The arrangement for water transport, which brought some food and more coal to Berlin, was at least put on paper. It was no more satisfactory in practice. There was no Allied Control Council settlement; the British alone had negotiated with the Russians because most barge traffic carried coal from the Ruhr. It had taken until 26 June 1946 to get a series of written promises from the Soviet authorities. Thereafter, they were constantly broken. The Russians seldom provided information about traffic movements in their zone and consistently failed to send back empty British zone barges, which they seemed to regard as reparations.

Significantly, the means of access which was to keep Berlin alive in 1948 and 1949 and to defeat the blockade – the air – was the most easily negotiated and the least subject to limitation or irritation. Initially it had not been discussed. Western pilots simply flew in and out of the city when they pleased, following the railway and autobahn to and from Helmstedt. However, they had no navigational aids in the Soviet zone and bad weather or night flying was difficult or downright dangerous. So no one was at all surprised that the Russians kept complaining about the number of near misses in the air, thought it was odd that they cited "air safety regulations" when none existed. There was general relief, therefore, on 30 November 1945 when the Allied Control Council approved a paper drawn up by its quadripartite Air Directorate recommending the creation of three air corridors between west Germany and Berlin (though ideally the western Powers would have liked six in all so as to have direct flights to Copenhagen, Prague and Warsaw).[8] The three corridors funnelled traffic from Hamburg, Bückeburg near Hannover, and Frankfurt on Main in the American zone. Each was twenty miles wide and allowed the use of all airspace up to 10,000 feet. They met in a Berlin control zone, a circle with a radius of twenty miles from the ACC building, within which all traffic movements were directed by the four-Power Berlin Air Safety Centre. Rules for air safety within the corridors were codified by October 1946 and then enforced by the Air Directorate. In spite of initial Russian objection, it was tacitly agreed, though never written, that commercial aircraft might use the corridors.

It may seem strange that the air agreement should have been reached so calmly and in such a concrete form when there were still so many tensions and uncertainties about other forms of access.

But air transport seemed insignificant in 1945; it carried a few passengers and a little mail. No one imagined then that its role could be expanded. In establishing the three air corridors the Russians could feel they had made a cheap goodwill gesture and gained greater safety for their own aircraft and some privacy for their military installations. Road, rail and water transport for Berlin, on which the city and the allied garrisons really relied, were still under tight Soviet control. These routes could be cut at any time.

On the whole the western Powers humbly accepted this dependent position. Only very occasionally did they get tough. Sometime in 1945, for example, when the Russians were holding up traffic at Marienborn "on orders from Moscow," the RAF retaliated by withdrawing facilities for refuelling or repairing Russian long-distance aircraft at Gatow in the British sector. (Andrei Vyshinsky from the Soviet Foreign Ministry and his interpreter were said to have sat at the airfield for a day drinking two bottles of vodka while Marienborn was unblocked.)[9] But such confrontations were no more than tinkering with existing inadequate machinery. They could be interpreted by the Russians as indicating that the western allies were prepared to put up with what they had and would not press for anything better. The western Powers assumed that constant usage would establish rights de facto if not de jure. They could hardly believe that the Russians would ever consider preventing communications between the zones and Berlin or cutting the supply lines for the city. They had decided that the way to deal with the Russians was to win them over by patience, blandishment and constant demonstrations of tolerance. Russian co-operation was judged vital for coping with the immensity of the task facing the occupation Powers in Germany.

According to the potsdam agreement, Germany should have been run on a quadripartite basis, with uniform policies administered by central German departments supervised by the Allied Control Council. The ACC met for the first time on 20 July 1945. At a Russian suggestion (perhaps to suggest unselfishness, perhaps to keep Nosey Parkers out of their own area) the headquarters was set up in the American sector of Berlin, in the cavernous Kammergericht, once the highest court of Prussia, then the Appeal Court of Germany and finally, in Nazi days, the People's Court of Judge Freisler and the scene of his screeching tirades at the 1944 plotters against Hitler. The building had been badly damaged in the war; a combat battalion of US Army engineers needed nine months to restore its 550 rooms to house the innumerable directorates, committees and working parties spawned by the ACC. From the beginning, however, the four Military Governors were able to meet three times a month or more to discuss policy for Germany and engage in competitive hospitality. General Eisenhower acted as chairman for the first month, then his colleagues took over in turn. They sat at four tables arranged to form a square with a hollow centre. This was an unfortunate symbol of quadripartite government: four confrontational policies and no meeting in the middle. When Eisenhower's deputy, General Clay, was asked at a press conference in May about the chances for four-Power co-operation in Germany, he had insisted: "It's got to work. If the four of us cannot get together now in running Germany, how are we going to get together in an international organisation to secure the peace of the world?"[10] They never did get together. And just as the Kommandatura referred its frustrations up to the ACC, so too the Military Governors in their turn passed their deadlocks on to their governments.

For the first few months relations with the Russians in the ACC were cordial enough. Marshal Zhukov retained his charm; his western colleagues were still impressed by his military achievements and optimistic that four competent soldiers would soon pull together and draw up plans with staff college efficiency. When such hopes drooped, they could be refreshed with nostalgic chats about the dear old war days when they had fought the good fight together and won. Early straws in the wind passed by almost unnoticed. A hint by the Russians that Berlin as a whole was part of their zone of occupation slipped by, but the claim would be built on later. On 3 October the Russians turned down an Anglo-American recommendation that the University of Berlin be run by the city under Kommandatura supervision. The Russian excuse that Berlin was the one and only university in their zone was patently untrue, but not challenged.[11] Notice was taken, however, of a worrying Russian habit. As Clay observed, "We have not found them willing to discuss matters on a broad basis. Apparently they will discuss one topic at a time, and will proceed no further until that topic is resolved."[12] For a while this was taken to be plodding meticulousness; in time it would be recognised as a ploy for impeding any progress through an agenda. As yet, though, the Americans and the British did not regard the Russians as much of an obstruction in the ACC; they were having too much trouble with the French.

In September 1945 the French vetoed an American proposal for a central German transport agency; in November they refused to allow even an agency to control rail traffic – railways, said the French, were "war potential." In October the new French Military Governor, General Pierre Koenig, announced that he would block the creation of any central German administration whatsoever until there was international agreement on the western frontier of Germany. French officials had previously hinted that their main concern was to prevent Russian domination of central institutions;[13] now it was clear that their veto was a weapon to win the Saar and a Rhineland settlement. They held up business in the Allied Control Council's Finance and Economic Directorates. On 26 October in the Council itself they turned down a measure to permit the federation of trades unions and later refused to allow political parties to function on a national basis. In December, with Russian backing, they stopped the opening of zonal boundaries for the free passage of Germans. No matter that all this was contrary to the Potsdam agreement: the French had not been party to it. No doubt the Russians would have used their own veto more often had the French not been hamstringing the ACC for them. As it was, given mainly French intransigence, the Allied Control Council could not begin to run the country as a whole. Germany soon disintegrated into four separate units of military occupation with four distinct policies.

The French came to their zone as victors with rights of conquest. It was reckoned that the Nazi occupation had cost France in destruction and pillage something in the region of $40 billion worth of property at 1938 values. Until there was an agreed quadripartite policy on reparations, the French would strip what they could. And they would live off the country (like the Russians, but unlike the British and Americans who imported their own rations). Their zone had more officials per head of German population than any other, and each official brought his family: to avenge the humiliation of their own occupation, to exploit the black market, or in some cases to escape retribution at home for collaboration with the Nazi and Vichy governments. The first Military Governor, de Lattre de Tassigny, spent a high proportion of his budget on luxury and entertainment and his staff revelled in it. The grounds of his official residence outside Baden Baden were landscaped; distinguished visitors were greeted with ceremonial guards of Algerian cavalry bearing lighted torches and given banquets or operatic performances.

There was, however, conflict between those who relished this life style and elements in the civil administration under Emile Laffon, who called for restraint and consideration for the needs of the zone. Much of the luxury was, indeed, cut when de Lattre de Tassigny was sacked in July, but his successor, General Koenig, was an ardent Gaullist who was frequently at odds with his civilian staff and, for that matter, with Paris. As a result, though the quality of administrative personnel was high, uncertainty and dissension led to inefficiency. Economic policies remained punitive, except in the Saar where food supplies were kept higher, industrial dismantling lower and controls lighter in the hope of encouraging a desire for union with France. Harsh as French rule was in most respects, the cultural policy was conciliatory. There were twice as many school textbooks per child as in the British zone, seven times more than in the American. A new university was founded in Mainz. Generous opportunities were offered to young people to travel and to discuss serious issues. German professionals were encouraged to debate with their French counterparts. Exhibitions, concerts, a tour by the Théâtre National Populaire all catered to a German craving for contact with the outside world and a broadening of intellectual horizons. Though France continued to regard Germany with hostility, in this respect at least a foundation was being built for future rapprochement.

The British occupiers in Germany behaved less as conquerors, more like conscientious colonial civil servants. They were dedicated to sound administration, the creation of democracy in industry and government, the inculcation of liberal values, a mission to instruct and improve. The officials went about their task with thoroughness, painstakingly building from the bottom local government and shop-floor trades union groups. It was understandable, therefore, that they needed large staffs. It is less excusable that they should have been quite so huge. There were 22,000 British in the zone by 1946 to administer a population of 22.3 million. The Americans, admittedly with less detailed ambitions, managed with 12,000 dwindling to 5,000 by 1947 for 17.1 million Germans. Though the core of top civil administrators remained of high calibre, and was trained and experienced, new recruits for lower posts were too often job seekers; a few of those who went into industry were suspected by the Germans of feathering their nests. On the whole, however, the tone of the British Control Commission was studiedly correct. The zone was treated as a colony for which the administrators felt responsible, but for whose inhabitants they had no affection and little understanding. The British remained aloof in their clubs and requisitioned houses, viewing the Germans as natives: restless at times, benefited by British rule and useful as cheap servants. British intentions were basically decent and benevolent, but tended to be concealed by reticence. Individuals could be high-handed. Konrad Adenauer never forgave the British brigadier who sacked him as Mayor of Cologne (before the city was taken over by the Americans) with the words, "You have failed in your duty to the people of Cologne" in not demonstrating "proper supervision and energy." He told the man later that he had added to a folder in his desk marked "Dismissed by the Nazis," another: "Dismissed by the Liberators."[14]

Adenauer, like many Germans and most Americans, assumed that because there was a Labour government in London, policy in the British zone must favour socialism and the Social Democratic Party. In fact, the military and civilian administrators were apolitical in standard British tradition, and although the Labour Cabinet might hope to see eventual nationalisation and a German welfare state it had more pressing objectives. It wanted to get Germany moving again. It was the belief of Ernest Bevin, the Foreign Secretary, that European recovery was impossible without German revival and that Britain was dependent on both. It could neither afford the costs of occupation nor provide food for starving Germans. Such compelling arguments were needed to temper Bevin's instinctive reaction to the Germans. He used to tell the British Military Governor, Sir Brian Robertson: "I tries 'ard, Brian, but I 'ates them"[15] – not as a result of Nazism and the war, but because he could never forgive German socialists for backing the Kaiser in 1914. Ernest Bevin came as near as any man to being an elephant. He had the four-square baggy body, the rolling movements and the canny, bright eyes. His political nose had all the delicacy and sensitivity of a trunk. His memory was elephantine, especially for treachery. Whatever his mistrust of German socialists, however, it was noticed by Dean Acheson that he had "an even deeper one of the Soviet Union."[16] As far as Bevin was concerned, the Germans might have let down socialism on occasion but the Russians had systematically betrayed and besmirched it. In his view Stalin's regime had always been a dictatorship of the Left and quite as inimical to freedom as any dictatorship of the Right.[17] Germans had as much right to freedom as anyone, whatever their past behaviour. Bevin would fight communism in Europe as he had fought it in the British Labour Party and trades union movement. Germans must develop democratic institutions in which they could grow freely, then be admitted as partners in Europe. If they chose

democratic socialism, so much the better; but Bevin would not foist it on them.

The man who administered Bevin's policies in Germany seems a strange contrast to his political master, but the two men worked in harmony and genuine affection for each other. General Sir Brian Robertson was fifty-one when he was promoted from being Montgomery's deputy to Commander-in-Chief and Military Governor of the British zone in November 1946. Robertson was the son of a Field Marshal (one who had risen from the ranks in the First World War and by extraordinary coincidence had then been commander of British occupation troops in Germany). Robertson had fought from 1914, then spent the years of peace running the Dunlop Rubber Company in South Africa. He returned to military life as a first-class manager and by 1944 was chief administrative officer to Field Marshal Alexander in Italy. In spite of his trim moustache and fastidiously pressed uniform, he never quite seemed a soldier. He was soft-spoken and extremely reserved. The few who got near found him perceptive and kind. He could be magisterial – laying down the law about who the selectors should put in the Test team, fixing stakes for bridge for his staff – and he was stiff on social occasions. But to his job he brought a flexible mind and a readiness to listen. He had calm common sense and the analytical clarity and drafting ability of a top-rate civil servant. As a natural bureaucrat and a trained soldier, Robertson was willing to carry out whatever orders were given, but he knew when it was his duty to give advice and warnings. He saw the day-to-day affairs of the zone as his own responsibility and did not refer details to London. Higher policy he thought a political matter and left to Bevin. He gave the Foreign Secretary devoted service and the loyalty which Bevin so prized. In return, Bevin gave Robertson total respect and backing; his first response in any German crisis was "What does the General think?"[18]

Such a close working relationship, direct communication and clear definition of roles were all advantages denied to the eventual Military Governor of the American zone, General Lucius D. Clay. It had been assumed in most quarters in Washington before the end of the war that the American zone would be run by a civilian High Commissioner and that a small American team would supervise an existing German administration. However, since no such administration survived, the military had to pick up the pieces. John McCloy, the Assistant Secretary of War who had been earmarked for the post of High Commissioner, strongly recommended that only a general had the authority to command a military bureaucracy. Though General Eisenhower had always said of the occupation, "Thank the Lord that will not be my job,"[19] he was obliged to become Military Governor. His duties at SHAEF and elsewhere meant that his deputy had to take over most of the running of the zone. Clay came to Germany for that task.

He was a military engineer who had been loaned to Washington in the 1930s to work with Harry Hopkins and to direct civilian engineering schemes, culminating in the building of the Red River Dam in Texas in 1938. In 1940 he took over the emergency Defence Airport Programme. When the United States entered the war, his constant requests for transfer to active service were turned down. He was sent to the War Department as chief of military procurement and became the Army's representative on the War Munitions Productions Board. Eisenhower poached him in 1944 and Clay was made supply chief at SHAEF, unsnarling the blockage in the port of Cherbourg and ensuring the flow of equipment to the front. Still begging to fight, he was dragged back to Washington to be deputy to James Byrnes at War Mobilisation and Reconversion. Byrnes was impressed, as everyone was, by Clay's vigour and competence. "Give him six months," he told Roosevelt, "and he could run General Motors or US Steel."[20] Clay was remarkable enough as an engineer and an administrator. What was exceptional in a soldier was that, as McCloy observed, "he seemed to have a real knowledge of how ... the federal legislative and executive systems worked."[21] He had, in fact, been brought up with them. His father was three times Senator from Georgia and young Clay had spent much of his boyhood in Washington; he had also worked closely with politicians, bureaucrats and industrialists during the war. It is not surprising that Byrnes could say: "I found no army officer with as clear an understanding of the point of view of the civilian"[22] and recommend him as Eisenhower's deputy and prospective successor. Clay ruefully admitted later: "I wasn't interested in the job. It was the last thing I wanted."[23] But he had a long record of taking on unpalatable tasks if they were defined as his duty.

Throughout his period in Germany Clay was subject to two Departments in Washington – State and War – and to their different instructions. He was on the spot and faced with practical realities; Washington officials were remote and inevitably less well-informed. He had to wrestle with them at long distance, unlike Robertson for whom it was easy to phone or fly back to London for consultation. Clay could hold a "conference" with the War or State Departments

55

by teleprinter, but given the time difference between Washington and Germany one set of participants was working in the middle of the night and not in the best of moods. Such working conditions would have tried a patient man; Lucius D. Clay was a "doer" – energetic, incisive and expecting instant action. The delays and confusions inherent in his relationship with Washington sharpened a naturally autocratic temperament. By contrast with the other Military Governors, Clay was not left to use his own initiative over the details of running his zone. He was confined by a set of official instructions in a directive of the Joint Chiefs of Staff known as JCS 1067. He found it an intolerable restraint and one, furthermore, which did not meet Germany's needs as he defined them and which embodied an attitude he found repugnant.

JCS 1067 had been drafted on the initiative of the War Department, in co-operation with the Department of State and the Treasury, as a counter to the Morgenthau Plan, but it still bore strong traces of Morgenthau's intention to bring retribution on Germany. Most of the provisions were punitive and concentrated on destruction. The Military Government was commanded to decentralise political and administrative structures, break up cartels and dismantle any plant capable of war production. It was forbidden to take any steps to rehabilitate the German economy, except in agriculture, or to take any financial measures to prevent inflation. There must be no action "that would tend to support living standards ... on a higher level than that existing in any of the neighbouring United Nations." JCS 1067 was not issued to key occupation staff until 21 May 1945 and it was immediately condemned by them as irrelevant to actual circumstances. Lewis Douglas, the Financial Adviser to the Military Governor, was contemptuous: "This thing was assembled by economic idiots. It makes no sense to forbid the most skilled workers in Europe from producing as much as they can for a continent which is desperately short of everything."[24] He demanded adaptations; when they were not made, he resigned. Clay thought the tone of JCS 1067 was inappropriate: "I realise the necessity for stern and Spartan treatment," but "retribution now is far greater than we had realised ... and our planes and artillery have really carried the war direct to the homes of the German people." There was no point in fixing a low standard of living: what little industry remained "even when restored will suffice barely for a very low minimum" subsistence.[25] He went to Washington in May 1945 to argue for reconsideration of JCS 1067 in the light of German circumstances. Discussions on changes began, but quietly (for fear of adverse public reaction) and tentatively (to avoid interdepartmental strife). The process was slow. JCS 1067 was not officially replaced until July 1947.

Until then Clay had to cope with his instructions by finding loopholes in them. Since JCS 1067 conceded that some central control might be necessary over railways, communications, power, finance and the distribution of essential commodities, Clay could at least get some movement back into the zone. To prevent mass hunger he interpreted as broadly as possible the section of JCS 1067 which permitted economic measures "to prevent starvation or such disease and unrest as would endanger" the American forces. Thanks to the vagueness of a reference in the instructions to an "eventual reconstruction of German political life on a democratic basis," Clay felt justified in forming German administrative bodies: "There can be no real start on restoring the German economy until governmental machinery has been re-established."[26]

As Clay wriggled against the constraints of JCS 1067, they were somewhat loosened for him by others. His legal adviser, Charles Fahy, assured him that the Potsdam call for prompt action "to effect essential repairs of transport, to enlarge coal production, to maximise agricultural output and to effect emergency repair of housing and essential utilities" overrode the dictates of JCS 1067 and that he might build up the economy to the point where Germans could subsist without external aid. In June 1945 President Truman was so alarmed by the west European shortage of coal that he ordered an increase in American zone production even if this involved constructing mining machinery, supplying extra food and clothing to miners and producing some incentives such as consumer goods. By December the Department of State had so revised its thinking on Germany that it issued a statement that there was no intention to hurt the economy permanently, resources would be left to enable the country to exist without outside help and indeed there would be capital to produce exports to pay for food. It even promised that the Potsdam standard of living would be regarded as a floor not a ceiling.

This remarkable series of shifts in American policy to Germany from the rigours of the Morgenthau Plan in 1943 to the leeway permitted to Clay from late 1945 was to a large extent motivated by practicalities. There was, however, a strongly humane inspiration for the adaptations. When Clay first visited Berlin in June he was moved: "My exultation in victory was diminished as I witnessed this degradation of man," he wrote later. He vowed to remember

57

that "we were responsible for the government of human beings."[27] Responsibility for the defeated had a very personal significance for Clay. He was a Southerner. He had been reared on stories of the Civil War, the excesses of Northern troops and Yankee exploitation in the ante-bellum period. Truman, too, the man from Missouri, came from a family which remembered the suffering of that time. Both understood the bitterness of defeat and the arrogance of occupation. When Clay moved quickly to stamp out rape and looting in the American zone, he was not just acting as a military disciplinarian; he was following a deep instinct. The spirit of the Morgenthau Plan and JCS 1067 was alien to both Clay and Truman.

And it went against the grain of many of the Americans in Germany. They had not known Nazi occupation or bombing. The war was over; they wanted to shake hands and make up. JCS 1067 forbade fraternisation: no Germans could live in a building where Americans had quarters, German staff could not eat in the same room or use the same lavatories or lifts as Americans. There should not even be conversations between occupiers and occupied, except in the line of business. But Americans are naturally outgoing and friendly; not passing the time of day seemed downright rude. They had none of the British colonial attitudes of "them" and "us"; since the Germans were not black there seemed no justification for segregation. It was irresistible to give gum or a chocolate Hershey bar to a child – who can think of a ten year old as a Nazi? No young soldier of any nation can resist a pretty girl. When one puzzled soldier asked an officer what "fraternisation" meant, he was told: "Well, it means when you stay on for breakfast." Americans took for granted the luxuries of the PX shop on all their bases, and it was a long time before they understood why Germans scrabbled for scraps in the dustbins behind the canteens. Once they did, they wanted to relieve such misery. They could not bear to see a mess and not try to sort it out: they itched to get things working again, and better than ever. Americans respected German efficiency, hard work and skill. They were prepared to work together. This reaction at least coincided with official Washington policy. The job of Military Government had been envisaged as supervising, not running, the zone, hence the relatively small staffs, mainly professional civilian experts or graduates of the School of Military Government of the University of Virginia. They concentrated on constitutional and legal engineering, decentralisation and decartelisation – making a framework within which Germans would operate. The aim was to move as quickly as possible from military to civilian government, from American control to German self-help and responsibility.

Though policy in the American zone developed gradually in response to perceived needs and through debate between Washington and the occupation headquarters in Frankfurt, the Soviet zone gave the impression of firm commitment to one line from the very beginning. Indeed, Germans in the early months of defeat used to mock the uncertainty and blundering in the western zones and say that only the Russians had a plan for Germany. The Soviet Military Administration applied it without consulting the western allies or referring to what the Powers had agreed at Potsdam.

Stripping of industrial plant continued in the Soviet zone at the rate it had begun, to the increasing anger of the Germans. An officer of the Political Administration of the Red Army once pointed out some new houses in the Russian sector to Wolfgang Leonhard of the Moscow cadre. "That's where the enemy lives," he commented. "Who?" asked Leonhard. "The Nazis?" "No, worse still, our reparations gang."[28] A new means of ensuring reparations in the form of manufactured goods was devised. From the end of October 1945 all industrial property belonging to the German state, the armed forces, banned organisations, or former Nazis and convicted war criminals was sequestered. Some of the enterprises were handed to German administrations under SMA control; others were formed into SAG (*Sowjetische Aktiengesellschaft*), Soviet limited companies. The Soviet Military Administration was, in fact, nationalising industry and taking reparations from current production without quadripartite agreement.

The Russian grip on the population was tightened and protest stifled. Some police units were armed and a new political section was added to the zonal police – K5, which worked under the NKVD. Suspected dissidents, former factory and land owners, teachers, doctors and police officials were branded as "Nazis" or "undesirables" and sent for "re-education". It was not necessary to build new educational establishments for the purpose: old concentration camps like Buchenwald and Sachsenhausen were conveniently available. It has been reckoned that between 1945 and 1950 as many as 200,000 people from the Russian zone were sent to the camps; up to a third died there.[29] For the rest of the population the rationing system was sufficient discipline. Those in the top of the five categories got 2,485 calories a day – these included politicians, officials and intellectuals as well as people doing manual labour. Those in the bottom two categories were labelled "useless" – the old, the unemployed and anyone who had incurred official displeasure. They received only 1,248 calories a day.

Even such meagre rations were threatened when land reform began in the Soviet zone in the autumn. Any land in excess of a 100-hectare holding was confiscated and put into a fund together with former state and Nazi property. By December this fund held 3.5 per cent of all the agricultural land in the eastern zone. Of the total 3.3 million hectares taken, 1.1 million stayed under central or local authorities and was used to set up collective farms. The rest was distributed among 560,000 applicants. As a result, 42 per cent of all farms in the zone were now under 10 hectares – a major factor in the fall of output in 1945 to 35.5 per cent of 1938 production. This drop was in part intended. The KPD (Communist Party) assumed that uneconomic farming and poverty would force the peasants to collectivise. Unless and until they did, there would be hunger.

The political parties in the eastern zone proved more resistant to Soviet pressure than the economy. Though land reform was backed by all parties, the means of carrying it out cracked the "Anti-Fascist" bloc. The CDU (Christian Democrats) objected to confiscation without compensation. The SMA silenced complaints by sacking the party chairman and his deputy and replacing them with men expected to be more compliant: Jacob Kaiser and Ernst Lemmer. (Neither turned out to be easy to handle.)

There was, however, a far stronger challenge to the Soviet attempt to control the zone through the KPD: from the Social Democrats. The SPD had more or less the same number of members by the end of 1945 as the KPD and it was enrolling at a faster rate, in spite of the fact that the SMA made sure that the communists got all the resources: paper for leaflets and posters, cars for campaigning in the countryside, accommodation for offices and meetings, let alone special rations, housing and the pick of good jobs in the bureaucracy, industry and education. Indeed, part of the SPD success came from this favouritism: to the man in the street the KPD was the "Russian party," the main support for the hated occupation force. The SPD, on the other hand, was a German party with strong links with its national organisation and policies which were not framed by the SMA. Though its eastern zone members were further to the left than the party elsewhere in Germany, they differed from the KPD in one essential: insistence on democratic, parliamentary means to achieve socialism. They also posed a threat to the very nature of the KPD: many communists dreamed of a German road to socialism and hoped that union with the SPD would free them from the Moscow line.

Collaboration with the KPD was resisted by the SPD national leader, Kurt Schumacher, a man who before the war had described communists as "nothing but twin editions of National Socialists, varnished with red,"[30] and who had not changed his mind after twelve years in concentration camps. To his hatred of communists was added extreme distaste for Russians. Schumacher was born in Kulm (Chelmno) in West Prussia, twenty miles from the Russian border, among Poles who had for centuries fought the Russians, been partitioned by them and had suffered the consequences of the Nazi-Soviet pact in 1939. Schumacher detested all occupiers of his country, but his hatred for the Russians was deeper seated. In September 1945 the eastern SPD was attracted by a KPD offer of fusion, but Schumacher turned it down. In October he insisted that any union must be on the all-German basis (well-knowing that the KPD was weak outside the Soviet zone). He took the same stand when a joint conference was held in Berlin in December, and added protests against the harassment of SPD members in the east and preferential treatment of the KPD by the Soviet authorities. For the moment fusion was blocked. There was no doubting that this was a setback to the hopes of Ulbricht and the SMA.

The western Powers made little or no protest about the policies being implemented in the Soviet zone. They could have accused the Russians of breaking the Potsdam agreements: denying freedom of press and speech, imposing high levels of reparations in advance of quadripartite agreement, maintaining a deliberately low standard of living. They might have claimed the Russians were breaking the promise of common treatment in all zones by deliberately building up quite separate economic and social systems. But the western allies were not in a good position to complain. They too were running their zones on different lines, albeit reluctantly, so could also be accused of failing to provide uniform treatment for Germans. And for the first six months of occupation the British and Americans saw the French, rather than the Russians, as the main obstruction to common policies. The Russians, they hoped, could eventually be beguiled rather than bullied into co-operation.

This optimism was maintained as Zhukov handed over to his deputy, General Vassily Danilovich Sokolovsky. The General had been a company commander in the Russian Civil War, fought on the western front against the Nazis, taken part in the assault on Berlin and been present at the surrender of the city. Western colleagues found him genial, well-mannered and dignified. He might be a high-ranking Soviet official, but he was credited with being "western-minded" and certainly not a "hard-liner." British and American associates appreciated his pleasant sense of humour and his ability to quote not just Russian proverbs but Jane Austen. Robertson thought it was possible to talk to Sokolovsky and that he was trustworthy, up to a point. Clay felt more warmly: "I learned to respect his ability and Mrs. Clay and I both developed a genuine friendship for him and Mrs. Sokolovsky."[31] (Social relations with the Robertsons remained formal and polite.) Sokolovsky always gave the impression, even in the most heated argument in the Control Council, that he was only carrying out his orders and that there was a decent, reasonable man underneath.

The membrane of confidence in ultimate common purpose in Germany was stretched thin by wrangling and obstruction in the Kommandatura and the Allied Control Council. But it was possible for a time to believe that the deadlocks could be eased at the highest level – by the national governments acting in the spirit of wartime co-operation. This belief was badly shaken when the Foreign Ministers of the United States, Britain and the Soviet Union met in London for three weeks from 19 September 1945, following a decision at Potsdam to hold regular meetings in a Council of Foreign Ministers to prepare a European peace settlement. The Foreign Ministers achieved nothing in London. They spent their time bickering over possible treaties with minor powers. The Russians refused point-blank even to discuss Germany until all their other demands were met, though they made passing reference by accusing the other Powers of holding up the reparations agreement.

In London the western delegations began to learn something of Foreign Minister Molotov's wide repertoire of tactics to delay and frustrate. His requests to consult Moscow over details were constant and shameless. One day he would appear to make a concession over an item on the agenda, the next he would behave as if he had never wavered and would start discussion from scratch. If cornered, he used the word which became a music-hall joke: "*Nyet,*" "No." His name expressed his negotiating style: "Molotov" means "a hammer" (it was his revolutionary nom de guerre; his family name was Scriabin). Coldly self-possessed himself, Molotov seemed to take a certain delight in making others lose their temper. At the London Conference he worked hard on Bevin until he provoked a massive outburst. He then dismissed Bevin curtly: "Eden is a gentleman, Bevin is not." Ernie, not one to be sat on, commented that Molotov's methods were reminiscent of Hitler's.[32] The acrimony of the Conference was not much sweetened by social gatherings. Bevin's rendition of "Cockles and Mussels" one evening was hardly likely to cheer (not with that girl dying of a fever and no one being able to save her), and although he once persuaded Molotov to join in the chorus of "Roll Out the Barrel," the "gang" never really "got the blues on the run." In fact, James Byrnes recorded that he went back to the United States "exhausted in patience and depressed in spirit."[33]

The London Conference had shown the new conflicts between the wartime allies. Russia would brook no interference in her east European satellites and was prepared to use Germany to get her own way. France had again not been invited and by now was regarded by the other western Powers as a positive nuisance. Britain and the United States were growing mistrustful of each other. Britain feared America would do a private deal with the Soviet Union and pull out of Europe, destroying the balance of power and any hope of economic recovery. The United States was tired of feeling like a dog wagged by the British tail and wanted freedom of action. The Americans increasingly viewed the vaunted "special relationship" as a one-way process, which only gave special benefits to the British: subsidies and unwarranted influence in policy as well as the illusion of being a great Power. Yet Byrnes had grown less tolerant of the Soviet Union than the British realised: "We had emphasised patience long enough," he decided; "henceforth we should stress firmness as well as patience in our relations with the Russians."[34] Firmness "as well," be it noted; not "instead." The Americans, like the British, were still willing to keep trying. The possibility of a complete breakdown of relations with the Russians was too frightening.

Yet the particular mixture of firmness and patience was to prove inadequate in Germany in the next two years. Conditions there did not improve. The Powers might have decided against dismemberment in principle, but they had allowed it to happen in practice, and Germany was an organic whole with each part too dependent on the others to survive in isolation. The Americans and the British had drifted into being doctors; the French and Russians had not striven officiously to keep Germany alive, but had not actually delivered a death-blow. They all now had to assess their treatment as Germany went into steep decline, Europe suffered a crisis and the alliance broke down.

4

The Patient Sinks

During the first months of allied occupation Germans were hungry. Food was bound to be scarce given dislocation of transport, loss of land to Poland and the arrival of millions expelled from eastern Europe. But occupation policies had made the situation worse – each zone fended for itself and there was neither a mechanism for national distribution of supplies, nor any common rationing policy. The Germans could not buy food from abroad: industry was either being dismantled as military, stripped as reparations (though in advance of agreement), or lying idle waiting for coal and an official decision on what it would be permitted to produce. So by the beginning of 1946 Germans were almost starving. Though the United Nations recommended an average daily ration of 2,650 calories, in January the French Military Government was begging the Americans for supplies to avoid cutting rations in their zone from 1,380 to 1,145 calories.[1] General Clay grumbled that the French had brought the trouble on their own heads by living off their zone, but that very month he himself had to start importing food from the United States to keep the American zone's ration up to 1,550 calories and by late March knew it would have to be cut to 1,275. In the British zone things were even worse. In late February Robertson announced a drop to 1,000 calories. Only 700 of these could come from local sources; the rest must be imported from Britain.[2] By comparison the steady ration of 1,500 calories a day in the Soviet zone seemed a positive cornucopia.

The western occupation authorities were shamed by the human

distress; they were also aware of the dangers of hunger. A report on the three western zones in spring 1946 from the allied Nutritional Committee prophesied what Clay called "a nutritional disaster."[3] It recorded rickets and retarded growth in children, anaemia and symptoms of acute malnutrition in people of all ages, and even famine endema in some urban areas. A population so weakened was already riddled with tuberculosis and vulnerable to every kind of epidemic. It certainly could not work. Though rations for miners were kept high, coal production was dropping. Inevitably, therefore, electricity supplies were cut, industrial output dwindled and the whole European economy experienced new setbacks. Prolonged hunger was bound to have political repercussions. By April 1946 Ruhr miners were on strike for food. It was reckoned to be only a matter of time before the rest of the population was driven by desperation to unrest. And for most people, as Clay put it, "There is no choice between becoming a Communist on 1,500 calories and a believer in democracy on 1,000 calories."[4]

Common decency and self-interest, let alone the Potsdam agreement, all dictated that the Germans must be fed. From June 1945 to April 1946 the British sent a million tons of food to their zone, costing something in the region of £80 million a year; the British Chancellor of the Exchequer, Hugh Dalton, called it "paying reparations to the Germans."[5] It was a barely sustainable expense at a time when rations at home were even lower than in wartime and the country was virtually bankrupt. The United States might be well able to afford the $200 million emergency support given by July, but it was nowhere near enough.[6] And it seemed ridiculous to both the British and Americans to go on subsidizing Germany when the country had all the potential to produce exports and buy its own food.

Action from the Allied Control Council was needed to realise that potential. But as Germany got hungrier and weaker, the ACC failed to reach agreement on quadripartite policies to improve agriculture, distribute food and raw materials, or to co-ordinate transport. The Russians resisted any suggestion of pooling resources or drawing up a joint export-import programme so that food could be bought abroad; the French vetoed any move towards the establishment of German central administrative bodies. The four zones operated in isolation from each other and withered. The Soviet zone was so insulated that it took Clay months of argument before even the American Graves Registration teams could visit it to locate their dead.

The one fundamental quadripartite decision reached only made the situation worse. On 26 March the Allied Control Council accepted the report of the Reparations Commission on the future level of industry for Germany. Not only was the production of armaments prohibited, but also any aircraft or ship building, the manufacture of radio-transmitting equipment and synthetic fuels, rubber and oils. The overall level for permitted industry was fixed at half of the production in 1938, but steel was limited to about a third of pre-war output, chemicals to 40 per cent and machine-tools to 11.4 per cent. Only the coal mines were allowed to produce as much as they could. Any productive capacity surplus to the agreed levels must be destroyed on the spot or dismantled and distributed as reparations. It was a harsh settlement, smacking of French and Russian fears and the lingering wish to punish rather than convert Germany to peaceful contribution to Europe's needs. Though the Reparations Commission had spent nine months investigating the German economy, it seemed to have taken no account of the loss of eastern territory and ignored the fact that the 1938 level of industry had supported 39.3 million people whereas the population had risen to 43.7 million.

In the ACC, Clay, with British and occasional French backing, argued that there was, in fact, no point in talking about limiting industrial production when the levels set seemed hardly obtainable. He recommended instead the full Potsdam formula: treating Germany as a single economic unit with shared resources, establishing uniform standards of consumption and using proceeds from exports to buy food. The Russians turned his proposal down and insisted that exports and imports must stay a zonal affair until there was a balanced German economy and all reparations had been paid. Their stress on reparations infuriated Clay. As he pointed out, by dismantling factories for them in his zone he was depriving it of the chance to trade and so obliging the United States to pay for its food and to subsidise Russian reparations.[7] The Russians would not budge. On 3 May they again refused to pool resources. Furthermore, though challenged for the umpteenth time, they would give no account of the plant or product they had stripped from their own zone so far.[8] Clay snapped. He told the Russians he would send them no more reparations from the American zone. Next day he announced he would stop dismantling "until the economic unity on which reparations are based has been attained."[9]

He had hit the Russians where it hurt, but not hard enough to force them to co-operate. By May 1946 Clay was warning Wash-

67

ington that "next winter will be critical under any circumstances"; a failure to get economic agreement before then could "make it almost unbearable." He wanted to end dismantling, introduce fiscal reforms and announce that the Ruhr and Rhineland would not be detached.[10] He gave notice that inflation, barely restrainable in Germany since before the war, was now beginning to bolt and that the Russians were using captured plates in Leipzig to print whatever occupation currency they needed – without giving a tally to the ACC. Clay knew that inflation could bring total economic collapse. He remembered family stories of what had happened in Georgia once Confederate money became worthless.[11] On the advice of experts Clay and Robertson wanted to replace the old Reichsmark immediately with a new Deutschmark, to be issued under four-Power supervision.

Since the Allied Control Council was clearly incapable of getting to grips with such matters, it was up to the allied governments to take them over. Yet relations between them had deteriorated alarmingly, and a year's experience had aroused deep anxieties in the West about Soviet policy and ambitions.

Since the end of the war western complaints about the unrepresentative nature of governments installed in eastern Europe under Soviet control had been ignored. The West was disturbed in early 1946 by Soviet reluctance to withdraw from northern Iran, occupied during the war to forestall a German invasion. They were increasingly alarmed by Russian influence in Turkey and Greece and strongly suspected a policy of expansion around the eastern Mediterranean. Any confidence in Stalin's willingness to do business was shaken by a speech he made on 9 February 1946, blaming the last war on "capitalist monopolies" and warning that, since the same forces still operated, the USSR must treble the basic materials of national defence such as iron and steel, double coal and oil production, and delay the manufacture of consumer goods until rearmament was complete.

By the time Churchill in his celebrated speech at Fulton, Missouri, on 5 March 1946 used his trusty metaphor of an "iron curtain" across the Continent and warned that though the Russians did not want war they did want "the fruits of war and the indefinite expansion of their power and doctrines," others had reached the same conclusions. George Kennan, now Counsellor at the US embassy in Moscow, had sent a "Long Telegram" of analysis to Washington in February, describing what he saw as a traditional Russian "neurotic view of world affairs," springing from a permanent sense of insecurity which was "impervious to reason." He stressed that the Soviet Union was "committed fanatically to the belief that . . . there can be no permanent modus vivendi with the United States."[12] Ernest Bevin in April advised Attlee, "The Russians have decided on an aggressive policy based upon militant Communism and Russian chauvinism . . . and seem to be determined to stick at nothing, short of war" to get what they want.[13] Truman's optimism about co-operating with the Soviet Union had taken a knocking in disputes at the United Nations and by the revelation that twenty-two Russian agents had been arrested in Canada and charged with spying on American atomic secrets.

Kennan and Churchill seemed to make sense of the experience of the previous nine months. Both called on western governments to get tough with the Soviet Union at a time when patience was wearing thin – Truman had barked in January, "I'm tired of babying the Soviets."[14] They also offered reassurance – that the Russians would not take wild risks; they would stop short of war. But, as Kennan put it, the Soviet Union "is highly sensitive to the logic of force." Why not try applying it? Stand up to the Russians for a change and show them it was time for some give as well as take.

When the Council of Foreign Ministers met in Paris at the end of April 1946, the American Secretary of State James Byrnes made a final test to see if Russian co-operation could still be won by reassurance and goodwill. He offered all his allies a treaty to guarantee German disarmament for twenty-five years and the promise that "this time the United States was not going to leave Europe after the War." Molotov behaved as if he had not heard. He made no acknowledgment of the offer, and, instead, churned out accusations that the western Powers were failing to demilitarise Germany. On all other German issues he simply stalled. Not until 9 July did Molotov make clear what he was playing for: $10 billion of reparations and a part in four-Power control of the Ruhr. It was Bevin's turn to say "No" – not as long as the Russian zone was a closed shop and there was no sharing of resources or a joint export-import programme.

So on 11 July Byrnes made in public a proposition he had been floating in private since the conference opened: "Pending agreement that Germany be treated as a whole I am ready to enter into agreement with any other zone for the treatment of the two zones as an economic unit."[15] For the second time he met silence. The French preferred stagnation to any form of dreaded unification.

The Russians probably felt they could gain nothing from zonal fusion and would lose the secrecy and economic monopoly they maintained in their own zone, never mind what hopes they had of profiting from economic distress elsewhere. Bevin, however, though he feared a breach with the Russians and division of Germany into two blocs, was impressed during the conference's recess in June by evidence that the coming winter would bring disaster to the British zone unless there were rapid economic development, and by Foreign Office and press opinion that zonal fusion was a *pis aller*. On 25 July the British Cabinet approved the principles of bizonal economic unity. Given the imminent breakdown of the Paris talks without any progress on Germany, Bevin decided to suspend reparations to the Soviet Union from the British zone. Formal negotiations between the British and Americans for economic fusion and bizonal agencies began on 9 September.

The Soviet Union denounced each move in the Bizone as contrary to Potsdam principles, but was met by the same reply: the offer to join was still open; this was the only way to achieve the Potsdam aim of economic unity, and it was better to take some action on Potsdam lines than none. Molotov, however, played on German fears that the Bizone was intended to divide their country and claimed that the true custodian of German unity was the Soviet Union. In a subtle speech on 10 July in Paris, carefully circulated in advance to the press and clearly aimed at the Germans, he gave an assurance that "it would be incorrect to adopt a course of Germany's annihilation as a state or that of its agrarianisation," the country must be developed as "a democratic and peace-loving state" with its own industry and foreign trade. He did not promise early withdrawal of occupation forces: "Even when a German government has been set up," he warned, "it will take a number of years to determine what this new German government represents and whether it is trustworthy." Nevertheless, he was publicly talking about a German substitute for military rule, and that was a prospect no one else had yet opened up.

Byrnes was warned by his advisers that Molotov's speech had made a strong impression on German opinion. So he decided to go one better than Molotov and speak directly in Germany itself. He travelled to the American zone from Berlin on Hitler's old train (armour-plated with black marble sunken baths) and on 9 September appeared in the Stuttgart Opera House before an audience of nearly 2,000 – mainly German politicians and local government officials. Clay sat with them to watch their reaction. He had made sure that everyone had a German transcript of Byrnes's speech and that it was broadcast with a translation.

Byrnes offered his listeners rehabilitation and respectability, a chance "to apply their great energies and abilities to the works of peace and in time to take an honourable place among the members of the United Nations." He explained: "Germany is part of Europe and recovery in Europe ... will be slow if Germany with her great resources of iron and coal is turned into a poorhouse." He promised a standard of living comparable to that of other European nations and the chance to produce surpluses to pay for imports. He was less grudging than Molotov over how much authority could be handed to the Germans; indeed, he announced that under safeguards they should now be given "primary responsibility for the running of their own affairs," in other words internal self-government. Not that Byrnes contemplated leaving them to it in the near future: "As long as an occupation force is required ... the army of the United States will be part of that occupation force." In that single sentence Byrnes had offered both security to his allies and a pledge to the Germans that his promises would be carried out.[16]

Byrnes had also demonstrated the new Washington policy of plain-speaking and given the go-ahead to those authorities in Germany who had so far only dared to undertake hesitant measures of reconstruction. He had heartened Bevin by his commitment to European revival and defence and so cleared some of the mistrust which had recently muddied Anglo-American relations. In his response to Molotov he had raised the bid for Germany. But after an initial flurry of interest in what the Powers had to offer, the Germans soon settled into cynicism. They wanted food not speeches. And it was all very gratifying to be competed for, but not if you were torn in two as a result. The division of Germany seemed a growing possibility. It was regarded as a particular threat in the place most in danger from allied traction – Berlin.

Berlin had been the scene of intense political campaigning since Kurt Schumacher had blocked the merger of the east zone Social Democratic Party with the communist KPD in December 1945. The communists had stepped up pressure for fusion of the two parties. In the Russian zone they were confident of success. They received all the facilities they needed from the Soviet Military Administration, had backing from the Russian-licensed media and the willing ear of the zonal SPD leadership. It was a different picture in Berlin. Here the KPD still benefited from SMA help, five Soviet-controlled newspapers, and the monopoly of Radio Berlin. But they were up against a different breed of Social Democrats. There were 50,000 members of the city party by March 1946 in what had always been an SPD stronghold. The officials were highly experienced and hardened by long years of Nazi persecution. Suspicious of KPD blandishments, they had kept their distance. Powerless to resist the forced move of their headquarters by the SMA to the Soviet sector, they had kept their old building in the British sector and built up duplicate records there. Apprehensive that their zonal party would lose its independence, they planned to fight to keep their own within the city. The strategy was discussed on 24 February 1946 in a living-room behind the textile shop belonging to an SPD member. Some of those present suggested an appeal for help to the western allies. The rest persuaded them to rely on their own efforts: the western Powers treated German politics as a matter which should not concern military government and would take time to learn that the SPD struggle with the KPD was more than a private quarrel.

On 1 March nearly 2,000 SPD party workers assembled and opened the battle. Their chairman was Franz Neumann, an unsophisticated working man with simple manners described in a Foreign Office briefing as "by no means an intellectual" but "an accomplished and aggressive orator," whose "commanding presence and transparent honesty make him a natural leader."[17] The meeting agreed to a secret ballot on party merger of all Berlin members on 31 March.

It was a clever tactic. A referendum would give the chance to debate the issue and rally party allegiance. The idea appealed to Berliners at large, who up to now had been apathetic about anything other than physical survival and who were jaundiced by political experience since the 1920s. It aroused some interest from the western authorities, who felt they had a duty to nurture democratic processes: the American-licensed newspaper, *Der Tagesspiegel*, was encouraged by the US Military Commandant to give equal coverage to Berlin and zonal parties' views; the British provided several tons of newsprint and licensed a new paper, *Der Sozialdemokrat*. The campaign flushed out the SMA's attitude to democratic procedures: SPD speakers in the Russian sector and zone were arrested, meetings to oppose merger were banned. There was no Soviet attempt to restrain communist threats or even outright physical assaults in all sectors. The western authorities were drawn to intervene. Their military police drove off men under the communist police chief Markgraf who browbeat SPD activists, and they arrested eleven

KPD officials who were intimidating opponents. Several SPD officials whose lives had been threatened were flown to the western zones.

The Americans and British sent guards to the polling stations in their sectors to keep the peace on 31 March. The SMA closed all the booths in their sector with the explanation that "the regulations have not been complied with." In the three western sectors three-fifths of all registered SPD voters went to the polls. Sixty-two per cent of them voted in favour of a proposition for "an alliance which will guarantee co-operation and exclude fraternal strife," but that is the kind of phraseology which gets plebiscites a bad name. On the clearer issue – "Are you in favour of an immediate merger of the two workers' parties?" – there was a resounding reply: 19,256 Berlin SPD voters (82 per cent of the poll) voted against fusion with the KPD.

A vote in Berlin, however, was not enough to save the east zone SPD. Otto Grotewohl, its chairman, dismissed the referendum as "irrelevant." On 21 April he, Wilhelm Pieck (the nominal head of the KPD) and Walter Ulbricht (its éminence rouge) spoke in favour of fusion to delegates from both parties in the Admirals Palast in the Russian sector. Then in a two-day ceremony which pulled out every emotional stop – the overture to *Fidelio*, the commemoration of Lenin's birthday, even the presentation of a wooden club made by the nineteenth-century socialist Bebel – the Social Democrats and Communists joined in a new Socialist Unity Party of Germany, the SED. It was immediately recognised by the SMA and, after some hesitation, given permission by the western Commandants to operate in their sectors. But in Berlin it had a rival. The March referendum had ensured that the SPD lived in the city to fight another day.

Both parties were fiercely engaged in the next battle, the municipal election on 20 October 1946 in which Berliners chose their City Assembly. The SMA did its best for the SED: closed halls booked for SPD speakers in its sector and arrested SPD members in the zone. It beat the electors with new sticks: there was a sharp reduction of the electricity supply to the western sectors from Russian-controlled power stations, and the rumour was spread that the western allies would withdraw from the city two months after the election. But new carrots were dangled too. Literally; the Soviet authorities announced that at the request of the SED they would issue fruit and vegetables throughout the city. This sudden shower of greengrocery came in addition to the drinks available to all and sundry in SED offices, the notebooks distributed to schoolchildren, and the coal briquettes stamped "SED" which passers-by received with more enthusiasm than traditional party pamphlets. The SMA clearly did a lot to stimulate interest in the election – 92 per cent of the electorate voted on 20 October. Over 48 per cent of the poll was for the SPD, 22.2 per cent for the CDU and 9.3 per cent for the Liberal Party. The SED got 19.8 per cent of the votes in the city as a whole and only 21 per cent in the Soviet sector, which gave them 26 seats in the Assembly where the SPD held 63, the CDU 29 and the LPD 12.

Berlin had given a slap in the face to the SMA and the SED, who were already far from happy with the results of elections at various levels in the Russian zone that autumn. Here the SED had done well in some rural areas where land reform was popular and other parties were badly organised, and inevitably so in those districts where the SMA had held up registration of CDU and LPD local associations so that the two parties were unable to put up candidates. But in no Land did the SED secure a clear majority of the seats, and in cities such as Dresden and Leipzig they were noticeably outvoted. At least steps could be taken in the zone to guard against a repetition of such failure. Nominal or "Little" Nazis, who had been obliged to join the Nazi Party but played no active part, were welcomed into the SED to swell its ranks and give the impression of tolerance and understanding. (Even so, one local SED group boggled at the suggestion of a slogan from a new member: "The SED – the Little Nazis' Greatest Friend.")[18] Never again would voters be allowed to choose between parties: for future elections there would be a single list of candidates. But there seemed no hope now of absorbing Berlin into the Russian zone system by methods which might pass as democratic. Indeed, there was every expectation that newly awakened political aspirations would be directed to the west, to national party leadership and to the promise of prosperity and liberal institutions in the Bizone. The city presented a set of alternatives to Soviet policies and did so flat in the middle of the Soviet zone, whose voters had just shown they were far from enamoured of SMA or SED policies.

For the moment the SMA could only make the best of a bad political job and try to limit the SPD zeal of the new city government by nobbling its executive, the Magistrat. It used a phrase in the city's constitution: "The resignation of the Magistrat or one of its members, as well as the appointment and discharge of leading persons in the city government, may take place only with the permission of the Allied Kommandatura of Berlin." The Russian Commandant, Kotikov, construed this as meaning that all officials, appointed or elected, must have quadripartite approval. His western counterparts interpreted it differently: their control could only be exercised over full-time professional bureaucrats; the Magistrat itself should be freely elected by the Assembly. They agreed to a compromise, however, after six weeks of dispute. An executive of eighteen, three of them SED members, was allowed to take office, but three candidates unacceptable to the Russians were declared ineligible for office. One of them at least had been rightly spotted by the Russians as a menace to them – Professor Ernst Reuter.

His danger lay partly in the fact that he knew them so well. Reuter had been converted to Marxism in a Russian prisoner-of-war camp in the First World War. He was taken to Moscow during the Revolution and met Lenin and Trotsky. By 1918 he was serving under Stalin as Commissar for the Volga Germans and in the early years of peace was secretary of the Communist Party, first in Berlin, then at national level. But Reuter broke with the Party in 1921, revolted by its violence and by the subjugation of German working-class interests to the machinations of Moscow. So it was as a member of the SPD that he served in the City Assembly and ran Berlin's transport. The Nazis drove him out of the city, then out of the Reichstag and finally, in 1935, from Germany itself. He spent the war mainly in Turkey and had only recently been permitted to return to Berlin. Reuter's early political experience made him a hated and effective opponent of the SMA and the SED. He had studied communism and been rewarded with high office, but had rejected both. He was well-versed in Marx and Lenin, but inspired by Goethe and Homer. He could use the dialectic with skill, but did so to argue against Soviet policies. He spoke Russian and expressed love of the Russian people, but always distinguished between "Russian" and "Soviet." He extolled socialism not in terms of class struggle, but of the intellectual and moral aspirations of the individual. Reuter might now be without an official post, but the SMA would learn that he was not without a mind, a heart and a magic tongue.

The new City Assembly avoided clashes with the SMA for several months. The administration hoped to make itself acceptable to a broad spectrum of party allegiance and to all the occupation authorities. Its leader, the Oberbürgermeister, Dr. Otto Ostrowski, was an uncombative SPD member with a conciliatory temperament. He openly expressed a wish to steer a middle course between East and West, Left and Right, and to concentrate on the physical needs of the city. His deputies held a political balance: Heinrich Acker of the SED, Ferdinand Friedensburg from the CDU (as keen a bridge builder as Ostrowski) and Louise Schroeder, a pugnacious SPD veteran whose formidable energies were for the moment focused on the welfare problems of the city. Few at this stage would have argued for political conflict or a show-down with any of the Kommandatura members. There was such an obvious need to tackle Berlin's appalling conditions.

Berlin in late 1946 was still a city of rubble. On one calculation the wreckage was being shifted at 1,000 tons a day, mainly by hand, and it would take thirty years before it was cleared.[19] There was virtually no rebuilding: there were so few construction materials. The Berliners' struggle against cold and hunger had gone on drearily since the end of the war. In the winter of 1946–7 it became frightening. Day after day the city was gripped by 30 degrees of frost. The snow went on until March, and when the thaw came it brought floods and bitter winds. There was little coal, and electricity supplies were cut for at least four hours a day. The Magistrat diverted fuel from domestic use and industry to heat public buildings so that Berliners could huddle together for warmth. Rations plummeted. Winter vegetables were frozen into the ground, stocks were ruined, transport was at a standstill. By the end of March there had been no meat at all in the shops for nearly a fortnight and none was expected for another ten days. From February a small block of chocolate was issued to schoolchildren every five days. It had to be eaten on the spot for fear it was seized at home and sold on the black market – but there was precious little to be found there either.

In the zones the distress was no less. In Hamburg it was even worse: two-thirds of the city's population was without much gas or electricity throughout the winter and meals could only be cooked every third day unless coal were stolen or bought on the black market; food processing had to stop after Christmas and did not begin again until late March. Nowhere in the Anglo-American Bizone could the official 1,500-calorie ration be met, even though the British imported 25 per cent of the required food, and the Americans, even more. The average ration fell to 900 calories a day. By spring there were hunger marches in many urban areas. Every effort was made to feed miners – never had coal been so necessary for survival – but still they went absent, foraging for their families. When their rations deteriorated from meat and fats to bread and

potatoes, there were strikes and increasingly violent demonstrations. Ex-President Hoover, investigating the food needs of
twenty-two countries that winter, found nowhere more desperate
than Germany. In the report he gave to President Truman on 27
February 1947, he called the German housing situation "the worst
that modern civilisation has ever seen," described over half the
children as being in "a deplorable condition" and the death toll
among the aged as "appalling." Truman had rather hoped that
Hoover would find ways to lift some of the burden of aid from
American taxpayers. Instead, Hoover recommended the immediate
supply of £77 million worth of food, "if we want peace, if we want
to preserve the safety and health of our army of occupation and if
we want to save the expense of an ever larger military force to
preserve order." Furthermore, he insisted that "the productivity of
Europe cannot be restored without the restoration of Germany as
a contributor." Only the United States could afford to get the
system working again. After bearing the brunt of the war, Europe
did not have the resources for the construction of peace.

Of nowhere was that more true than Britain. By January 1945
the British were indebted to other countries to the extent of £3,355
million. The war had soaked up not just loans but something like
a quarter of all national wealth. Lend-Lease had ended without
warning in August 1945. The American loan which replaced it was
absorbed by the rising price of imports, which nearly all had to be
bought in dollars and was tied to a promise of sterling convertibility
by July 1947 which led to an instant rush from the pound and
imminent financial ruin. The impoverished country had still got an
empire and had not yet surrendered the role of world Power. There
were British troops in Burma, Malaya and Hong Kong, in Egypt
and Palestine; occupation forces in former Italian colonies, Japan,
Trieste, Austria and Germany; and military assistance was being
given to Turkey and Greece against Russian-backed communists.

Faced with financial collapse, in mid-February 1947 the British
Cabinet was obliged to inform Washington that it must stop aid to
Greece and Turkey within weeks. The crisis brought to the boil a
major decision which had been simmering at the back of Truman's
mind for many months. On 12 March he told a Joint Session of
Congress: "I believe it must be the policy of the United States to
support free peoples who are resisting attempted subjugation by
armed minorities or by outside pressures. I believe that we must
assist free peoples to work out their own destinies." He asked
Congress for $400 million for Greece and Turkey to be spent in the

next twelve months as aid "essential to economic stability and orderly political processes."

The Truman Doctrine of positive action to check the spread of communism and his challenge to the American people to take on new responsibilities was enunciated two days after the opening of the Council of Foreign Ministers in Moscow. Bevin was to write in his summary of the Moscow Conference that chances of Russian agreement on major questions of principle "were quickly lost when President Truman made his announcement" and that once news of the speech was received "the whole scene of the conference changed."[20] It is hard to believe him. The mood would have inevitably darkened after two days of formalities and polite platitudes. *Izvestia* certainly denounced the speech as announcing "a fresh intrusion of the United States over the affairs of other states," but Molotov and Russian officials made no reference to it at all. The discussions which took place show no signs of new antagonism. They were carefully prepared restatements of old positions. President Truman had just thrown more grist into the mills which had been grinding for two years.

The obdurate arguments in Moscow from 10 March to 24 April 1947 had a new witness. James Byrnes had resigned as Secretary of State in January and been replaced by General George C. Marshall. Truman had brought into office a man whom he could call without fear of contradiction "the greatest living American" and in whom he had total trust; someone with long experience of reconciling international interests and of the weight needed for top-level negotiations; a universally esteemed public servant of renowned integrity who could ensure bipartisan support in Congress and respect overseas. General Marshall revered the Presidency and respected Truman; he was happy to share with him the development of foreign policy and to use the professional expertise of the State Department. With these energies concentrated, a new purposive drive was brought to American foreign policy.

General Marshall had been Chief of Staff of the American Armed Forces during the war and Churchill had paid tribute to him as the "organiser of victory." His new right-hand man at the State Department, Dean Acheson, noted that though the General had been a soldier all his life there "was no military glamour about him and nothing of the martinet." But he compelled instant respect. "His figure conveyed intensity which his voice, low, staccato and incisive, reinforced.... It spread a sense of authority and calm."[21]

Marshall told Acheson when they began to work together: "I shall expect of you the most complete frankness, particularly about myself. I have no feelings except for those I reserve for Mrs. Marshall." The instruction was typical – the American team in Moscow was instantly delighted by its new leader's encouragement to speak out and offer criticisms. So was the phrasing – direct and correct ("Mrs. Marshall"). Everyone was treated alike by the General: with courtesy, by title or surname, and without favouritism.

Before coming to Moscow he had been on a mission in China and had had no time for a full briefing on the conference. Robert Murphy thought it "must have been galling to his pride to lead debates in which it was evident to everybody that he was unfamiliar with relevant facts."[22] Marshall's only pride was professional: he was used to being on top of any subject he dealt with and did not usually need notes for even the most complex discussion. It did not take him long to master the main themes of the negotiations and to reverse everyone's poor opinion of his initial performance. Perhaps his biggest contribution was his fresh eye: he saw the issues in stark clarity and had not been conditioned by previous conferences to expect nothing but futility and backbiting.

The Council of Foreign Ministers in Moscow discussed every aspect of the German problem in forty-four main sessions, and innumerable committees and informal meetings. By the time it broke up on 24 April, it had reached agreement on only one matter: all German prisoners of war would be released by 31 December 1948. For the rest, six weeks of discussion were fruitless. When Marshall repeated the American offer of a treaty to guarantee German disarmament, Molotov, who had been deaf to Byrnes in Paris, chose to hear but condemned the offer as "inadequate." He claimed that the Polish frontier had been settled at Potsdam. Faced with a proposal to reduce all occupation forces, he would only accept a reduction which gave parity between the Soviet zone and the Bizone – 200,000 each. When the nature of a future constitution was the topic, the western delegates all agreed that Germany should be a federation (though they differed on how loose), but Molotov stuck out for strongly centralised government which the others saw as vulnerable to takeover by a minority. Molotov pushed relentlessly for a part in four-Power control of the Ruhr, but Bevan resisted him and wrote to Attlee: "It is quite clear what the Russians are after, namely to get into the Ruhr, to make our Zone impossible to work, and to create a disturbance so as to get a grip on that great area."[23] He told Molotov that there would be no Soviet share in

79

the Ruhr until there was genuine four-Power control in all the zones of Germany.

But the fundamental cause of stalemate in Moscow was disagreement on economic policy. Molotov called for the abolition of the Bizone. He was invited to join it, but refused. The Americans and British pressed for economic unity throughout Germany and Bevin emphasised the importance of a German "peace potential," arguing that if "the standard of life in Germany is reduced to too low a level, if she becomes an economic cesspool in the middle of Europe, we shall sow the seeds of war just as if we were to leave her with a potential for making armaments." He called too for a revision of the Level of Industry Plan so as to make Germany self-sufficient. And Marshall assured the Russians that with the treaty he had offered them "a reasonable increase in the level of industry should not endanger European security but should contribute materially to European recovery."

None of this swayed Molotov. What he wanted was resumption of reparations deliveries from the Bizone, confiscation from current production and full payment of $10 billion to the Soviet Union. "It is well-known," he kept saying, that all this had been agreed at Potsdam. Not to the Americans or British – quite the reverse. What they did know for sure was that any traveller by rail from Berlin to Moscow passed sidings crammed with rusting machinery hacked to pieces in Germany; what they suspected was that the Russians now needed German goods because they could not reassemble that machinery and had ruined the industry of their zone. The western allies were not going to let Molotov ruin their own zones too, not when the Russians would not account for what they had taken already and the Bizone was being so heavily subsidised. Bevin summed up Molotov's demands as an attempt "to loot Germany at our expense." Marshall did, however, go so far as to offer a limited quantity of reparations from current production if, and only if, the Soviet Union agreed to forgo plant scheduled for dismantling. There was no response from Molotov.

To some extent it might be thought that Molotov made a miscalculation in Moscow: a less extortionate demand for reparations could have secured resumption of deliveries from west Germany and encouraged further talks on the Bizone and the constitution. It could be argued that he paid an even higher price for his greed in turning down a French request for economic fusion with the Saar, which the Americans and British were willing to consider but which would have cut off reparations from the area. Molotov's refusal deprived the French of their last hope of playing both sides against the middle; from now on they made tentative approaches to the Bizone and seldom gave tactical votes to the Russians.

It was, however, possible to interpret Molotov's tactics not as economic obtuseness but as deliberate political strategy. Bevin certainly reached the conclusion in Moscow that the Soviet Union's "underlying motive was to cause such confusion in Germany as to reduce the influence of the western Powers in the western zones and eventually to induce the Americans to clear out of Europe."[24] Marshall too decided that the Russians were deliberately aiming at economic chaos for political ends. On 18 April he paid a courtesy call on Stalin. He found him looking old, grey and careworn, but cheerfully doodling wolf heads in red pencil. Marshall was shocked by Stalin's relaxed view of the conference's failure.[25] The Generalissimo and old world leader was patronising to the General and new Secretary of State and dismissed Marshall's urgent pleas for action to avert European collapse: "It is wrong to give so tragic an interpretation to our present disagreements." Never mind if there were no settlement now; "when people have exhausted themselves in dispute they recognise the necessity for compromise."[26]

This conversation made up Marshall's mind. All the way home he told his party that Stalin was happy to let things drift and wanted economic collapse and social misery, because these were the conditions in which Kremlin policy could triumph. Marshall himself wanted an initiative to prevent a complete breakdown in western Europe.[27] On the way back he stopped in Berlin and instructed Clay to strengthen the organisation of the Bizone and get an upward revision of the Level of Industry Plan. In Washington he told the American people in a nationwide broadcast that the United States and Britain could not go on pouring money into Germany without four-Power action to promote a healthy economy. He emphasised the alarming decline on the Continent: "The recovery of Europe has been far slower than had been expected. Disintegrating factors are becoming evident. The patient is sinking fast while the doctors deliberate." And he produced a variation on the words of Stalin which had made such a deep impression on him: "Action cannot await compromise through exhaustion."

Action had been so long delayed in the Bizone that by May 1947 the average ration was only 1,100 calories a day and in some large industrial cities it was barely 900 – in spite of increased imports. One British official warned, "We are living from ship to ship";[28]

General Clay reported that the American zone only had three or four weeks' supply of bread grain and would be dependent on imports until the harvest in late August.[29] Strikes and hunger marches were rife; coal production was dropping. Any treatment of the economy would take time to show results. To be effective, the occupation authorities believed, it must be accompanied by measures to lift the Germans from their sense of helplessness.

To encourage self-confidence the Germans were first given a say in the running of the economy. On 29 May 1947 the military governments of the Bizone reached an agreement to establish a German Economic Council made up of fifty-four-delegates from the Länder (provinces) to be responsible for drawing up policies, subject to allied approval, for economics, finance, transport, communications, food and agriculture. An Executive Committee, with one representative from each Land, would direct the administration of these policies and have the right to make recommendations to the Council. Next the Germans were given something to work for. By mid-July there was a new Level of Industry Plan, allowing an increase of production to almost 75 per cent of the pre-war level, leaving undismantled enough steel capacity to double output and abolishing many of the restrictions on industries concerned mainly with exports. In August it was announced that management of coal production would be transferred to Germans, supervised by a joint Anglo-American control group.

Not surprisingly all these measures provoked strong Soviet protest. The Russian Military Governor, Marshal Sokolovsky, denounced them in August as "witness to the fact that the US and British military administrations have taken the road of a complete breaking away from the decisions of the Potsdam conference." His western counterparts might well have argued that they were acting wholly in the spirit of Potsdam if only in part of Germany. Clay's answer to Sokolovsky was firm: "We do not propose to let continued and indecisive discussions draw the US zone into a state of economic chaos which would retard the recovery of Europe as a whole."[30] As ever he made it clear that the invitation to join the Bizone still stood. It was refused. And the Soviet Union had already turned down another offer, which even at this late date could have restored the unity and prosperity of all Europe and the co-operation of East and West. The Russians had rejected the Marshall Plan.

Within two days of his return from the Moscow conference General Marshall had acted on his belief that immediate steps must be taken to avert total European catastrophe. He had instructed the

Policy Planning Staff under Kennan to study means for economic revival. Marshall developed their ideas in a speech at the Harvard Commencement ceremonies on 5 June. Here he spelled out that American assistance to Europe must no longer be piecemeal and improvised in response to sudden emergencies, but comprehensive and once and for all: "a cure rather than a palliative." He made it clear that help must be available to any state "willing to assist in the tasks of recovery" and that the policy of the United States was "directed not against any country or doctrine but against hunger, poverty, desperation and chaos." If Europeans themselves agreed on an analysis of needs and the contribution each country could make, the United States would give financial backing for their programme. "The initiative, I think, must come from Europe," said Marshall.

These last words were a clarion call to Ernest Bevin, who heard a report of the speech early in the morning, listening to the radio in bed. He seized the initiative, informed Washington immediately that the message had been understood and arranged with Georges Bidault, the French Foreign Minister, to meet Molotov in Paris at the end of June to discuss joint action. But here Molotov denounced Marshall's offer as a weapon of imperialist expansion. He refused to discuss a joint plan, insisted that each country should present a separate list of requirements and argued against any aid for Germany. He made dark hints at nasty consequences for any state which joined the plan. He could not frighten Bevin or Bidault. They were determined to act on the terms Marshall had set and to do so with or without the Soviet Union. They called a conference in Paris in July of all the states of Europe. The Russians did not come. Furthermore, they stopped the Czechs, Poles and Finns attending.

As Bevin had listened to Molotov's tirades against the Marshall Plan in June, he had whispered to a Foreign Office official: "This really is the birth of the western bloc."[31] Even France and Italy were now secure parts of it, after years of political instability and endemic social unrest when it seemed likely that strong communist parties and unions would tip them into Moscow's orbit. As the western bloc formed, the eastern bloc hardened. It had to: the satellites of the Soviet Union must be shielded against the attractions of Marshall Aid, with its promises of prosperity and free development, and locked into Moscow's economic system. The democratic fig-leaves in east Europe were removed: by the end of 1947 Bulgaria, Hungary and Rumania were one-party states, the leader of the Polish Peasant Party had fled his country under threat of execution and the Greek communists had proclaimed a provisional government. The eastern states were brought together not in a joint task of reconstruction but under the aegis of the Cominform (Communist Information Bureau), a reincarnation of the old Comintern (Communist International) which had promoted the spread of revolution. When the Cominform was set up at the end of September 1947, Communist Party members were called upon "to take the lead in resisting the plans of imperialist expansion and aggression."

As Europe cracked in two, the threat of a permanent rift in Germany loomed. Already the gap between the western and Russian zones was wide: the systems had been radically different from the start of occupation. With Marshall Aid available only in the western zones that gap must widen. Furthermore, in response to the new Bizonal institutions, the SMA on 14 June set up the DWK (German Economic Commission) in which representatives of the SED, communist-led trades unions and others would co-ordinate planning and oversee the central economic agencies. Both sets of institutions, east and west, could be seen as embryonic and rival German governments and bureaucracies.

Even so, the British and Americans dreaded an irrevocable division of the country. As Robertson explained in a broadcast on 3 November: "We aim to see a united Germany not merely because we believe that the Germans will not be happy until they are united ... but also because we hold that the future stability of Europe demands a united Germany."[32] The expectation of aggressive German nationalism in response to partition was strong; but if anything, belief in the need for a full German contribution to Europe's economy was even stronger. In contradiction to these arguments, however, economic pressures drove the British and Americans to consider further separate development in the Bizone. By autumn 1947 they knew that the year's industrial production would not have risen above 47 per cent of 1936 levels and that barely half the pre-war output of coal would have been mined. Already two-thirds of the 1,000-calorie ration was being imported and prospects for the harvest were dim indeed – prolonged drought after the terrible winter had ruined crops. The situation encouraged political as well as economic fusion of the Bizone to harness German energy to the full. General Clay argued in November that such political development need not necessarily provoke the Russians; they were still at liberty to join, and if they chose not to then the split of Germany would be their responsibility. Economic rehabilitation and sound political growth in Germany, he suggested, "can be successful only if directed under our supervision by a German government."[33]

Germans, however, were far from sanguine at the prospect. Of course they wanted the chance to run their own affairs, but not at the price of a divided Germany. And by autumn 1947 they feared the division would come whether they played a part in it or not. In a poll in the American zone in August, 150 businessmen were reported to be "strongly opposed to a final division of Germany" but to see "such a development as inevitable." They did not want to stave it off by concessions to the Russians and thought it prudent to compensate for the split by speeding up Trizonal fusion.[34] *The Times* noted in late September the increasing numbers leaving the Russian zone for the west sensing that a split was "inevitable and near at hand."[35]

As German fears of division grew, the Soviet zone took on itself the role of champion of unity. In September the SED called for a national referendum on the formation of "a unified German democratic state with a decentralised administration." On 26 November Grotewohl announced a German People's Congress "for unity and a just peace." It met in Berlin on 6 and 7 December. Only KPD representatives came from the western zones. There were few Christian Democrat delegates from the Russian zone. Jacob Kaiser and Ernst Lemmer, who had been installed to run the CDU as SMA yes-men, had worked hard to please and appease in the hope of preserving some alternative to the SED. But they had reached their sticking-point: they would not back a movement to unite Germany on Soviet terms. Kaiser and Lemmer were sacked by the SMA and other CDU officials were threatened. A few stayed as a rump in the Soviet zone, claiming independence but toeing the SED line; the rest preferred expulsion from the zonal party and the leaders moved to west Berlin.

Here, of course, fears of partition of Germany were particularly acute and were intensified by the belief that it would result in the incorporation of the city into the Soviet zone. This belief was fed by stories starting in the spring of 1947 in the Russian-controlled press that the western Powers were about to leave Berlin. There had been signs too in the Kommandatura which suggested Russian plans for a takeover. In May, for instance, the Russian representative had criticised the western authorities for giving too much leeway to the city government and suggested that if they found the existing constitutional arrangements burdensome they should renegotiate

85

four-Power control.[36] In August visits by Berlin officials to the Bizone to discuss food supplies for the western sectors were denounced by Soviet spokesmen as opening moves in the merger of the western sectors and the zones – an example, as the western authorities saw it, of a standard Russian tactic of accusing others of what you are doing yourself. In October Kotikov, the Soviet Commandant, introduced a fourteen-point programme for the improvement of the city's working and living conditions. On the face of it this was a useful move; these were matters the western authorities very much wanted to discuss. It soon became apparent, however, that Kotikov would only allow his fourteen points to be accepted or rejected as a package and as they stood. In so doing, he blocked any discussion of alternatives for months and presented the deadlock to the Berlin public as evidence that only the SMA cared about their welfare and only the withdrawal of the western Powers would ensure its improvement.

Berliners had less and less faith in western readiness to stand up to the Russians. They were dismayed that no public protest was made over the kidnapping of opponents of the SED from all parts of the city and that no support was given to the City Assembly's calls to discipline Colonel Markgraf, whose police from the Soviet sector were known to be involved in the abductions. Western protests were in fact made, but only in the secrecy of the Kommandatura – in the interest of quadripartite solidarity. That left Berliners with the impression of lack of concern and weakness.

So too did the handling of a crisis over who should become the city's Oberbürgermeister. Dr. Ostrowski, who took the post after the 1946 election, had hoped to stay politically neutral and concentrate on uncontentious practical policies. He discovered that there was no middle course. The SMA hauled him to their headquarters night after night. He was alternately plied with drink, interrogated, or threatened with the exposure of family skeletons until he agreed to work with the SED on a common programme for three months. That was totally unacceptable to the City Assembly. A vote of no confidence was passed against him; Ostrowski resigned in April – or thought he did. Kotikov invoked the Russian interpretation of the city constitution and refused to approve the resignation. And, when the SPD on 24 June chose Ernst Reuter as their candidate for Oberbürgermeister, Kotikov vetoed him. The western Powers argued with Kotikov – but again behind the closed doors of the Kommandatura – and finally appealed to the Allied Control Council where Kotikov's right to veto was upheld. As far as the City Assembly was concerned, if they could not install Reuter, they would leave the post vacant. In the coming months Reuter was regarded by Berliners as their Lord Mayor, but his functions had to be taken over by his deputy, Louise Schroeder. The western allies may have thought it better to avoid precipitating a breakdown in four-Power government and splitting the city. Berliners thought they had seen another demonstration of craven western submission to the Russians and a sign that sooner or later the western Powers would succumb to pressure and leave the city.

No one, least of all Berliners, had high hopes that any fundamental German problems would be eased by the Council of Foreign Ministers' meeting in London from 25 November to 15 December 1947. Anyone could have written out the arguments of both sides in advance. Molotov's demands were the same as ever: four-Power control of the Ruhr, the end of the Bizone and half the total of $20 billion of reparations. So were the replies of the western ministers. There was even more abuse than usual. Molotov accused the western governments of using Germany as "a base for the development of war industry and Germany's reactionary forces as a support" in taking over Europe. Bevin gave as good as he got. (He was the first to admit that shouting at Molotov did no good, but he found it therapeutic.) Even Marshall, who found such slanging matches distasteful, was stung by Molotov into retorting that his charges were clearly designed for another audience in another place and that delivering them in the CFM made it difficult to respect the Soviet Union – at which, Clay noticed, Molotov "winced perceptibly."[37] The only significant difference between the London Conference and all its barren, bad-tempered predecessors was that it adjourned without any arrangements being made for another. Everyone had lost faith in conferences and lost any hope of agreement. They would go their own ways.

There was no western sense of merciful release. Clay described leaving London "not with exhilaration but with sadness."[38] But there was a reluctant admission by the Americans and British that the only course open now was to concentrate on the Bizone and keep hoping that the French and Russians would be won over.

Everyone knew this was a dangerous course to take. Germans, occupation authorities and allied governments alike thought that at the very least the Russians would now try to push the western Powers out of Berlin. Admiral Hillenkoetter, the Director of the

CIA, suggested to President Truman in a memo on 22 December that the Russians might well "undertake a programme of intensified obstruction and calculated insult in an effort to force withdrawal"; they would certainly use Berlin as a lever to check allied plans for west Germany. He warned that if communications with the city were disrupted, it would be impossible to feed it by air alone.[39] Bevin told the Cabinet that the Russians saw continued western presence in Berlin as "fatal to any plans which they may have for the political assimilation of the Eastern zone." At the same time, he thought that an attempt to "squeeze us out by direct pressure on our communications or by cutting off our supplies in Berlin would be very risky and might even lead to war." He guessed that the Soviet Union would stop short of that and might not even risk losing steel supplies from the Ruhr or the hope of eventual reparations from the west. It seemed more likely that they would "pursue their tactics of undermining us with the Germans in order to make our position in Berlin as uncomfortable as possible, and ultimately to convince us that we should lose more face by staying on in the city than by evacuating it."[40] One Washington official judged that the Russians were trying to establish a totalitarian regime in their zone, which could "not reach maximum effectiveness without Berlin as its capital." He predicted that they would either boycott the ACC and Kommandatura and wait for the western allies to give up, or would cause such difficulties over the supply of the city that the allies would be driven out.[41] However, General Walter Bedell Smith, the US Ambassador in Moscow, warned against concessions: to "think in terms of appeasing the Russians in order to maintain our position in Berlin seems to me to ignore what experience in dealing with [the] Soviet government should have taught us."[42] Nearly everyone had reached the conclusion that if the western Powers were to leave Berlin, it would be a grave blow to their prestige in Europe and would almost undoubtedly result in the whole of Germany coming under the control of the Soviet Union.

In Berlin itself the American Commandant, Colonel Howley, made a public promise that the allies would stay under the same agreement which gave the Russians the right to be present and that they would defend their "investment in democracy" in the form of the $100 million of food so far delivered to the city.[43] But a leading article in the *Tägliche Rundschau* threatened that Bizonal, let alone Trizonal, government would lead the Soviet Union to re-examine quadripartite administration of the city. Other Russian-controlled papers began a war of nerves, retailing new rumours of western withdrawal.[44] In official quadripartite circles there was a struggle to maintain an appearance of four-Power friendship. At the last meeting of the Kommandatura for 1947 Howley, as chairman, thanked the other members for their co-operation so far and expressed his "extreme affection for his Soviet, British and French colleagues" (at which someone wrote in the margin of the Foreign Office copy of the minutes: "Oh, I say. Steady on.").[45] But the underlying mood was deeply pessimistic. No one doubted that the coming year would see a Russian offensive to drive the West from Berlin. Berliners were not alone in wondering if it could be withstood.

5

Putting on the Squeeze

The Russians did not make any direct attack on the western Powers in Berlin during the early weeks of 1948; indeed, Robert Murphy, General Clay's political adviser, noticed that it was a "relatively harmonious period" in the Allied Control Council and the Kommandatura.[1] Instead, they maintained steady pressure against the morale of Berliners. A favourite device was a dropped comment to politicians – they were good loudspeakers. When an SMA official at a Liberal Party meeting in the Russian zone on 6 January remarked that the Soviet Union would soon be the only Power in Berlin, the whole city knew about it in no time.[2] In addition, the Russian-licensed press kept up its effective campaign suggesting that quadripartite administration would soon end and that the western Powers were already leaving the city.[3] Berliners believed it. Well aware that large numbers of British and American staff were moving out, they were too nervous to accept the true explanation: that the officials were being transferred to the expanding administration in the Bizone. A survey of public opinion in the city in the second half of January suggested that Berliners viewed the future as gloomy whatever happened: either the western allies would be driven out and the Russians would take over, or they would stay with their communications cut and supply themselves by air but be unable to feed the population in the western sectors.[4] Berliners had recently had a sharp reminder of their isolation in the middle of the Russian zone and their dependence on imported food. On 15 January the Russians had issued an order that all vehicles moving in or out of the city must carry a green pass signed by the SMA.[5] It took time and trouble to get the pass. As a result, fewer people were travelling into the east zone to see friends or to barter and fewer food lorries were coming into the city.

Meanwhile the mood in the western zones was, in Clay's view, "more tense than at any time since surrender."[6] The cause was the old intractable problem: hunger. When Murphy was tucking into a US Military Government dinner one night, he was told by the Minister President of North Rhine – Westphalia that in his Land the official ration was no more than 900 calories a day.[7] In the Ruhr the average ration seldom reached 1,200 calories in January. Miners were still relatively well-fed, but for weeks the old and those who did light work got only bread and cereals, no meat or fats (even on the black market there was hardly any butter). So there were strikes: in the Ruhr 150,000 people downed tools for twenty-four hours on 16 January; in the Bizone two and a half million stopped work on 4 February.[8] The occupation authorities had not only failed to relieve hunger, they had failed to explain to Germans why it was endemic. A survey of 3,100 adults in the British zone in January revealed that 46 per cent of them believed that "starvation and wrecking the economy" were the actual objectives of allied occupation. Significantly in the British sector of Berlin, where political perceptions were sharper, only 19 per cent thought so, and 44 per cent believed the purpose was "building democracy and fighting communism."[9] Starvation and such a degree of political alienation had to be tackled quickly and radically. It was no real answer just to import more food, though for the moment that was what the British and Americans had to do. Germans themselves must produce more food, or earn foreign currency to buy it.

For the moment there was no incentive for farmers to produce more. Any money they earned was rapidly losing value through inflation. They were not bothering to slaughter what animals they reared and they were storing crops or keeping them for their own consumption. They were not even selling much on the black market, where it was reckoned that four million cattle, pigs and sheep had disappeared in 1947.[10] There were few goods in the shops to tempt anyone to earn, few being produced for export. Manufacturers were stockpiling their rare raw materials rather than make goods for worthless money. Currency reform could break this log-jam. Clay and Robertson had pleaded for it in the Bizone when they were in London for the Council of Foreign Ministers at the end of 1947. Marshall and Bevin had persuaded them that it made political and financial sense to have one last attempt to get a four-Power scheme for a new national currency.

The matter came on to the agenda of the ACC in January 1948. The prospects for a quadripartite policy seemed good. The Russians quickly dropped their argument that it was possible to have a uniform currency whilst they themselves continued to print their own notes in Leipzig; they began to discuss seriously western proposals for a single financial administration and one central bank of issue. By 11 February there seemed to be an agreement in principle. Only technical details now needed to be sorted out and these were handed to the ACC's Financial Directorate. Sokolovsky even accepted Clay's suggestion that a limit of sixty days be set for finding final agreement.[11] Some western observers were suspicious about this sudden Russian reasonableness and wondered if it were a delaying tactic, or whether the Soviet authorities actually wanted a quadripartite currency reform so as to keep a finger in the western economic pie and frustrate recovery.[12] Having got this far, however, it was not possible to break off discussions – that would give the impression that the West was looking for an excuse to widen the division of Germany. Even so, given doubts about Soviet intentions and bitter experience of Russian ability to spin out any negotiation, it seemed prudent to start planning a separate Bizonal currency reform, just in case.[13]

It also seemed essential to bridge the rift in the Bizone between the population and government. Germans themselves must be given fuller powers to improve food production and distribution and get the economic system working. On 7 January 1948 in Frankfurt, Clay and Robertson met the eight Ministers President of the Bizonal Länder and put to them a series of proposals for strengthening administration and increasing the part played in it by Germans. In so doing, they were pointing the way to eventual German self-government. They recommended that the Bizonal Economic Council should double its representation from the Länder from 52 to 104 members and be given full control over customs and the right to levy taxes. A new Legislative Council – a Länderrat – with two representatives from each Land would protect the interests of the states and have power to initiate legislation on matters other than revenue and to veto the Economic Council unless overriden by its absolute majority. The old Executive Committee should take full control of departments to administer the Bizone's finance, food, agriculture, economics, communications and civil service, and a High Court should be set up to adjudicate in disputes between these agencies and the Länder. It was further suggested that a central bank be established to handle currency and funds for exports and imports, staffed by Germans and owned by the Land banks, though still under the ultimate control of the Military Governors.

These Frankfurt proposals were clearly an offer of viable though as yet unborn German government: the Economic and Legislative Councils were essentially two chambers of a parliament, the Executive Committee was a virtual cabinet. The eight German politicians took two days to consider the ideas, grumbling the while about the speed of the changes and the lack of time to prepare for them.[14] In fact, they were frightened by the proposals. They dreaded widening the division of Germany, and no amount of reassurance from the Military Governors that the western allies were not writing off the east zone and still aimed at a united Germany made them feel any better. The Ministers President well knew what accusations the Russians and the SED would make about the changes and they expected a hostile public reaction in their states. It would have been so much easier for them if they had been handed an allied diktat: then they could have stood aside and let the British and Americans bear the brunt of criticism. But the whole point of the allied exercise was to make the Germans take responsibility. With reluctance and deep anxiety they did so. On 9 January their spokesman, Dr. Hans Ehard of Bavaria, accepted the Frankfurt proposals on the grounds that the present distress of the population demanded instant financial and economic remedies. This fiction to cover the constitutional content of the reforms was carefully maintained by Germans and occupation authorities alike in the coming weeks.

It deceived no one. However, public opinion in west Germany was much readier to look on the bright political side of the Frankfurt decisions than the Ministers President had expected. *Die Zeit* took the view that union of any sections of the country was a move towards final complete unity. *Der Tagesspiegel* decided that Germany could hardly be more divided than it was at present and that anyone who thought there was not already an east German government (in SED headquarters) was talking through his hat. It was left to the Russian-controlled newspapers to deliver the expected onslaught on "the establishment of a western state and the complete partition of Germany," condemning "the treason of Frankfurt against German unity" and reserving special venom for the Ministers President as "Quislings" engaged in "clandestine treacherous activity" in the "Frankfurt conspiracy." Several east zone papers reprinted a leader in the *Tägliche Rundschau*, which called the Frankfurt proposals the most flagrant example of Anglo-American violations of Potsdam and warned, ominously, that they must lead to changes in the running of Berlin: the city could not continue to be the focal point of intrigue by those who supported German partition.[15] Yet as Clay put it: "Anything we do to strengthen the Bizonal administration will create a hazard with respect to the USSR in Berlin"; but, on the other hand, appeasement would make Bizonal reconstruction "difficult if not impossible."[16]

Were the newspaper threats anything more than indignant noise? Perhaps not, since the Russian zone press gave up stories of western withdrawal from Berlin for several days. Certainly the challenge to the allied position in the city was not repeated at an official level. When Marshal Sokolovsky read a statement to the ACC about the Frankfurt proposals on 20 January, he stuck to criticism of bipartite action "behind the back" of the Control Council and, in terms implying sorrow rather than anger, bemoaned the fact that the western Powers had turned down Molotov's offer at the London Foreign Ministers' meeting of a central German government and, instead, had taken "a new step towards the splitting of Germany."[17] He made no reference to the terms of their presence in Berlin.

That might seem reassuring for his western colleagues. Sokolovsky had just returned from a visit to Moscow, where presumably he had discussed the response to the Frankfurt proposals. Conceivably the Soviet government had decided against an ultimatum: give up Bizonal development or leave Berlin. Or had it? Was the message being put across in a different way? On 20 January, the day Sokolovsky made his relatively mild objections in the ACC, a Russian liaison officer told CDU officials that the Soviet occupation authorities would not hesitate to close Berlin's road and rail corridors in the event of a western currency reform or moves to split Germany.[18] Then on the night of 23 January a British military train from Berlin, which included two sealed coaches carrying 120 German passengers, was held up at the Russian checkpoint at Marienborn. Russian guards wanted to board it and inspect their documents. They claimed that German passengers should have interzonal passes as well as the usual permits to travel on official allied business. It was the third time in ten days that they had tried to do this. On the two previous occasions there had been a few hours of argy-bargy and the trains had moved on. This time, however, when the British escorting officer refused to let the Russians enter the train and insisted on the standard procedure of handing over movement orders for inspection on the platform, the train was shunted into a siding and left there for twelve hours until the section with British passengers was allowed to move on but the two German coaches were sent back to Berlin.[19]

Yet if the SMA was trying to tell the western Powers something, it was not doing so very clearly. These two incidents were noted only as further skirmishes in the war of nerves. Nor did the western allies make it clear enough to Germans that they would not be bullied out of their rights and responsibilities in Berlin. Clay issued a statement that if the Russians interrupted rail communications he would bring in reinforcements and supplies for his garrison by air, but at the same time he threatened to hand over the feeding of his sector to the Russians, which simply strained Berliners' nerves further.[20] Robertson, for his part, after more hold-ups of British trains, decided on 13 February to stop carrying German passengers for a while. He personally may have thought it sensible to keep the traffic moving and send German travellers by road. Berliners took it that the western Powers were all too ready to give way to Russian pressure.

The Russians might well have been arguing by early 1948 that the really big pressure in Germany was on them. They had seen the creation of the Bizone, the ending of reparations deliveries from the west, the announcement of a German part in the Marshall Plan, and the Frankfurt proposals. Now, in mid-February, they learned that the western Powers were going to hold a conference in London to discuss Germany – without inviting the Soviet Union. They protested. A duel of diplomatic notes was held. The Soviet Union made the first thrust on 13 February, communicating in Washington, London and Paris its displeasure at only hearing of the meeting in the press, calling the conference a violation of Potsdam and warning that any decision in London would not be regarded as legal. The western governments parried with arguments that Potsdam did not preclude Powers separately discussing Germany, that the Soviet Union itself had violated Potsdam by preventing economic unity and that steps had to be taken to check German economic deterioration for the sake of all Europe. By March the Soviet Union was lunging back with warnings that western policies were "pregnant with consequences which may be useful only to all kinds of incendiaries of a new war."[21] All to no avail. The London meeting went on regardless. Talks about Germany between the United States, Britain and France would always have angered the Soviet Union. As it was the conference gave an added cause for alarm. Belgium,

95

Holland and Luxembourg were invited to join. They were, after all, Germany's neighbours and old trading partners and had a strong interest in problems of security and the success of the Marshall Plan. It must have looked to the Soviet Union as if western Europe was ganging up against her.

The London talks began on 23 February in India House. The building, with its portraits of governors and viceroys, was still redolent of the old Empire, but it was now the offices of a new little bureaucratic empire, the German Section of the Foreign Office, whose staff was the size of the rest of the Foreign Office put together. Politicians and diplomats held continuous sessions. The Military Governors and their advisers flew back and forth to Germany, a shuttle which Clay lamented had "helped to contribute substantially to Murphy's support as I was unable to win a single game of gin rummy from him in the entire period of the conference."[22] The delegations faced the traditional English dilemma: whether to sit near the fire and roast or away from it and freeze. They might have been expected to be even more uncomfortable with an agenda which was full of contentious issues: control of the Ruhr, the German part in the European Recovery Programme, closer French links with the Bizone, security and reparations, the form of a future German government. But, by the time the conference went into recess on 6 March so that governments could consider its interim agreements, Bevin was able to record that it had been "more successful than had been expected"; everyone had been much readier to make concessions than had appeared likely.[23]

Delegates had no excuse for self-congratulation, however. Their spirit of unanimity had not sprung from their own altruism. It had been provoked from outside. Indeed, the conference might well have adjourned with a vote of thanks to the Soviet Union. For in the third week of February, as the talks began in London, the Czech Communist Party, supported by a Soviet Deputy Foreign Minister in Prague and units of the Red Army on the border, had carried out a coup and seized full control of Czechoslovakia. In the same week news also reached London that Stalin had written to the Finnish President proposing a pact of friendship and military alliance and pressing him to visit Moscow – the sort of invitation known to put the visitor in the predicament of Little Red Riding-hood. (A fortnight later the Norwegians were faced with similar propositions.) These moves created such a sense of threat and outrage at the London talks that the delegations had been pushed into agreements unimaginable otherwise. Probably the Soviet

Union's moves in northern Europe and Czechoslovakia had happened together and at the same time as the London talks by pure coincidence; conceivably they were not intended as warnings against west European change, but as logical measures for east European security. Given the timing, the west European states drew quite opposite conclusions. And their fears led not just to major decisions on Germany; they triggered a new concern for western solidarity.

Western Union was a project on which Bevin had been ruminating ever since the failure of the Council of Foreign Ministers at the end of 1947 persuaded him that the intended post-war settlement of all Europe by the four Powers had been aborted and that an alternative settlement must be conceived – less extensive than had been hoped for, but still capable of safeguarding west European interests. From the end of the war it had been assumed that the main threat to west Europe was Germany. Increasingly, Bevin had come to think that the real menace was the Soviet Union. Not that he expected a military attack: the British Chiefs of Staff estimated that given conditions in Russia that was unlikely before 1957 or even 1960.[24] But, as he told the House of Commons on 22 January, the Russians must not be allowed to think that they could intimidate west Europe by political upsets, economic chaos and revolutionary methods; the time was "ripe for consolidation" in west Europe and its states should not only draw together, but also reach out for ties with Africa, Asia, the Commonwealth and the Americas. He wanted a defensive relationship with any nation where parliamentary and liberal institutions flourished and a warning to the Soviet Union not to try to undermine them. He thought, furthermore, that "war was less likely if we acted firmly now than if we allowed matters to slide from crisis to crisis as had been done in the '30s."[25]

Bevin was not specific about the form Western Union should take. The old elephant liked to amble along within broad principles, chewing over possibilities, nosing out the feelings of his friends and enemies. He was not a believer in rigid institutions and rules of procedure as incubators of genuine co-operation and mutual help. As one Foreign Office official spotted, Bevin did not like words such as "organ" or "organisation"; he preferred "organism," something with a life of its own which could grow and adjust to its environment.[26] Bevin also had practical reasons for staying vague. He saw a strong Germany as an essential element in Western Union, but knew the French would shy away from the idea; they would have to be led to it in slow stages. He wanted to involve the United States, as the greatest liberal power and the mightiest military

97

force, but the Americans had always avoided overseas peacetime commitments; they would have to be lured in gradually.

In the event, enticing France and the United States took much less time and patience than Bevin had envisaged. The Soviet Union did the job for him with the Czech coup. From January 1948 he had been making quiet and cautious approaches to France and the Benelux countries (Belgium, The Netherlands and Luxembourg) while the United States looked on benignly from the sidelines. The diplomatic machine was slammed into top gear by the news from Prague. On 8 March, while the London talks were in recess, Britain, France and the Benelux countries began formal meetings in Brussels. On 12 March General Marshall sent word to London: "We are prepared to proceed at once in the joint discussions on the establishment of an Atlantic security system." On 17 March the west Europeans signed the Treaty of Brussels and promised to aid each other against any armed aggression. Their agreement was hailed that day by President Truman in a speech to Congress, in which he recommended that the determination of the "free countries of Europe to protect themselves" be "matched by an equal determination on our part to help them to do so." It was not yet certain that the President could deliver support in the form of military assistance – he would have to get Senate and public approval for an historic reversal of foreign policy and unpalatable taxation first. In the meanwhile, he asked Congress for immediate legislation to permit selective military service to keep US forces up to strength (around one-and-a-half million men by comparison with an estimated four million Soviet troops). On 22 March talks began in Washington between the British, Americans and Canadians to explore the possibilities of an Atlantic pact. The Americans were leery. If they were to be persuaded to join, one State Department official thought, much would depend upon whether some "fresh Soviet action maintained the present tense atmosphere."[27]

There had been a noticeable increase in the tension in Berlin since the London talks had begun. After a lull of a few days from 20 January the Russian-controlled press had resumed its prophecies of imminent western withdrawal from the city. Russian interference with traffic had increased. When the Magistrat totted up the sum effect of the hold-ups, it found that the freight moving in and out of the city had dropped from 8,806 tons in the first ten days of January to 2,457 in the last.[28] Food was noticeably lacking even on the black market. Not only Berliners were feeling the strain now.

Murphy observed a steady deterioration in relations in the Kommandatura from the end of January "to a point at which it appears that agreement is impossible on even the most routine questions." He reported at the beginning of March that the Russians were returning time and again to accusations that the western Powers were breaking allied agreements, trying to disrupt quadripartite administration of Berlin and using the city to meddle in the affairs of the Soviet zone. Murphy reminded Washington that past experience showed: "The Soviet government (like the Nazi government) charges the other person with those things it itself intends to do." He suspected that present Russian tactics were "designed to irritate, confuse and tire the other three" (and with Commandants' and Deputies' meetings lasting anything up to eleven hours, tired they must have been), in the hope of "trapping them into ... some precipitate reaction upon which the Soviets could seize as a pretext for breaking up the Kommandatura."[29] Many British observers suggested that the Russians would find a pretext for taking over Berlin with the implementation of the new Frankfurt proposals or western plans for currency reform.[30] At the Commandants' meeting on 2 March there was the clearest indication yet that the Kommandatura was in danger. The Soviet Commandant, Kotikov, said his western colleagues had reduced "the principle of quadripartite control to a farce" and that the only question which remained was "whether or not it could now be preserved."[31]

At the Military Governors' level the atmosphere had become equally unpleasant and forebodings were strong. Clay felt so disturbed that on 5 March he wrote to the Director of Intelligence of the US Army General Staff that though he had always believed war unlikely for at least ten years, within the past few weeks he had "felt a subtle change" in the Soviet attitude which suggested that war might come with "dramatic suddenness"; he sensed a "feeling of new tenseness in every Soviet individual with whom we have official relationships."[32] His assessment was taken seriously in Washington. It undoubtedly influenced Truman's request for selective military service and Marshall's interest in an Atlantic pact. Both Clay and General MacArthur in the Far East were instructed to brush up their emergency plans.[33] The British were less alarmed about the Russian mood. Even so, they were very worried about their position in Berlin. As Robertson pointed out, the western presence there was "a serious inconvenience to say the least" for the Russians and an obstacle to "the final absorption of the Eastern zone in the Soviet orbit." He warned that once quadripartite currency negotiations broke down (possibly in April), or there was an offer of a fuller constitution to the Germans in the Bizone (some time in midsummer when the London talks wound up), the Russians might well bring matters to a head, either by calling on the western Powers to leave or by cutting communications to reduce them "to a position of humiliating discomfort."[34] Strang, agreeing with Robertson's analysis, added that though the Soviet Union had the military resources to drive the westerners out of Berlin, they would not risk war. He thought that for the time being the Russians would concentrate on sapping German morale and try to get more control over Berlin whether the western Powers stayed or not.[35]

Through February and early March Strang seemed to be right. The SMA leant heavily on all political leaders who opposed the SED. Parties could seek permission for meetings in the Soviet sector only three days in advance, which left them little time for publicity or booking rooms. SMA officials turned up even to ward committee meetings and tried to fix agendas; one local SPD chairman was threatened with prison when he threw out an SED interloper. Prominent members of the CDU and LPD were increasingly summoned to interviews at local Russian Kommandaturas, often during the night. They were questioned, shouted at and menaced with loss of rations. A Liberal Bezirk chairman, Herr Sonk of Weissensee, was forced to attend such sessions almost every day, sometimes twice a day. He ran a petrol station, but also owned a lorry for contract haulage work. In January the papers for his lorry were confiscated. It took a month to get them back, during which the Russians told Sonk the process would be quicker if he were "for us"; they also dangled the advantages of joining them by offering clothing coupons for his wife and daughter.[36] The LPD, the smallest party, felt particularly vulnerable and isolated: in February its members in the east zone were forbidden to attend their national party rally in the west and did not dare to disobey. By the beginning of March it was expected that both the LPD and the CDU would soon be banned.

The SMA and the SED made every effort to persuade politicians of all parties to attend the second People's Congress in Berlin on 17 and 18 March. The date and the place had been carefully chosen. It was the hundredth anniversary of the first German parliament, the symbol of liberal and nationalist ideals. That parliament had met in Frankfurt, now the administrative centre of the Bizone and expected seat of a future west German government. It had died there, and with it hopes of unification for a couple of generations.

By choosing Berlin for the Congress, the SMA and SED were reminding people of Frankfurt's failure and of Berlin's former position as capital of a united Germany while trading on fears of a split country. No amount of emotional manipulation, however, could turn the People's Congress into a genuinely national event. Of the 1,989 delegates who arrived at the Staatsoper in the Russian sector, over a thousand were from the east zone and most of the representatives from the western zones were members of the KPD.

The assembly set up a People's Council – a Volksrat – of 400 members, which was to form committees (more or less government departments) and elect a Praesidium (more or less a cabinet). The institutions were obviously a counter to those proposed for the Bizone and claimed to represent Germany as a whole. Furthermore, the Congress called for a constitution for a German republic and the abolition of the Allied Control Council at the earliest opportunity. As a first step the Congress announced that a nationwide plebiscite on the issue of independent national government would be held between 23 May and 13 June, with signatures collected house to house, factory to factory.

The patriotic fervour in the People's Congress failed to attract the democrats of Berlin: the SED's idea of a united Germany seemed too like a Soviet Socialist Republic. The opponents of the SMA and SED were called out on to the streets on 18 March by the Berlin SPD to show that there was a different way to cherish the aspirations of 1848. It was the first in a series of epic demonstrations in which Berliners would stand up to be counted and assert their values. From all parts of Berlin, 30,000 people came in the cold and the rain to the space in front of the ruined Reichstag and heard speakers from all democratic parties call for the unity of Germany, but not on communist terms. Franz Neumann, chairman of the SPD, reminded them that the freedoms fought for in 1848 did not exist in eastern Europe. Jacob Kaiser of the CDU, an exile from the Russian zone, warned that if totalitarianism triumphed Europe would be split and with it Germany and Berlin itself; "We want a free Germany and a free Europe." Carl Hubert Schwennicke, chairman of the Berlin LPD, urged that there could be no compromise with communism, that freedom could not be sacrificed for unity. Finally, Ernst Reuter displayed his gifts for seeing into the hearts of Berliners and putting into words their hopes and fears. He talked to the crowds in his simple, direct way about the pressures they were under, about how Prague had been overrun and Finland might well be. But, he told them, if the question were now put,

"Who will be the next, we can answer firmly and confidently: it will never be Berlin." They cheered him, but Reuter had another thought to offer – his vision was always wider than the bounds of the city. "If the world knows this then we will not be abandoned by the world." He had given notice that Berliners would fight alone if need be, but that the Berlin struggle was the world's struggle.

Within two days of Reuter's speech the conflict of the Powers in Europe, which had recently taken the form of distant manoeuvres in Frankfurt, Prague, Helsinki and London, became combat at close quarters in Berlin.

Marshal Sokolovsky, as the month's chairman of the Allied Control Council, had called a meeting for 20 March. It was a slightly intriguing summons: an addition to the meetings already scheduled and with no announcement of an agenda. The western Military Governors were not apprehensive. Nor were they surprised when at the beginning of the session Sokolovsky asked for a full briefing on the decisions reached so far at the London talks. This was a reasonable request, and they could reply quite honestly that they themselves were not yet fully informed but would pass on the details as soon as they were. There was nothing unusual about the argument which followed, with Sokolovsky accusing his colleagues of unilateral actions in west Germany behind the screen of the ACC, Clay retaliating that the Russians had put up a screen round their own zone, and Robertson wading in with allegations that the SMA frequently took unilateral actions without advising the others. And there was nothing remarkable about Sokolovsky then reading a long statement charging the London participants and his western colleagues with taking decisions contrary to agreements on quadripartite government and arguing that the ACC "no longer exists as an organ of government." Sokolovsky had delivered his set piece with a distinct air of unease – an indication that he was acting on precise orders from Moscow, which always earned him sympathy from his opposite numbers. Everything up to now had been predictable and depressingly familiar. Suddenly there was a nasty shock. As Robertson began to reply to the Russian statement, Sokolovsky and his advisers stood up. "I see no sense in continuing this meeting," said the Marshal. "I declare it adjourned." The whole Russian delegation then walked out.[37]

Those who stayed behind steadied their nerves with the rule book: they decided that a unilateral adjournment was "improper" and closed the meeting by the normal procedure of a vote. An immediate thought struck them: they had not been offered the customary "refreshment," the sweet champagne and caviar which usually helped them to swallow a Russian rebuke. Then another more serious thought occurred: Sokolovsky had not mentioned the next Council meeting. Would there be one? Had he really meant that the ACC no longer existed?

There was one sign he had. A few hours before the Russians walked out Otto Grotewohl had told the SED Central Executive, using many phrases identical with those in Sokolovsky's written statement, that quadripartite government was at an end.[38] Yet, on the other hand, there were several indications of business as usual. The Russian member of the ACC secretariat turned up for a meeting the following day, and though several meetings of Kommandatura committees were then postponed by their Russian chairmen, others continued normally.[39] Furthermore, Sokolovsky's Chief of Staff, Lieutenant-General Lukyanchenko, told the Russian-controlled press that the Soviet Union would support the Allied Control Council as long as it was not used as "a cloak for unilateral action by the Western Powers in their zones."[40] So it was still possible to hope that Sokolovsky was just making a short demonstration. His western colleagues made their own: on 23 March they refused to attend quadripartite directorates, which handled such essentials as taxation, until the ACC met again.

It never did. Several weeks went by before everyone finally grasped that four-Power government had ended. Some people in Berlin wondered if that had really been the Russians' intention, or whether they had stepped out of the ACC as a short-term ploy and events then moved so quickly that they could not scramble back.[41] The Russians may, indeed, have made a tactical mistake – Clay's early reaction to the walk-out was: "I do not see how the Russians can block things more effectively by postponement of meetings than they have done by attendance."[42] If anything their move accelerated decisions at the London talks and in the Bizone. Given the timing and the nature of Sokolovsky's attack, most people had assumed that the walk-out was a gesture against Bizonal development. Was it also a challenge to the four-Power presence in Berlin? If so, why not make it in the Kommandatura?

As it was, in the absence of a clear Russian signal, let alone statement, the western Powers had to keep reading the runes. These suggested a definite threat to quadripartite occupation of the city even if no one could decide whether the Russians wanted allied withdrawal as a desirable end in itself or were naming the price of west German government. An article in the *Berliner Zeitung* on 20 March, clearly written with the knowledge that Sokolovsky intended to walk out of the ACC, had stated that if four-Power control of Germany ended, so too did four-Power occupation of Berlin. Russian officials in the offices of the *Tägliche Rundschau* were talking openly of the western allies being ejected from the city. There were innumerable rumours that Berlin was about to be incorporated into the Russian zone.[43] At one time all these stories would have been dismissed as bluff. Now it was feared that the Russians did, indeed, intend to take over. When? The betting was that the push would come some time in June when the decisions of the London talks were announced. How? By demanding western withdrawal? Infiltrating city institutions and political parties? Cutting communications with the western zones and either making life uncomfortable or actually threatening the survival of the city? No one expected the use of force. The Soviet Union might have something like 324,000 men in Germany (much the same number as the other three Powers) and their troops might be organised tactically rather than as quasi-police units, but it was not thought the Russians would use them – that would be to risk war and be blamed for it. Occasional troop movements were reported, but Russian supply dumps of fuel seemed no bigger than was necessary for peacetime needs and there was no build-up of bridging material or other supplies for a military offensive.[44]

With that thought as their only comfort, the western allies began to think seriously about how to cope once their position in Berlin was seriously threatened. On one thing they were agreed: they wanted to stay. As far as the French were concerned the best hope was to soft-pedal in the Bizone and give the Soviet Union no pretext for a move.[45] For the British and Americans that was conceding the game to the Russians; they wanted firmness. On 22 March Clay made a public statement: "We came into Berlin by right and we have every intention of staying." Two days later Whitehall passed on a message to Robertson: Bevin had said, "We must stay in Berlin ... he did not want withdrawal to be contemplated in any quarter."[46] It was relatively simple, however, to commit American and British staffs to putting up with whatever discomforts and dangers might arise – they were small, mainly military and could be supplied by air. But if the Russians cut electricity supplies from their sector or food from the western zones, what hope was there for the two-and-a-half million Berliners in the western sectors? A US Army General Staff study back in January had been emphatic that it was impossible to feed the civilian population of the city by air alone.[47]

On 23 March it was agreed that the British, French and American Commandants, Herbert, Noiret and Howley, should start to discuss secretly ways to keep the city alive.[48] Robertson warned that if a word of these talks got out he would stop them – he did not want Berliners alarmed. After a week Herbert gave a résumé of the difficulties they had envisaged should the Russians merely incorporate their sector into their zone and increase interference with traffic: food shortages would be inevitable and electricity supplies would be cut and could not be replaced for long by the obsolete power stations under western control. He feared it was "highly improbable that the western sectors could hold out through a winter on this basis, even leaving out political repercussions." The chances were that given power cuts, hardships and unemployment for a few months, Berliners "would prefer to have the Russians." Even so, Herbert just wondered if he were "underestimating the nerves and toughness of Berliners."[49] Indeed, he was – and also the seriousness of the crisis they would face. As Herbert wrote his report on 30 March the prologue to that crisis had begun.

For several days there had been more hold-ups than usual at Marienborn. These were seen as little more than a nuisance caused by over-zealous Russian officials. But they came at the same time as the rerouting of many trains in the Soviet zone to bypass Berlin, which meant that Berliners were often dependent on hitch-hiking to get in and out of the city. There was a brand new press campaign: on 24 March all Russian-licensed newspapers reported a sudden increase in murders, robbery, banditry and black-marketeering on the borders of the east zone, warned that food stocks were being drained by an influx of "starving thousands" from the west and called for stricter guarding of the zonal boundary.[50] (There had been previous scare stories along these lines, but they had stopped on 21 March and been replaced with articles praising the restoration of orderly traffic.)[51] Western observers had reckoned for some time that food was short in the Soviet zone thanks to the previous year's bad harvest, muddled direction of agriculture by the SMA and the dislocation caused by land reform. So they assumed that the Russians were just making excuses and blaming the West. But the press stories were taken up by various SED spokesmen ("alarming increase in the number of armed assaults in the Thuringian frontier districts," "removal of food and industrial equipment by sinister elements," "criminal elements including Fascist activists expelled from the Soviet zone ... perpetrating acts of violence on foreign orders").[52] It began to look as if a case was being built up to tighten border controls. A case was, indeed, put at length by Lukyanchenko to the press on 30 March, when he stated the need for "appropriate measures" to deter "starving hordes" and "criminal elements" – seemingly a retrospective case since extra Russian guard posts had already appeared and there were new intermediate checkpoints between road junctions leading from Berlin to major east zone cities.

Then in the night of 30 March – very late, a popular time for major SMA announcements – the western Military Governors received a letter from General Dratvin, Sokolovsky's deputy, giving them twenty-four hours' notice of "certain supplementary regulations" for traffic between Berlin and the west. He explained that these were necessary to cope with the "considerable increase in communications" and the needs of the Soviet zone economy, and would provide a "greater degree of organisation, system and control" to ensure "the safe carriage of freight" and to prevent the "rise of various rumours calculated to sow mistrust in relations between the occupation authorities."[53] The tone was reasonable; the "supplementary regulations" were not. They amounted to a thoroughgoing revision of the Berlin access arrangements. They laid down that all road and rail passengers, civilian or military, should submit individual documentation and most of their belongings for inspection at Russian border checkpoints, and that all items of freight, including those carried by military trains for occupation use, should be authorised by separate SMA permits. In other words, nothing would move without Russian say-so.

"I view this development very seriously," Robertson cabled to London. "It is plainly intended as the first move in the squeeze on our communications and it will not be long before there is another." He had acted calmly, however, and sent a restrained reply to Dratvin that the British were perfectly willing to discuss new regulations if they were given a fortnight to think about them, but would not accept this unilateral decision nor the Russian claim to control persons and goods, and least of all interference with British military trains.[54] Clay too saw the new regulations as "the first of a series of restrictive measures designed to drive us from Berlin." "Unless we take a strong stand now," he told Washington, "our life in Berlin would become impossible." A retreat from the city would have "serious if not disastrous consequences in Europe." Unlike Robertson, he was not satisfied with restraint. "It is my intent to instruct our guards to open fire if Soviet soldiers attempt to enter our trains." Clay knew the possible consequences of firing, but thought that if the Russians wanted war "we might as well find out now as later."[55]

This was pushing things a bit far for Washington. Bradley told Clay that the matter must be taken up with the Joint Chiefs of Staff and others; the evening US military train from Frankfurt must be delayed until instructions were sent from the Army Department.[56] Service chiefs, State Department officials, the President and his advisers held several urgent meetings to consider a response to the crisis. Should the President send a message to Stalin warning that the new orders could create an incident leading to war? Perhaps that was the impression Stalin wanted to create. Should the President consult Congressional leaders? That might cause public hysteria. Devise a joint response with the British? Certainly. Let Clay send through an armed train? Shooting by either side for whatever reason could well make the situation even more perilous.[57]

In three teleconferences that day Clay kept pleading to be allowed to send through his armed train. "I do not believe this means war," he argued, "but any failure to meet this [situation] squarely will cause great trouble." There could be no question of letting the Russians board allied trains: "It will only be a day or two before one of our people is pulled off on trumped-up charges.... There is no middle ground which is not appeasement." The "integrity of our trains as part of our sovereignty is a symbol of our position in Europe." By the last teleconference of the day, however, Washington approved a reply to Dratvin which Clay had reluctantly suggested: the right would be conceded to the Russians to check the identities of car passengers, but not to inspect their belongings; the Americans would supply passenger lists and movement orders for their rail travellers and manifests of cargo, but not allow Russian guards to board. A clamp was put on Clay's armed train: he must not increase the number of his guards or the weapons they carried and no one was to fire unless fired upon – and that, as Bradley was careful to stress, was the policy agreed by President Truman.[58]

During the night of 31 March and 1 April six allied trains arrived at the Russian checkpoint at Marienborn. The French train was stopped. After a short delay the guard allowed Russians to board, inspect documents and take off sixty-seven German passengers. It then went on its way. A British military train from Berlin arrived at 2 a.m. and was halted. The wing-commander in charge argued sharply for three-quarters of an hour with the Russians, who then gave up trying to climb on the train but would not allow it to proceed. What the *Daily Telegraph* called "a young lady from Bexleyheath" climbed off and, helped by some soldiers, lit a bonfire on the tracks so that food and tea could be distributed to the passengers.[59] This picnicking could have gone on – the train had been stocked with supplies for seven days – but at 3 p.m. an order was sent to return to Berlin. The second British military train was the long-distance shuttle through the zone. Its passengers were used to frequent stops, so few of them stirred when it stuck at Marienborn. They were rather bewildered, however, to find themselves still there next morning. "April Fool," they decided. At about 10 o'clock they got bully-beef, biscuits and tea; by lunchtime they had made friends with American passengers parked alongside and discovered how to heat US tinned steak-and-kidney pudding on bonfires and eat it with nail-files and toothbrushes.[60] The train sat there until late afternoon, then rolled back into the British zone; the passengers flew to Berlin instead. Two American trains had already backed out of Marienborn after refusing to allow Russians on board; the one from Frankfurt had a round trip of twenty-nine hours. A third had gone through in disgrace. Its commander, a lieutenant, had allowed the Russians on. Clay was furious, threatening court martial. (It would have been a good idea if someone had suggested putting a more senior officer in charge on such a crucial day.)

Clay was not going to risk that kind of humiliation again, or even give the Russians the satisfaction of seeing his trains in retreat. On 1 April he cancelled all US military rail transport.[61] The British followed suit next day after repeated hold-ups at Marienborn. They laid on a daily bus service for ninety passengers between Berlin and Helmstedt to connect with zonal trains, and regular RAF flights for priority travellers and mail.[62] But with only two Dakotas and an Anson they could not carry much. The Americans could do rather more: they got thirty C-47s flying in and out of Berlin at fifteen-minute intervals and in two days had delivered 55,000 lbs of food for their garrison.

For the rest the travel picture was confused and no one could be certain what the Russians would do next. Non-military trains seemed to be moving normally and, indeed, allied coaches could still be coupled to the Soviet zone train which connected with the Nord Express for Paris (until the Russians suspended the service on 23 April). Allied cars were getting through at Marienborn, but many German drivers were being turned back unless they had "proper authorisation." There was a new inconvenience for allied road travellers, however: on 2 April the SMA gave notice that they would close the two western aid stations on the autobahn, rightly pointing out that the agreement with the British and Americans specified "seasonal occupation" which meant winter use only. General goods traffic was suffering sporadic interference. On 1 April it was banned by the SMA on roads through their zone between 11 p.m. and 6 a.m., and twenty-four barge skippers were forbidden transit on the grounds that their permits were "invalid." Yet both these policies were abandoned on 5 April and replaced on the 9th with an SMA order that all goods travelling between the zones must have consignment notes signed by the Russian authorities. This, it was noted, gave the Russians "a complete stranglehold over the flow of goods from Berlin."[63]

But did they intend to keep it? The Russian-controlled press gave no indication of a permanent policy; all the articles were still written in terms of "disorderly and uncontrolled traffic" and "illegal operations" by "shady individuals." The Moscow papers too talked only of traffic control, the seepage of food to the west and the escape of "speculators and war criminals" from the Soviet zone.[64] Colonel Tulpanov of the SMA had said at a party on 3 April that the restrictions would be ended in a couple of weeks and that the Russians would then fire off another blank, but he was reported to have been "slightly intoxicated" at the time and a "blank" suggested bluff.[65] Were the traffic restrictions merely to test western reactions?

There were two incidents which certainly looked nothing more than probes. On the morning of 1 April Russian soldiers set up a post at a crossroads just inside the British sector near Gatow airfield, stopped some passing British vehicles and held their drivers. That afternoon a British officer came round to remind them whose sector they were in. When they refused to leave without their commander's permission, he closed off three of the roads and left one open to show them the way to go home. They took it that evening.[66] The next day eight Russians took up position in the American sector offices of German Railways – because, said Kotikov, "a group of criminal Germans in the Russian sector were scheming to enter the building and destroy valuable documents" in what he was often pleased to call "the Soviet military railway headquarters." Colonel Howley put his own men round the building, left some food on the steps like cheese for mice, and ordered that no one might enter but anyone could leave. When Kotikov complained directly to General

Clay about "encirclement," Clay did not deign to reply but let it
be known "it is not expected that he will be able to give his attention
to it until he has solved the problem of free entry of American
supply trains into Berlin." Early in the morning of 4 April the
Russians crept out and were picked up by a Red Army lorry.[67]

Such silly little confrontations were perfectly familiar to the
Americans and British and could be dealt with quickly and firmly.
It was not so easy to decide what to do if the Russians kept their
grip on Berlin's traffic; worse, if they tightened it. The British were
in favour of trying to talk to the Russians. Clay was dead set against
the idea. He saw it as a British "wish to propose compromise" and
thought it could not "serve any useful purpose except humiliating
rebuff."[68] Robertson was, in fact, no more in favour of concessions
than Clay was, but that was something he failed to get across
to the General whose attitude he found "most pessimistic and
bellicose."[69] He hoped to sound out Russian intentions and perhaps
offer them a discreet way out if they were regretting their behaviour.
Since there was no longer an Allied Control Council where matters
could be raised, Robertson's deputy, General Sir Nevil Brownjohn,
went to see Dratvin on 1 April. Brownjohn got nowhere at all. An
alternative to negotiation was retaliation. President Truman had
asked the Department of Commerce for their views on limiting
exports to the Soviet Union back on 26 March.[70] Bevin, too, considered cutting trade at the risk of losing Russian wheat, timber
and oil products, but got a doleful Foreign Office response: "We
have no good cards to play," the Russians "would not mind over-
much" and there was nowhere in the world they could be put in as
much difficulty as they themselves could cause in Berlin.[71] Clay had
suggested that the Russians could at least be inconvenienced by
limiting their use of the Panama and Suez canals and bunkering
facilities.[72]

There was something to be said for evacuating allied dependants
from Berlin – the presence of women and children added to the
strain and the supply problem. When the suggestion was put to
Clay in the first tense days of March, he cabled that evacuation
"would be politically disastrous ... would create hysteria
accompanied by rush of Germans to communism for safety."[73]
When the idea was revived during the teleconferences on 1 and 2
April, he was adamant: "Evacuation would play into Soviet hands"
and frighten Europe. He was certain "our women and children can
take it" and had told his staff that it was "unbecoming to show
signs of nervousness," but they were at liberty to leave – if they

chose not to return.[74] Even so, he had looked at the logistics of a total withdrawal. There were nearly 10,000 Americans in Berlin, 1,933 of whom were civilians and 2,602 dependants. They could probably be got out minus luggage in thirty-six hours by air and in twenty-four hours if all forms of transport were available; but on the assumption that rail transport was unusable and only aircraft and road vehicles were employed, it would take up to seven days to move personnel and all their property into the American zone.[75] The British would be hard-pushed to do it as quickly. They had three battalions of troops, 2,461 Control Commission staff and 466 wives in Berlin, but fewer vehicles or aircraft than the Americans. To add to their problems they had long since decided never to withdraw without taking "our Germans" – staff who had worked for the British Element of the ACC, trades union leaders and politicians.[76] No one, however, was contemplating withdrawal except as a remote contingency should the Russians force them to it.

Clay, indeed, wanted to take the Russians on: to form an Anglo-American convoy, arm it and force a way through the checkpoint at Marienborn and up the autobahn to Berlin. "I can see no future in this," commented Robertson, "because a few tanks across the road at a defile will soon bring it to a halt."[77] It was a "Boys' Own" image of wily Pathans and craggy mountain passes wholly at variance with geographical realities, which offered no opportunity of an ambush from the occasional incline, the foot-deep ditch either side of the road, the clumps of birch trees or the cabbage fields round Magdeburg. Robertson was nearer the mark in suggesting that "the Russians might get the best of a shooting match." But Clay got more and more excited about his scheme. By 12 April he was suggesting that the three western allies each bring a whole division to the crossing-point. General Bradley turned down the idea on 14 April.[78] As he recalled in later years, "The Russians could stop an armed convoy without opening fire on it. Roads could be closed for repair or a bridge could go up just ahead of you and then another bridge behind and you'd be in a hell of a fix."[79] Not that there were many bridges along the autobahn and Clay was itching to let his military engineers use their equipment.

Clay did not give up his pet project. Then and later there were many who thought he should have been allowed to try it. Murphy wrote in his memoirs that he himself ought to have resigned when permission was refused; that the Russians throughout the year judged the American response to be weak so kept up the pressure.[80] But in the opinion of another State Department official – and most of Washington, civilian and military – the "forcing of the blockade had the attraction of being a clear, firm and courageous decision. But it carried with it the risk of placing the onus on us for another world war."[81] To do anything more than bluff Clay had to be prepared to shoot his way out of trouble. He did not believe he would have to, but was simply guessing. What if he were wrong? In any case, shooting often starts not because an order is given but because someone gets nervous.

So, with options narrowed, much travel restricted, stocks of food in Berlin for only forty-five days and a belief that an airlift could do little more than temporarily sustain the allied garrisons, in the first week of April the western allies could do only one thing: sit tight and wait to see what the Russians would do next.

6

A War of Pinpricks

Thanks to Sokolovsky's walk-out from the Allied Control Council and the interference with traffic from 1 April, everyone, German and ally alike, was braced for a major Russian offensive to drive the western Powers out of Berlin and to incorporate the city into the Soviet zone. The attack did not come. Indeed, for two months or more it was scarcely hinted at. Russian sources stuck to the story that traffic restrictions were needed to prevent "all kinds of illegal operations" by "criminal and other restless elements";[1] they made no overt challenge to western rights in the city. So April and May were almost an anti-climax. But no one could relax: a Russian assault seemed inevitable, and there was no certainty it could be withstood. While they waited for it, Berliners and the western authorities endured what the French President called *"une petite guerre à coups d'épingles"*[2] – constant pinpricks, bearable in themselves but nerve-wracking nevertheless.

The new SMA traffic regulations remained in force. Western occupation officials travelled between the city and the zones by air or road, though the Military Governors maintained their right of access by running their official trains along the designated line across the Soviet zone. Western freight trains, sealed and escorted, gradually resumed their shuttle and Russian guards gave up trying to inspect them. Germans had to come to terms with the irritation of applications for travel permits and searches at the border. Occasionally a German lorry was turned back at Marienborn on the grounds that its papers were incorrect; on 8 May two freight wagons were returned to Berlin because their consignment notes did not have the signature of the latest SMA official.[3] Incidents like these were rare. They seemed to be caused by the nitpicking of individual Russian officers rather than deliberate SMA policy to interrupt the passage of freight. There was a minor alarm in the middle of April when the Russians stopped British zone barges returning to Hamburg from the Soviet zone and Czechoslovakia. By 21 April fifty barges were stuck at Wittenberge on the Elbe, while their skippers waited in Berlin for the SMA to issue a "new transit document." The British military government doubted one would ever come and suspected the Russians might be trying to seize a new form of reparations, so they suspended all their water traffic through the east zone. After a few days, however, the transit document did appear and on 27 April barges were moving normally again.[4]

Within a week the parcel post was not. During the night of 4–5 May the central post office for the Soviet zone announced that any parcels sent from Berlin to the western zones containing food, spirits or spices would be confiscated and that all parcels for the west must be presented at one of five post offices in the Russian sector for examination and a permit before they could be sent off.[5] The western Commandants protested. The Soviet Controller of Posts said he was too busy to meet them. Once wagon-loads of parcels had accumulated in the Soviet sector, the Russian Commandant, Kotikov, explained that 70 per cent of them contained food – concisely insinuating that his own zone was being stripped and the western zones were starving.[6] For Berliners the solution seemed simple: fly the parcels out. For the western Powers there was no answer: they lacked both aircraft and weight to put behind their protests.

These restrictions were not only irksome, they slowly sapped Berlin's morale. As the weeks went by Berliners told themselves that the allies, for all their public statements about staying, were "allowing themselves to be manoeuvred out of Berlin."[7] Anxiety about the city's ultimate political fate began to affect its economy (though it is worth asking whether this factor was as debilitating as the failure to do anything about inflation and currency reform). After two months of transport restrictions, goods were piling up in the factories: electrical and mechanical engineering firms had 110 per cent of their average monthly turnover stuck in warehouses waiting for dispatch; there was a backlog of 50 per cent in the chemical works; seven scrap-metal dealers had two million Reichsmarks' worth of material lying about. As a result, capital reserves were blocked too and future production threatened – all the more so because west German suppliers were increasingly reluctant to send raw materials to Berlin. For the time being industry could take the strain: firms were producing even though they could not deliver, and little or no labour had been laid off.[8] But how long before that strain began to tell? There was a suspicion that it was being eased by sending Berlin's goods east rather than west. The western authorities were disinclined to stop this: any outlet for the city's industry was better than none.

The western Powers themselves were mainly concerned with making sure that their garrisons and staffs could be supported if and when traffic restrictions got worse. The thirty American C-47s kept up their daily round trips. The British planned to increase their own capability from its present measly two Dakotas and an Anson. On 4 April HQ BAFO (British Air Force of Occupation) was asked to consider a proposal from HQ British Army of the Rhine that the Berlin garrison be supplied by air in the event of a full blockade of the city. On 15 April a conference was held at HQ BAFO in Bückeburg to discuss requirements. BAOR thought that a long-term airlift would have to deliver 87 tons a day, for a shorter period the garrison could manage on 65 tons; the chances were the operation would last a month. The plan must envisage the possible evacuation of 2,000 dependants, each with 65 lbs of luggage (heavy kit would be left behind and guarded by the army). BAFO and Transport Command in the UK went to work and produced Operational Instructions Nos. 12/48: No. 46 Group of Transport Command would provide a small operating HQ, a servicing echelon, and two air movement sections of six officers and fifteen men with sixteen aircraft, eight of which would put in three daily return flights each from Wunstorf in the zone to Gatow in the sector carrying 130,050 lbs a day (food, POL and mail) and enough fuel for the round trip. The operation would be controlled by Air HQ BAFO and was given the glorious title "Operation Knicker."[9]

The British and Americans were thinking in the most limited terms. Anything more ambitious was still inconceivable. Their air transport was designed and operated for the specialised purposes of military support, not for prolonged relief of civilian distress and certainly not for the complex task of maintaining the life, production and trade of a great city. They had few spare aircraft in Germany. Even if they could get some transferred from other theatres, no one believed they could meet Berlin's needs adequately.

And a shocking incident made it distressingly clear that air communications were particularly vulnerable and at the mercy of the Russians.

On 5 April a scheduled BEA passenger Vickers Viking was coming in to land at Gatow when a Soviet Yak fighter, which had been observed for some time performing aerobatics in the area, suddenly dived, passed underneath it, then rose sharply and ripped off the Viking's starboard wing. Both planes crashed. The Russian pilot, the British crew and seven passengers were all killed. The Viking came down just inside the Soviet sector. When the British Commandant, General E. O. Herbert, arrived at the scene, he found a Russian guard on the wreckage and was refused permission to touch it or to remove the charred bodies. He left one of his men as an observer and mounted a guard on the Yak remains in his own sector, with the excuse of "stopping German looting" but the real purpose of making sure the Russians could not tamper with the aircraft, above all with its undercarriage, to give the impression that the Yak had been innocently preparing to land.[10]

Robertson immediately ordered fighter escorts for British transport aircraft (Clay would follow suit as soon as he could get some fighters) and then blazed round to confront Sokolovsky. He found the Marshal "ill at ease and on the defensive," showing little conviction in his argument that the Yak had obeyed safety regulations but had been rammed by the Viking, and obviously anxious that the British should believe the crash was a pure accident; the SMA, Sokolovsky said, had no intention of interfering with western aircraft.[11] Given that assurance, Robertson and Clay called off their fighter escorts. However, the Marshal's tone changed dramatically in the next twenty-four hours. (There were strong rumours later that he had been genuinely upset by the crash and wanted to apologise and give written guarantees, but had been overridden by hardliners in the SMA.)[12] In reply to Robertson's letter asking for a quadripartite commission of enquiry into the crash, Sokolovsky lambasted the British for "not informing" the Air Safety Centre of the arrival of the Viking and claimed that the Yak (posthumously converted from a fighter to a "training aircraft") had been getting ready to land when the Viking burst out of a cloud and hit its tail. His story was patent nonsense. Many witnesses had seen the collision; the Air Safety Centre knew that the Yak had given no notification of its presence whereas the scheduled Viking had been monitored and cleared to land; and as a civilian aircraft it had right of way in any case. It was already established that visibility at the time of the crash was five miles and that there was a good 1,500 feet of cloud-free sky above the aircraft when they collided. Once experts inspected the Viking, they confirmed that its wing had given way under a blow from behind and below.[13]

Clay was infuriated by Sokolovsky's bluster and called his letter "entirely unsatisfactory and in fact insulting."[14] He was made even angrier by Robertson's reply: no attempt to contradict the Marshal's version of events, promises the British would observe air safety rules and no demand for guarantees of free passage for western aircraft. This, thought Clay, was "an appeasement reply," an indication of "weakness which will expedite rather than defer Soviet pressure" and possibly even "an opening breach in our hitherto solid front."[15] In all probability Robertson was counting on Sokolovsky's verbal assurances (he had kept his word in the past) and was offering a helping hand out of an untenable position dangerous for all. He certainly hoped to make it easy for the Russians to agree to an investigation of the crash: he wanted the British case on the record.

A commission of inquiry was, indeed, set up. It was not the quadripartite body Robertson had asked for as the Russians would not accept French or American members (though two Americans had been killed in the crash). Nor did it review all the evidence – the Russians would not hear German witnesses (though they rapidly withdrew their comment that Germans were "unreliable"). Separate British and Russian reports were finally written – for all that General Dratvin originally argued they would only be needed "if the experts had been briefed in the spirit of an unobjective view."[16] Yet though the proceedings were symptomatic of poor allied relations, they served a useful purpose. The alternative evidence and arguments were available for all to see and both versions led to the same conclusion: the crash had been an accident, not a malign Soviet attempt to disrupt western air communications. That cleared the tension. Indeed, it was possible to believe that the accident had had a salutary effect. Kit Steel, Robertson's political adviser, reckoned that the strength of public reaction in Britain and the United States had impressed the SMA; there was every likelihood that the Russians would try to avoid such happenings again.[17] When people puzzled in the coming year over the freedom of movement of western aircraft, they felt it dated back to the moment when Robertson and Clay had ordered fighter escorts – the Russians must have decided that a premeditated attack would provoke a tough response and might even be seen as a casus belli.

117

Even so, the Russians did keep trying to frighten western aircraft. From time to time in April allied planes were buzzed in the corridors, but by pilots with the skill and sense to keep a safe margin. In early May there were daily declarations that Russian fighters would be exercising in the approaches to Berlin.[18] On 4 May the Soviet representative at the Air Safety Centre breezily informed his colleagues that allied night flying across the Soviet zone was no longer acceptable. That caused no flurry: "We propose to pay no attention to this advice," Clay told Washington.[19] The Russians next accused the western allies of violating safety rules and threatened to withdraw from the Air Safety Centre until present "chaos" was straightened out.[20] To vary the intimidation the SMA suggested that all civilian air traffic should be rerouted from Gatow and Tempelhof in the western sectors to Soviet airfields at Schönefeld or Aldershof; even that all allied military aircraft should be concentrated in the Soviet sector at Dalgow.[21] They were ignored. Yet some people asked if the SMA would soon try to ban all commercial air traffic with Berlin or reduce the number of allied air corridors.[22] Recent pressures suggested the Russians were well aware that air traffic was "the all-important gap in the iron ring" they were constructing round the city.[23] Would the ring be completed? How tight would they make it?

Most western observers agreed that the Russians would try anything short of war. Berlin was a prize in itself and taking it would secure the Soviet zone and the east European satellites. Forcing western withdrawal would deal a blow to confidence in west Germany and the rest of Europe. Perhaps more: Clay warned that after "Berlin will come western Germany, and our strength there is relatively no greater and our position is no more tenable than Berlin"; thereafter west Europe was open to communist takeover.[24] In depressed moments Clay even feared it was "so vital to get us out of Berlin that they will face the prospect of war in doing so."[25] But in early April the CIA and the Armed Services Intelligence Agencies reported to President Truman that though the Russians had the capability to overrun western Europe and the Near East, they were unlikely to use it.[26] No western politician or official was talking about the deterrent effect of the atom bomb. Everyone was banking on the belief that the Soviet Union had still not healed from the last war and would not risk the opprobrium of causing another. All the same the Russians were expected to probe for weak and sensitive spots. As Bevin put it to Marshall, the Russians would get up to "every devilment," do all they could to wreck European recovery and "cause us the greatest political embarrassment everywhere, but without pushing things to the extreme of war."[27]

That, of course, is a dangerous game; like doing stunts round an airliner it can well prove fatal. Bevin warned that the Russians "may miscalculate and involve themselves in a situation from which they feel they cannot retreat"; it was important not to trap them in a corner. By corollary, the western allies themselves must make sure they were not "provoked into any ill-considered action." This demanded cool nerves and infinite patience. When Clay put the question which was worrying many people in April and May – what happens if some jumpy or trigger-happy young soldier uses his rifle? – Strang and Robertson were firm: isolated shooting incidents need not lead to war unless one side or the other wanted it.[28] No one looked forward to what Clay called "having to take humiliation without retaliation,"[29] but virtually no one in the west was spoiling for a fight either; certainly not Clay, though he feared one might come. The British embassy in Washington did notice in early April that one or two "Russo-phobe hotheads in Congress" were calling privately for shooting a way through to Berlin and never mind the consequences;[30] and later in the month Churchill went on a solitary rampage, growling that the Russians must be told to retreat from Berlin and east Germany or "we will raze their cities."[31] These were lone voices.

Not that the western attitude was passive. There were limits to how much the West would tolerate. Lewis Douglas, now the American Ambassador in London, cabled to Washington at the end of April: "the British will go to war in event clear organised act of war is committed against them by the Soviet. They probably would not commit organised act of war against Soviet to preserve position in Berlin."[32] That was Marshall's policy too: "We intend to stay in Berlin and ... we will resist force with force"; but not initiate it.[33]

The British and Americans might be of one mind over strategy; they did not always agree on tactics. Given their shared determination to stay in Berlin, the Americans wanted to put it on the line to the Russians. A note they drafted for delivery in Moscow saying they would not budge from the city and had every right to stay there alarmed the British. Whitehall thought it should be toned down, especially the last sentence expressing the expectation that the Soviet government would not permit actions by "its military commanders inconsistent with the unquestioned rights" of the western Powers – in London's view implications of military action by either side only raised the temperature. Bevin warned against wording the communication "too forcefully without making sure that we had the necessary force with which to back it up."[34] Privately he thought the note a waste of time and was uneasy about constant assertions of allied rights and intentions. His instinct, he told Attlee, was to "sit it out" quietly and "take any reasonable opportunity which occurs of trying to come to terms with the Russians on disputed points" as long as principles were not sacrificed.[35] The Russians would become pigheaded if harried, but biddable faced with imperturbability and firmness.

The Americans learned painfully the dangers of exploring for opportunities to come to terms. By late April Truman and Robert Lovett, the Under-Secretary of State, wanted the Soviet Union to understand that, in spite of recent attacks on their foreign policy by Henry Wallace (former Secretary of Agriculture and now a Democratic presidential contender), most politicians of every hue backed their government's stand in Berlin, opposed the extension of totalitarianism, did not want war but did hope for friendly relations with the USSR. Truman and Lovett probably thought they could loosen the deadlock in Soviet-American relations too. A personal and candid approach was chosen. The US Ambassador in Moscow, General Walter Bedell Smith, was instructed to see Molotov privately. On 4 May he read the Foreign Minister a three-and-a-half-page statement of the American case, suggested that recent alarm in western Europe had led to a drawing together for protection and explained American opposition to the foundation of two Continental blocs or the maintenance of big military establishments. Since Molotov then asked for time to consult the Politburo, Bedell Smith left a copy of his statement for study. Five days later he went back to the Foreign Ministry where, with a little preliminary sugar about the Soviet Union's wish for better relations, all he got was a large dose of blame for the present crisis and accusations that the United States was building bases and sponsoring alliances against the USSR.[36] The exercise had been pointless.

Worse was to follow: while flying next day to a holiday in France, Bedell Smith heard a Radio Moscow broadcast about Molotov's tirade; the Russians also released titbits from the American statement selected to persuade the British and French that the United States had proposed talks and a settlement behind their backs. Bedell Smith was shocked and embarrassed: some people in the State Department had warned that the Russians might breach diplomatic confidence for the sake of propaganda, but he himself had been confident that the Kremlin was punctilious in these matters.[37] General Marshall was appalled by the damage done to allied relations. He quickly issued a denial that Bedell Smith had asked for bilateral negotiations with the Soviet government. The French and British were incensed. Once they had time to read the full American statement, they accepted that Washington had not proposed separate talks; but why, oh why, had the Americans not consulted or at least warned them about the approach to Molotov? Resentment did not last. Like the Yak incident the Moscow fiasco brought its benefits. Bevin now encouraged frank exchange of information and views between Washington and London; Marshall was at pains to keep his allies informed and with him. The hammer blow to Anglo-American relations in May actually forged a stronger partnership better able to withstand the stresses of the next twelve months.

At bottom, of course, the Americans and British were friends with shared interests and a common purpose; when they quarrelled it was over nuance and style, not fundamentals. That was not true of their relationship with France. The French were pursuing very different ends in Germany, national aims sharpened by historic insecurity. While the Anglo-Saxons calculated that everyone's safety and prosperity would ultimately be safeguarded by holding out in Berlin and making no concessions of principle, the French added up the risks and reached the opposite conclusion. At the end of April General Koenig pleaded with the other Military Governors to discuss with the Russians how to make the western presence in Berlin more acceptable to the Soviet Union. Otherwise, as he saw it, the prospect for the city was economic death and the West, he argued, did not have enough force in or out of Berlin to maintain an uncompromising stance.[38] The French Ambassador in London, Massigli, "rather shocked" Sir Orme Sargent, the Permanent Under-Secretary at the Foreign Office, with his opinion that the western allies must prepare to leave Berlin because the Russians "could and would make it impossible for us to stay and it would be far more ignominious to be driven out by Russian pressure than for us to withdraw in good order and of our own free will"[39] – a distinction he may have thought subtle, but which others might find illogical.

It is not surprising that from April onwards whenever Foreign Office papers referred to French trepidation or rationalisation for withdrawal, someone jotted: "just like 1938," "1939," "1940." This was not merely a xenophobic sneer: typical of the French to lie down and be trampled over. It was a shorthand reminder that everyone was in danger of being involved in a rerun of the old drama: Munich. No one wanted to revive that tragedy (even the French were simply trying to rewrite the last act). It had been played only ten years before; all the main actors now had had minor parts then or had watched others declaim "appeasement" and millions die on the European scene. The Russians, of course, had missed Munich. They had acted in a two-hander, the Nazi-Soviet Pact, and toured Poland and the Baltic States instead. The Soviet Union totally failed to realise what a formative western experience Munich had been and that the Kremlin was now being cast in place of Hitler.

As the western Powers laboured to write a new script, the role of Berlin was crucial. Everyone saw it differently. From Washington's standpoint there might be a new European tragedy unless Berlin's dilemma were resolved quickly. For Bevin, on the other hand, Berlin's predicament contained potential for good. He suggested to Marshall that the greatest danger to Europe could well be sudden conciliatory moves by the Russians, encouraging the western states to "ease up on the creation of solidarity" through self-defence pacts and co-operation in the European Recovery Programme. The Military Governors were primarily concerned with the interaction between Berlin and their plans for currency reform and German self-government in Frankfurt. Clay suspected that the present Berlin problems had been "designed to scare us away from these moves" and that further steps in the zones would "develop the real crisis."[40] He pressed his colleagues for a clear declaration: would they stay in Berlin come hell or high water? Robertson doubted they would have to play a heroic role; indeed, he thought the "greatest danger was that we should be made to look silly." He shared Clay's belief that the Russians were trying to block west German progress, but held out the hope that if the allies stuck to Berlin and doggedly built up their zones there was a good chance that in twelve to eighteen months the Russians would accept the faits accomplis and give up in Berlin.[41]

While they waited for the next Russian move against the western sectors of the city, Clay and Robertson considered the narrow range of practical steps they could take. Neither man thought it wise or even necessary to evacuate all the western dependants, and they were particularly anxious not to alarm Berliners. Nevertheless, during April and May they did not check the natural flow of their

staffs to Frankfurt where they were needed; this was also a way, as
Robertson said, to "clear the decks so that we can prepare ourselves
to take on the struggle with resolution and without embarrassment."[42] It was not so easy to find ways to prepare the Berliners.
Robertson asked himself constantly how much they should be asked
to take. Clay was more optimistic and thought it improbable that
the Soviet Union would stop food supplies to the western sectors –
the Russians could not feed the whole city themselves, unless the
next harvest were infinitely better than expected; in his view, they
would not risk alienating German opinion by letting Berliners
starve. And German support, Berlin support above all, was going
to be the vital weapon in the struggle between the Powers. As
Robertson saw it: "So long as the majority of the Berlin population remain firm in opposition to the Communists the Russians will
not get their way."[43]

Quite obviously the Russians wanted to soften up that opposition.
To the inconvenience and worry of the creeping blockade they
added coercion. Throughout April and May there was a marked
increase in the number of Berliners summoned to local Soviet
Kommandaturas and bullied. Kidnappings multiplied: on 22 April
the Americans published a list of forty-nine people who had recently
disappeared from their sector.[44] All too many of the cases implicated
police headquarters in the Russian sector. Western protests in the
Allied Kommandatura drew nothing more than denials of police
guilt or accusations of western intimidation. When Kanig, the head
of the Protection Police (a rare non-SED official at Markgraf's
headquarters), actually disciplined an officer for enticing a German
from the French sector, he was grilled by his boss and finally fled
to the west. His flight, as someone observed, was "scarcely an
inspiring spectacle" given his job, but he must have known that his
days as a conscientious officer were numbered and was perhaps
aware that his predecessor had been arrested in 1945 and never
heard of since.[45] Rather late in the day the western Powers
announced on 25 May that they would put liaison officers into
Markgraf's offices. These had no deterrent effect.

Democratic politicians were now being subjected to uncomfortable stress. East sector members of the CDU who wanted to attend
the Berlin party conference on 10–11 April were threatened with
losing their homes if they went. Most of them took the risk and a
unanimous resolution was passed to sever connection with the CDU
Russian zone party.[46] On 23 April a pro-SMA splinter group formed

in retaliation. Seven CDU party officials who refused to join it got visits from Bezirk employees, who measured their homes and made inventories of contents.[47] The LPD too was cracked by the pressures. On 27 April five out of eight Bezirk chairmen (but a smaller proportion of their committees and members) accepted SMA control. Herr Sonk of Weissensee, who did not, had his phone cut and his flat measured; he was told his furniture would be confiscated and his ration card was scaled down from Grade I to Grade III. His deputy was warned that another family would be moved in to share his flat unless Sonk found himself in a position to supply alternative accommodation.

It is tempting to believe that there was a touch of desperation in this bullying of the democratic parties. Since 1945 the revolutionary zeal of the proletariat, which any good communist had been taught to expect, had been disappointingly tepid. Recently the SED was reported to be chagrined by some local elections in the Bizone: their candidates won only 7.9 per cent of the vote in Hesse and a paltry 3 per cent in Bavaria.[48] The decision in May to change the name of the KPD in the western zones to the SVD (*Socialistische Volkspartei Deutschlands*, with "Communist" dropped) was unlikely to awaken the consciousness of the working classes with a jump. For the time being in Berlin some waverers could be rounded up and brought into the SMA fold; most seemed to be slipping away.

Berliners were having to choose which political side they were on. The old hope of politicians that they could get on with practical matters and avoid ideological wrangles had gone; so too had the belief that it was possible to co-operate with all four occupation authorities. Berliners were involved in a Big Power conflict and the middle ground was disappearing fast. A man like the Deputy Mayor, Ferdinand Friedensburg, who had on some occasions tried to be a bridge between the western and eastern authorities, on others to profit from their differences, was now dangerously straddled. He was attacked in several west sector newspapers for going to Soviet zone CDU meetings without informing the Berlin party and failing to attend the CDU conference in April where others had risked their necks or at least their homes. There was no point in him complaining to a western liaison officer that it was his public duty to be a link, that he could not declare his allegiance openly but knew in his heart where it was.[49] He called himself Coriolanus; others called him a trimmer, even a traitor. As the political lines hardened there was no place for neutrals.

124

For the moment, however, Berliners were not called on to fight with their fists. The western authorities feared there might be a battle on May Day. This traditional occasion for mass demonstrations and calls for workers' victory seemed a likely time for the SMA and SED to spill out a parade from the Lustgarten through the Brandenburg Gate and into the British sector to occupy the old Reichstag. General Herbert planned "extensive precautions with troops at very short call but tidied away out of view."[50] Men of the 1st Battalion, the Royal Norfolk Regiment, crept into the Reichstag in the night of 30 April, groped through the rubble of artillery-blackened rooms and set up their weapons where they could find solid floor, prepared to fight for their sector.[51] This was a particularly nasty job for the Norfolks: their regiment had been captured in the fall of Singapore, and many of the men now in Berlin had only recently returned from Japanese prisoner-of-war camps. Fortunately they spent a quiet day. The east sector demonstration was a lack-lustre affair. There were relics of former delights in the decorated floats, flags and the two-hour parade of 120,000 marchers, but the traditional sweets and sausages could only be had on ration cards, the children and 500 blind passed in front of the tribune several times like the Grand March from *Aida* in a cheap tour, and the crowd listened apathetically to mundane speeches. A counter-demonstration of no more than 80,000 on the other side of the Brandenburg Gate heard some oratory of little more fire, then everyone wandered home, east and west, lethargically.[52]

Clearly the SMA did not think a coup appropriate. Against all recent evidence, they must still have believed that the popular will would eventually deliver what they wanted – ideology, after all, taught that the people would reach the correct conclusion even though methodology suggested they might need help to get there. Huge resources of energy and ingenuity were invested in the campaign for national unity and a just peace, proposed by the Soviet zone People's Congress in March, which was to take the form of a country-wide collection of signatures to a People's Petition between 23 May and 15 June. Moves to whip up public interest began early in May. Fearing violence by campaigners, the French and Americans banned the Petition in their zones and sectors. On 22 May the Berlin City Assembly forbade the collection of signatures in municipal buildings – a ruling they could not enforce in the Russian sector. However, the Speaker of the Assembly, Dr. Otto Suhr, took the view that official opposition to the Petition gave it undeserved importance; he himself hoped for an official result of 99 per cent support, to show what a fraud it was.[53] The British too decided against dignifying the plebiscite with official interdict, though they speculated that failure to accept its result might lead to a final Russian break with quadripartite administration and possibly an "all-German" government in Berlin.[54]

As a result of the ban on campaigning, the French and American zones and sectors remained relatively quiet for the three weeks the Petition was touted (though twelve men and fifty-four women were arrested in the US zone for trying to get signatures). Elsewhere the SMA and the SED gave a dazzling display of chicanery. Not satisfied with door-to-door canvassing armed with electoral lists, nor with sessions in factories carrying the payroll, collectors added uniformed Russian escorts to their own persuasive powers. Citizens who wanted time to consider whether to sign were speeded up by having their latest ration card withheld or the revelation that a list was being compiled of "saboteurs of democracy." Children helped the petition: signatures of fourteen year olds were welcome, and they could encourage their parents thanks to six hours of instruction in all schools in the Russian sector on the merits of national unity and a just peace. Clergymen were asked to extol the virtues of signature, doctors in Dresden were told they would lose their licences to practise unless they signed, post-office workers and policemen discovered that their jobs depended on it, and patients in mental hospitals perhaps found the chance to sign remedial. Others were spared any decision about the Petition: they signed a list brought round by "social workers" said to be a request for higher rations, or put their names on slips offered by "health inspectors" which were said to declare their homes had been checked for "pests." One group was delighted to sign: German-speakers expelled from eastern Europe were told the petition would improve their chances of returning home. Individuals clearly enjoyed doing so: a radio reporter signed four times. Everyone who gave a signature got a receipt, free; those who did not sign could buy one on the black market for 50 to 100 marks. The SPD considered spreading the benefits of ownership by printing a few thousand receipts themselves.

By the end of the campaign, which had demonstrated such imagination and individual initiative, the Soviet zone press proudly announced that thirteen million signatures had been collected, three-quarters of a million of them in Berlin. Unfortunately these were not available for contemplation: the People's Council had decided that only certified statements on the number of names would be presented for inspection, the signed lists themselves would be treasured in its archives.[55]

Whether they would eventually be brought out to demonstrate the people's wish for an "all-German goverment" or the expulsion of the western allies from Berlin remained to be seen. Meanwhile the western Powers had to rely on their permanent barometer of Russian pressure, the Allied Kommandatura. During April the Russians were found "fairly cordial" on the whole, sometimes "wooden" but showing "no signs of working for a break."[56] Granted, there were rows about the parcel post. Furthermore, for two weeks the Russians wanted to close down eight sub-committees, which suggested they were abolishing the Kommandatura by stages; but once persuaded to cut only one and redistribute the work of the others, it looked as if their claims to be short of staff were genuine.[57] There was also a squall in a Deputy Commandants' meeting, ending with the Russian, Colonel A. I. Yelisarov, shouting that the British had stood aside in 1945 and "watched the Red Army bleeding," hence "no British graves in Berlin."[58] Yet all in all the meetings had been no more unpleasant than usual, though no more fruitful either. The sessions were perhaps longer – the Deputies met for six, nine, eleven hours and had a grand finale on 28 April, when they started at 10 a.m. and finished at 5 a.m. the next day – but even this was unremarkable.

Tiny details did disturb western observers, however. Yelisarov, for instance, who used to busy himself making notes for his replies, now played with his pen and paper and used prepared statements. By the end of the month the Russians insisted on every interpreter putting his own Commandant's words into the foreign language (which was slow and inaccurate) and tended not to shake hands at the end of a session. More importantly, Kotikov was getting obstreperous about including other people's items on the agenda and would only fix one meeting in advance instead of arranging the schedule for a month.[59] Even so, in western opinion, the SMA had been unhappy about Sokolovsky's walk-out from the Allied Control Council and wanted to avoid responsibility for breaking up the Kommandatura.

In May it looked as if the Russians were trying to make the western allies do the breaking. There was an unpleasant scene in the Public Safety Committee on 14 May, when the British representative began to question Colonel Markgraf about a senior police officer with a known criminal record, and the Russians shouted him down and took their leave. They refused to meet again unless the British member were reprimanded for his "brutal and incorrect behaviour,"[60] and everyone wondered if this was a new way of abolishing committees. The meetings of the Deputy Commandants too, thought Murphy, suggested that the Russians were "making deliberate and determined efforts" to bring them to a halt. Those of the Commandants themselves became more bad-tempered – significantly Clay dropped into one as an observer, presumably to sniff the atmosphere for himself.[61] Kotikov managed to prevent the dispatch of business by refusing to discuss anything but his fourteen points and had at his elbow a new assistant, whose official position was unknown but whom the French Commandant called "a killer."[62] On 28 May, after a fifteen-hour scrap about east sector police with criminal records, Russian charges that the American and British sectors were being incorporated into the Bizonal economy, and accusations that low standards of living were deliberately maintained in the west, Herbert, who had been baited throughout by Kotikov, finally barked the fundamental question: Were quadripartite agreements on Berlin still valid? He got no reply.[63]

By now western officials all felt that the Russians would soon make an open challenge to quadripartite government and the right of the western Powers to stay in Berlin. No one had forgotten that Sokolovsky had walked out of the Allied Control Council over the issue of the London talks on west German government, the Ruhr and the German part in the European Recovery Programme. Those talks had adjourned in early March, but they reconvened on 22 April. This in itself was a goad for the Soviet Union. To make it more painful, any newspaper reader could see that the talks were going to reach agreement on all the main matters. Could the Russians tolerate a major settlement made without them? Could they passively accept separate west German development, exclusion from the honeypot of the Ruhr, growing western co-operation and prosperity? It was unlikely. And the western allies knew only too well that if the Soviet Union made one last throw for its ambitions in Germany and Europe, it would do so in Berlin.

That in no way made Clay and Robertson waver from the conviction that all the items on the London agenda were essential for the well-being of western Germany and were worth any rumpus the Russians kicked up. Germans, on the other hand, were growing noticeably worried that the London agreement would result in the partition of their country and the loss of the Ruhr. They expressed resentment that they were not consulted and that little had been said about the nature of future allied occupation or a peace treaty.[64] But a *Times* correspondent was not alone in spotting that though German politicians would not publicly support the idea of a separate state, most privately had "already written off the east for the purposes of immediate planning."[65] Kit Steel was told by Carlo Schmid of the SPD that his party was reconciled to the establishment of a west German government; the only worry was "the manner of its presentation" – Berlin and east Germany must not be alienated.[66] Several other SPD officials emphasised to members of the Allied Control Commission the moral and political importance of a western stand in Berlin.[67] It was a responsibility stressed particularly by Berliners, who understood better than anyone the danger to their city once the London agreements were announced. Jacob Kaiser, the Catholic trades union leader and elder statesman of the CDU, toured the American zone preaching the need to hold on to Berlin if west Europe were to control its own future and he then went to tell the French that the fate of Paris was tied to that of Berlin: for the Russians Frankfurt would be only a stop-over between the two cities.[68]

This was a bit of stiffening much needed by the French, who had been thrown into a tizzy by the nearness of agreement in London. Massigli suggested to the other heads of delegation at the talks that west German government should be postponed.[69] The Foreign Minister, Bidault, sent notes to Washington and London warning that constitutional development would provoke a dangerous Soviet reaction which the western Powers lacked military strength to fend off; they might well be driven from Berlin.[70] The Americans and British were far from sympathetic towards French fears. They reckoned they were exaggerated to squeeze concessions in London to France's demands for a weak German confederation and frontier adjustments, and to extract American armaments and a quick helping of Marshall Aid. In London Strang and Douglas rallied Massigli: internationalisation of the Ruhr was just as provoking to the Russians as a constitution; the Brussels Pact and American commitment to Europe would guarantee France's safety; delay in west Germany would be seen as weakness by Germans and Russians alike and was riskier than action.[71] In Washington Lovett gave it to the French Ambassador, Henri Bonnet, hot and strong: France was unlikely to get any American help if she wrecked the London talks; Capitol Hill was sick of spending so much on European recovery and now being asked for arms as well; a weak and impoverished west Germany was ripe for Soviet takeover – and surely the French did not want that. Bonnet slipped in a poignant comment about French psychological problems. Lovett was stony-hearted: "I said we were well aware of the French psychological problem but that they would do well to bear the American psychology in mind as well."[72]

It dawned on the French that if they did not co-operate in London, the others would leave them out – then more than their feet would get cold. When the London talks ended on 1 June, France had not been given any part of the Rhineland but had agreed that the Ruhr would remain part of Germany, with resources owned and managed by Germans but allocated throughout western Europe by an international authority. Some of France's fears were calmed by the creation of a Tripartite Military Security Board to supervise German disarmament and a pledge that the occupation Powers would not withdraw until the peace of Europe was secured.

Under the London agreements the Military Governors were instructed to see the Ministers President of the western Länder no later than 15 June and call on them to convene a constituent assembly by 1 September to draft a constitution for a federal state "best adapted to the eventual re-establishment of German unity at present disrupted." This constitution must protect individual freedoms and local rights, yet give "adequate central authority." It should be approved by the Military Governors and ratified by two-thirds of the Länder. A "Letter of Advice to the Military Governors" outlined the elements to be included in the constitution: a two-chamber legislature with one house to represent the Länder; no federal control of education, culture or religious affairs; restricted central control of taxation; an independent judiciary with the right to review the exercise of executive power and to resolve disputes among the Länder or with the federal government. This Letter emphasised that there were many ways to design a federal state and the Military Governors must judge the constitution as a whole and on broad principles. They themselves should start work on an Occupation Statute to define the powers they would retain and explain it to the Ministers President and constituent assembly. They would conduct foreign policy, but limit their interference with foreign trade and the economy to ensuring the wise use of aid, and stay responsible for enforcing reparations payments, the Level of Industry Plan and security measures. For the rest the Military

Governors could hold only emergency powers and must accept within twenty-one days any legislation submitted for their approval unless two out of three of them voted against it.

Most Germans greeted the London settlement as "diktat," which in the case of some politicians was almost a term of approval. There was a strong reaction against the Occupation Statute as a symbol of Germany's conquered status, and fears that any reserved powers would be made all-embracing. The SPD Executive Committee would have preferred an "administrative statute" rather than a "constitution" to express the lack of national independence, and the party as a whole was dissatisfied with the potential weakness of a federal system. Konrad Adenauer of the British zone CDU talked of the "gilded annexation of the Ruhr," complained of finding no trace at all of self-government in the proposals and threatened non-co-operation in the constituent assembly. One LPD zonal chairman called the settlement an "instrument of perpetuated distrust." Such a general German outcry was an expected reflex. What really mattered was whether the Military Governors would show goodwill in their drafting of the Occupation Statute and tolerance in judgment of the constitution, and whether the constituent assembly showed good sense and public spirit in its work. Both sides had to demonstrate a sense of responsibility and wisdom; the London agreements had left them a lot of leeway to find a settlement satisfactory to all.

Predictably the main attack on the London proposals came from the communists. The party in west Germany condemned "an obvious violation of the Potsdam agreement," warned that the country was being torn to pieces, and called for the immediate withdrawal of occupation troops and a free decision by Germans on their country's future. The Praesidium of the People's Council in the east zone used more or less the same ideas and phrases, while the headlines in the press were more colourful: "Control of Ruhr under Terror," "Rape of Germany by Western Powers," "Occupation to Last for Ever."[73]

The Military Governors could ride the storms. They looked forward to an immediate meeting with the Ministers President, who were not expected to make political capital out of the situation and who had the prestige to persuade others to seize the opportunity of shaping the national future. The occupation authorities wanted to start the constitutional process straightaway. They now had no doubt at all that they would face a major confrontation with the Russians soon. For, by an extraordinary piece of timing, on 1 June –

131

the very day the London talks ended – the western allies had at last agreed to reform the currency in their zones. They were challenging the Soviet Union not just with radical political changes, but with separate economic development in the west – both at once. The simultaneous ripening of the two policies was coincidental. To some extent, however, it was desirable: political and economic changes would secure and nurture each other; it could even be argued that all crises might just as well be got over in one. Nevertheless, by facing the Soviet Union with such far-reaching and independent decisions, the western Powers had ensured a massive retaliation. It was bound to come in Berlin.

The western allies were quite ready to take the consequences. Moves to west German government had been eagerly awaited; currency reform was long overdue. By spring 1948 industrial production in the Trizone was still at barely 50 per cent of its 1936 level. Admittedly the figures had shown a marked improvement in recent months: coal production had shot up to 74 per cent of pre-war output, exports had increased so food could be imported and rations had risen at long last. Ultimately Marshall Aid would benefit the country enormously, but only if the economy was in a fit state to gain from the financial transfusion. That was doubtful. Given no confidence at all in the inflated Reichsmark, manufacturers were stockpiling raw materials and finished goods; the population preferred barter to money transactions. The Bizonal occupation authorities had had contingency plans for a new mark since autumn 1947. They polished them as rumours spread from October that the Russians themselves were preparing a new currency for their zone. In the new year a western Deutschmark was printed in the United States and, in the highly secret "Operation Bird-dog," was sent to Frankfurt. Ideally it would not be needed: the Allied Control Council would agree on a uniform currency for the whole country. But once Sokolovsky left the ACC in March, currency negotiations stopped. Each side waited nervously to see what the other would do.

Both faced a particularly perturbing question: what currency would be used in Berlin? A western Deutschmark or an eastern new mark would bind the city to the economy of west or east; the very name and design of the note would be an emblem of sovereignty. Two currencies circulating at once would fight each other and signify a split city. Even after the collapse of the ACC, the western Powers still hoped for a uniform currency for Berlin; a Soviet mark

132

would be tolerable as long as it was issued under quadripartite supervision. Clay was told by Washington at the end of April that if the Russians tried to impose the sole use of an East mark or dual currency, he must push for a special "B" for "Berlin" note. If he failed to get it, he might have to accept the use of a perforated or overstamped Deutschmark in tandem with the Soviet note. Washington understood the difficulty of two currencies, feared that an influx of Soviet marks would cause inflation, and took Clay's point that any defacement of the Deutschmark suggested a temporary arrangement and possible western withdrawal from the city. They kept hoping for a sensible arrangement with the Russians instead.[74] The British shared American anxieties and conclusions. The French dithered. Having accepted the plan for currency reform in early May, on the 21st they asked for a postponement; having got one, they tried to sell their support in exchange for Anglo-American tax changes in the Trizone. Again it had to be made clear to the French that they could join in or be left out, and that any crisis in Berlin could and would be lived with.

If anyone had a right to worry and complain it was not the French but Berliners. They had all the added anxiety of not knowing what the western allies intended to do. (It might have been a slight consolation to them had they known that all the currency negotiations were kept so secret that most high occupation officials were not privy to them either.) If the city were left out of western currency reform, the chances were that not only its economy but its democratic institutions would be drawn into the Soviet system; if it were included, the Russians would probably try to take over the city anyway. Either way, few Berliners expected the western Powers would stay long; the only question was whether they would be eased out slowly or given one quick shove.

In early May there were plenty of hints in the Soviet zone press of imminent eastern currency reform; Berliners guessed it would come as soon as the People's Petition was over.[75] Possibly it would give the final excuse to seal off the Soviet zone and sector – and, indeed, American intelligence had reports of extra troops on the zonal frontier.[76] Dratvin told the press in the middle of May that western currency reform was due any day, which was seen by Berliners as a warning of what the Russians themselves intended to do.[77] The announcement on 28 May of a new central bank for the Soviet zone seemed to clinch the argument that the Russians were ready to introduce new currency. On that assumption some western sector companies were making arrangements with Soviet zone firms and getting promises of raw materials from the eastern Economic Council.[78] It seemed unlikely to Berliners that their city would be included in western reform: a Magistrat delegation to the Bizonal Economic Council in Frankfurt was told firmly that its participation would be unworkable. Most Berlin politicians in May and early June warned against a western reform at all because of dangerous Soviet reaction. Some of them advocated a special "Bear" mark, a reference to the belief that "Berlin" was derived from "Berlein," a little bear which was the city's symbol. Only a few opposed any delay or compromise and demanded full incorporation into the western currency and economic systems. Since this small group included Ernst Reuter and Dr Klingelhöfer, the head of the Magistrat Economics Department, its views carried weight and added a new financial compulsion for Berliners to take sides in the struggle for their city.[79]

The SMA was insinuating by early June which side had the big guns. On 4 June the Russians held at Marienborn three German trains bound for the west with freight and mail. Two were finally allowed to go on, but five wagons were detached from the third because their labels were "incorrect."[80] There were more delays for the next forty-eight hours, then traffic flowed normally. Just as people were deciding that the stoppages had been caused by muddle, freight was held up again, and on 11 June none at all got to Berlin.[81] Thereafter it dribbled through, but by the second week of June manufactured goods were piling up in the city without transit permits and there was an alarming shortage of raw materials.[82] From the beginning of the month more and more German motorists were turned back at Russian checkpoints on the grounds that their passes had been stamped not signed, and the British warned people to think twice before applying for interzonal permits.[83] Nearly a hundred barges were tied up near Hamburg on 10 June waiting for their papers to be processed by the Soviet zone authorities.[84] There were fears it would soon be impossible to move perishable or even semi-perishable goods to Berlin by water.[85] There was no point in Berliners dreaming that their food could come by air instead. The Americans were stretched to build up supplies for their garrisons alone; the British had no prospect even of putting "Operation Knicker" into effect until their new runway at Gatow was finished, and it was expected to be fit only for emergency landings at the end of July.[86] Nor could Berliners look forward to comfortable rail journeys: on 14 June the SMA ordered all Berlin passenger trains to start from the Friedrichstrasse station in the Russian sector and not to stop at two picking-up points in the British sector. Within three days of this decision the trains were reduced by four coaches because the Friedrichstrasse platforms were too short.[87] By then freight was barely trickling to and from the city: 250 wagons had been stopped at Marienborn between 12 and 16 June because of "mechanical defects" and there were 116 wagon-loads of parcels stuck in the Russian sector.[88]

The western Powers, as well as Berliners, were feeling the pinch. In the first two weeks of June Russian guards again tried to claim the right to inspect sealed wagons on military trains. In addition, the SMA published the information that from Wednesday 16 June the autobahn bridge over the Elbe at Hohenwarte (the only link with Berlin for allied travellers) would be closed for repairs. It was undeniably in need of them, for it was just a temporary structure put up by the Americans after retreating Germans had blown up the old bridge. The closure, as the Foreign Office confessed, had "been anticipated as a development, but unfortunately no counter has been thought of."[89] Bevin quickly thought of a solution and instructed Robertson to offer the Russians another temporary bridge and help to overhaul the old one.[90] Sokolovsky turned down the offer most politely on 22 June. The alternative river crossing he provided for western travellers was a ferry platform attached to a buoyed cable, held at an angle to the current and nudged across by it. This ramshackle construction could hold only two buses or six cars. The ramps either side were in poor condition and unlikely to stand up to heavy traffic, and the approaches to them were along second-class roads which added a diversion of fifteen miles or so. The whole journey was now expected to take anything up to an extra two and a half hours.[91] One British traveller going down to the zone on 16 June had to queue for a mere thirty minutes to cross the river; another encountered an entire battalion of the King's Own Scottish Borderers on the opposite bank and took rather longer.[92] In later years they could count themselves lucky to have had a rare experience. When they returned to Berlin in a few days' time, their only means of access was by air.

By the end of the first week in June the economy in Berlin had frozen to a standstill while Berliners waited for currency reform in east and west. The American and British Military Governors waited too – for the French to join their financial plans, which they finally did in the second week. Though very few people knew it, new Deutschmarks were already in Berlin. Ten planeloads of them had been flown to the city recently and German financial experts, who had told their families they were off on a trip to Frankfurt, were lurking in a "cage" in York House in the British sector working on the details of distribution in case no four-Power agreement was found.[93] The western allies, like Berliners, worried about the Russian response to their zonal currency reform. Bevin told Attlee that the introduction of an East mark was probable, but added: "We cannot foresee in what other ways the Russians may react. The problem is really a part of the general Russian reaction to the London talks."[94] Tension increased as details of the western reform leaked to the press; everyone suspected the new currency would come at the weekend of 19–20 June. German newspapers were told to stand by on Friday for a 6,000-word announcement.[95]

As if this suspense was not enough, a flash of melodrama was thrown in. On 16 June the Allied Kommandatura gathered for a regular meeting. Only two of the four Commandants were present at first: Brigadier Benson stood in until Herbert arrived in the late afternoon; Kotikov was ill (or "ill") and was represented by his deputy, Yelisarov. The meeting began at 10.05 a.m. There was formalised wrangling about the parcel post, a long ritual argument about nationalisation of Berlin industry, a break for lunch, followed by barren discussion on minor topics until 6 p.m. Then came a real surprise. Astoundingly, the Kommandatura began to agree. For three whole hours the four representatives talked about increasing the city's rations, with what an American listener praised as "a great deal of honest and imaginative horsetrading," and they not only drew up a uniform scheme of rations but even settled the details of which category of people should get what. It was the first time the Kommandatura had reached any constructive decision for months. With so much achieved it seemed almost cosily familiar that they then reverted to squabbling for a couple of hours. The mood "grew steadily heavier, although not unusually so for the Kommandatura," the American noticed.[96] They got through to the last item on the agenda: any other business.

Howley protested that the meeting had gone on quite long enough. Yelisarov promptly circulated a long document on wages and social welfare – a rehash of Kotikov's fourteen points which had held up business for months. Ganeval and Herbert demurred: perhaps this could be postponed. Howley stated he had heard enough pointless discussions; he was tired and was going home because he had to be up early in the morning, but his deputy, Colonel Babcock, would remain. He was on his feet and off to the door, without shaking any hands, before the Russian interpreter had finished translating his remarks. Whether he then slammed the door or, as he claimed later, yanked it "because it was stuck" remained debatable. Ganeval as chairman beckoned to Babcock to take the American seat and began a statement. Yelisarov sat quiet "with a somewhat baffled expression." Only when asked for a comment a few minutes later did he listen to a whisper from an aide and blurt out: "I do not understand Colonel Howley's hooligan manners. If Colonel Howley does not apologise we will not attend future meetings." He stood up, shook Ganeval's hand and, with his team trailing behind, moved to the door. Herbert cut in: the next meeting had not been fixed. Yelisarov paused. He "looked very helpless, made a vague movement with his left hand, and finally left the room."[97]

What on earth was going on? Ganeval decided that the meeting was suspended because the Russians had left. Howley, he pointed out, had nominated a deputy. (Benson, he could have added, had been perfectly acceptable to the Russians for eight hours.) All the westerners at the meeting agreed later that there was no reason to believe the Russians had planned to wreck it but, as Murphy explained, it was "impossible to say whether the Soviet action was dictated by pique or . . . a decision to capitalise on an incident which could easily be misinterpreted in the press as a walk-out of the American commandant."[98] Had Yelisarov thrown in his policy document to spoil a good meeting or to grab the rare chance of an amicable mood? Should Howley have realised how he would provoke Yelisarov; was he genuinely too tired to wrap his departure in the usual polite formalities (though not too tired to go to the press camp and give his usual half-hour briefing)? His own memoirs put a brave face on the whole affair and give the impression he was glad of the Russian reaction. He claims to have told Clay's Chief of Staff: "If it hadn't been this incident it would have been something else," and to have replied to Clay's complaints that he was not contrite about the mess he had caused: "You're too damned right I'm not." He wrote in his diary: "I think it has been a disgrace for an American representative to sit for six months and listen to the abuse of the American people, the American army and all our concepts of democracy." However, he was not hearing any abuse at the time he left the Kommandatura; anyway, as Clay told him firmly, "Your job is to sit there and take it."[99] Most people decided Howley had been thoughtlessly rude and had not expected such a strong Russian reaction.

The really important question was how strong and lasting the Russian response would be. Did Yelisarov just hope to see the Americans eat a little humble pie, to remind everyone that quadripartite administration depended on Soviet goodwill? Or had he been unable to resist the opportunity to break up the Kommandatura and blame it on someone else? No one knew. For two more weeks the main Kommandatura did not meet, but its committees functioned normally. The western allies waited to see if the crisis would be used as a lever against currency reform and as an argument against their presence in Berlin. There was still a possibility that the whole thing would blow over, that the Americans and Russians could get together and make up. If not, there was at the very least a tricky constitutional problem: you can hardly have a four-Power administration with only three members, yet the Kommandatura had been set up by one quadripartite agreement so could only be dissolved by another. As it happened, such knotty legal problems did not have to be untangled. They were cut through by events.

On 18 June each western Military Governor sent Marshal Sokolovsky an explanation of the currency reform to be introduced that day into their zones. They emphasised that the new notes would not circulate in their sectors of Berlin and expressed the wish for a uniform currency for the whole country. Later in the day, as soon as the banks closed, the details of the reform were broadcast. Every inhabitant of west Germany could change 60 old Reichsmarks for 40 new Deutschmarks on Sunday; the other 20 would be distributed later. Employers would get 60 new marks for every employee. (60 old marks would hardly buy a packet of black-market cigarettes; the immediate import of twenty million American cigarettes would bring their price down while the new mark floated up.) Since such a tiny amount of currency would be in circulation, old notes of small denomination could be kept for change, but at a tenth of their face value. There was the same swingeing devaluation of deposits and pensions – hopes for the future had vanished, but they had been the mirages of inflation.

All weekend Germans scurried hither and thither spending: getting their hair permed, buying new false teeth, making down payments for future appendix operations.[100] The occupation authorities piled on reassurance. The currency reform, promised Clay, was a "technical, non-political measure"; Berlin, stressed Herbert, was not involved. These were at best disingenuous comments; few could be convinced. The worries of most west Germans for the moment were concentrated on their savings and the paucity of

138

ready cash available, but the population was reported to think that the gravity of the economic situation had justified the severity of the measures. The SED, on the other hand, called currency reform "a most terrible blow against the German people," a policy to make them "pawns of foreign interests," and warned on 18 June that the time was coming when "the great democratic people's movement led by the People's Council" would put an end to "Protectorate Government" in Frankfurt.[101]

And that same evening, 18 June, the SMA stopped all traffic from west Germany to Berlin. Everyone on foot, in train or car was turned back at Marienborn and at every minor crossing. At midnight the Russians issued new regulations: all passenger trains in or out of their zone would stop forthwith; no cars with passes issued in west Germany would be admitted; all freight traffic by rail or canal must submit to rigorous inspection of cargo and crews' personal belongings. Great numbers of extra Russian and German frontier guards appeared. The electricity supply to the western sectors of Berlin began to flicker: "coal shortages," explained the SMA. Sokolovsky issued a public statement: western marks would not be permitted to circulate in the Soviet zone or, he stressed, in Berlin, "which lies in the Soviet zone of Germany and economically forms part of the Soviet zone." That was a resounding assertion.

The western allies made no immediate protest. For a few days they were willing to give the Russians the benefit of the doubt and treat the new traffic restrictions as an excusable defensive measure to protect the Soviet mark; as Clay argued, "Were the situation reversed we on our side would have been required to take similar precautions."[102] In the meanwhile, the West still hoped to get the Russians to agree to a uniform currency settlement. A meeting of financial experts from all four Powers was arranged, ironically in the Allied Control Building. Meanwhile, in the western zones, twenty cigarettes were costing only 5 new marks and black-market butter had plummeted to 4 or 6 marks having once reached a peak of a full thousand.[103] Goods had magically appeared in the shops overnight; it was, people said, like Christmas in June. In Berlin word was seeping through that local Kommandaturas in the Soviet zone had rounded up hundreds of people to stick stamps on to old mark notes: if a Soviet currency for Berlin could be introduced before the western mark, it might well sweep the board.[104]

Against that background the financial experts of the four Powers argued for seven hours on 22 June. As they aired all the old pros and cons for uniform, mixed or a special currency for Berlin, it became clear that the Russians would accept only their own mark in the city. Though the western Powers still offered to accept the Russian mark if subject to quadripartite supervision, their advisers were increasingly doubtful that the controls would work and feared that sooner or later Soviet currency would make the western allies guests in Berlin. They did at least put it to the Russians that if the Soviet mark were introduced to the city unilaterally, they would retaliate by bringing in their own currency.[105]

It made no difference what they said. Some time before their meeting ended the acting Mayor, Louise Schroeder, was summoned to the City Hall by a Russian liaison officer. She and Friedensburg, who went along for support, were given an order from Sokolovsky for the introduction of a new East mark throughout the city, a set of implementing regulations dated 21 June from the east German Economic Commission, and a handwritten note from the Chief of Staff at the SMA containing the comment "the Soviet Military Administration does not doubt that the Berlin City Assembly will carry out its instructions."[106] When the financial experts broke up their meeting at about 11 p.m. without arranging another, they went home and heard on the radio that Soviet currency reform would be announced next day and would apply to the whole of Berlin.

This new currency was to be the sole legal tender for the city. Soviet-controlled enterprises, SED groups and their officials would exchange one old mark for one new; other groups and individuals would have a less favourable rate. Private firms would receive just enough currency for their immediate needs. Persons and companies classed as black-marketeers, manufacturers of Nazi war materials or profiteers would get no currency whatsoever. Berlin's special status was to be acknowledged by a thumb-sized paper stamp stuck on the new notes with potato glue – "wallpaper marks" Berliners called them. This stamp, it was soon discovered, fell off after three or four exchanges, but by 25 June you could stick on your own, a neat little forgery bought at a reasonable price on the black market.[107]

Western Deutschmark notes for the city had already been inde-libly stamped with a circle and a "B." On the morning of 23 June the western Powers announced that they would be issued immediately in their sectors. Still hoping for eventual agreement with the Russians, they would permit the use of both currencies for food, rent, taxes, power and coal.

With two competing forms of currency in Berlin and two sets of mutually exclusive regulations for their issue, which would Berliners choose? On 23 June the Magistrat passed a resolution asserting the four-Power status of the city and its unity, and Ernst Reuter led the way in insisting that both currencies must circulate. The City Assembly was asked to ratify these decisions and, by so doing, defy the SMA. A meeting was called for 4 p.m. that afternoon in the Stadthaus. An hour before, SED and communist trades union members surrounded the main door, crammed into the spectators' gallery, and flooded the chamber and passages. East sector police made no attempt to hold back the crowds or help Assembly members through the crush. Wagner, the new head of the Protection Police, came into the building with a couple of men, but Dr. Suhr, the Speaker of the Assembly, asked them to wait in an office while he and Frau Schroeder tried to restore order in the hall. By the time Suhr admitted defeat, the officers had disappeared; neither Wagner's deputy nor any other senior policeman answered phone calls. The French liaison officer, Captain Hector Ziegelmeyer, appealed to his Russian counterpart to help clear the floor of the chamber; the Russian refused to act. It took two hours before the Assembly meeting could begin and, to an accompaniment of barracking from the gallery, it voted to uphold the Magistrat's decision that two currencies must circulate in the city.

When the Assembly members then tried to leave, the mob outside turned very nasty. It charged at the main entrance and blocked the way. Cyclists patrolled the other doors and shouted for reinforcements if anyone tried to get out. In the car park thugs kicked and punched those caught making for their cars. Jeanette Wolff, an SPD representative, was called "*Judensau*" and beaten up, just as she had been in the 1930s before going to a concentration camp; she recognised the reincarnation of the SA. Those stuck inside the building could get no police escort. When Friedensburg finally got through on the phone to Wagner and shouted "My life is threatened," Wagner was unmoved: "It's not so important; don't be so afraid." It was late at night before Suhr, Friedensburg and a handful of others could slip out, thanks to the help of an SPD police officer and five men.[108]

And in the early minutes of 24 June the Russians stopped all rail traffic at Marienborn and cut the supply of electricity from eastern power stations to the western sectors. There was no hope now that this was the passing whim of individuals: the SMA officially announced that "technical difficulties on the railways" meant that

141

they would be closed "for a long period"; chronic fuel shortages "prevented resumption of electricity." West Berlin had stocks of food for roughly thirty-six days and enough coal for forty-five. No more would be allowed in by the Soviet authorities. Nothing could move to or from the western sectors except by air.

But the people of Berlin demonstrated on 24 June that they were not afraid, that they knew the bully-boys of old, had stood up to the Nazis in the past and would stand by their Magistrat and Assembly now: 50,000 of them packed into the Hertha Stadium in the French sector and 20,000 more crowded the street outside. They listened to a long, calm, reasoned address by Reuter in which he welcomed western currency reform, explained why the difference between the eastern and western economic systems made unified currency impossible, and suggested that Russian sanctions and yesterday's mob proved that the real issue was not currency but Berlin itself. The crowd cheered when he called on the world to help the Berliners "in the decisive phase of the fight for freedom."[109] How could the western Powers possibly resist such an appeal or be unmoved by such courage?

7

Scramble

There was help on its way to Berlin. On the morning of Thursday 24 June, Clay telephoned to General Curtis LeMay, commanding General of the United States Air Forces in Europe, and asked him to start flying in food for Berlin.[1] British military vehicles blossomed with bloomers from their radio aerials – "Operation Knicker" was under way.[2]

Yet this was help of a pitifully limited kind. Six British Dakotas would ply back and forth from Wunstorf in the zone to Gatow ferrying supplies for the garrison; a squadron of eight more Dakotas and their ground crews had been ordered from RAF Waterbeach; a further squadron, in training since mid-June, would come to Germany shortly. The RAF airlift had been planned only for the restricted needs of British civil and military staffs and their dependants in Berlin, and immediately available aircraft could supply little more. The Americans had to hand 100 C-47s, their own transport versions of the Dakota, battered old "Gooney Bird" veterans of Sicily, Normandy and Arnhem. The USAF had a bigger transport, the C-54, but there were only two of them in Germany.[3]

Such a small, decrepit contingent could not possibly sustain the two-and-a-half million people blockaded in the western sectors of Berlin. These sectors usually imported 12,000 tons of supplies a day, 75 per cent of them from the west.* Their basic need was, of

---

* All tonnage figures are given, where possible, as short tons (2,000 lbs). In the early stages of the blockade the USAF, RAF and the German authorities all had different definitions of a ton. Ultimately the two air forces kept their own records in short tons but provided figures for the Germans in metric tons.

course, food. Thanks to Russian insistence in 1945 that the western allies feed the parts of the city they occupied, it was known how much food was necessary: 641 tons a day of flour, 105 of cereals, 106 of meat and fish, 900 of potatoes, 51 of sugar, 10 of coffee, 20 of milk, 32 of fats, 3 of yeast.[4] Once the figures were rounded up, the western allies faced a frightening total – west Berlin had to have 2,000 tons of food a day. Dakotas and C-47s could each carry about 2.5 tons. Arithmetically allied planes could almost nourish west Berlin if requirements were cut to the bare minimum and each aircraft put in several round trips a day. Realistically they could not: pilots could not fly for twenty-four hours day in day out, aircraft would have to be taken out for regular servicing and would break down anyway, adverse weather conditions would prevent landings.

Furthermore, cities do not live by food alone. They need a whole range of other domestic goods, raw materials and machinery for industry, equipment for public services, spare parts and medical supplies. Western Berlin had reasonable stocks of fuel for its buses, cars and lorries; with careful allocation these might stretch to four or five months' supply of diesel, three or four months' of motor oil, but only seven to eight weeks' of petrol.[5] Even more vital to Berlin's existence was coal. The first rough estimate of stocks had suggested they would last for forty-five days. Once the various qualities for different purposes were taken into account, the situation for some users was less rosy. Those domestic consumers who burned coal for heating or cooking and industrialists who fuelled their boilers with it might expect hard coal for another thirty-five days, coke for forty-nine, brown (lignite) briquettes for twenty-five. If gas pressure were reduced and domestic cooking permitted for only short periods, perhaps gas-works could keep going on 1,000 tons of hard coal a day, in which case their reserves would last for forty-eight days. Since the gas supply was on a city-wide basis, it was tempting to lower the pressure and suck gas through from the Russian sector, but there was always a danger that the SMA would play the same game.[6] Waterworks and sewage plants relied on coal too. Berlin's water had to be pumped from deep wells through a natural filter of sand and gravel. On 24 June housewives rushed to fill every bath, bucket and basin with water. They came near to draining the system before the authorities announced that there were ample reserves and people should use as much as they wanted. That stopped the panic and spared householders the knowledge that the waterworks had only enough coal for thirty-five days, after which the pumps would stop. The sewage plants could last out that long too, thanks to a decision to stop treating sewage and use coal only to siphon it raw into the river and canals.[7]

The prospects for generating electricity were even more disturbing. On 26 June electricity restrictions were introduced: consumption had to come down to 75 per cent for cooking, hospitals and schools, 50 per cent for domestic lighting and for transport, and 25 per cent for municipal buildings. Industrial users were to be severely limited though food processing was given priority.[8] Even so, power stations still needed at least 1,650 tons of hard coal a day and at present rates could last out for just over three weeks.[9] The generating stations faced a further problem. Before June most electricity in Berlin had come from the Russian sector; that supply was now cut off. There were eight power stations in the western parts of the city. In theory, they had the capacity to meet a half of normal summer demand. In fact, they were small and obsolete and had been used only to boost supply at peak periods: they were unlikely to stand the strain of constant production.[10] In days gone by the Berlin West power station in the British sector had supplied a quarter of the electricity for the whole city. The Russians had stripped it bare in June 1945. The western allies had struggled ever since for a quadripartite decision to re-equip it. In April 1948 the British gave up the attempt to get one and decided to go ahead themselves with the rebuilding. The site was ready, the plans drawn up. There seemed no way now to bring in steel girders, mountains of concrete and cumbersome machinery to a city cut off by land and water.

All in all, doubtful though the chances were that west Berlin could be fed by air, there seemed even less possibility that the tonnage of other commodities – coal especially – could ever be flown in.

The history of airlifts was not particularly consoling. In spring 1945 the RAF had dropped 1,560 tons of food in two days over starving Holland. That had needed 650 sorties by Lancaster bombers. The Americans had flown as many aircraft a day over "The Hump" of the Himalayas from India into China from April 1942 to support Generalissimo Chiang Kai-shek and the US forces who were pinning down Japanese armies. The RAF too had supplied British troops fighting their way through Burma to Rangoon. These two operations had transported over a million tons of food, arms and equipment across vast distances and in

145

appalling climatic conditions. They were great achievements, but only possible because of detailed forward planning and the use of the immense resources released in wartime. By contrast there was no preparation for feeding the west sectors of Berlin in 1948 (the western Powers had expected an assault on themselves not the civilian population); British and American air transport services had been wound down rapidly at the end of the war, aircraft had been scrapped and replacements built for small peacetime needs.

Flying in and out of Berlin involved particular difficulties. Over "The Hump" transports had flown in corridors never narrower than fifty miles and ultimately 200 miles wide; the allies had achieved the run of the skies. To get to Berlin, on the other hand, they must use three corridors merely twenty miles wide and fly across the Soviet zone on Russian tolerance. Once over the city western aircraft shared airspace with seven Soviet airfields, three of which had circuits intersecting or perilously near those of Tempelhof and Gatow. For the support of troops in China and Burma the allies had custom-built, fully supplied home bases. Rhein Main, where LeMay intended to concentrate his 60th and 61st Troop Carrier Groups, had been built pre-war as a base for lighter-than-air Zeppelins; since then it had been used by the Luftwaffe and the USAF as a fighter station and been expanded for American civil operations too. Its one runway was of good length – 6,000 yards – but it was made of Marston matting, a steel mesh giving a level surface and grip which was not designed for heavy use and which subjected tyres to terrible wear. RAF Wunstorf, the British zonal base, had been laid out as a grass airfield in 1934, first used by a bomber group, then in wartime as an operational fighter station. The British had concreted the 2,000-foot runway and covered it with tarmacadam. Wunstorf had well-built messing for a couple of squadrons, a spur to the railway and six hangars, but little hard-standing for parked aircraft and loading and no solid track for taxiing or the use of motor vehicles.[11]

In comparison, facilities at Tempelhof in the US sector were positively lavish: a vast curving operations and administrative block designed and constructed between 1934 and 1939 for Berlin's civil airport and thought to be one of the biggest buildings in the world. Much of it was underground, where during the war there had been a hospital and Messerschmidt factory. The long arc of the roof had been intended for restaurants and seating for spectators at air and ground displays; its cantilevered width now sheltered a great stretch of parking for aircraft and vehicles. There was a concrete block apron and taxiway, but the 4,987-foot runway was surfaced with pierced steel planking (PSP) – a menace to tyres especially on an aircraft which braked hard – and it was laid on a relatively unstable foundation. Landing there was always tricky and in bad weather impossible – traffic often had to be diverted. For Tempelhof was flat in the middle of the city. The best approach, from the west, required careful positioning between seven-storey blocks of flats on one side and, as a reminder to avoid them, a cemetery on the other. Alternative approaches involved dropping sharply over the buildings to use a good length of runway. As a final refinement of hazard, pilots had to avoid the 400-foot chimney of a nearby brewery. Its proud owner had resisted American appeals to demolish it with a series of excuses about its aesthetic contribution to the city and economic importance to Germany which he had been embroidering ever since Hermann Göring first tried to get rid of the obstacle.

Landing at the British airfield at Gatow, on the other hand, was easy – a *"morceau de gâteau,"* as the pilots said. The approach was clear – it could be made in comparatively poor visibility – and the chief danger came from minor slips in navigation which landed pilots at the next-door Russian military airfield, Staaken. Again, however, there was only one runway. Its 1,500 yards were covered with PSP laid directly on the sandy soil. The RAF had decided in 1947 to supplement it with a 2,000-yard concrete runway with connecting perimeter track. By June 1948 the runway was three-quarters complete, but the track had not been started. Gatow, a former Luftwaffe training college then fighter base, had provided excellent accommodation for an RAF station of 580: a large administrative building, agreeable barracks scattered among trees and lawns, ten good hangars and underground fuel tanks with parking above for a dozen aircraft. But it had never been intended for freight handling: the off-loading area was made of bricks resting in sand and could not stand up to much weight or vibration. Unusually for a German-designed airfield there was no spur to a railway. In compensation, though, there was the Havel lake just to the east with waters connecting to the River Spree and the network of canals which covered Berlin. The blockade of 24 June had trapped forty barges on the Havel; on 28 June ten more slipped into the city.[12] One tug could pull 3,000 tons for twenty-four hours while consuming only a ton of coal; diesel lorries needed 5 tons of fuel to do the same work; petrol-driven vehicles 15 tons.[13] The Russians had provided the western sectors of Berlin with one asset.

But their blockade had left the city with little else. The municipal authorities took what immediate action they could to conserve resources: froze food stocks and cut fuel supplies. The British dosed the Russians with a bit of their own medicine and stopped coal and steel deliveries to the eastern zone; the Bizonal Economic Commission introduced further restrictions on trade. Even so, the outlook was bleak indeed for Berliners. When a British liaison officer saw Frau Schroeder, the acting Mayor, at 11 p.m. on 24 June, he found her "calm and cool, but not in a confident mood." She and other members of the Magistrat were desperately worried about the problems of food and coal. They could think of no way short of war in which the western Powers might force the lifting of the blockade, and war would inevitably destroy their city and open west Germany to Soviet invasion.[14] The alternatives to a short ruinous fight between the Powers seemed to be lingering death for Berliners or surrender to the Russians. Reports were already coming through from the east sector that the Soviet authorities would not themselves try to oust the western allies; they would wait until food shortages became acute, then foment civil disturbances and incite the population to seek salvation by combining with the Russian zone.[15] Frau Schroeder told an American liaison officer: "Unless provisions arrive in Berlin in the next three weeks or so there will be no need to stage riots as it will be a case of real riots" – hunger and unemployment would spare any Russian effort.[16]

Throughout the first day of the blockade, 24 June, the western authorities tried to cheer Berliners with reassurance and promises. They gave pretty cold comfort. Clay told the press that only war could force the United States out of Berlin – a statement which could be read as callous indifference to the suffering of Berliners and which was contrary to his real feeling: "I propose to stay until [the] starving German population asks us to go."[17] Herbert broadcast to the city: "There is enough food to avoid immediate anxiety" – which could only raise the question whether Berliners should start worrying next day or next week. Howley vowed, "The people of Berlin will not be permitted to starve," yet was in no position to say how they could be helped to eat.[18]

For as yet the western allies could do no more than fly in a few tons of food a day. This was simply a gesture of commiseration, like a bunch of flowers for a mortally sick man. On 25 June the first C-47s with food from the American zone landed at Tempelhof; the regular half-dozen Dakota flights from Wunstorf came in to Gatow.

There would be more RAF sorties soon: a new Transport Command squadron with eight aircraft and ground crews arrived at Wunstorf that day. It came without the Royal Army Service Corps men from 749 Company who should have travelled with it and taken over the loading of aircraft. Their movement order had been cancelled that morning: the Treasury refused to pay for their flight. So they set off by train from Salisbury to Harwich, across by ferry to the Hook, then trundled by rail to Wunstorf where the station commander tore strips off them for being late.[19] To compensate for paucity of aircraft, the British were scratching around for ways to maximise their effort. Bevin was sending dried milk, eggs and other concentrates to Berlin – he was particularly anxious about the plight of babies, small children and nursing mothers.[20] He had every reason to be: on 25 June no fresh milk at all reached the city. On 26 June a British pilot did a recce to see if supplies could be dropped on Berlin.[21] Sites like the old Olympic Stadium offered plenty of room on the ground but hopelessly constricted airspace. Later experiments proved that dropping, regardless of packing or method, too often delivered smithereens.[22]

Clay believed at this stage that air transport could neither meet Berlin's pressing needs nor solve the basic crisis. He told the Department of the Army on 25 June: "As matters now stand the German population will begin to suffer in a few days and this suffering will become serious in two or three weeks. I am still convinced that a determined movement of convoys with troop protection would reach Berlin, and that such a showing might well prevent rather than build up Soviet pressures which could lead to war."[23] While waiting for official approval to send an armed convoy, he discussed with his officers the creation of an allied task force, of 5–6,000 men with tanks and artillery, to deliver 500 tons of food and fuel. It was assumed the Russians would block the route so engineers must be taken and bridging equipment carried, which would have to be brought from the United States.[24] Many of Clay's Berlin staff, including Howley, doubted the convoy would get through.[25] If it did, there was no guarantee that the blockade would collapse at once, so the first convoy would have to be followed by others. But there was too little military transport in west Germany to maintain Berlin and a shortage of troops for holding the 120-mile autobahn. Should the allies make the huge military effort that Clay envisaged just to force through 500 tons of food a time to a city which needed 12,000 tons of supplies a day? Even if the risk of war were taken and it paid off quickly, the operation would take time to prepare.

149

Berlin needed food now. It could only be supplied by air.

Clay understood the urgency all too well, but he had to ask himself how much the people of Berlin should be asked to suffer so that the western allies could maintain their right to be in the city. He saw Ernst Reuter on 25 June and put the stark situation to him: whatever the allies did, Berliners were going to be hungry, cold and without electric light. Could they put up with that? What price would they pay to maintain their independence from the Russians? Reuter was unshaken. Willy Brandt who was with him remembered his reply: "Do what you are able to do; we shall do what we feel to be our duty. Berlin will make all the necessary sacrifices and offer resistance – come what may."[26] Reuter had made it clear: the city would hold out whether the allies stayed or not. That was what Clay needed to hear. He rang LeMay: every C-47, every man available must be put on the Berlin run. The chances were that seventy aircraft making a total of 100 round trips a day could bring in 225 tons of food every twenty-four hours. If another thirty planes were brought to Germany, the shipment would go up to 500 tons.[27] It was little enough. But it might slow down the rate at which Berlin crumbled and give a few more days to find a real solution.

On 26 June the C-47s brought 80 tons to Berlin; the RAF Dakotas managed 13. Air Officer Commanding-in-Chief RAF Transport Command was ordered to replace "Operation Knicker" with a plan to supply not just the garrison but the sector. This new operation was to be called "Carter Paterson," the name of a well-known British haulage firm. As the Russians soon pointed out, the company was best known as a removals firm; the British, they sneered, were organising a flit. "Carter Paterson" was soon re-christened "Plainfare." Under its original title it was approved by the Cabinet on 28 June. That day the second Dakota squadron left Britain for Wunstorf, and a conference at HQ 46 Group in Bückeburg was told that 38 and 47 Groups were joining in and sending thirty-eight additional aircraft within twenty-four hours.[28] Meanwhile, on the 28th, the C-47s flew 384 tons in 100 sorties, with LeMay throwing in every aircraft which could limp off the ground and every desk-bound man who had ever learned to fly. The RAF sweated round the clock and delivered 44 tons in thirteen Dakotas, making the best of each flight by tearing out safety equipment to make more room for freight.[29] The possibilities of landing flying boats on the Havel were also being explored.[30] The British Yacht Club could provide moorings; Finkenwerde on the Elbe was to be surveyed as a base for Sunderlands.[31]

The British, with so few resources, were thrown back on ingenuity. They could not depend on many more aircraft from the UK – a crippling dock strike had begun on 22 June (and would last until the 29th) and the Cabinet must reserve some air transport in case the military had to take over domestic food supply. The Americans were going great guns with the aircraft they had available. There was no certainty, however, that they could use more, though Clay asked the Department of the Army for fifty extra on 27 June.[32] Limited facilities on the ground might well hinder their operation; short runways would prevent the use of the biggest transports. There was, furthermore, some reluctance in Washington to supply them. Admiral Leahy, Truman's Chief of Staff, warned that an airlift was a dangerous enterprise and could spark off military conflict; a memo from USAF Plans and Operations advised that it was a diversion from planning for a war which could well develop from the current crisis.[33] Americans and British alike had to weigh the needs of Berlin and the city's political and strategic importance against their commitment to supply bases in the rest of the world and the danger that the Russians might strike somewhere other than Germany. Putting everything they had into the Berlin effort could well cause even worse problems.

Ernest Bevin, however, always saw the airlift as the cardinal priority, the means to secure not just Berlin but much more besides. When explaining his foreign policy he was fond of the metaphor of a table with four legs: the European Recovery Programme, the Treaty of Brussels and Western Union, American military commitment to western Europe and the organisation of west Germany. If one leg were weakened, the whole structure would collapse. The Russian blockade had exposed the frailty of the Berlin strut and was intended to show the inability of the West to prop it up. But, Bevin believed, as the American Ambassador Lewis Douglas reported, that an airlift would "reinforce the morale of the Germans in Berlin, already high, and what was even more important, demonstrate to the Soviet* and to its satellite countries that we are not powerless but on the contrary possess a wealth of technical ability and spectacular air strength."[34] It could more than compensate psychologically and politically for its physical and economic shortcomings.

* Douglas, like Robertson, clung to doomed accuracies: he spoke of "Russians" or "citizens of the Soviet Union" but very properly used the word "Soviet" as a noun to refer to the government of the USSR, and "Soviet" as an adjective related to nouns connected with that system of government.

When news of the Russian blockade broke on 24 June Bevin was on holiday – such was British readiness for a sudden blow from the Soviet Union that the Foreign Secretary was taking a few days' break at Sandbanks and the Prime Minister was arranging a visit to army bases in Germany the following week.[35] Bevin rushed to London for a Cabinet meeting, fizzing with vigour and ideas, an advertisement for the bracing effects of Dorset sea air. The Cabinet was briefed on 25 June by Robertson's deputy, General Sir Nevil Brownjohn. In his opinion Berliners were calm and the majority "ready to resist Russian orders if they were confident that they could continue to receive the support of the western Powers."[36] There was no doubt in Bevin's mind: that support would be given. Brownjohn warned, however, that it was not practical to bring in trains or road convoys by force, "save as a major military operation," that there were too few troops in the city to handle more than minor civil disturbances, and that there were no countermeasures to shake the Russians which would not involve risk such as the cutting of allied communication cables. Above all, Brownjohn stressed that it was impossible to supply Berlin fully by air, even if returning aircraft were packed with Berliners willing to leave the city and reduce the need for provisions. This was all pessimism which Bevin refused to share. He demanded the biggest possible force of transport aircraft to be made available at once and ordered the Chiefs of Staff to prepare plans for supply as a matter of urgency. He called for immediate consultations with the Americans and French to pool ideas and resources for air provisioning. Meanwhile, a group of ministers would keep the situation under review and channel information and authorisations with all possible speed.[37] (Three members of this Committee of Ministers on Germany – Attlee, Herbert Morrison and Bevin himself – had served in the wartime Cabinet; they were used to acting decisively and cutting peacetime corners.)

"I really frightened that Brownjohn," Bevin used to remember gleefully.[38] It was more likely that Brownjohn had been delighted by a minister ready to listen to warnings and then to release the energy and means to fight the problems. Bevin galvanised everyone in the next few days. On 26 June he issued a press communique stating Britain's determination to stay in Berlin. He kept Parliament up to date and, by the time he told the House of Commons on 30 June that it "could not abandon those stout-hearted Berlin democrats who were refusing to bow to Soviet pressure," members from both sides were ready to back him to the hilt. He put it to them frankly that "a grave situation might arise" and the government "would have to ask the House to face it." They cheered and Harold Macmillan, for the Opposition, assured him that force could not be met without preparedness to risk war. Members cheered again when Bevin told them that the alternative was surrender, "and none of us can accept surrender."[39] Meanwhile, he had raced around securing other support. He saw the Commonwealth High Commissioners, impressed on them Britain's resolve to help Berlin, passed on intelligence reports that the Soviet Union intended to have the western allies out of Berlin by August, and gave notice that any Russian interference with the air corridors "would be treated as acts of war."[40] He appealed to them for help with aircraft and supplies; Canada offered dehydrated food on 1 July.[41]

Above all Bevin worked to strengthen the bond with the United States and to make sure the Americans were fully committed to Berlin. He told Lewis Douglas on 25 June that even if "the Russians held the cards ... we could bluff them out of their hands by convincing them that we meant business." He recommended that the combined Anglo-American Chiefs of Staff in Washington should make an appreciation of the situation and discuss air transport for Berlin.[42] Next day he proposed a western co-ordinating body in London: Strang, Massigli (the French ambassador) and Douglas should oversee all allied information and planning. The idea made obvious sense: London provided easy communication with Germany, and the three men had a record of working effectively together and great experience of German problems (Strang and Massigli since the days of the European Advisory Commission, Douglas through negotiations for Marshall Aid and at the London talks). Bevin liked and respected all three; in return they admired his expertise and judgment, but would not be used as doormats. Such a body would certainly give him a grip on the crisis. Through Strang and the German section of the Foreign Office he had access to Robertson and via him to Clay. In Massigli he had a "reliable" Frenchman – in other words, one who did not share the "Munich" views of some of his colleagues and political masters and had disobeyed instructions from the Quai d'Orsay from time to time. (As it happened France was entering yet another political crisis and would be without a government for nearly two months from July; a steady French representative would turn out to be invaluable.) Douglas was a friend. His mind was educated, logical, clear – very different from Bevin's, which was instinctive and often expressed in rambling periods blurred with mixed metaphors. Yet the two men tended to reach the same conclusions and could enjoy unusual candour on the way. Douglas once explained that Bevin "would blow his top, shout a bit and curse the Americans, but I did the same and neither of us ever walked out of the house."[43]

The role of Douglas, Strang and Massigli was approved by Marshall on 27 June.[44] In the coming months, under Bevin's beady eye, they gathered the complex strands of the crisis: made their governments' cables available to each other, drafted joint diplomatic notes and assessments, and struggled to keep awake on a sofa in Douglas's office while he held teleconferences with Washington into the early hours. Their professionalism made a great contribution to the smooth running of the political and diplomatic operation, their personal relationship prevented many a misunderstanding.

Bevin had set up a conduit for joint allied policies and started an all-out effort to supply Berlin by air. He was not satisfied. He also wanted to confront the Soviet Union with a show of military might, not as a threat but as a statement of determination and power. For that he needed US fighters and heavy bombers in Europe, based if necessary in Britain. "This might help to persuade the Russians that we mean business," he explained to Douglas on 25 June.[45] Washington was more than willing to send air reinforcement: a fighter group of F-80s was standing by, and three bomber groups each with thirty B-29s, which were potential carriers of atomic bombs though not yet modified for them, could be ready at twelve hours' notice. American officials, however, must have been rather startled by Bevin's request for US military aircraft, let alone willingness to house them: states are more used to pleading for bases than being begged to set them up. Marshall asked Douglas to check that the arrival of B-29s was really acceptable to the British government.[46] A conference of State Department and military officials on 27 June considered the pros and cons of stationing them in Britain or Germany.[47] Truman gave permission on 28 June for their dispatch to Europe, and the Committee of Ministers on Germany approved an American suggestion that one group be kept in Britain and the others stop in transit to Germany, with the proviso that the Americans should fuel them since British oil stocks were dangerously low.[48]

In the event, the B-29s did not yet leave for Europe. Bevin began to have second thoughts about timing: since the Russians had not yet made any military moves he did not want to give them an excuse to send troops westward, nor did he want to jolt diplomatic contacts just established.[49] Marshall too reconsidered the wisdom of immediate dispatch: nuclear-capable aircraft would be vulnerable in Germany and provocative in Britain, and he preferred to prepare American public opinion first.[50] In the next two or three weeks the Americans wondered if they had lost their opportunity of a British base and a chance to make the planes what the Secretary of Defence James Forrestal called "somewhat of an accepted feature" in Britain.[51] Bevin, however, did not change his mind on the principle. Even though he had delayed the bombers, the press on 30 June announced that they would come to Europe. His point had been made: the West had strength and was agreed on using it.

What Bevin was also looking for was a public declaration from the Americans that they would stay in Berlin and use their vast resources to do so. In the first few days of the blockade only Britain had spoken out: in Bevin's statements to the House and press releases. He himself, through Douglas, certainly knew that Washington shared London's resolution, but the rest of the world did not. He pressed for a clear, firm statement. He even suggested it might include a compliment to the Berlin SPD, "the best element in the country," in his opinion, which had stood out longest against Hitler and was now standing up well to the Russians (though he recognised that the word "socialist" did stick in American gullets).[52]

While he waited for the Americans to break their silence, Bevin enjoyed another chance for general-frightening. By coincidence General William Draper, the Under-Secretary for the Army and Lieutenant-General Albert Wedemeyer, the Director of Plans and Operations, Army General Staff, were visiting Europe. Douglas brought them to see Bevin on 28 June. Draper, a trusty comrade of Clay and a former Economics Director in the U.S. Military Government who had negotiated the feeding of Berlin with the Russians in 1945, proudly referred to the tonnage the Americans were already lifting to Berlin and promised it would soon be 1,500 tons a day. Not enough, snapped Bevin, then played every trick in his repository of low cunning: flattery (America, the world's greatest air power), cajolery (surely they could do better), pathos (look at what poor little Britain was managing) and nostalgia (think how the two countries had struggled together in the War).[53] Wedemeyer, who had worked on the airlift across the Himalayas, promised they would do at least as well as over "The Hump." The two men came out of the room, as Bevin's Private Secretary remembered, shaking themselves like dogs out of a pond.[54] Probably, like Brownjohn, they had been told what they wanted to hear and were glad of political drive behind the military effort.

They had had less encouragement so far from Washington. Certainly Truman had decided on 26 June that the airlift should be put on a fully operational basis and that every aircraft in the European theatre should be pressed into service.[55] The reaction to the crisis in other official quarters had been less decisive. It was one of cautious appraisal sprinkled with recrimination. The State Department's first suggestion to Clay on 25 June was that he should slow down the introduction of reformed currency. That, as Clay pointed out, came rather late in the day.[56] Other officials fretted over the United States' legal right to be in Berlin and sought documents on allied access agreements, even cabling Douglas to ask if the British had any.[57] So vague was their understanding of their position in Berlin that on 25 June, Forrestal, Kenneth Royall, the Secretary of the Army, and Lovett talked only of messages between Roosevelt and Stalin and verbal promises given to Eisenhower by the Russians. What is remarkable about this conversation is that according to the edited version of Forrestal's diary Truman was present and could have well pointed out that he himself had had correspondence with Stalin on access and presence. Furthermore, the President did not correct Lovett's opinion that the present sorry mess was all the fault of "the attitude prevailing at the time in the minds of Roosevelt, Stimson, Hopkins, Eisenhower etc., that we would have no trouble in dealing with the Russians"[58] – though his own administration had taken that line and had done little to improve allied rights obtained in June 1945. Indeed, the buck was being passed by everyone at this time. Murphy, with the clean nose of a man who had criticised allied access arrangements from the start, blamed the present crisis on "a defective agreement negotiated by Mr. Winant and others in 1944 in an outburst of faith and goodwill designed to induce the USSR to work in Germany" in co-operation with the West.[59] There was to be a peptic spasm from a legal official in the Foreign Office complaining: "I personally am getting a little tired of being treated at the Club and elsewhere including, if I may say so, at a public dinner ... to remarks about the failure of Foreign Office lawyers ... to cause proper agreements to be made." Lawyers, he wished it to be known, had given proper advice but had been brushed aside by the military.[60]

Fortunately there was too little time in the early days of the blockade for much of this backbiting. Current problems were compelling. On 27 June, Forrestal, Royall and Lovett with the three

American military chiefs appraised a range of solutions. Should they withdraw from Berlin? That would have enormous repercussions on west Germany and Europe. Should they stay and break the blockade by force, with Clay's armed convoy, for instance? That involved the risk of war. Could they stay and use local contacts or international diplomacy to assert their rights and seek a settlement while topping up Berlin's stocks by air for at least sixty days? This raised all kinds of questions about diplomatic and technical means.[61] When these options were put to Truman next day, his reponse was instantaneous and unequivocal. Forrestal recorded it as "we were going to stay – period." Never mind Royall's scruples that the threat of war must be considered from the start: "We would have to deal with the situation as it developed," insisted Truman.[62]

On that firm foundation Marshall could at last publicly outline the United States' policy on 30 June and proclaim American determination to uphold the right to stay in Berlin. His statement included the announcement that air transport would supply Berlin. "It has been found," Marshall indicated, "that the tonnage of foodstuffs and supplies which can be lifted by air is greater than had at first been assumed."[63]

That was a veiled sentence, giving no figures of needs or aircraft, and it concealed the fact that the Americans and British still had no idea of how nearly they could meet Berlin's requirements nor for how long. Yet it was true that in a mere week from the total blockade of the city the whole concept of air supply had been transformed. The United States would soon be able to airlift 1,000 tons a day – C-54s with a capacity double that of the C-47 were on their way from Panama, Hawaii and Alaska; Rhein Main and Wiesbaden were expanding to house them, Tempelhof was priming to receive them. The main limitation on the American effort now seemed to be shortage of trained men for servicing and flying.[64] By 29 June the RAF was averaging 75 tons daily and within two days was expected to be up to 400 tons thanks to the arrival of four-engined Yorks, which in the passenger-cum-freight version could carry 15,000 lbs and as freighters pure and simple 16,500. At the end of the first week in July Gatow's new runway would be open and the British could then handle 750 tons a day.[65] The Dutch and Belgians were being asked for supplies and the possible use of their ground staff.[66] Some improvement on the ground was certainly needed and staff alone would not provide it. An officer who arrived at Wunstorf on 30 June found that aircraft could hardly be loaded at night because lighting was inadequate until two floodlights were brought in next day, refuelling was chaotic given only one bulk issue point, telephones were few and often failed to connect, and there was an acute shortage of starter trolleys and wheel chocks.[67] For both the Americans and the British ambition and aircraft numbers were beginning to outstrip the means to handle them. The organisation had to catch up.

In spite of all the efforts so far the airlift was barely keeping abreast of Berlin's most basic needs. Food stocks in the city were dwindling. Reserves outside had to be rifled. Much of the flour delivered by the Americans had come from their Army depots; not until the second week in July did a ship dock at Bremen with any replacement.[68] It had been possible to fly in 84 tons of dried potato only because west German miners sacrificed a consignment ear-marked for them.[69] The authorities were having to learn that some provisions could not be supplied at all. Fish in barrels, for example, was too awkward to load; it would have to be tinned and packed in boxes. Butter in barrels too was inconvenient; furthermore, the barrels burst and there was no cold storage at either end of the lift.[70] Difficult though it was to deliver food, other commodities had so far been ignored because they created such problems. Newsprint came in rolls which weighed nearly 4 tons each. That was tonnage best reserved for food, so Berlin newspapers would soon go out of production.[71] Medical supplies were leaching away at an alarming rate. An urgent signal from Berlin on 3 July warned that some stocks would be exhausted at the end of the month and that the city needed 1,270 kgs of ether a month, 6,000 litres of alcohol, 20 or more tons of plaster of Paris, 20,000 square metres of X-ray film[72] – all bulky and difficult to handle. The great necessity still to be tackled was, of course, coal. Given power cuts and rationing plus the discovery of a few hundred tons here and there in mer-chants' yards, Berlin had kept going. But by 5 July generating stations had only enough coal to last until the 27th.[73] Industry was already suffering badly from coal and electricity shortages and lack of raw materials. It was doubly squeezed by its inability to export goods: aircraft turned round as quickly as possible to get back for more food. A little mail had been sent out, however, and by 1 July Herbert was recommending dispatch of a few high value exports and goods vital to the west German economy.[74]

The airlift had grown dramatically in terms of tonnage during the week since total blockade on 24 July. It must now both make a quantitative leap and develop sophistication of planning never previously imagined. So far the operation had been improvised in the heat of crisis and offered a few days' hope to Berlin. If it could mature into a more complex, longer-term affair, that hope would be extended. And the western Powers would have a chance to set up diplomatic negotiations and look for a way to persuade the Soviet Union to lift the blockade which did not entail sacrificing western rights in Berlin and objectives in west Germany and Europe.

It was, however, still far from clear what the Soviet Union hoped to achieve through the blockade. The SMA and the Russian-licensed press all talked about protecting east German currency and "technical difficulties" in maintaining power and communications: local and temporary problems. Clay, for one, was prepared for a day or so to accept that the Russians were only concerned with the immediate financial issue. He told Royall on 25 June: "I still doubt the Soviet intent to drive us out by starving Berlin"; it was more probable they wanted "to frighten Berlin people so that they would not accept western currency."[75] Yet even if Russians on the spot gave no hint of broader aims, there was a strong indication from outside that the Soviet Union's blockade of Berlin was a major instrument of policy.

On 23 and 24 June the Foreign Ministers of the USSR, Poland, Czechoslovakia, Hungary, Rumania, Bulgaria, Albania and Yugoslavia met in Warsaw. At the end of the conference a Declaration was issued, which denounced the London talks for excluding the Soviet Union, liquidating quadripartite administration in Germany, planning Germany's "dismemberment," and proposing an Occupation Statute to prolong the state of war rather than preparing a peace treaty. The western Powers were accused of subordinating west Germany's economy to their European Recovery Programme and turning the Ruhr into "a weapon for the restoration of Germany's war potential." The Warsaw Declaration called for complete demilitarisation, four-Power control of the Ruhr, the fulfilment of reparations obligations, a provisional "democratic and peace-loving" German government composed of representatives of political parties and "democratic organisations," and a peace treaty to be followed within a year by the withdrawal of all occupation forces.

The Declaration laid many baits for Germans: unity, independent government, peace, the end of humiliating occupation. It was not difficult to see, though, that the Warsaw settlement would renew Russian stripping of the west German economy for reparations, give the Soviet Union influence in the Ruhr and in German government through communist and Front representation, and leave Soviet troops on the Oder, only forty miles from Berlin. Once the British and Americans had mulled the document over they reached the same conclusion: the Soviet Union wanted to reopen the whole German question and hoped for a new meeting of the Council of Foreign Ministers to thrash it out. London and Washington remembered previous CFMs as occasions of frustration and delay. Both reckoned that a future Council would be used by the Russians to demand suspension of the London proposals in return for lifting the Berlin blockade. "That, of course," said Marshall, "is out of the question."[76] Bevin was not prepared to discuss anything with the Russians until the blockade was up; as an old trades union poacher turned ministerial gamekeeper he insisted "there must first be a return to work, after which one could talk."[77]

Yet the Soviet Union had not spelled out clearly and directly that the price of lifting the blockade was a CFM. Ideally the western Powers would have liked to solve the crisis in the city itself. A settlement between the Military Governors would revive quadripartite relationships and contain the problem as a narrow legal question of access and presence rather than dilate it into a confrontation over the future of Germany and Europe. They were not optimistic that a solution could be found at the local level. Even so, they went through the motions.

On 25 June Robertson sent a conventional note of protest to Sokolovsky about the new traffic restrictions. Clay disapproved of the approach and thought the note could be read as "an indication of apprehension on our part."[78] He preferred to wait for a few days to see if the Russians came to terms with the new currency position and lifted the blockade of their own accord. Robertson had to wait five days for a reply. On 30 June Sokolovsky informed him that the traffic restrictions were of "a temporary nature and designed for the protection of the currency of the Soviet zone," though having conceded they were deliberate SMA policy he still referred to "technical difficulties" on the railway. Without a blush the Marshal expressed satisfaction that there were adequate stocks in Berlin "for several weeks." With a fair degree of brass neck he praised the measures "now being taken by the British and American authorities for maintaining communications with the western zones by air," and added a schoolmasterly hope "that the rules of air safety will be fully adhered to."[79]

British and American reaction to Sokolovsky's reply was unanimous. In Douglas's words Bevin saw it as a characteristic Soviet tactic, "giving us a sense of false reassurance ... inducing us to relax our efforts."[80] Lovett dismissed it as merely holding out "relatively vague hopes."[81] The three western Military Governors decided Sokolovsky had offered "no promise of compromise" though his reply had been "carefully worded not to entirely lock the gate."[82] It was noted that Sokolovsky had not even hinted at talks, local or international, had promised ultimate restoration of rail travel without mentioning the rights of allied trains to move without check, and had said nothing about electricity supplies. The Americans and British agreed on policy: what Robertson called "full steam ahead" with air supply and a show of force.[83] The Americans would have liked to leave things at that: Sokolovsky's letter was better ignored in their opinion. However, they tolerated Bevin's wish for a reply because he had promised the House of Commons to see the whole procedure through. "I understand the British position," said Clay. "Anyway they are in it with us all the way now. Of that I am sure, and that's what really counts."[84] These were generous feelings he could not extend to the French. "My British colleague has been splendid throughout," he told Royall one day, "but neither he nor I get any support even moral from the French."[85]

While the paper formalities plodded on Clay and Robertson considered whether all four Military Governors should meet. They anticipated little from quadripartite talks but, as Clay put it on 25 June, "the conference might develop more fully the extent of Soviet intransigence and Soviet intent"; it would at least show willingness to "prevent suffering by a helpless German population caught between us."[86] The idea was tossed about in cables between Germany and the western capitals for a few days then abandoned. Everyone agreed with Clay's view on 29 June that another approach to Sokolovsky was "not yet timely," and accepted his request to wait until the airlift had been substantially increased and the Ministers President briefed on the London proposals for west German government.[87]

By a strange accident Clay himself had just met Sokolovsky. It was a reunion which in other circumstances might have been amusing. Some weeks before, the Americans had lost patience over arrests of their personnel while visiting the Russian sector of Berlin — ninety-three were held for short periods in the first half of 1948. They decided to get a bit of their own back. Knowing that Russian officers often drove at dangerous speeds across the US sector from their headquarters in Potsdam to offices in Berlin, Clay ordered patrols to flag them down and ask for identification. On 26 June a US jeep observed a speeding Soviet military car, which refused to stop. The jeep radioed ahead to an armoured car and the Soviet vehicle was intercepted. Out jumped Sokolovsky. From the car behind out jumped his bodyguard, guns at the ready. The patrolman was unimpressed. He put his gun in the Marshal's stomach and held him until an American officer came along to give identification.[88]

Clay was embarrassed by the incident and two days later paid a personal call on the Marshal to explain and apologise. The two men were old friends and Sokolovsky had always been pleasant and humorous. So Clay was upset by the frosty reception he got: official politeness but no cordiality, no acceptance of his apology, not even the usual offer of a drink. Neither man referred to the Berlin crisis, though Clay had the impression that Sokolovsky hoped he would raise it. He came away feeling that the Marshal "is set on his present course but is by no means happy or confident."[89] Their meeting was a sad end to a friendship and illustrated the deadlock former allies had reached.

Any flickering hope it might be eased by the remnants of quadripartite machinery was finally snuffed on 1 July. Colonel Kalinin, the Russian Chief of Staff at the Kommandatura, called his western opposite numbers to a meeting in the building, giving them just half an hour to get there. He read them a short statement, the meat of which was in one long sentence: "The well-known behaviour of Colonel Howley and the lack of reaction of the British and French representatives to the protests made by the Soviet authorities, as well as the separate actions of the French, American and British authorities in introducing currency reform of the western zones into Berlin, a city which is part of the economic system of the Soviet occupation zone, have resulted in the fact that the quadripartite meetings in the allied Kommandatura cannot take place any longer." Lest there be any doubt what he was driving at, he added "the Soviet representatives will no longer participate in the quadripartite meetings of the Allied Kommandatura in the city of Berlin. That is all." One question was put to him: did the Kommandatura no longer exist? "That is correct," said Kalinin,[90] though it took until 13 August before the Russians cleared their red flag and sentry from outside and all their files from inside the Kommandatura.[91]

The western allies were depressed by this final annulment of all quadripartite administration for Berlin, though they can hardly have been surprised. The Military Governors felt it was the first move in the current crisis which was entirely irrevocable. They feared it presaged a Soviet threat to the Magistrat and an attempt to make the city the seat of an "all-German" government. Koenig was particularly morose and lamented that the Russians "are determined to evict us from Berlin and nothing we can do locally will deter them." He cheered up a little when Clay gave him the latest figures for the airlift and the promise that it was extending time for seeking a settlement.[92]

It was soon certain that any settlement would have to be sought outside Berlin. On 3 July the three western Military Governors went to see Sokolovsky at his headquarters. Their conversation lasted only half an hour, but for the first time they actually got some indication of Soviet policy from a Russian horse's mouth. Most significantly Sokolovsky made no specific reference to currency. He still talked about "technical difficulties" on the railways, but once pressed would not guarantee that present snags would not be followed by new ones. It was noted with relief that he did not call for the withdrawal of the western Powers from Berlin. There was no comfort, however, in his long exposition of how economic disorders had been created in the Soviet zone as a result of decisions at the London talks, where his government had not been represented and the interests of his country had been ignored.[93] The western Governors left Soviet headquarters sharing Clay's opinion that Sokolovsky was "under instructions which permit him no latitude in negotiating the transport question alone or even in connection with other subjects unless there is a complete discussion of the German problem"; the Soviet government "has no intention to settle the Berlin problem except as part of the settlement of the German problem."[94] There was no point at all in trying further moves in Berlin.

Perhaps it would be effective, therefore, to lay the Berlin problem before the United Nations. The Americans still maintained some of their early hopes of that institution. The British had always been sceptical; experience of the UN's lumbering procedures and the destructive use of the veto had deepened their mistrust. On 28 June the UN Secretary-General, Trygve Lie, suggested to the American and British delegates that Article 99 of the Charter might be applied to the Berlin crisis – the clause which permitted him to "bring to the attention of the Security Council any matter which in his opinion may threaten the maintenance of international peace and security." The Foreign Office thought it "inappropriate" to the situation and the British delegation considered the Security Council "not a very suitable body" – not least because its present chairman was a Ukrainian.[95] Gradually the State Department came to agree with Bevin that it would be foolhardy to go to the UN until the allies could speak from strength: they must build up the airlift and show they were undaunted in west Germany first.

So the only diplomatic move still open was direct communication with Moscow. The Americans were keen to send a note to the Kremlin stating the western position. The British were not: the Russians, Whitehall argued, would try to expand talks to the full range of disagreements and west German development would be delayed; the allies should wait for a firm bargaining position. Bevin warned that once the "note was delivered we should no longer have any freedom of manoeuvre"; it would mark a "definite and final taking up of position."[96] Yet the Americans had been patient over Bevin's wish to continue the correspondence between Robertson and Sokolovsky; the British owed them a similar courtesy now. Once the meeting with Sokolovsky in Berlin had failed, they dropped their objections to writing to the Kremlin.

On 6 July the three western allies handed versions of the same note to Soviet Ambassadors in their capitals. These laid out protests against the blockade of Berlin, a city which they insisted was not part of the Soviet zone but an international area of occupation where all four Powers were present as a result of agreed and established right and to which the western allies had access in consequence of their withdrawal to the zonal frontiers in 1945. The western Powers would not be induced by threats or pressure to forgo their rights in Berlin. They were willing to negotiate on outstanding problems if and when free communications with the city were restored.

There was not the slightest chance that the Soviet Union would ever reply to any letter by return of post. The western allies would have to wait for a response to their notes, and Berliners would have to endure more uncertainty and more privation. It was likely that the Russians would want to negotiate before lifting the blockade – any talks, however amicable, would take yet more time and involve still more suffering in Berlin. The only palliative for the stress of time was the airlift.

Yet when Robert Murphy reviewed the condition of Berlin on 9 July, he had to report that "time is working against us." The situation in the city had "deteriorated with alarming rapidity within the last two weeks and, more particularly, within the last few days."[97] Faced with the coal crisis the authorities had slashed power supplies further. Domestic consumers were limited to four hours of electricity a day, on a rota which sometimes meant they had to cook in the middle of the night. Electric trains, trolley buses and the U-bahn (underground railway) started at six in the morning and ended at six in the evening. Buses could not take over: most were off the road waiting in vain for delivery of spare parts or tyres. Generators were being flown in for hospitals, telephone exchanges and a few vital offices, but industry must lose 80 per cent of its electricity. Since power cuts meant breakdown in radio services, the British and American military were going to send round broadcasting vans to relay the latest news.[98] It was painful to see a city which had struggled for three years to restore normal life reverting so quickly to misery. No wonder the British embassy in Moscow reported that the Russians were confident the airlift could not supply Berlin and the western Powers must soon leave.[99] Murphy, too, reckoned that given the inability of the allies to keep pace with the city's needs, "within a week or so we may find ourselves faced with a desperate population demanding our withdrawal to relieve their distress." The western allies might have a legal right to be in Berlin; did they have a moral right to stay there at the cost of so much anguish?

Fortunately Murphy's report of 9 July dealt with the past not the present. He recorded the early results of the airlift which had been cobbled together on the spur of the moment with puny resources of aircraft, crews and ground staff, with no existing logistical organisation, and totally inadequate airfields and traffic-control methods. During the last week in June, when only C-47s and RAF Dakotas were flown, the combined Anglo-American airlift had carried a mere 1,404 tons into Berlin. In the first week in July thirty-five USAF C-54s and the first RAF Yorks arrived in Germany, but the total tonnage did not reflect the increased number and capacity of aircraft. There were neither systems nor facilities to use them properly.

Extracts from a diary kept by Group-Captain Noel Hyde, appointed on 29 June as Officer Commanding Transport Wing at Wunstorf, give some idea of the confusion and limitations which hamstrung the early operation. 1 July: "Well behind schedule chiefly owing to loading difficulties.... P[etrol] and F[uel] section completely overworked and in a muddle...." "Yorks going to be difficult to handle with present congestion on airfield. Insufficient oil and petrol bowsers...." 3 July: "Gatow asked if we could speed up

165

rate of flow at night to one every 10 minutes. P and F could not cope.... Plumbers behind with serviceable a/c [aircraft], chiefly rectifications.... It appears that night flying under present conditions costs us more than we gain because of difficulties of loading, servicing etc. at night.... Big gap of over an hour in flow due to unserviceability and P and F loading u/s [unserviceable] aircraft." Later in the day he observed that there were now plenty of serviceable aircraft, but "Army cannot cope with both Yorks and Daks." 4 July: "Combined ops. room not working well as Flying Control cannot cope with traffic and let operations know when a/c are taking off and landing ..." – there were not enough people to man the telephones – "... telephone went u/s at 17.20 hours. Tried to get it repaired but army apparently have no one available." 5 July: "Part of Dakota parking area badly cut up – arranged to have it covered with PSP." 7 July: "Army lent us two jeeps and trying to get us a walkie-talkie set.... Wing-Commander Tech[nical] says we cannot with present manpower cope with 10-minute intervals between take-offs. Marshalling and refuelling are the difficulties."[100]

In those first two vital, chaotic weeks the British and Americans had to scour their records for men of every expertise: air-traffic controllers, mechanics, electricians, drivers, staff experienced in loading. They rummaged stores for spare parts, PSP, radios, fuel lines, marshalling bats, flares, cords for lashing down freight. They rounded up lorries, jeeps, cars; signed on thousands of Germans and Displaced Persons as labourers and loaders; found stoves, pots and pans to feed the sudden influx on to the airfields.

As if manpower, equipment and organisation did not present problem enough, the airlift faced truly appalling weather. In what was supposed to be the height of summer there were thunderstorms, snow and heavy icing, fog if the wind dropped, continuous low cloud which was often below 200 feet and incessant driving rain. For three weeks and more, aircraft struggled to and from Berlin against conditions in which, as a British officer admitted, crews would not normally be asked to fly.[101] Some American pilots encountered such icing that they had to maintain full power just to stay in the air; when they used their de-icing equipment, great lumps of ice would crack off the wings and thud down the fuselage. The RAF could seldom meet its target of 160 sorties a day because of poor visibility which prevented landings or because Gatow was closed while sheets of water were swept from the runway. Tempelhof was unusable for hours at a stretch thanks to dense cloud or violent tailwinds.[102] Everyone on the ground was soaked to the skin – little or no protective clothing could be found. Rain seeped into the aircraft and engines would not start – on 2 July twenty-six Dakotas were out of service because of electrical faults caused by damp.[103] Aircraft and motor vehicles churned the airfields into quagmires, then skidded and bogged down. Bulldozers laboured night and day to flatten the fields; PSP, rubble and bricks were thrown down to give some solid-standing. Crews waded to their aircraft through heavy, glutinous sludge, then flew in caked wellingtons or boots which glued or even froze to the rudder. Wunstorf was encapsulated by the RAF's pet cartoonist, "Frosty" Winterbottom: a lake across which a crew had just been rowed by dinghy to a half-submerged aircraft, where they perched on the fuselage reading their manual "All Weather Flying."

The only thing not dampened was morale. Men worked round the clock without grumbling or slacking. Pilots flew every hour the weather would let them and took frightening risks to land in minimal visibility. A Flying Control Officer at Wunstorf was on duty for fourteen hours non-stop. Drivers worked for twenty-four hours without a break. Ground staff put in regular sixteen-hour shifts. High-ranking officers stood in the pouring rain and marshalled aircraft or exchanged their warm offices for a freezing aircraft packed with flour for Berlin. US airmen gave up their Independence Day holiday and kept flying – the *New York Times* commented: "We were proud of our Air Force during the war. We're prouder of it today." Even when there was some time off, there was little rest. Aircraft and motor vehicles kept up an incessant din. American aircrews lay in rows as Nissen huts were hammered together around them and men clattered in and out, on and off duty at all hours; RAF pilots climbed ladders into attics at Wunstorf to sleep on the floor and be trampled on by people looking for a space to lie down. Other ranks, American and British, settled into sodden tents and tried to rest on the soggy ground. Everyone kept going on adrenalin. Old hands recognised "a flap" and responded to it as they had in the war; young recruits were excited and keen to show how good they were. On paper the odds against the airlift being able to feed Berlin were impossible; the results of the first few weeks were paltry. The people involved saw only a challenge and leapt at it. Never mind the problems: "Do your best," "Every little pound helps." Men who only three years before would have set out to bomb Berlin were now using all their skill and energy to feed it. It was a target into which they put their hearts.

And by the second week in July the airlift began to show signs of coming to grips with its problems, even though they were far from solved. Systems for handling freight had been developed, staffs of all kinds expanded, air-traffic control improved, equipment scrounged or indented for. The C-54s and Yorks were being integrated into the operation. On 4 July half-a-dozen Sunderland flying boats landed at Finkenwerde on the Elbe and next day made their first trips to the Havel. The Russians protested at their use of the lake and claimed to control all Berlin waterways (and they were right), but they were ignored.[104] Sunderlands could carry 10,000 lbs in their lower decks and bomb compartments. Their primary use would be to transport salt – they were anodised against salt water and their controls were tucked up out of reach of cargo so that, unlike other aircraft, they would not be corroded. They soon settled to taking other freight as well: meat, cigarettes, sanitary towels. The Havel made a natural flying-boat base: calm, thanks to the shelter of low hills on all sides, with a long take-off run (often afflicted with crosswinds) and deep moorings close to the shore. Finkenwerde, on the other hand, was not ideal. The Elbe was choppy and strewn with wrecks and rubble. There were no facilities for refuelling, and the job had to be done by hand from 40-gallon drums until REME mechanics brought out a barge with a pipeline floating on jerrycans.[105] Objectively the Sunderland itself was something of a liability – slow and ponderous, it presented scheduling problems because its run had to be slotted between those for Gatow and Tempelhof. Yet it did much to cheer the Germans, who saw it as a sign that efforts were being made and that resources were available. The ten daily Sunderland landings on the Havel attracted crowds of delighted spectators, and children especially were enchanted by this new monster duck.

With more and bigger aircraft and better back-up, allied tonnage figures started to rise. On 8 July 1,117 tons were flown into Berlin; next day the total dropped to 819; but on 11 July it was 1,264 and by 15 July 1,480.[106] Obviously this was still short of the 2,000 tons of food needed every day, let alone the 12,000 tons of goods in all. Even so, measured against the 1,404 tons brought in during the whole of June, it was quite an achievement.

As the airlift grew, so did ambitions. The allies were no longer satisfied with just trying to feed Berlin. At the beginning of July Yorks carried 100 emergency generators. Pilots watched with horror as two of these 6,000-lb machines were swung by crane into their holds without the slightest regard for the standard load factor or the usual rules for distribution of weight, and they wondered if they

168

would get off the ground without the cargo dropping through the floor. The Americans and British flew in petrol – a dangerous, volatile consignment which had to be carried in heavy metal drums taking up valuable space and difficult to load and secure. The backlog of letters and parcels from Berlin was cleared and more industrial goods were brought out, though the British drew the line at transporting an upright piano and a baby grand destined for export to South Africa.[107]

Most dramatically, the decision was taken early in July to fly in coal. The Americans had practised in their zone dropping it from the bomb bays of B-29s, but faced at the receiving end with piles of dust they soon gave up the scheme. The first coal landed at Tempelhof on 7 July packed in old service duffel bags. Nobody, two weeks before, had dreamed of bringing fuel to Berlin. Even now no one imagined that they could ever meet minimal needs. Nevertheless, coal was a new demonstration to the Russians of allied determination and capability, a new offer of hope to Berliners, another way of giving time to the politicians and diplomats to get the blockade lifted.

8

A Cushion of Time

In mid-July 1948 western politicians and diplomats needed all the time they could get in which to search for a solution to the Berlin crisis. It was clear that the Soviet Union did not need a quick settlement and was, indeed, prepared to stretch out the crisis in the hope of forcing the western Powers to withdraw from the city or negotiate on the full range of disputed German issues.

On 14 July the allied capitals received a reply to the case they had put to the Kremlin eight days before. This Russian note was totally uncompromising. It insisted that Germany had been split by western introduction of separate administration and currency; that Berlin was "the centre of the Soviet zone"; quadripartite control of the city was "an inseparable component part of the agreement on quadripartite administration of Germany as a whole"; and since the western Powers had broken that agreement, they had undermined the "legal basis on which rested their right to participate in the administration of Berlin."[1] The reply expressed willingness to negotiate only on condition that discussions covered Germany as a whole – presumably with the agenda of the Warsaw Declaration – but made no offer to lift any transport restrictions before talks began. Passing reference was made to the Soviet Union's wish "to protect" Berlin and the Russian zone at the time when western currency was brought in, but it was obvious that currency was not the main bone of contention.

The western allies had not hoped to gain much from their own note. Even so, they were taken aback by the Soviet response. It was worse than propaganda; it was a flat rejection of western proposals and claims and implied complete confidence that the Soviet Union had the upper hand and would soon realise its ambitions in Germany. None the less, allied principles remained firm: the allies would stay in Berlin and supply the city by air; would not negotiate on any matter until the blockade was lifted and no party was under duress; and would not sacrifice plans for west Germany in order to win a Berlin settlement. As Under Secretary of State Robert Lovett put it, the western Powers would not yield even if they risked war.[2] Marshall publicly expressed allied determination in a statement to the press on 21 July: "We will not be coerced or intimidated in any way under the rights and responsibilities that we have in Berlin and generally in Germany." Every diplomatic means, he promised, would be used to resolve the Berlin emergency and to avert the tragedy of war. But, he repeated, "We are not going to be coerced."[3]

These were brave words. But the allies well knew that they were in a tight corner. No one cared to calculate how long Berlin could be kept alive by the airlift: supply was difficult enough now and was presumed to be impossible in winter. The longer the crisis lasted, the more likely it would lead to war. Marshall talked of "diplomatic means." There seemed all too few of them.

Bevin, in fact, took the view that the diplomatic process might just as well stop since neither side was willing to make any concession. By all means send a pro-forma reply to the Russians' note in due course, but keep them waiting for it; show "no concern or fuss" and improve the airlift to strengthen the allied hand first.[4] The Americans, however, wanted action. Specifically they wished to make a direct approach to Stalin to warn of the dangers of war and impress upon him that the western Powers would not be bullied out of Berlin or into negotiations under the duress of blockade. Marshall thought there was just a possibility that the Soviet Union would welcome a tactfully presented opportunity to back down. If not, it was still worth sounding out Stalin's position. A personal approach by the three allied Ambassadors in Moscow would, in the State Department's view, be quick, flexible and private. It must not involve questions of real substance – full negotiations must wait until the blockade was lifted – but it would open up communication with the one man who had the power to change Soviet policy.[5] If nothing else, a meeting with Stalin would assure the American public that every effort was being made to reach agreement.[6]

Bevin was dead set against the proposal and used every argument, good or bad, to oppose it. He called the personal approach "a weak way of doing things"; why, he asked, "should we go cap in hand to Stalin?" The Soviet leader, as far as Bevin was concerned, was "a bit down" at the moment in the eyes of Europeans and of communist parties in particular, thanks to the recent expulsion of Yugoslavia from the Comintern; so leave him down, don't puff him up.[7] Stalin, Bevin kept warning, would exploit any meeting to get further talks, then insist they took place in Moscow and pin everyone to his own agenda.[8] As Bevin ran out of better ammunition against the proposal, he tossed in the idea that Stalin would never agree to see the three Ambassadors at once and the suggestion that it was essential to talk to Molotov first, otherwise his nose would be out of joint.[9]

Washington, perfectly reasonably, thought the "susceptibilities of the Soviet Foreign Office … of minor importance."[10] The State Department argued that the oral approach had proved fruitful in the past (conveniently forgetting the bitter fruit of the Molotov-Bedell Smith meeting); thought Bevin's draft reply to the Soviet note so weak as to look like retreat; wanted tough talking not compromise with Stalin; and even considered going it alone if Bevin would not join in.[11] Not that the Americans believed a meeting with Stalin would solve everything on the spot; it was simply an option which had to be explored. Given the possibility of failure in Moscow, they kept in reserve their plan to refer the whole case to the United Nations.[12] Here again they ran up against Bevin's opposition: all his old arguments about the futility and stagnation of the UN procedure. The United States clung to its ideals and commitment to the institution. It was, however, undeniable even in Washington that the Berlin situation would deteriorate during the inevitably long process.

The British and Americans could agree on only one immediate response to the Russian rebuff to their case. Squadrons of American B-29s must now be stationed in Britain. Bevin had asked for them the day before receiving the Soviet reply; the National Security Council in Washington agreed on 15 July that they should be sent.[13] Bevin gave the impression of being a little nervous about the political repercussions of offering British bases for nuclear-capable American bombers. He looked for a cover story and suggested to Douglas that all publicity should avoid mention of Berlin and "take the line that these are long-range heavy bomber exercises."[14] He deceived no one. The arrival of two squadrons of B-29s in Britain on 17 July (to be followed by a third in August) was front-page news in the British press for two days; everyone took it for granted that the aircraft were a counter to the Soviet threat in Berlin and every newspaper, including the Labour *Daily Herald*, welcomed their deployment.[15]

As far as Clay was concerned the B-29s were an inadequate display of force. He was also dissatisfied with the plan to meet Stalin – it was not likely to produce any results and "should not be permitted to delay our plans for west Germany" – and he feared that referral to the UN would be equally barren and allow Berlin conditions to worsen "especially if discussions last into winter." For Clay there was only one way to break the present deadlock: tell the Soviet government that "we propose on a specific date to send in a convoy accompanied by the requisite bridge equipment to make our right of way into Berlin usable."[16] He had been excitedly redesigning his armed convoy in early July. It was now envisaged as 200 lorries escorted by a US constabulary regiment, rifle troops and an engineer battalion, and reinforced by a British infantry battalion and a French detachment of anti-tank troops. "Loss of equipment," said Clay confidently, "would not be serious"; loss of personnel would reduce "combat effectiveness by perhaps 10 per cent."[17] Washington had tried to put the damper on his zeal with the standard warnings about lack of troops and transport and the risks of being trapped. Nothing quelled Clay, and indeed once the Russian note of 14 July was received he became more insistent and Washington's interest was at last tickled. The Army chiefs produced a memorandum on 17 July recommending that the scheme be considered, and on the 19th the Secretary of the Army Royall suggested to his department that an armed convoy might be used if the Russians kept stalling and the application to the United Nations failed.[18]

Even so, there was still a strong feeling that any attempt to force a way through to Berlin could precipitate a war. That was an abhorrent prospect. Memories of the last war were too strong and were kept fresh by the destruction and mutilation all around. Renewed fighting, it was believed, would bring final, irreparable disaster to Europe. A war which began in Berlin would be downright folly: the allies had only 6,500 combat troops facing 18,000 Russians in the city itself and an estimated 300,000 more in the east zone. The inevitable first stage would be Russian capture of the very city the allies were fighting to retain. In Montgomery's very Monty-esque words: "The city has NO military value; it is in fact a first-class military liability," and fighting a convoy up the autobahn was "not a good way to start a war."[19] Some, like Clay, did not believe that war was likely, but thought the risk had to be run if the Russians were to be stopped.[20] Others took seriously warnings such as that given by the British Chiefs of Staff on 7 July: anything other than diplomatic activity "would almost certainly lead to an incident and the opening of World War III."[21] Sombre thoughts of war were probably more frequent in July 1948 than at any other time during the Berlin blockade or since 1945. Revulsion at the possibility was universal.

The more experts appraised the outcome of a battle with the Soviet Union, the more pessimistic were their conclusions. There was no point in harping on about Russian technological backwardness, lack of long-range aircraft, or poor training and equipment of troops. The stark fact was, as the British Chiefs of Staff told the Cabinet: "Our forces in their present state are not in a position to fight with what we have got"; a Soviet attack would trigger "complete disorganisation leading to disaster."[22] Continental states could give no help: Montgomery reported, "Our allies in the Western Union can be classified as quite useless from the military angle."[23] Nor could the United States, for all its vast wealth and resources, pull European irons out of the fire. James Forrestal, the Secretary of Defence, told Truman on 19 July that they had merely two-and-a-half divisions in reserve, only one of which could be committed with any speed.[24] Though Marshall retorted that this made the odds better than in 1940, in more reflective moments he reckoned that the Americans would need eighteen months to prepare for a war over Berlin.[25] In July 1948 standing orders for western commanders in Germany in the event of Russian attack were to withdraw rapidly to the Rhine and fight a defensive battle. There was a good chance they would lose it. They would certainly already have lost Berlin.

The West did, of course, have one hideous bulwark against defeat: the atom bomb. Would it be dropped if the Russians held Berlin and its allied garrisons hostage? Would it be dropped in Germany or the Soviet Union? Did the Berlin issue justify the destruction which would follow? There were no answers prepared to these questions. One had to be found immediately: who was to have charge of the Bomb? On 21 July President Truman turned down a request to hand over control to the military. He made it clear that responsibility for the weapon was his and he intended to keep it – a typical example of his sense of personal accountability given characteristic colour by his remark to Forrestal that he was not going to have "some dashing Lieutenant-Colonel decide when would be the proper time to drop one."[26] The Joint Chiefs of Staff were asked to study when or whether an atomic bomb might ever be dropped. Its use was never contemplated by anyone in authority as a solution to the Berlin crisis.

Since the confrontation with the Soviet Union had exposed the weakness of western conventional forces, the post-war policy of reduction had to be checked and the United States and Britain began to agonise over how to improve them. Nineteen forty-eight was presidential election year. In July Truman was already way down in the opinion polls and big military spending would probably sink him. The Republican majority in Congress had tried to enforce a 26 per cent cut in the first American contribution to the European Recovery Programme, and although the Vandenberg Resolution of 11 June permitted the President to develop regional arrangements for collective self-defence, it stressed the need to work within the United Nations and certainly did not authorise blank cheques for European rearmament. At meetings in Washington from 6–9 July with a Canadian representative and ambassadors from the five Brussels Pact countries, State Department officials had insisted that the United States would give no military Lend-Lease or unilateral guarantees to Europe. On the contrary, the Americans would offer nothing at all until Europe proved it was making every effort for itself; thereafter, any aid must be approved by Congress and the new President, so would not be available before 1949. All the same, the international working party in Washington, which began to examine details of possible American and Canadian involvement in a North Atlantic alliance, met in the apprehensive atmosphere of the Berlin crisis and dismay at the parlous condition of western defences. The European members found it easier to woo the North Americans than they would have done only a few weeks before.

In the meantime, on 15 July Britain invited the United States to join Western Union military talks. General Lemnitzer arrived to discuss ways to meet the present emergency and improve allied armed forces. Urgency was given to the wish of the British Chiefs of Staff for a unified headquarters in Europe and the appointment of a supreme commander.[27] The British Cabinet anxiously reviewed schemes to stop demobilisation, call up selected reservists, bring back technicians from industry and increase stocks of military equipment[28] – all without alarming the public or sparking off a political outcry. By 22 July a rough-and-ready plan for selective mobilisation was almost prepared, and there was some awareness of what supplies were needed though no confidence that they could be obtained.[29] Britain was already spending more than she could afford on the armed forces (a higher proportion of the national income than the United States) and a sudden increase in expenditure might easily shatter her weak economy. Throughout July quick and cheap decisions had to be made: to overhaul radar installations, refit small craft, accelerate orders for fighter aircraft, repair seaward defences and military communications, and fill 100,000 rounds of anti-aircraft ammunition. The underlying poverty of British resources was revealed by a report from the Ministry of Defence at the end of the month that in "the event of an early emergency, considerable reliance would have to be placed on existing types of piston-engined aircraft, e.g., Spitfires ... at present in store," for which there were no adequate stocks of spare parts.[30]

The western allies in July knew they could not fight the Soviet Union and would be foolhardy to bluff. They had run up against a diplomatic brick wall. There was only one area where they could still invest fresh resources and see immediate benefits: the airlift. Britain had already put nearly all its military transport aircraft to work. If a massive increase in tonnage were to be effected, only the Americans could do it.

On 21 July Clay and Murphy flew to Washington for talks on tackling the Berlin crisis. Clay took the chance to plead for his armed convoy. He undoubtedly damaged his case before an already sceptical audience by arguing that the chances of provoking war were one to four (good enough?), that the French would fight (would they and with what?), and that the Russians could be held on the Rhine by twenty divisions (whose?).[31] Next day he and Murphy were present at a meeting of the President, State and Defence Department officials, and the Joint Chiefs of Staff where all the possible options were assessed. Truman and the military firmly vetoed an armed convoy. As second best Clay begged for expansion of the airlift, explaining that it was already capable of carrying 2,500 tons a day but could manage 3,500 tons if given seventy-five more C-54s. This would be adequate for summer needs, but would still fall short of winter requirements and did not meet the daunting challenge of fuel supply. The service chiefs sniped to defend their broad interests: sending more aircraft to Berlin would disrupt regular military transport around the world, strip reserves needed in the event of war, choke the city's existing airfields and possibly provoke the Russians into closing the air corridors. President Truman overrode them. The airlift, he said decisively, involved fewer risks than an armed convoy. The Air Force must give fullest support.[32]

The military, having very properly drawn attention to the dangers, now cheerfully accepted the President's decision and set about making a thorough job of the airlift. Clay would not only get seventy-five more C-54s but the wherewithal to build a new airfield at Tegel in the French sector. The notion of an armed convoy was kept simmering in case all else failed, but with the caveat that full preparations for war must be made before it was used. The Joint Chiefs of Staff were certain that the airlift in itself could not solve the Berlin problem – only diplomacy could do that. They were, however, "firmly of the opinion that air transport should be continued and should be augmented." It would give a "cushion of time," they said, while a real solution was sought.[33]

In the second and third weeks of July, even without additional C-54s, the airlift cushion had already been plumped up. On 17 July 1,582 tons were delivered to Berlin (650 by the USAF, 932 by the RAF); on the 19th 1,660; on the 20th 1,171; next day 1,447, with the Americans handling 1,089 and the British 358.[34] The steady flow was almost keeping up with Berlin's food needs. By 20 July the city's stores held enough flour and grain for thirty-six days, fats for fifty, sugar for sixty, meat and fish for forty-six, dried and skimmed milk for thirty-eight, coffee for fifty-nine and yeast for eight.[35] The situation was still precarious, however. The string of aircraft was all too easily snarled by operational difficulties and especially by bad weather – by 7 August Berlin's stocks had dropped dangerously to less than two weeks' supply of milk, meat, flour and cereals, and a month of fats.[36] Food had been the airlift priority so far. As yet the quantities of coal being lifted were hardly measurable, for all the RAF had joined in and landed their first consignments at Gatow on 19 July.[37] Fuel deliveries could not be increased until there were more and bigger aircraft.

The backlift of industrial exports was being encouraged and in the second week of July 30 tons of freight were flown out daily.[38] But there was debate about whether backloading was worth the effort. Keeping aircraft on the ground in Berlin while oddly-shaped and unpredictable loads were laboriously packed inevitably delayed their turn round and lessened their chances of bringing another delivery that day. The Americans constantly argued that the backlift was a waste of time, and, at one stage, calculated that for every 100 tons taken out of Berlin 40 tons of imported supplies were lost.[39] The British questioned the figures and believed that Berlin's economic and psychological gains from backlifting were well worth the cost; they saved precious time by restricting backloading to the last Dakotas of the day.[40] On 15 July the RAF extended the service to several thousand west Germans who had been stuck in Berlin since the full blockade,[41] for all there were doubts about the legality of using military planes to carry German civilians and anxieties over what would happen if an aircraft were forced to land in the Russian zone where travellers would not have Soviet transit documents.[42] Transporting people, however, had an unforeseen snag. On 5 August a passenger arriving at Wunstorf was found to have polio. The station's medical officer slapped the entire shift into quarantine and disrupted several days' operation.[43]

Any expansion in the airlift so far had come mainly from hard sweat. It was achieved in spite of constant foul weather, an acute shortage of aircrew and skilled personnel, and a chronic dearth of spare parts which left aircraft idle on the ground. Methods of air-traffic control and loading and unloading were still primitive. Given the adverse odds it was extraordinary that so much was done and so cheerfully.

Only ingenuity, stop-gaps and sheer grind surmounted the difficulties. As often as not solutions threw up new problems. For example, thanks to finding some spare aircraft and making minor improvements in servicing and ground procedures, the American bases in Wiesbaden and Rhein Main and the RAF airfield at Wunstorf were already congested by early July. They could neither cope with the traffic nor find room for the back-up. The British created some space for them by opening up an old Luftwaffe training field at Fassberg, north-east of Hannover, where in a matter of a couple of weeks the railhead and runway were renovated and extended, new sidings built, PSP laid in the operations area, hutting erected, landing lights installed and a 1,400-metre access road constructed. The RAF transferred their Dakotas to the new base from Wunstorf on 16 July; eighty or more USAF aircraft would join them on 27th.[44] British and Americans were going to have to learn to live together, sort out tricky demarcations of command and harmonise operating procedures.

It was quite complicated enough to bring USAF aircraft to the northern corridor with their different cruising speeds and own navigation and flying methods. To add to the confusion the British were about to introduce a whole pot-pourri of aircraft types and fliers – chartering civilian firms to compensate for lack of RAF planes and aircrew. The first company to join the airlift was Flight

Refuelling, who would deliver petrol to Berlin. Its owner, Sir Alan Cobham, who was a pioneer of inflight refuelling in the 1930s, had volunteered two Lancastrians (the civil version of the old Lancaster bomber) which he had adapted for carrying bulk liquid fuel. Flight Refuelling would relieve the military of a dangerous and specialised task for which they were not equipped. On 27 July one of the Lancastrians flew direct from Tarrant Rushton with a consignment of petrol. Once the second arrived in Germany, each would do three sorties a day from Bückeburg. Here supplies were being concentrated, but there were no underground storage installations.[45] At Gatow, where underground tanks did exist, they had to be filled by gravity feed through 400 feet of refuelling hose, which for various reasons could neither be cut nor replaced. It took a whole hour to empty each aircraft.[46] More civilian aircraft would join in soon, some for the wetlift, others for all manner of freight. Talks went on in mid-July between the Foreign Office, Air Ministry, Ministry of Civil Aviation and BEA to plan the civilian charter. By 21 July six Yorks, thirteen Halifaxes, four Vikings and two Hythes had been found. Their proud owners boasted they would put in a total of 120 sorties a day;[47] time would tell a less happy tale. Whatever the advantages of increasing the fleet, it was already obvious that so many varied aircraft with so many individual and individualistic owners, outside service authority and disciplines, were going to make a difficult operation even more intricate.

Even an improvement in the weather was a mixed blessing. Once the rain stopped, men who had struggled through mud had to battle against a new torment – dust. Dust blew up from the airfields, where the filter of grass had been pounded away by aircraft, motor vehicles and bulldozers. It filled eyes, nose, throat and clothing. Dust flew out from flour bags and coated men and machines. It trickled from coal sacks and turned everyone and everything black. Coal-dust was not just unpleasant; it was dangerous. It penetrated into each cranny, stuck fast to the electrical contacts and eroded them, glued itself into the lubricating fluids on the controls and jammed them. It would not dissolve, and spraying the holds merely sluiced it into parts where it could do most damage. American mechanics tried crafty ways to get rid of it. One passed the end of a rubber hose through a porthole in the hope that the slipstream would vacuum clean the aircraft on its way home; another stretched a 36-foot sheet of anti-icing cloth over the fuselage and set teams on either side to pull like Lilliputian shoeshiners.[48] Nothing really

179

worked except pernickety hand brushing. As an aircraft landed, two women had to dart inside and sweep. Their gleanings of coal-dust would make a briquette or two and keep a fire going for a while. A scientific alternative to manual drudgery on the outside surfaces was to be installed at Fassberg: steam from the central boiler powered kerosene sprays at two aircraft at a time, the kerosene being retrieved for further use.[49]

To the inbuilt difficulties of the airlift the Russians added others but not, fortunately, one which had been feared – balloons. A few barrage balloons, let alone a net of them, would have made the air corridors unusable. Robertson told the RAF on 28 June that any they spotted must be shot down.[50] Clay wanted permission to give the same order, though he acknowledged the danger of starting shooting.[51] The Joint Chiefs of Staff thought the problem was being exaggerated (there was no actual evidence that the Russians were planning a barrage) and the British government was persuaded to instruct Robertson not to shoot unless authorised by a joint Anglo-American decision.[52] Such permission never had to be given; Soviet barrage balloons were not launched.

The Russians had plenty of other ways, however, to make flying nerve-wracking. To the accompaniment of orchestrated complaints in their press and at the Air Safety Centre about western infringements of safety regulations in the corridors, Yak fighters intermittently buzzed allied transports. On 6 July there was heavy, and unannounced, Soviet fighter activity in all the corridors. Next day the Russians interfered with Tempelhof's radio.[53] On 17 July the Soviet military announced a programme of night flying in the corridors without providing any details of numbers or positions.[54] Two days later a formation of eight or ten Yaks performed aerobatics at 500 metres over Gatow; soon after, one Russian pilot carried out air-to-air firing exercises with a towed target in the northern corridor and another enjoyed some bombing practice.[55] Both must have known that all training in the corridors was forbidden; neither had notified his presence.

To be absolutely fair, allied flying was not always strictly according to the rule book. Many a pilot enjoyed a detour low down the Unter den Linden in the Soviet sector, giving rude wiggles of the wings.[56] Many a crew cheered itself up on a dreary return journey at night by picking on a Russian barracks, throttling down and dropping to 300 feet or less, then opening up the engines hard to climb and make sure everyone was woken up and reminded that others were still working.[57] Slipshod navigation often led to aircraft blundering about and peering for Gatow or Tempelhof: there were reports in mid-July of a Sunderland at 600 feet over the Russian airfield at Dalgow and an American plane at 300 feet over Aldershof.[58] Yet allied naughtiness or carelessness was one thing. Russian behaviour in the corridors too often seemed another: deliberate intimidation and the threat of worse to come. Running an airlift was quite hazardous and difficult enough without that.

Logically it might seem that the best way to ensure maximum delivery of supplies to Berlin would be to send thick formations of aircraft by the shortest route at the fastest speed they could manage and taking off the second they were loaded. In reality, all this was impossible. Aircraft could not take the shortest route: they were confined to the three air corridors across the Soviet zone. When the airlift first started the Americans flew the southern corridor, the RAF went to Berlin on the north side of the central corridor and back to Wunstorf on its southern side.

The corridors could not be filled with dense formations: they were only twenty miles wide and everyone had to pack in to the twenty-mile radius of the Berlin control zone and be landed in tightly confined runway space. So for safety and efficient handling, aircraft flew and landed one at a time. In theory it was possible to dispatch and receive one aircraft every three minutes. In the early months of the airlift that was rarely practicable: loading delays and sudden servicing problems were frequent, poor visibility and makeshift ground control reduced landings in Berlin to one every fifteen minutes. In very bad weather, of course, hours and hours of flying were lost. To avoid mid-air collision, aircraft had to be spaced horizontally as well as vertically in the air. The Americans were originally assigned individual altitudes – high because of the mountains in their zone. The first man flew at 5,000 feet, the second at 6,000 and so on up to 10,000 feet, after which the pattern was repeated. This was all very well en route, but caused confusion when descending to a common approach height. With more experience and tough discipline the system could ultimately be revised: first to five altitudes, then three, and finally two with a six-minute gap between aircraft at the same height. The RAF began by flying all its Dakotas to Berlin at 3,000 feet and back at 4,500 when they were light and could easily gain height; the Yorks went at 1,500 feet and returned at 2,500.

Ideally traffic would have been rhythmic and non-stop. Both Americans and British would have liked a continuous dispatch system – aircraft taking off at short and regular intervals twenty-four hours a day – to achieve the fullest utilisation of machines and time. The system could not be made to work. In the infancy of the airlift, night flying was not always feasible. When the RAF tried continuous dispatch for several weeks with six-minute intervals between Dakotas by day and fifteen-minute gaps at night, the pattern was constantly broken by servicing and loading problems and by bad weather. Once Yorks joined the operation and began night flying from late July, the pattern would not fit. The loading time for a York was slower than for a Dakota but its cruising speed was faster, so the two types of aircraft had to be sent off in separate waves to avoid leapfrogging or fast Yorks flying into the rear of slow Dakotas. When the weather was poor the Dakotas, as the smaller load-bearers, had to be taken out of the operation and the airtime used by the more capacious Yorks. The Americans were never able to employ continuous dispatch. They did not have the navigational equipment to guarantee precise spacing in the air and regular arrival times.[59]

USAF aircraft carried two pilots and an engineer but no navigator because their instruments did not justify one. To find the way to Berlin they had a low-frequency radio link with the ground and what was misleadingly called a radio compass – not a compass in the usual sense but a radio tuned into medium-frequency ground beacons along the route which sent out continuous signals. As an aircraft passed over a beacon the radio compass was activated and the pointer on the cockpit's instrument panel turned through 180 degrees from full ahead to dead astern. (It was advisable to be ready for a beacon and avoid blinking: the pointer whizzed round pretty quickly.) An American pilot flying from Rhein Main was briefed before take-off on his route, flying speed, and the wind and weather conditions. He climbed first to the Darmstadt beacon, adjusted course for the Aschaffenburg beacon where he took up his assigned altitude, then made for the Fulda beacon and lined up for entrance to the southern corridor. At Fulda he listened on the radio for the time and position of the plane ahead, checked his own and reported it. Thereafter, he was on his own down the corridor: no more beacons, only dead reckoning to keep him on course. He knew his indicated course and speed, allowed for airstream course and speed, and calculated true course and speed, making constant adjustments for turbulence or gusts of wind. By keeping to an exact 170 mph over the ground, he would be able to contact Tempelhof in forty minutes and get a height and time check. Once at Wedding beacon he slowed to 140 mph, let down and waited for final landing instructions. Going home he flew straight back along the central corridor, turned south after the Braunschweig beacon, passed over Fitzlar, then lost height before Staden beacon after which he was picked up by his base control. One more beacon at Offenbach and down.[60]

Given the rudimentary navigational aids of the C-47s and C-54s, the round trip depended on the perfect reliability of the radio compass and the precision with which pilots timed and calculated their course. Radio compasses were simple but sturdy; the USAF trained its men rigorously, and they flew with concentration and accuracy. With less impeccable flying there would have been US aircraft strewn all over the Russian zone and into Czechoslovakia, and constant mid-air collisions. For all the admirable skill of the pilots, however, they could not possibly be sure of reaching Fulda and Tempelhof with split-second timing.

Punctuality was less of a problem for the British. The RAF benefited from an array of navigational equipment and navigators willing and able to display arcane arts with map, compass, watch and pencil if all else failed. Transport Command aircraft had radio compasses and used them to check turning-points. More sophisticated and in constant use was the Rebecca-Eureka system – a radar direction and distance finder. The Rebecca set in the aircraft interrogated a Eureka beacon on the ground (a small, neat machine with which pathfinder parachutists had dropped during the war). Two antennae either side of the aircraft's nose received two signals from the beacon and transformed them into a blip on the navigator's screen. The blip's position showed the distance from the beacon: if it was longer on one side of a vertical line than the other the pilot adjusted his course until both sides were equal. There was a Eureka beacon at Gatow and each base in the British zone, as well as at the start of the northern corridor and the turning-points on the run in. For final approaches the navigator could tune to BABS (Beam Approach Beacon Systems) and a single antenna transmitted to the screen two beams from the ground, the first a string of short pulses, the second of long. The aircraft was turned until both pulses were the same size and a perfectly accurate position obtained. When the airlift began there were already BABS installations at Gatow and Wunstorf; others were put into RAF bases as the operation expanded and a mobile BABS was flown into Tegel in November 1948. York navigators loved BABS; it was their standard landing device and they practised with it even in perfect visibility. Most RAF transport aircraft also had Gee equipment to receive two simultaneous signals from the ground – the aircraft was perfectly positioned if they arrived at the same time but had to be adjusted if one came before the other. The Gee chain was helpful in the zone, but less so in the Berlin area which was outside its effective range.[61]

Thanks to all their technical devices RAF pilots needed no great effort to find their way to Berlin and back with exact timing regardless of weather (though one crew had a difficult time when they took a glider pilot along with them, until they discovered what his hobnailed boots were doing to their wonderful scientific equipment). From Wunstorf the journey was in short legs with checks over beacons at Celle, Danenberg and Frohnau ("The Fraulein"). There was little excuse for inaccuracy and, for example, turning outside a beacon and being late or cutting inside and jumping ahead, but it was possible to slow down or speed up at any stage to correct the timing. Twenty miles before Frohnau the aircraft called Gatow to state its cargo and give prior warning to the unloaders; at the beacon it reported again and requested permission to carry out the final approach. The final turn was made and, if all went according to plan, the aircraft approaching the runway saw the aircraft ahead rolling to its end, and the one ahead of that taking up position on the unloading apron. Then it was touch-down, brake along the runway, taxi to the apron, and off to the Malcolm Club for tea and a bun.[62]

Though British and American aircraft got to Berlin by different routes and means, once over the city they shared a technical blessing – GCA (Ground Controlled Approach), invaluable for giving traffic controllers a view of the arrival pattern and vital for landing aircraft in poor visibility. The GCA truck parked at the side of the runway at Gatow or Tempelhof was equipped with a radar screen showing the height, bearing and distance of all aircraft within forty miles. Pilots could be directed by radio to adjust their course and speed to ensure separation and regular arrival at the airfield. At twenty miles, incoming aircraft were picked up on an azimuth tube, which gave an amplified picture of the immediate approach. If visibility was too bad for the pilot to land without help, the GCA controller then made contact. He told the pilot his distance from touch-down, whether he was left or right of the centre line for approach, how many degrees to turn to regain it and what height to maintain. Once the aircraft was about six miles off, the controller instructed the pilot to check his wheels were down and locked and his flaps set for descent. Constantly monitoring the screen, the controller fed the pilot with information on changes to height, position and speed and talked him along the glide path: "A mile to go, half a mile to go, coming over the end of the runway, look ahead for touch-down." Landings could be carried out virtually blind – the eventual minima were 200 foot cloud base and 800 yards horizontal visibility. Everything depended on the controller acting with calm and assurance to win trust from pilots who had to fly with his eyes and carry out his instructions to the letter. In the early days GCA could handle one aircraft every fifteen minutes; with more experience and more staff the rate was improved to one every five minutes.[63]

Success and safety in the airlift, however, could not depend on hardware, however sophisticated, or skill, however polished. System was essential. In the first weeks when the airlift ran on energy and enthusiasm, men tended to grab a plane as soon as it was loaded, fly as best they could to Berlin, circle over the city waiting to land, then hustle to get back and loaded for another trip. USAF aircraft, Yorks and Dakotas milled about in the Berlin control zone one on top of the other. RAF pilots in the corridors, over-secure in their navigational equipment, were tempted to choose their own operating heights and bob up and down to avoid icing, thunderstorms or thick cloud. In an excess of zeal to get to Berlin, too many fliers passed the aircraft in front or cut corners at beacons. In poor visibility they might well bunch up and only realise it when they felt the slipstream of a neighbour. Stacking over Berlin was potentially lethal, especially in thick cloud. Initiative and keenness are all very well in their place, but they are a menace in congested airspace.

In all this muddle it is something of a miracle that there were so few fatal accidents. The RAF lost more than one plane by running off the runway or hitting a lorry, and a Dakota crashed near Fassberg when its engine caught fire but the crew got out alive.[64] Three members of the USAF were killed on 8 July when their C-47 crashed into a hill north-east of Wiesbaden on return to base. On 25 July another C-47 hit the flats on approach to Tempelhof and two more men died.[65] The Mayors of the six American Bezirke called on Howley to express their sympathy and letters of condolence poured in to Clay. A plaque was put up on the site of the crash by an unknown Berliner: "Two American officers became victims of the Berlin blockade here. You gave your lives for us. The Berliners of the western sectors will never forget you. We stand deeply moved on this spot dedicated by your death. Once we were enemies and yet you gave your lives for us." Day after day fresh flowers were laid on the scene. When a newspaper reported that both airmen were fathers of small children, money was sent from all parts of the city to help them;[66] 3,000 Germans came to their funeral at the beginning of August.

As the number of aircraft in the operation built up, types proliferated, new airfields opened and the Americans began to fly from the British zone, confusion and danger were bound to increase. In addition, the strains of running on adrenalin rather than system were beginning to show. So far there had been no shifts for aircrew; they flew until they dropped. Aircraft touched down and by the time the loaders met them the pilot was fast asleep. A man at the controls would nod off in mid-air and be jerked awake when the aircraft suddenly lost height. One American captain who flew 156 hours in the first month, most on instruments, wondered why he felt so bad-tempered. "Pretty soon I said to myself, 'Boy, you aren't grouchy, you're just about on the verge of being done in.'" A USAF surgeon found some men flying a seven-day week and lucky to get seven hours sleep out of thirty-two. They were shaky with coffee and tortured by plugged-up ears.[67] Food for both services was poor, cooked on field equipment and gobbled in crowded shacks amid all the noise and bustle at the edge of runways. The issue of vitamin pills to the Americans helped a little. The British were not even getting wartime rations; indeed, there was a hard fight to stop the government cutting their existing bacon and meat allowance in August. Too many of them lived off Malcolm Club snacks until an order was given that no one must fly more than two sorties without having a proper meal. Most Americans had arrived in Germany as temporary duty personnel with a baggage limit between 45 and 65 lbs, which often included toolkits. They were short of clean clothing, as were the British, who had been told to pack for ten days.[68]

The weariness and its dangers were revealed in the anonymous answers to an RAF medical questionnaire during July and August. Unit medical officers considered that pilots were "flaked out" and noticed that although the men were eating more they were losing weight. Station commanders and Wing-Commanders Flying all recorded that aircraft were landing faster and more bumpily and that taxiing was careless, especially on the last trip of the day. Pilots were said to be "gasping a bit" on the radio, seemed "a bit done in" and not anxious to talk when they landed. Crews described the pilot on his third sortie: "He is slower in his movements at the controls and seems to fumble and hesitate"; he "forgets to reduce the take-off engine boost" or "to feather engines or to put down flaps." "He is more irritable than usual. If what he considers to be

186

a silly order comes up on the air, instead of questioning it as he would normally he says, 'Let's cut the bloody thing off.'" Pilots admitted: "I feel definitely fatigued on the last trip"; "I have a feeling similar to oxygen lack"; "I also notice that when I am tired, people I normally dislike mildly I begin to dislike very much indeed." They were well-aware that exhaustion was leading to sloppiness: "For example, I know I am landing a bit faster than usual, though I feel I shall probably get away with it."[69]

Things could not go on like this. More aircrew had to be found, conditions for proper food and sleep created, rotas drawn up and leave period introduced, otherwise the airlift would literally fly itself into the ground. So far marvels had been accomplished by men's wits and nerves. Now, to integrate new aircraft and get the best use from them, disciplines must improve and better traffic control evolve. Pilots themselves were already working out ways to improve their performance – Squadron-Leader Eric Best and others at Wunstorf, for instance, had begun to radio their positions at fixed points and any changes they intended to make in speed so as to prevent bunching and ensure accurate spacing and timing. More routines like that were needed and they would have to be standardised. When Major-General William H. Tunner, recently Deputy Commander for Operations of Military Air Transport, arrived at Wiesbaden on 29 July to set up an Airlift Task Force independent of HQ USAF, he observed the airlift with the sharp eye of the man who had run the lift over "The Hump." He summed it up in one pithy phrase: "a real cowboy operation." The early days with their bustle, jumble and excitement had been an adventure, no doubt. But in Tunner's considerable experience, "a successful airlift is about as glamorous as drops of water on a stone." "The real excitement from running an airlift," as he well knew, "comes from seeing a dozen lines climbing steadily on a dozen charts – tonnage delivered, utilisation of aircraft – and the lines representing accidents and injuries going sharply down."[70] Despite all the discomforts and fatigue of the first weeks, the airlift had actually been enormous fun. It now had to become serious and professional.

Few Berliners believed after three or four weeks of the airlift that it would ever be more than a temporary expedient. They were being fed, but only just; if they were to survive long, the blockade must be lifted. A US Military Government opinion poll in July recorded that 84 per cent of Berliners thought that the allies could fly in adequate rations for them, though 15 per cent did not and among these were the most educated of the sample. Eighty-six per cent of those questioned, however, judged that the city could not last out the winter and feared that within a few months Berlin would have to capitulate to the Russians.[71] In a public discussion after the relay of a Voice of America broadcast, most of the audience wondered how long people's nerves would hold out, how soon before they said, "Better a live dog than a dead lion."[72] As Dr. Suhr, the speaker of the City Assembly, put it to a British liaison officer: if the Russians in their sector created fuller employment and a better standard of living people would join them eventually.[73] Not that they wanted to. Berliners were ready to fight for their city's independence from the Russians and communism, but wondered how long they could keep up the struggle.

To make matters worse, Berliners had little confidence in the western allies. In Suhr's view it was assumed that they would sooner or later "give in and quit Berlin." Certainly, as a British report noted, the airlift had done "considerably more than pronouncements of Anglo-American leaders" to persuade people that the allies wanted to stay – but not enough. Berliners felt that the western Powers must "bare their teeth still further before the Russians will make any concessions and many still believe that there will be a withdrawal"; they were deeply "suspicious of the West's record for compromise."[74] They had been cheered by the dispatch of the B-29s, but they were amazed that an armed convoy had not forced through the blockade and convinced that the Russians would not have tried to stop it.[75]

For Berliners a symptom of allied shilly-shallying was the British failure to do anything about a running sore in their sector: the Russian-controlled Radio Berlin in the Rundfunkhaus. Like the Soviet war memorial in the British sector to which Russian soldiers goose-stepped several times a day to change guard, the Rundfunkhaus was an unpalatable reminder of the early days of occupation when the West bent over backwards to placate the Russians. The SMA was in possession of the building when the allies arrived and had been left there, running the radio station ever since, though the Americans had bypassed Radio Berlin with their own RIAS (Radio in the American Sector). The British had long tolerated Radio Berlin's stream of Soviet propaganda and the use of the premises for meetings of communist front groups and the collection of signatures for the People's Petition. From April to June Berlin and London had argued about whether it was time to expel the Russians. Against the wishes of many in British Military Government nothing was done for fear of provoking the SMA.[76] On 25 June the Cabinet expressed the view that any move against the Rundfunkhaus would lead the Russians to cut allied communication cables between the city and the outside world.[77] This may have seemed a sensible precaution to British officials; Berliners found it grotesque that the Russians were allowed to use a western building to make virulent attacks on the allies and to poison the morale of the civilian population.

To Berliners' general mistrust of western intentions and contempt at weakness was added profound irritation over what was seen as allied mismanagement of the city. Most aggravating for the Berlin municipal authorities was the existence of two currencies, East and West, bringing chaos to already complicated finances. The last thing the Magistrat wanted to see was the East mark becoming the de facto official currency for the city; yet the western Powers permitted its use for the payment of rents, public service bills and most goods. The East mark flowed into municipal coffers while the city government pleaded for the issue of more western Deutschmarks to pay wages and contractors' bills; the western allies resisted their arguments on the grounds that the value of the new notes must not be inflated.[78] On 7 July the Magistrat reluctantly decided that its bookkeeping and financial transactions would have to be in East marks and all its Deutschmarks converted one for one. It was a painful decision forced on them by the need to persuade the SMA to release credits from the city treasury in their sector for municipal wages – so far the city had only been able to pay half of what was due for June.[79] Berliners were furious that the West seemed to be throwing them on the financial mercies of the East and allowing the Deutschmark to disappear either into the pockets of hoarders or into the maw of the east zone. (Enormous numbers of Russian cigarettes – perhaps twelve or fifteen million of them – were being sold on the black market for western marks only, and everyone knew by whom and why.)[80] It was rumoured that Ernst Reuter would resign unless more Deutschmarks were issued soon, and Louise Schroeder berated an American liaison officer: "If the British and Americans don't produce more money in Berlin, you can take over the duties of the Magistrat yourselves."[81]

The financial worries of the Magistrat increased as the blockade choked industry and caused unemployment – 75,737 were out of work in the western sectors by the end of July.[82] The Russians had made it clear to the city government that they would release no funds for unemployment pay,[83] and there was no joy in hearing that the

FDGB (the communist trades union) was ready to provide benefits. Non-communist union officials (from the rival UGO) persuaded their members to work shorter hours, take longer holidays and do routine maintenance work in the hope of keeping firms open. The Magistrat wanted to employ 100,000 people on municipal schemes such as rubble clearance and to pay up to 60 per cent of normal wages to those for whom work could not be found.[84] But the western Powers would not issue any more notes for the city. The German financial authorities in the Bizone were just as austere in their views on the need to limit Deutschmark circulation. The Ministers President of the western zones sympathised with Frau Schroeder's appeal on 11 July for DM 100 million as aid, but simply did not know how to raise the money. On 29 July finance ministers of the west German states offered to guarantee the loan from their new central bank, but the bank did not consider their security adequate. All Berlin could get was dribs and drabs: DM 20 million from the Bizonal Economic Council, a few credits from the Ministers President to relieve unemployment, some profits from German exports diverted by the Military Governors and small loans from individual state banks.[85]

Exasperated by the western Powers' financial stringency and by their apparently myopic inability to understand that dependence on Soviet East marks would lead to political subservience, the Berlin Magistrat was further plagued by the confusion of its relationship with the occupying authorities. There was no longer an Allied Kommandatura to draw up unified policies for the city; eastern and western authorities sent out contradictory instructions on all aspects of city government including two irreconcilable sets of financial orders for the control of the two currencies. To make bad worse, the western Powers themselves seldom co-ordinated the administration of their sectors and, what was intolerable for the Magistrat, tended to ignore the city government and deal direct with Bezirk Mayors.[86] The all too obvious mess would have been avoided, as Berlin leaders never tired of pointing out, had the western allies persuaded the Russians during the last couple of years to write a new city constitution which properly defined the responsibilities of occupiers and occupied and devolved powers to the elected government. In its absence Berliners now wanted a joint committee of sector Commandants and Berlin representatives to harmonise administration and tackle the problems of the blockade efficiently. The Americans were prepared to back the idea. The British stonewalled, parroting "provocation" and arguing that the Russians would welcome an excuse to wreck the Magistrat and Assembly and seize control of the city government.[87]

By July, though, there was every sign that the Russians would soon attempt to take over Berlin, provocation or no. It was the opinion of many that only the weakness of the SED and FDGB machines had so far saved the Assembly from violent overthrow,[88] and the Russians already seemed to be trying to get their grip on the Magistrat, department by department.

Throughout July, Russian intimidation made the lives of Magistrat officials a misery. At one Magistrat meeting, for example, an SED member made a vituperative attack on Dr. Friedensburg and promised to "take care" of him at a later date.[89] On another occasion Holthöfer, the head of the Post Office, clashed with an SED member who then threatened: "I shall arrest him wherever I can lay my hands on him ... because he has allowed himself to be caught up in the toils of the Americans." Holthöfer went to confront the fellow (prudently taking a couple of staff along), apparently in "hilarious spirits" and recommending that if he were taken into custody the British should arrest one of his employees, a renowned Russian lickspittle.[90]

It was more difficult to cope with longer-lasting strains, as when Russian officers came to squat in offices and loom menacingly over work. A certain Major Bakaroff turned up in the Education Department, accused its head, Dr. May, of "sabotaging" education and discriminating against "progressive educators" in favour of SPD members, and demanded to see all May's plans for city schools. May managed to remain "very cool and not the least intimidated" though as his home was in the Russian sector he must have felt very vulnerable. He challenged Bakaroff to repeat his accusations in the presence of a western officer. The Major left a few days later complaining that he had not been given the information he needed and whining about being "badly treated."[91] It was not so easy to get rid of another Russian cuckoo who came to nest in the Food Department on 14 July. Major Klimov was a much tougher bird than Bakaroff. He accused employees of the customary sabotage and told them they "deserved to have their heads shattered against the walls or to be bayoneted," which put quite a few of them off going to work and brought the deputy head close to a breakdown.[92] The head himself, the propitiously named Dr. Füllsack, not only had to endure such threats but an interview with the Deputy Soviet Commandant Yelisarov, who charged him with "political sabotage" on the orders of an unnamed power ("But I know who," hinted

Yelisarov). Füllsack expected arrest and a "spectacular" show trial at any minute. Frau Schroeder was completely unsympathetic: she thought he was making a fuss and doubted that any Magistrat official would be touched while the western allies remained in Berlin. Füllsack's nerves, she said dismissively, were getting the better of him. Füllsack did what he could to calm them: on 24 July he stopped going to his office in the Russian sector and moved to the west in the hope of working in peace.[93]

The poor man had run the Food Department for eighteen months. His job had never been easy, but the blockade had made it a nightmare. The Russians were not content with bullying; they then tried to pull the rug from under him. On 21 July the Soviet Military Administration offered to feed the whole city from the beginning of August. All inhabitants of the western sectors, it was announced, would be allocated a district in the Soviet sector where they could register for rations including fresh milk, which had been virtually unobtainable since the start of the blockade. It was a beguiling proposition for people who had seen little meat or fresh food for a month, had been living on dehydrated vegetables, egg, milk and coffee, and who were promised only 1,080 tons of food a day in August when the airlift would diversify to build up coal stocks.[94] The SMA, however, had failed to take into account that Berliners were not easily impressed (*"na und"* – "so what" – was a favourite expression) and were not predisposed to accept Russian blandishment. They well knew that the SMA was failing to look after its own people:[95] by 26 July two of the east sector Bezirke had been without meat for a week,[96] potatoes were scarce throughout the sector, and there was a chronic shortage of grain in the zone which was being met by deliveries from Russian reserves and purchases in eastern Europe.[97] The Economics Office of the Magistrat reckoned that to feed the western sectors the SMA would have to dig deeper into Soviet stores and deprive their own zone; even so, they could not back up their grand gesture if more than 10 per cent of western residents applied for rations.[98] That small SMA gamble paid off – a mere 2,050 had registered for Soviet rations by 31 July. But the bigger political gamble clearly failed: 80,000 had voted SED in 1946 and these had not signed on. The small take up of Soviet rations was not a relief for the SMA, it was a humiliation. The Russians tried to claw back some lost influence by sticking a former SED Mayor of Mitte, Paul Letsch, into Füllsack's empty office at the Magistrat. He summoned the heads of branches of the Food Department, called himself Füllsack's successor and asked for loyalty. All he got was a declaration that they were bound by the Berlin constitution: city officials had to be appointed by the Magistrat and confirmed by the full Kommandatura.[99]

When the offer to feed Berlin was made, a significant limit to Soviet munificence was noticed: there was no mention of supplying coal or power to the western sectors. Yet these were the city's greatest needs at the time. Food, after all, was being flown in; coal was not, and no one expected that it could ever be airlifted in sufficient quantities. To give the Russians their due, they had begun to supply all the current for the S-bahn on 9 July when it was feared that the railway would close because of the severe electricity cuts announced two days before.[100] This had done little, however, to relieve the general hardship. There was still no public transport after 6 p.m., domestic consumers got only four hours' supply of electricity a day, and 148 firms had closed by the second week of July because of shortage of power. On 9 July the gas supply was cut by 50 per cent. That was not enough to staunch the drain on coal stocks. A few days later the allies examined plans for even worse electricity restrictions, which would further damage industry and be a blow to dairies, bakeries and hospitals.[101] No wonder that when Friedensburg was made an offer by an official from the generating authority in the Soviet zone he was all ears.

What the official wanted was 1,000 tons of western hard coal a day – he was at the moment buying Polish coal at the extortionate price of $11 a ton. This would be used at the Klingenburg power station and supply the Russian zone with 250,000 kwh a day, leaving a surplus of 1,050 kwh which could be passed to the western sectors. Friedensburg was tempted by the offer and argued that it must at least be discussed: after all, Berliners could not keep going for months under the present circumstances and although, he said, he himself did not support the East nor want Berlin to become part of it, he did want to do something for the people.[102] Others sensed a Soviet trap. Reuter thought it was a bargain which would mainly benefit the Russians: "Let them raise the blockade altogether and the coal difficulty would solve itself."[103] He refused even to see the east zone officials: "The Russian-controlled press would immediately say the Magistrat 'was coming again to Canossa,'" and that was a political gift he would not give. It made much more sense to Reuter to cut the current from the Lübeck power station which the British supplied to West Mecklenburg in the Soviet zone.[104]

Friedensburg's interest in the proposition revived the mistrust which many felt about his motives: it was never easy to decide if he was a moderator or a man of no scruple, altruistic or driven by vanity and ambition. Herbert discussed the coal offer with him and commented: "I remain suspicious of him altogether ... If not actively pursuing Soviet policy he produces a series of compromise solutions which are liable to obscure a plain issue." Herbert had undoubtedly been needled because Friedensburg had taken the opportunity of the interview to air one of his favourite grievances: how he was consistently ignored by the British in favour of SPD leaders.[105] This was a typical example of tactlessness from a man described by Louise Schroeder as having two left thumbs and two left feet, all of which spent most of the time in his mouth.[106] As so often, his manner on this occasion destroyed whatever virtues there may have been in his case. He was forbidden to take the coal proposal any further.

Whatever damage the coal affair might have done to Friedensburg's reputation was more than compensated for, however, by his handling of a major storm in the Berlin police force. It had long rankled with the Magistrat that the Police President, Markgraf, eluded their authority and answered only to the SMA. The conduct of his subordinates was intolerable: they abducted west sector residents, stood by while citizens were beaten up, and on the 23 June abetted the mob which attacked the City Assembly. It was always feared that Markgraf's men, many of whom were armed, would be used in a violent coup against the city government. When a purge of non-SED police officials was carried out in July (160 Protection and 80 Criminal Police were sacked in the first few days alone), it was suspected that Markgraf was stripping his force for action.[107] The Magistrat could not dismiss him – only the joint decision of the Allied Kommandatura could do that – but it could call for his resignation. Although the Americans encouraged this, the British yet again opposed it with the old argument that the SMA would be given an excuse to attack the city government.[108]

With or without allied backing, Friedensburg resolved to take action against Markgraf. He won support from Reuter and Schroeder for the organisation of a body of police loyal to the Magistrat and stationed in the west of the city to be on hand in case of a repetition of the violence of 23 June.[109] On 26 July he sent a letter to Markgraf announcing that he was suspended from office because he employed and dismissed officials without consulting the Magistrat or Kommandatura, had failed to control the Assembly incident or to punish those responsible, and had shown "lack of discipline

...undemocratic, anti-social and un-German conduct."[110] In theory Markgraf's duties would be taken over by his Vice-President Johannes Stumm, a policeman since the 1920s who had received the accolade of dismissal by the Nazis in 1933. But Markgraf refused to regard himself as suspended or to move out of his headquarters. Kotikov, the Soviet Commandant, instantly instructed the Magistrat to sack Stumm.[111] In effect there were now two police forces in Berlin, each with different allied recognition. On 2 August Stumm warned every policeman against accepting Markgraf's orders and insisted that all matters should be referred to his office in the American sector; Markgraf issued the same but contradictory instructions and began to arrest officers loyal to Stumm for "stealing equipment," in other words carrying police files to the west.[112] Throughout the tussle Friedensburg stood firm in the face of diatribes from the eastern press and threats from the Soviet authorities. His refusal to give way won him respect all round. It was felt that he had now decisively thrown in his lot with the West. No one blamed him for splitting the police force; it seemed he had taken a brave and sensible precaution.

Even so, the wrestling over the police had given new urgency to the question of how long the Magistrat could or would be allowed to go on claiming to run the whole of Berlin, east as well as west. The war of nerves in the Magistrat departments must surely force them to move west soon to avoid a Russian takeover. As far back as 4 July the western Powers had offered accommodation to any administrative department which wanted it.[113] Frau Schroeder expressed the common opinion: Let the Russians themselves dismantle the Magistrat, no one else should do it for them.[114] The allies also recommended the Assembly to seek refuge and they made a building available in Schöneberg. Again the offer was turned down: the Assembly would not budge until it was shoved. How soon before that happened? Rumours flew that a coup would be staged on 29 July.[115] Herbert was worried enough to tell Reuter and one or two others not to attend that session.[116] They ignored his advice. As it turned out the only incident at the meeting was a walk-out of the SED group when the SPD put a resolution which called the blockade of the city a crime against humanity. Some doubted that the SED would ever come back. Many wondered if they would return in force and expel the democratic parties. Berliners and western occupation officials feared the worst, and any day now.

*　　*　　*

195

While Berliners held out tenaciously against the sapping effects of hunger, cold, dark and anxiety, they were observed from afar in west Germany with somewhat less compassion than they deserved and were sent rather less practical help than they might have expected. True enough, in the early days of the blockade, west Germans had been shocked and indignant at the plight of their fellow countrymen. Declarations of solidarity with Berlin had been passed in local Landtage, money was collected and food sacrificed. As the weeks went by, interest cooled. People in the west were too engrossed in the effects of currency reform and the abolition of price controls which had occurred at the same time. They were upset that their savings had been wiped out, but amazed by the miraculous appearance of goods in the shops and the rapid increase in employment, wages and rations (in July the meat ration in the Bizone actually doubled). Some expressions of fraternal sympathy and food parcels were still sent to Berlin, but demonstrations were poorly attended; there were sneers at the new-found friendship of the western allies for the city and a tendency to shrug off Berlin's problems as something the Powers had to solve.[117]

West German politicians, however, could not ignore the crisis. Murphy reported that "the Berlin situation and the current tension between the western Powers and the Soviet Union are exercising a profound effect."[118] The Ministers President met the three Military Governors on 1 July to receive the London proposals that they should draw up a west German constitution and accept an Occupation Statute. They had agreed beforehand to show no reaction and to ask for time to consider. So the Ministers President withdrew to Koblenz from 8 to 10 July for private discussion. Their instinct was to postpone a national constituent assembly, indeed any constitutional development, until an all-German scheme was possible and the allies were persuaded to reserve few powers for themselves. They were undoubtedly influenced by an appeal from Louise Schroeder to do nothing which could be interpreted as abandonment of Berlin or provocation to the Russians to take violent action against the western sectors.[119] A British observer, however, reckoned that the Ministers President were "all cheerfully prepared if the Military Governors should say that they do not like their proposals to be told that they must get back to the London framework and carry on with it."[120] There was a strong impression that the west German politicians preferred to be ordered rather than authorised to draw up a constitution so that they could disclaim all responsibility for unpleasant consequences.

When the Ministers President met the Military Governors again on 14 July, they expressed their fears that a west German constitution would split Germany irrevocably, argued for economic rather than political fusion in the western zones, denounced the Occupation Statute as a denial of sovereignty, and opposed the idea of submitting any draft constitution to a referendum because this would give undue weight to what they wanted to call merely a *"Grundgesetz,"* a "Basic Law." Clay told them firmly that whatever they did they would be accused of splitting Germany, so they might just as well get on and create a strong and prosperous state as a rallying-point for the whole nation. A further meeting on 20 July failed to resolve the arguments and, at Robertson's suggestion, the Ministers President went away again to think things over. At Rudesheim from 21 to 22 July they retreated from their Koblenz position, pushed by Reuter who took a very different line from Frau Schroeder and urged speedy establishment of effective institutions in west Germany as the best contribution to solving the Berlin crisis.[121] At last on 26 July the Ministers President told the Military Governors that they would go ahead with the London recommendations – a decision eased by allied agreement to disguise the constituent assembly as a "Parliamentary Council" and the constitution as a "Basic Law" (with "Provisional Constitution" added in brackets).

The west Germans had been led to the constitutional water and had taken a nervous sip. Would this incite the Russians to crush Berlin's independence? Or would it persuade the Soviet Union that the blockade had failed, that it had strengthened allied enthusiasm for separate development rather than scared them off it? The western Powers would soon have a chance to sound out the Soviet reaction.

On 26 July Bevin finally threw in the towel and agreed to a joint allied approach to the Kremlin. The three western Ambassadors in Moscow would make a statement to Molotov and ask him for an interview with Stalin. If this were refused, the western statement would be left with Molotov as an aide-mémoire and the allied governments would take their case to the United Nations. Bevin accepted this plan with bad grace: a discussion he had with American representatives about what to say in Moscow was glossed over in the British record as "long and somewhat difficult."[122] Douglas summed up his own talk with Bevin on the matter as characterised by "a considerable amount of petulance at times" and frequent "plaintiveness."[123] The American Ambassador was so touched by all this misery that he slipped back later to assure Bevin that he need not give way if the idea made him so unhappy. Bevin's histrionics had, in fact, won him two things he had always wanted: the first approach to be made to Molotov not Stalin, and a written rather than purely verbal account of western arguments. Nevertheless, he was genuinely unhappy about the whole business. He thought it pointless; it went against his negotiating instincts to force an issue when it was not crystal clear what could realistically be hoped for. He did not need Reuter's warning in a speech at the Berlin SPD Party Day Rally against "rotten compromise" nor the pleading of another speaker to avoid "four-Power negotiations under pressure of the blockade."[124] Bevin was all too aware of the dangers of supping with the Russians. But what alternative was left? And if this approach did not loosen the blockade, how long could Berlin survive?

9

Amiable Bears

After all the arguments about approaching Moscow, the travail over drafting the allied statement, and the hopes and fears surrounding what might be the final chance of a Berlin settlement, the first contact of the western representatives with the Kremlin was a moment of bathos. Molotov, they were informed, was "not at present in town." They were not told where he was or when he intended to return, though they guessed he was at his dacha just outside Moscow and could be back in his office in half an hour if he chose.[1] The best the Soviet Foreign Ministry would offer was an interview with Zorin, not just a mere Deputy Foreign Minister but a lowly one at that. The Russians had played a diplomatic variation of switching the points on an allied train at Marienborn: the West's envoys had been shunted down a branchline.

They had to make the best of it. On 30 July the American Ambassador, General Walter Bedell Smith, went to see Zorin, delivered the allied statement and requested interviews with Molotov and Stalin. Bedell Smith had long experience in tricky negotiations. In his wartime job as Eisenhower's Chief of Staff he had been better than most at dealing with difficult customers like Montgomery and had soothed Soviet fears of a separate western peace with the Nazis. He had had close contact with the Russians in Germany in 1945 and since March 1946 had been Ambassador in Moscow. He knew Soviet leaders and understood the pace and style of their negotiations. He handled Stalin skilfully: played the game of old generals and offered tasty morsels of military fat to chew, which flattered the Generalissimo with implications of strategic wisdom and gave him the pleasure of mocking the ignorance of his civilian underlings. For the moment, however, Bedell Smith could only use his arts on a Deputy Foreign Minister, whose initial response he found "uncompromising." Zorin shrugged off the request to see Molotov with the curt comment that he was not expected in Moscow in the near future. He suggested that since the western statement showed no change in the allied position on Berlin, there was nothing to discuss with Molotov let alone Stalin. Bedell Smith put down a personal trump: when he first came to Moscow as Ambassador, Stalin had promised he could have an interview at any time. Zorin softened enough to agree to forward his request, but offered no hope it would be granted. Bedell Smith knew enough about Soviet psychology to leave it at that: "I did not make any request for an estimate of when a reply might be expected and refrained from giving any other indication of eagerness or anxiety on our part."[2]

The French Ambassador came next to Zorin's office. Yves Chataigneau was in an awkward position: there had been no French government for several weeks, so he had no proper negotiating instructions or indication of future French policy. To increase his discomfort he had only recently taken up his post in Moscow and was new to the Soviet game. Fortunately he had already "become a valued friend," said Bedell Smith, "in whose judgment I had great confidence."[3] Chataigneau knew and got on well with Americans – he had been a liaison officer with their forces in the First World War and won the American Distinguished Service Cross. His British counterpart, Frank Roberts, was meeting him for the first time but took to him immediately. The Frenchman went through the agreed procedure, presented the joint note, and asked to see Molotov and Stalin.

Frank Roberts, who followed, was not the British Ambassador (Sir Maurice Peterson was in London for treatment after a heart attack and had been advised by his doctors not to risk the long flight back); nor was he the Minister at the Embassy (Geoffrey Harrison had just been appointed and lacked the background for these talks); but he was Bevin's Principal Private Secretary. The British need to field a relatively junior official had its advantages. Bevin, for a start, must have found it satisfactory to send someone who knew his mind intimately, had studied every detail of the Berlin crisis and been privy to every decision, and in whom he had total trust (for as Roberts knew, "Ernie had a great gift for suspicion").[4] It is tempting to believe that Bevin would have relished conducting the Moscow negotiations himself – while they lasted his trunk twitched to catch every whiff of change, nosed out every trace of weakness and trumpeted over every allied point scored. As it was, he could enjoy the next best thing: watching his ideas being tried out and acting as trainer to a shrewd young practitioner. Stalin himself was to comment to an interpreter that Roberts was "a very able chap."[5] Bedell Smith had spotted him in 1946 as "one of the best of the younger British career diplomats"[6] while Roberts was serving as Counsellor at the British embassy in Moscow and acquiring a good working knowledge of the Soviet Foreign Ministry and its ways. During that period Roberts, for his part, had developed admiration and genuine affection for the American Ambassador, whose quick temper sharpened by stomach ulcers could offend those who did not know him.

Tolerance and mutual respect between the three western envoys was going to count for a lot in the coming weeks while they lived and worked at close quarters and under considerable strain. They would have to withstand Russian attempts to crack their united front and the attempts of their political masters to pull the negotiations in every national direction. It was a great help too that Roberts and Chataigneau could acknowledge Bedell Smith as the Moscow doyen. He had the habit of command; furthermore, it was tactically desirable that one man should present a joint case and that it should be the American – as Roberts was well aware, "The Russians are mainly concerned with American reactions since America alone is powerful enough to stop them."[7]

Roberts's talk to Zorin on 30 July yielded no more positive results than those of his colleagues. Even so, when the three envoys compared notes that night, they decided that Zorin had become "more talkative and less uncompromising" in the course of the evening and had been reasonably friendly.[8] They did not expect an early reply to their requests for interviews at a higher level – the Russians liked to keep people waiting and guessing.[9]

So it was a surprise when Bedell Smith was rung next day, 31 July, by the Foreign Ministry to be told that Molotov would see him at 7 p.m. that evening, Roberts at 8 and Chataigneau at 10 o'clock. They prepared a uniform approach – this was, after all, the second time they had been given separate invitations and they did not want to be picked off one at a time. Each was greeted very affably: Molotov, thought Roberts, was "in his friendliest mood throughout." This was something of a relief. Molotov could be outrageously rude on occasion and seemed to take a delight in smiling and puffing away at his interminable cigarettes while driving an adversary to lose his temper. Molotov's geniality this evening, however, could not be allowed to disarm. His visitors knew that he was devious. He had the reputation of being coldly self-possessed – not for him the usual Russian bouts of drunkenness – and real emotions seldom showed on his face, though he might betray occasional anger by a sudden attack of stuttering. The western representatives were dealing with a man of dangerous calibre. He had no real diplomatic creativity, nor great finesse, but he was always methodical and well-prepared, cunning and relentless in pursuing his aims. Molotov initiated nothing – Soviet foreign policy was made by Stalin – but he carried out his instructions without question, apology or modification. Like many Russians he did not treat diplomacy as a method of finding compromise but as war conducted by other means.

At this first meeting with him, on 31 July, the western diplomats all felt that Molotov was trying to "manoeuvre one or the other of the representatives ... into stating definitely the position of the western Governments."[10] They avoided telling him – Molotov, after all, was a sprat to catch Stalin. With Bedell Smith, Molotov probed: the allied aide-mémoire was not very clear, he complained; exactly what discussions did the Americans have in mind, what "wider questions" were referred to in the final paragraph, what did he think about the Russian argument that talks about Berlin could only take place in the wider framework of talks about Germany? Bedell Smith fended him off: all the answers, he promised, would emerge in fuller discussions. Nor would the General be pinned to details by two comments flicked out by Molotov: a specific reference to the currency problem in Berlin and the charge that traffic restrictions had been made necessary by western acts since the London talks.[11] Roberts too managed not to disclose what discussions the West had in mind. He even cracked a brief smile from Molotov by saying, "We thought it better at this stage to talk over the problems rather than to continue exchanging notes," though he noticed that the Foreign Minister "checked his exuberance to add that it was certainly no more than exchanging notes."[12] With Chataigneau Molotov adjusted his technique and concentrated on French sore spots – the Ruhr and the dangers of German military revival.[13] The French Ambassador, like his colleagues, would not be drawn.

That evening all three felt fairly sure that Stalin would now agree to see them. In fact, Bedell Smith cabled to the State Department: "We are having a rehearsal tomorrow."[14] It was as well that they polished their act early. A summons arrived to see Stalin and Molotov together in Stalin's office in the Kremlin on 2 August.

The interview was arranged for 9 p.m. – a very Kremlin time. Stalin began work only in the late afternoon, but he carried on into the early hours of the morning, sometimes calling in his subordinates at 10 o'clock for heavy meals which might last for hours, during which he drank little but ate voraciously and squeezed out unguarded opinions from his increasingly tired and tipsy guests. If he granted an audience to a foreign ambassador – and he seldom did – it took place some time between 9 p.m. and midnight. Those privileged to meet Stalin went up in a lift to the second floor, then down a long, narrow, red-carpeted corridor dotted with guards in polished boots and pressed uniforms. Those used to the scruffy decrepitude of Moscow were disconcerted by this corridor. Like Milovan Djilas they were "astonished at the cleanliness ... not a speck on the carpets or a spot on the burnished door-knobs."[15] At the end they went through high double doors covered with dark-green padded leather into a suite of reception-rooms. The last of these was Stalin's study – long, modest, unadorned except for identically carved wooden frames for portraits of two military heroes of Imperial Russia, Marshals Suvorov and Kutuzov. Stalin himself sported the order of a Hero of the Soviet Union. During the war he had worn the plain Party uniform of buttoned tunic and khaki trousers; in peacetime he preferred to dress as a Red Army marshal.

The first glimpse of Stalin in the flesh was startling. Everyone knew the newspaper pictures and the vast icons which brooded on public buildings and flowed from banners across Moscow. They anticipated a massive figure with bristling black hair and warrior's moustache. They found a small, slight man, whose tunic seemed too big for him except across his paunch and whose arms and legs were disproportionately long. His face was pock-marked, and pallid except for red cheeks – the "Kremlin complexion" it was called and was attributed to long nights in airless offices. His hair was sparse on the head and wispy on the lip where it was streaked, perhaps by the smoke from his Dunhill pipes. Stalin's image, big and powerful, owed much to the art of Russian photographers. It had not been diminished by group portraits at wartime conferences because these tended to show the Big Three sitting in deference to Roosevelt's wheelchair. It was preserved in his rare public appearances by a diminutive entourage. (It was surely one of Molotov's virtues in his chief's eyes that he was barely 5 foot 4 inches high. Smallness is no small matter to a great dictator.) Once visitors adjusted to Stalin's scale they felt a strength in his physique, were impressed by his quiet and assured bearing, and often charmed by the seriousness with which he listened and by flashes of mischief or rough humour. His manner of a stern but benign peasant father was belied, however, by his teeth – inward-pointing, discoloured and sharp like a carnivore's – and by his eyes, which were yellow and could be pleasantly intelligent and expressive, but which sometimes sparked with menace or with sadism when he taunted one of his staff. It was all too easy to be attracted by Stalin's unassuming behaviour, his reasonable comments, his acute and decisive reactions. It was dangerous not to know that he was suspicious, vindictive, ruthless and a genius of duplicity.

The evening of 2 August found Stalin at his most beguiling; cordial and responsive throughout.[16] Bedell Smith read the allied statement, which emphasised the West's "unquestionable and absolute" right to be in Berlin and drew attention to the gravity of the crisis in the city. It suggested that if the blockade were the result of technical difficulties, these could be remedied; if a reaction to currency reform, then the matter could be sorted out in the city; if intended to force negotiations, then unnecessary since the allies were always ready to talk; but if designed to drive the western Powers out of Berlin, "it could not be allowed to succeed." The statement ended with the warning that useful discussions could only take place "in an atmosphere relieved of pressure": the blockade must be lifted before the allies were willing to go into any other matter. Stalin listened attentively but made no direct reply. Instead, he asked if the three envoys were empowered to negotiate and whether, once Berlin questions were settled, they could move on to wider German issues. Bedell Smith checked him: the western governments would not be committed at this stage; they only wanted to learn Stalin's opinion on possible bases for settlement.

Stalin seemed pleased to give his views. He grumbled for a few minutes about "technical reasons" for the blockade and western "stripping" of Berlin's assets. Yet he soon focused on the argument that the blockade was the consequence of decisions reached at the London talks: the introduction of western currency into "the middle of the Soviet zone" to "disrupt" its economy and the establishment of a separate west German state. He kept assuring his listeners that the Soviet Union had no wish to oust the western Powers from Berlin ("After all," he explained, "we are still allies"), but he stressed that they had forfeited their legal right to be in the city by their financial measures and the creation of a new German capital in Frankfurt. Finally he made it clear that he wanted to see the abolition of the western "B" mark in Berlin until all other German questions were resolved. Bedell Smith prodded: if the "B" mark were withdrawn, would the blockade be lifted? No, Stalin replied; first all London decisions must be suspended and the four Powers must meet. The American Ambassador explained events from the allies' perspective: all their moves in west Germany had been defensive and made after years of frustration and disagreement, and all their changes were designed to slot the three zones into a united country; the history of four-Power talks on Germany, he pointed out, was discouraging and the West would never negotiate under the duress of blockade. He applied a little duress of his own: the western allies would prefer not to supply Berlin by air, but they could fly in up to 10,000 tons a day if they had to. Then he made an offer: if the Russians opened communications with the city, negotiations on Berlin and Germany could begin immediately.

Stalin now bluntly put his own demands – more bluntly and finally than anyone realised. He asked for abolition of the "B" mark and suspension of all London proposals until there had been a four-Power meeting to discuss every contentious German issue including reparations, demilitarisation, government, control of the Ruhr and a peace treaty. Without actually saying so, he was trying to pick up where the 1947 Moscow talks depressingly left off. Bedell Smith cut in quickly to say that an agenda could not be fixed here and now, and that no talks could be arranged while the blockade was in force. Stalin seemed to take a small pace back: if the western mark were abolished in Berlin and the London decisions postponed, there would be no real difficulties over any other problem. Then, of his own accord, he gave much more ground: he conceded that he was prepared to accept a mere oral, confidential promise on the delay of west German government. Roberts slipped in a reminder that such matters were for discussion by Foreign Ministers; what the representatives wanted to concentrate on was the urgent problem of the pressure on Berlin. Stalin reacted as if ready to surrender. This was the moment warning bells should have sounded – he was retreating the better to jump. After a long muttered conclave with Molotov he threw himself back in his chair, lit a cigarette, smiled and asked: "Would you like to settle the matter tonight?" Indeed, they would. In that case, suggested Stalin, they should tell their governments that the blockade would be lifted the moment the East mark became the sole currency in Berlin and that, although he would not make suspension of the London proposals a condition for agreement, he wished this to be recorded as "the insistent wish" of the Soviet government. Only when Bedell Smith raised the point did Stalin add that he would also like an announcement of quadripartite talks in Berlin on the city's problems and a top-level conference elsewhere on the full range of German questions. No western envoy pursued the Soviet leader's seemingly casual reference to the East mark as the "sole" currency in Berlin. It was an omission which might be excused in the general excitement. It was to prove costly.

The account of this two-hour meeting on 2 August compiled from the notes of the English and Russian interpreters recorded that it "broke up in a very friendly atmosphere." The western diplomats went off to hold an inquest in Bedell Smith's office feeling most encouraged, and they chatted happily about how they would now handle the technical details of a draft agreement with Molotov. Their euphoria was understandable. Stalin had been remarkably welcoming and shown unusual readiness to get down to essentials. Given the way he had played down the difficulties, there seemed every chance that the blockade would soon be lifted. Surely no one since the war had had such a friendly, conciliatory discussion with the Soviet leader? The three western representatives were not alone in sensing Russian readiness to climb down. Charles Bohlen, the Russian expert in the State Department, also thought the outcome of the meeting highly satisfactory. In his judgment, thanks to recent reverses for the Soviet Union such as Tito's independent stand and the success of the airlift, the Kremlin had significantly modified its attitude.[17]

But had it? Or had the western envoys been temporarily blinded by Stalin's geniality and their own impatience for a Berlin settlement? A sharp eye, undazzled by the Soviet leader's smiling charm, could detect many a trap in the record of his conversation. Stalin had denied the right of the western Powers to be in Berlin; he would only let them stay on sufferance. Since the diplomats had failed to mention the problem of allied access to the city, he had been spared the need to discuss routes and guarantees for their unrestricted use. He had in no way conceded that west German developments were justified or that they provided a basis for uniting Germany. He had talked of "postponing" London proposals until four-Power talks took place without implying that the Soviet Union was ready to accept any of those proposals – indeed, his list of items to be discussed was a troubling reminder of Soviet rigidity and ambition.

The logic of his bargain to lift the blockade and start talking was that the blockade would be reimposed should the discussions not satisfy him. Most significantly Stalin had never relaxed his insistence that western currency in Berlin was unacceptable – and if the East mark became the city's "sole currency," as he had suggested, then Berlin would inevitably be sucked into the economy and under the control of the Soviet zone.

Several clear eyes spotted these snares, none clearer than Bevin's which were trained by decades of appraising political and trades union bargains and at their brightest when reading between the lines of minutes from smoke-filled rooms. He quickly drafted a telegram to Roberts reminding him of the basic western principles which must not be sacrificed: all transport restrictions in Berlin must be lifted before any discussions on other matters took place, and the western representatives must at all costs prevent Soviet currency under Russian control becoming Berlin's only means of exchange – if that were to happen, "I am afraid we may have lost the fight because economically and politically our position would be impossible ... and we should sacrifice the whole of the Berlin people who have been supporting us."[18] Lewis Douglas, as so often, agreed with him. If the Berlin mark were to be controlled by the Russians, he cabled to Washington, "we will have abandoned our clear right to participate in the Government of Berlin"; and, he added, if occupation of the western sectors were made dependent on cancellation of the London agreements, the western Powers would be reduced to the status of a "tenant whose lease had expired."[19] Clay too told the Department of the Army that without control of Berlin's economy the western Powers would have "no real say in Berlin Government." Furthermore, he drew attention to the probability that the blockade would be reimposed once west German government was set up and to the danger that any talks with the Soviet Union at this delicate stage might throw the western zones off course.[20] By 4 August even Bohlen had changed his tune. He wrote in a memo to Marshall that Stalin was angling for a halt to west German government; if he failed to get it, the logic of a split Germany dictated that he would try to drive western troops out of Berlin.[21] Marshall himself needed none of this advice. His eyes were as bright as any. On 3 August he sent a firm directive to Bedell Smith: "Our acceptance of Soviet zone currency in Berlin cannot be unconditional and its use must be subject to some form of quadripartite control." The allies, he maintained, must keep a free hand over west German government; Stalin must be persuaded that any constitutional arrangement would allow all German states to subscribe in time.[22]

These were not instructions that Bedell Smith was necessarily glad to receive. Although the formal account he gave to Washington of the Stalin meeting was the record agreed by all the envoys, he had sent a personal evaluation at the same time, said to have been prepared in the presence of his colleagues but significantly not passed on to London or Paris.[23] This cable began with a rider to the official optimism about the Russians' readiness for a settlement: "If one did not know real Soviet objectives in Germany [one] would have been completely deceived by their attitude ... literally dripping with sweet reasonableness." Thereafter Bedell Smith showed that he was not only undeceived himself about what the Russians were after, but he was perfectly willing to let them have it. He made no bones about declaring, "We are in a mess over currency in Berlin and might as well be out of it on Soviet terms." Not content with that, he argued that it would be a good thing to postpone west German government since once it was established the West would have "fired one of the last shots in their political locker." These capitulationist views were not an isolated outburst. They were based on strongly held convictions which were not shaken by subsequent experience. Nearly two months later Bedell Smith was reported as regretting that the United States was in Berlin – an exposed salient – and recommending withdrawal to zonal lines and the creation of a new west German capital. In his opinion, it suited the Russians to have the western allies in the city where they could be drained of resources needed elsewhere, it would be a good thing, therefore, to find an opportunity to get out soon.[24] Bedell Smith, for all his qualities and experience, was not, perhaps, the ideal man for tough talking with Stalin on this occasion.

Whatever his personal views, however, and despite the irritation he recorded in his memoirs at interference from "a lot of very able young experts" in Washington who thought they could handle the talks better, Bedell Smith was duty bound to carry out his government's wishes and answerable to Marshall – his senior in both military and State Department rank. And Marshall's orders were clear: the question of quadripartite supervision "must be clarified in order to avoid any possibility of the Soviets controlling the city of Berlin through use of currency." It was a pity that all three governments had not emphasised this point before their representatives spoke to Soviet leaders. For as Marshall cannily observed, "Past experience would indicate that Stalin will adhere

1. Playing airlifts was a delightful game for young Berliners.

2. Unloading sacks of coal for power stations at Tempelhof.

3. Making briquettes from coal dust and spillage.

4. Louise Schroeder, acting mayor and 'mother of Berlin', and (right) her deputy, Dr Friedensburg.

5. Ernst Reuter, for once without his black beret, the voice of Berliners and the conscience of Europe.

6. The last demonstration of Berliners' solidarity, outside the Rathaus Schöneberg on 12 May 1949 - not in protest, this time, but celebration.

7. With only four hours of electricity a day, listening to the news from the RIAS broadcasting van.

8. Ironing in the middle of the night.

9. Cooking with scarce fuel by the light of an expensive candle.

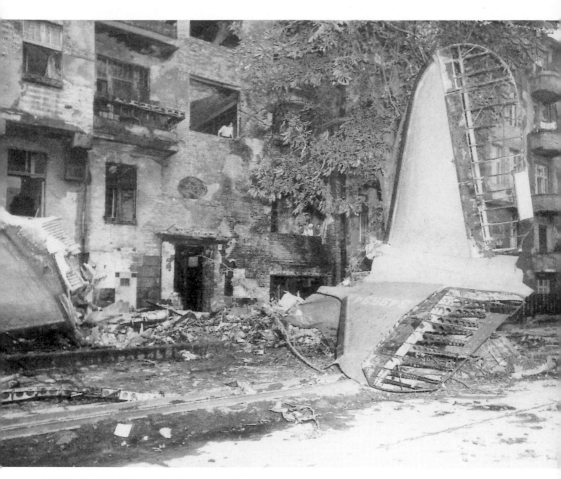

10. The first airlift tragedy. Wreckage of the C-47 which crashed on approach to Tempelhof,
5 July 1948.

11. There was no certainty that Berliners would get even 3 cwt of coal to heat homes throughout the winter.

12. Wood was rationed too, so even a few twigs were a welcome find.

13. Communal warming rooms were set up by the municipal authorities.

14. Lieutenant Halvorsen loads chocolate onto the parachutes he dropped for Berlin children.

15. Klingelhöfer receives a sack of flour from the crew of the York which had just landed at Gatow with the millionth ton airlifted to Berlin on 18 February 1949. By the end of the operation 2,325,808 tons would have been supplied.

16. Berliners celebrate the first departure in a year of a bus from Berlin to the western zones and proclaim that they are now living again.

to the proposals he made at the first meeting."[25] Stalin and his subordinates did, indeed, try from now on to treat the currency question as already settled on their own terms. The western envoys, without realising it at the time, had given dangerous ground when they thought they were capturing the heights of an agreement to lift the blockade.

All the same Marshall was still pleased with the general tone of the Moscow meetings so far and felt that Stalin was "near accepting what we hope to achieve through informal discussion."[26] Bevin was not so satisfied. He told the Committee of Ministers on Germany on 4 August that he was not willing to let Stalin get away with comments about the western Powers losing their rights in Berlin, nor to turn a deaf ear to the suggestion that western currency reform and the London proposals in some way "justified" the blockade.[27] Marshall might consider four-Power discussions on Germany; Bevin cabled to Roberts: "I do not want to be committed to a meeting of the Council of Foreign Ministers." Even so, Bevin did want to keep talking in Moscow and said: "I do not want to be hostile." Yet he stressed one overriding priority: "Try to keep in mind our obligations to the Berliners."

Roberts was never given the "freedom of manoeuvre" Bedell Smith pleaded for; Bevin's rein was tight. He cabled a stream of negotiating instructions to Moscow and advised: "If after doing your best you cannot get what we want, come back for instructions."[28] It was direction Roberts appreciated rather than resented and was often sweetened by the affectionate little phrases at the end of telegrams ("We all wish you good luck," "We are thinking of you here") which so endeared Bevin to those who worked for him. All the same, Bevin's attention to every detail caused Roberts some embarrassment with his colleagues, especially Bedell Smith. He had to send a hint to the Foreign Office: "[I] should warn you that despite our excellent personal relations, the US and French Ambassadors are becoming irritated by what they interpret as a tendency in London to 'impose our will' in regard not only to substance but to every individual point of drafting."[29] Bevin's thick skin was impermeable to hints.

Once the Moscow talks got down to details, the early western optimisim that the Kremlin wanted a settlement soon dissipated. An allied draft announcement of the lifting of the blockade and start of four-Power talks was discussed on 6 August with Molotov and a Deputy Foreign Minister, Smirnov, who was an expert on German affairs. Molotov would not accept it: "There is nothing here," he complained, "about the insistent desire of Generalissmo Stalin for the postponement of the decisions of the London conference." But, Bedell Smith pointed out, Stalin had not made his "wish" a condition for agreement. Molotov ignored the reminder. Again and again throughout the three-hour meeting he returned to this same point; every time, the western diplomats repeated that Stalin had only asked for his feelings to be noted. They kept assuring the Russians that the convening of the west German constituent assembly on 1 September was a far cry from the actual establishment of a government. Molotov appeared not to hear. Right at the end of the session he came back: "Tell me, do you or do you not intend to postpone the convocation of the Parliamentary Council on 1 September?" He was equally deaf to any argument about the need for quadripartite control of Berlin's currency: "The three western allies had and could have no function whatever in connection with the control of Berlin currency once the Soviet mark had been accepted." This, he said flatly, was "not a technical question but one of principle on which the Soviet government could not give way." When the allied negotiators pressed their case, Molotov expanded his: quadripartite control in Berlin no longer existed, though the Soviet Union had no wish to expel the allies from "the capital of the Soviet zone." He went further and asserted that since there were no longer four controlling Powers in Berlin, only two sides, any future discussions in the city should involve one Russian and only one western representative. The allied diplomats dug in their heels, defended their legal right to be in Berlin and threatened to increase the airlift rather than surrender them. Molotov would not yield an inch.[30]

The western envoys did not see Molotov's statements at this 6 August meeting as a precise definition of unalterable Soviet demands. Instead, they interpreted them as merely typical Soviet negotiating tactics. Both Bedell Smith and Roberts recorded their impression that Molotov was more sceptical about the chances of a German agreement than Stalin – seemingly forgetting for the moment that the two Soviet leaders often played hard and soft roles, with Molotov doing the dirty work and Stalin keeping his hands clean and his face smiling. They also agreed that these Kremlin negotiations would be lengthy, not least because the Russians were trying to settle details as well as general principles in Moscow rather than in Berlin.[31]

Washington and London on the whole approved of their envoys' handling of this session with Molotov. Marshall, however, warned against any weakening "in the face of these obvious Soviet tactics" and against letting the Russians drag the talks out while Berlin was still blockaded. Soviet control of the city's currency, he stressed, would be "the substitution of another form of duress for the blockade."[32] Bevin sensed that Molotov might give way on some issues but not without a great deal of pressure, and he told Douglas that every effort should now be made to increase the airlift.[33] He suspected that Molotov and Stalin underestimated allied ability to supply Berlin by air and that telling them the lift could be substantially expanded might "turn the scales in our favour."[34] A greater pessimist could have argued for the same policy for the opposite reason: if the Moscow talks failed, the West had only the airlift to fall back on.

Clay was delighted with Bevin's recommendation to develop the airlift. It gave weight to his own complaint that the authorities were not providing C-54s quickly enough. "Can you push them along politely?" he asked the Department of the Army on 7 August. "Yes," his old comrade Draper promised, and "not necessarily politely."[35] In fact, Draper did not have to push hard. When the Secretary of the Air Force, Stuart Symington, and its Chief of Staff, General Hoyt Vandenberg, saw Bevin on 9 August, they had already decided to build up the airlift.[36] In Germany next day Symington told the press that tonnage levels were now reaching the average carried over "The Hump" and that with more C-54s on their way winter supplies were guaranteed.[37]

It was a good thing he avoided facts and figures. The airlift was at present delivering only 3,000 tons a day; even if it could meet the minimum need for 5,500 tons in winter, there was no certainty, as Robertson pointed out, that Berliners could hold out long on such a low standard of living.[38] Experts were worried about maintaining a regular service in winter conditions, and they doubted that it would ever be possible to achieve a daily supply of 7–8,000 tons.[39] Whatever the professionals might think, Bevin was convinced that such a total was possible if the Americans put their backs into it. He argued passionately that "such a step might save the world" and "could not possibly cost a sum equal to a day's war."[40] For the time being, however, a headline in the Soviet-licensed Berlin paper, the *Tägliche Rundschau*, was painfully accurate: the airlift was not so much an Airbridge, or Luftbrücke as the Germans called it, it was more of a "Bluffbrücke."[41]

It was a bluff which did not deceive Molotov, to judge by the hard line he took at the next few meetings with Bedell Smith,

Roberts and Chataigneau. The proposals he offered them on 9 August included suspension of the London agreements but did not mention quadripartite control of currency at all. In discussion he maintained that Soviet control of Soviet currency was "natural and proper" and that if there was to be quadripartite control of any kind it should apply to Germany as a whole. (He must have enjoyed pointing out to Bedell Smith that four-Power supervision had never been mentioned to Stalin.)[42] Given Molotov's obduracy Bedell Smith feared that agreement was "not probable,"[43] and Bevin told Douglas "the negotiations in Moscow were now likely to break down."[44] No one was cheered up by the next session with Molotov on 12 August, though Bedell Smith thought the Foreign Minister "grew progressively more reasonable and mellow (if such a word can be appropriately applied to Molotov)."[45] On this occasion both sides stuck to their respective guns over currency and Stalin's "insistent wish" for suspension of west German government. Molotov pressed for a full agreement to be drawn up in Moscow while the western envoys wanted details to be settled in Berlin. A new wrangle developed about the specific date on which transport restrictions had been imposed in Berlin. Molotov, astonishingly, chose 15 August as the starting date; his opponents argued that interference had begun long before and that all restrictions must be lifted before a bargain could be struck. The British and Americans decided that Molotov was trying to bog the negotiations down. They must cut the process short and ask to see Stalin again.[46]

The western representatives made one last effort with Molotov. At their fifth meeting on 16 August they presented him with an unambiguous list of the items they insisted on: the lifting of all traffic restrictions imposed since 1 March; four-Power talks on Berlin and on Germany; the East mark as sole currency in Berlin but under quadripartite supervision; no discrimination against those holding western marks (at present illegal tender in the Soviet zone); currency, banking and credit to receive equal treatment in all four sectors and trade to be unhampered in the city; and the issue of enough currency for budgeting and occupation costs. Molotov wriggled over some points. For example, he wanted to substitute 18 June for 1 March as the start of traffic restrictions on the grounds that "this was the date on which the currency reform had been introduced which had brought about the complications." Surprisingly, however, he made no mention of the London decisions and the Soviet wish to see them suspended. Equally oddly, having previously insisted that a complete settlement must be shaped in

Moscow, he now suggested that any problems should be left to the Military Governors to sort out in Berlin. This shift became comprehensible when he suddenly scribbled out a proposed directive for the Military Governors: traffic restrictions imposed by both sides to be lifted; the western Deutschmark withdrawn and replaced by Soviet zone currency; agreement on all this to be reached "in the shortest possible time." Clearly he was hoping to sink the negotiations in an even deeper bog in Berlin than he could find in Moscow. The western representatives leaped in to complain that none of their own conditions had been mentioned. Bedell Smith politely wondered how long the Military Governors would take to find an agreement on currency. He turned to Smirnov and asked whether he had an opinion in view of his Berlin experience. This must have been one of the moments when Molotov began to stammer: any minion he took to a negotiating table had a purely decorative function, to be strong and absolutely silent. But he managed to laugh and suggest that "everything was possible" and that if "Mr. Smirnov had some views he could express them." Smirnov knew his place and what his job was worth. "No," was all he said. The four-hour meeting, described by Roberts as "all very hard going," adjourned with a western statement recording disappointment over lack of progress and the claim from Molotov that he had gone a long way to meet them but that "it takes two sides for an agreement."[47]

The western Powers were now convinced that the Russians did not want any agreement at all, indeed, would gladly prolong the Berlin crisis through the imminent General Assembly of the United Nations and sit back to see the effects of winter on the airlift and the economy of the western sectors.[48] Politicians and diplomats shared the view expressed by Bevin: "We cannot and will not agree to anything which will allow the Soviet Government to achieve by the means of their hold over the currency of Berlin that which they have not been able to achieve by their blockade."[49] To finish the negotiations and set a seal on their failure, the western representatives asked for a final audience with Stalin. While they waited for an appointment, they painstakingly prepared the ultimate statements of their position: a draft directive for the Military Governors on currency, trade and traffic matters and a press communique on the decision to hold four-Power talks.

When they met Stalin at 9 p.m. on 23 August he took the wind out of their sails. "Well," he remarked jovially almost before they sat down, "I have a new draft." It was, indeed, new and amazingly near to the western proposals. Furthermore, Roberts thought, "It was clear from the start that Stalin and Molotov, who were both on their very best behaviour, were out to reach an agreement." Stalin explained his proposed directive and communique logically and reasonably. In one place he had suggested that once the Military Governors worked out currency changes, the German Bank of Emission would then issue notes and a new four-Power Financial Commission would supervise its work and control the circulation of the money. On this crucial matter the western representatives wanted to make sure that quadripartite control would be built in to every stage and would be permanent. Stalin's reply seemed unequivocal: "This was, of course, the intention," he said, adding that he "did not mind using the word 'control.'" So far, so good, so very much better than anyone could have expected.

Then the dramatic tension of mounting agreement was jolted by a change of mood of almost Shakespearean piquancy. Stalin began to talk about the end of the war. He was led to it by the reminder that Bedell Smith had signed the agreement in 1945 to withdraw allied troops from German territory assigned to the Soviet Union. Perhaps the Ambassador hoped to lure Stalin into giving by recalling what he had once been allowed to take; all he managed was to stir up old rancour. Stalin retorted, though good-humouredly, that if the western allies had not withdrawn to their zones, they would never have been let into Berlin. As he and General Bedell Smith campaigned again at length, the American Ambassador suggested: "Mr. Molotov must be getting impatient" (and the final report does, indeed, note "signs of impatience"). But Molotov was in the Smirnov chair this evening and his possible discomfort was ignored. Strategy and tactics were analysed until the two old soldiers came to close combat: Stalin said the western armies could never have taken Berlin – they had only seventy or eighty divisions whereas the Russians had 280. Bedell Smith hit back: the West had eighty-six and each was twice the size of a Soviet division and, what was more, backed by air power. A truce was called on terms acceptable to both: all the allies "had done the best they could."[50]

It seemed almost as easy to find agreement when the negotiators finally returned to the hostilities of peacetime. Stalin was perfectly accommodating over the date on which the blockade could be said to have started. In spite of Molotov's insistence on 18 June, he himself suggested referring only to "the restrictions latterly imposed" and lightly agreed that this phrase would cover any which existed before 18 June. When the westerners expressed anxiety that talks in Berlin might be lengthy, he commented that the Military Governors ought to be able to settle the details within a week. On the question of suspending the London agreements, he repeated his "insistent wish" of 2 August but allowed that "if the western Powers thought it inconvenient to publish this from the point of view of prestige then ... it might form the subject of an exchange of confidential notes" (an idea which he credited to Bedell Smith). He then dropped the matter abruptly. Molotov picked it up just as the meeting was about to end. Bedell Smith was firm: the West would not make any promise to suspend constitutional developments. Stalin finally agreed to disagree.[51]

This conciliatory atmosphere carried on into an immediate drafting session with Molotov on the press communique and directive for the Military Governors. Here everything went so smoothly that Bedell Smith at last remembered one of Stalin's favourite proverbs: "An amiable bear is more dangerous than a hostile one."[52] But even with that in mind it was impossible to detect a trace of hostility in so much apparent amiability. He and his colleagues were delighted. It really looked as if the Kremlin had decided to climb down. Yet optimism at the moment sprang from casual remarks, tone of voice, veils over controversy. The actual directive for Berlin did not transmit any of these. Much still depended on Russian good faith and their interpretation of what went on to paper.

For that reason the Military Governors were chary. Robertson cautioned London against the belief that "everything is going to be easy from now on."[53] Clay was far from happy that there were no references to the legality of western presence in Berlin or guarantees of future access, and he bemoaned the fact that quadripartite control had been agreed merely for the limited area of currency. This, as he indicated, was only part of the issue: "There is involved the full political, governmental, social and economic life of the city." He feared that discussion in Berlin might do no more than put off the evil day when it had to be acknowledged that no settlement could be found.[54] The State Department was in complete agreement with him and cabled Bedell Smith to say so.[55] They found the Ambassador "somewhat captious in arguing with the Department on the line that they are being unnecessarily meticulous."[56] He quoted with approval Bevin's advice to Roberts at this stage: "we have a chance of wrecking the agreement if we put up a long series of amendments."[57] General Marshall, to the contrary, worried that the British and French were "prepared to go too far in order to get a quick agreement."[58] He had no real cause for anxiety. His allies were no more ready to sell out than he was; they just had a slightly different estimate of how far the Russians could be pushed to committing themselves in writing.

There was a salutary reminder at this point of the value the Russians put on their written word. Hugh Lunghi from the British embassy, who had been interpreting for the three western diplomats, wrote to Pavlov, his Soviet counterpart, on 26 August drawing attention to an extra paragraph which had appeared in the Russian version of the proposed communique which concerned suspension of the London decisions and had not been agreed at the drafting meeting. Pavlov was not shamed. "I do not consider it possible to enter into discussion of the question," he replied.[59]

Molotov, on the other hand, doggedly pursued the matter on 27 August when he spent three hours with the western representatives going over the directive and communique (with his deputy Vyshinsky taking the place of Smirnov). He clung to the view that suspension of the London proposals was an essential element in any agreement. At the same time he tried to drop from the drafts any clear definition of the roles of the German Bank of Emission and the Financial Commission. It was just as if the conversation with Stalin on 23 August had never taken place and Molotov himself had not agreed the drafts afterwards.[60]

The bleak prospect of futile Berlin talks was confirmed at the final meeting with Molotov on 30 August. Once again the Soviet Foreign Minister stood every previous understanding on its head. He opened by insisting on a reference to the London proposals in the communique, then suddenly opposed the idea of a communique at all: "It might create considerable misunderstanding." Finally he conceded that the press could be informed that high-level talks would take place but should not be told on what subjects. When the western diplomats pointed out that there was still nothing on paper about the functions of the Financial Commission, Molotov brazenly called this "wanting a new document." He led the argument round in circles for an hour until the westerners read him the record of the talk on 23 August and Stalin's exact words on the continuing control of the Commission. They even read out the section where Molotov himself had agreed that the Commission "would not only be a controlling body but it would supervise the introduction of currency and its continued circulation." No one's words, not even his own, would sway Molotov. The Financial Commission, he now contended, would have powers "only to the extent envisaged by the four Military Governors."[61] One decision alone was made and it satisfied everyone: the discussions in Berlin must be completed by 7 September.

The final directive for these talks stated that "subject to agreement being reached among the four Military Governors in Berlin for their practical implementation the following steps shall be taken simultaneously: A: Restrictions on communications, transport and commerce between Berlin and the Western Zones and to and from the Soviet Zone of Germany which have recently been imposed shall all be lifted. B: The German Mark of the Soviet Zone shall be introduced as the sole currency for Berlin and the West Mark 'B' shall be withdrawn from circulation." Later in the document there was an indication that "regulation of the currency circulation in Berlin is to be undertaken by the German Bank of Emission of the Soviet Zone" and that a quadripartite Financial Commission "shall be set up to control the practical implementation of the financial agreements indicated above."[62] But these clauses came at a dangerous distance from those concerned with the use of the East mark as the sole means of exchange in Berlin, and they did not specifically empower the Commission to supervise credit and trade. It was risky, furthermore, to allow the Russians to define the Bank of Emission as being "of the Soviet Zone." Most hazardous, however, was the opening phrase which set the foundation for the rest of the directive: everything was "subject to agreement" by the Military Governors – implying that, if they so chose, their talks would not be bound by any undertaking previously reached in Moscow. Stalin's apparently helpful phrase about restrictions "recently imposed" could now be seen as creating plenty of room for disagreement. The absence of any mention of allied rights in Berlin meant that these essentials need not be discussed. After a whole month of debate in Moscow and the raising of so many hopes this was the best the West could get from bears who had received them so amiably.

No wonder, then, that when all the Military Governors met at the Allied Control Council building on 31 August to plan how to carry out the directive, the atmosphere was strained throughout. Sokolovsky smiled pleasantly from time to time but, as Robertson observed, he was extremely cautious and "since seemingly restrained by the need to stick to rigid instructions from Moscow appeared slightly embarrassed." But the term "embarrassed," Robertson admitted, "probably applied to all of us." Clay came to the meeting grudgingly and arrived late. He refused to shake hands with Sokolovsky. Theoretically it was Clay's turn to take the chair; he

217

tried to refuse it, but since it was physically the only seat left he had to sit on it and Koenig was persuaded to preside. Clay remained silent for a long time, but thawed at last and began to intervene. "The fact is," thought Robertson, "his forceful and efficient mind cannot bear to see things going untidily." The meeting agreed to set up three committees – on transport, finance and trade questions – and to begin formal Military Governors' discussions next day.[63] Everyone had avoided the slightest comment about something which must have been near the forefront of all their minds: the appalling events in Berlin since the beginning of the Moscow talks.

For Berliners the negotiations in the Kremlin had seemed interminable. Many criticised the West for wasting time and letting the Russians prolong the blockade into the winter. Few expected any successful outcome to the talks and the comparison was constantly drawn between Moscow and Munich: people were anxious, said a British report on morale, "lest the western Powers make concessions to Russia – any such concessions it is felt will only be at the expense of Germany and will only lead to further demands."[64] Their apprehension increased as rumours seeped out from the supposedly secret discussions in Moscow and were readily believed by a population so mistrustful of western commitment to the city. (The Foreign Office reckoned the leaks came from the Soviet embassy in Britain and *Le Monde*'s London correspondent noticed how "more or less official Russians" in early August suddenly displayed unusual "talkativeness and sociability."[65] Many of the stories, however, must have been channelled direct to Berlin.) Most damaging to Berliners' confidence was the impression they got that the allies were ready to accept Russian terms on currency. The west sector press denounced any bargain over the mark: as *Der Tagesspiegel* put it, single currency was a Russian political weapon to subjugate Berlin.[66]

Currency – or rather the lack of it – was one of the major concerns of the Magistrat and Assembly throughout August. They could not pay the promised unemployment relief: 4.7 million marks were needed, but the Soviet authorities would only agree to release 3 million from the city bank, the Stadtkontor in the Russian sector, if west sector banks agreed to pay the rest.[67] Even more seriously: at the beginning of the month Dr. Suhr told the American liaison officer with the Magistrat that "Moscow or no Moscow, the wages for workers and employees in the western sectors must be paid on the coming Friday"; the previous Friday people had merely been told to wait a week.[68] The Magistrat had no hope of paying its wages bill – the monthly budget was about 125 million marks and on 7 August the City Treasurer had only 15 million.[69] The SMA had blocked all the city's funds in the Stadtkontor and, although 25 million marks were released in the first week of August, they refused to fund some wages such as those for the police; the following week they froze the entire account again.[70] Private firms in the western sectors were also tightly squeezed. If they banked in the Soviet sector their deposits were blocked from 6 August, unless they agreed to submit to control by the Soviet zone Economic Commission and to trade solely in East marks. Yet many of their workers refused to accept payment in East marks at all, even the 75 per cent insisted on at the time of allied currency reform. Faced with this emergency the western authorities stepped in and offered credits to allow firms to provide 100 Deutschmarks for each worker. That did not satisfy either the men (the democratic union UGO called for at least half of all wages to be paid regularly in Deutschmarks), nor the bosses, who had to pay the loan back in sixty days and who most of all wanted their money out of the Soviet sector.[71] On 23 August the Military Governors at last stopped further funds getting into SMA control by prohibiting the deposit of current Magistrat revenues in the Stadtkontor until all commitments in the western sectors had been met.[72] It was all rather little and late. Berliners' contempt for western financial management and kowtowing to the SMA had increased. Much of the credit won by the airlift was wiped out.

The city had lost for a time the courage and tenacity of Louise Schroeder, who had gone to Hamburg in mid-August for an operation. Once there her doctors decided she was too run-down and her heart was too strained for immediate surgery, so she endured the unpalatable treatment of four weeks' rest in bed – though Friedensburg suggested that a dose of DM100 million for the Magistrat would be the best medicine.[73] He himself took over the duties of Oberbürgermeister and had to remain healthy since his successor was Acker from the SED.

Whatever the official leadership of the city, however, there was a feeling that the people themselves were beginning to take over, and the allies worriedly discussed the danger of spontaneous anti-Russian outbursts by the population. An American assessment of the mood noted Berliners' increasing wish to "see the fight through," their belief that war was a minor evil compared with Soviet ascendancy and their frequent use of the old saying: "Rather an end with horror than horror without end."[74] Berliners were ready to push their leaders because they felt the Russians pressing so heavily on them.

Raids in the western sectors by east sector police or Russian troops reached frightening proportions in August. There were too few west sector police to defend their area against these regular incursions; those who did try to intervene were often dragged over the Russian boundary. Two Markgraf men who went into the American sector and tried to snatch a former city prosecutor were arrested.[75] But most stayed safely on the eastern side and pointed out western colleagues for Russians to kidnap.[76] Stumm's men got a little revenge when they spotted the SED head of the Criminal Police at a boxing match in the British sector and took him into custody. Markgraf became oracular: "consequences will flow."[77] The most frequent raids were on the Potsdamer Platz, where the Russian, American and British sectors met. The SMA claimed they were necessary for "rounding up black-marketeers." There were certainly plenty of illegal traders there, but surely never 2,000, which was the bag in one raid; indeed, Stumm told a press conference at the end of the month that out of 350 arrested on another occasion only two had been black-marketeering.[78] When a posse of east sector police was stoned by the crowd in the Potsdamer Platz, they opened fire, killing one person and wounding several more before the British military police moved in.[79] The fact that the British then gave their sector boundary a coat of white paint and the Americans festooned theirs with barbed wire was a hint to Russian troops, but no deterrent to Markgraf's men or any great protection for west Berliners.

A good stiffening of allied troops did rather more, but did not make up for an acute shortage of western police. Over half of Stumm's officers had followed him to the west, sacrificing their homes, accepting that the Magistrat could not pay them, and disregarding Markgraf's ominous warning that they would have to "stay in Berlin and that Berlin is part of the Soviet zone." Stumm himself had been ordered by the Soviet authorities to give up his house in their sector; they then refused to allow the removal men in, claimed he had disobeyed their orders so confiscated his furniture.[80]

Another Magistrat official who had moved to the west was also under pressure and finding it increasingly difficult to do his job. Dr. Füllsack, head of the Food Department, had hoped to run the city's Central Food Office from his new accommodation in the British sector. He soon discovered that the Russians intended to strip him not just of authority but of staff as well. Letsch, his self-styled "successor," issued a list of 468 key employees who were told they must accept his orders or resign by 7 August.[81] Of those named, a half would be expected to work on the Soviet scheme to feed the entire city, for all that 60 per cent of Berlin's population lived in the western sectors and the vast majority of them were still registered for rations there. Those on Letsch's list were not only faced with an unpleasant choice, they seemed likely to lose what little allied protection they had. On 6 August the Markgraf police tried to stop the American and British liaison officers getting into the Central Food Office. The American barged through, the Briton sneaked in as the gates were opened to let out a Russian lorry while passers-by on the pavement shouted "Bravo." Once inside they were told by their rebarbative Soviet counterpart, Major Klimov, that their offices were needed for the administration of the new ration scheme and that in future only employees on Letsch's list would be admitted to the building.[82] Half of these decided to disregard the instruction of the allied Commandants to stay put and ignore Letsch. They and many of their unlisted colleagues left and joined Füllsack, who had no offices for them, looked for new homes and worked without a guarantee of wages.[83] Major Klimov attempted to move in too, but found it impossible to roost in the West.[84]

Thus far, in spite of all the menace and vexation they faced, Magistrat officials had gambled that the Russians would not dare to lay hands on them while the western Powers were still in Berlin. But on 17 August the SMA ordered the Magistrat to sack Dr. Mückenberger, the head of the Coal Department, on the grounds that he had stored coal in such a way as to "encourage theft" and "cause spontaneous combustion." Three days later they arrested him in his office.[85] He was allowed no lawyer and his wife was only given permission to visit after she broke down and wept. She was able to leave books but no shaving kit and was desperately anxious because her husband, who had suffered from tuberculosis and had a bad heart, was now deprived of medicine.[86] Dr. Mückenberger was to be held in solitary confinement for ninety days before coming to trial. This nasty experience had a hidden benefit: those days counted as double when his sentence was assessed, so virtually cancelled out the prison term he finally received.[87]

Clearly the SMA and SED could continue to pick off one city official after another. Most people, however, thought they lacked the patience and that a major move to smash the entire Magistrat and Assembly was more likely. Warning of such an attack came on

25 August. A letter to Friedensburg from the Soviet Commandant, Kotikov, condemned as illegal recent actions by the city government, such as introducing the Deutschmark and splitting the police force; city officials, he warned, would be held personally responsible.[88] That day several reports came through that the SED intended to march on the Assembly next afternoon and that there had been calls for "action" in the streets against the "policy of sabotage" by the Magistrat.[89] Friedensburg contacted Wagner, the SED head of the Protection Police, and asked him to guard the Stadthaus. Wagner said he could not guarantee its security.[90] Given that refusal and the suspicious absence of the Soviet liaison officer from the Magistrat premises, the Council of Elders on the morning of 26 August postponed the Assembly meeting scheduled for later in the day.[91] Shortly before 2 o'clock that afternoon, processions converged on the Stadthaus. Anything up to 5,000 people, women and children among them, crowded outside with red flags, banners, and placards – "One administration, one currency, one food supply"; "Down with the bankrupt Magistrat"; "No Marshall Plan"; "No more airfields"; "A peace treaty for Germany"; "Through unity to socialism." Some 400 then crammed through the doors, up the stairs and into the Assembly chamber. Once their banners had been draped round the walls, Litke, chairman of the SED in the city government, called for the replacement of the Assembly by a special commission of councillors and citizens to carry out an emergency programme and co-operate with the east zone Economic Commission and "the great Soviet Union." A deputation of ten went to see Friedensburg in his office to tell him that the Magistrat should make room for other people. They were "quite harmless," commented Friedensburg; "I have already had worse experiences." Meanwhile, the demonstrators left the chamber shouting "Down with the Magistrat" and singing the "Internationale," and joined the crowd outside to hear some more speeches. By 4:30 p.m. everyone was drifting away, quiet and orderly.[92]

That evening 30,000 or more Berliners staged their own demonstration in front of the Reichstag. Ernst Reuter spoke to them and for them: "We Berliners have said No to Communism and we will fight it with all our might as long as there is a breath in us ... The Magistrat and the City Assembly together with the freedom-loving Berlin population will build a dam against which the red tide will break in vain." Tens of thousands were there to hear him though they were tired and hungry, they had every reason to be afraid, and twelve years of Nazi rallies had sickened them with public oratory and mass meetings. They hardly needed Reuter's words, but they were glad he spoke them. Berliners had come to show the Russians what they cared for. At a time when, however wrongly, they believe the western Powers were about to sell out to the Soviet Union, they hoped to draw attention to Reuter's call: "The struggle for Berlin is a struggle for the freedom of the world."

This awesome testimony to the people's wishes did not deflect the SMA and SED from their attack on the people's elected government. Next day, 27 August, the City Assembly intended to meet in the morning. By 9:30 a.m. a mob of between 500 and 800 was waiting in front of the Stadthaus. Though no attempt was made to obstruct the entry of members of the Assembly, it was decided to accept the wisdom of Dr. Suhr's decision to postpone the session until it could take place without a threat of violence. Assembly representatives left the Stadthaus, again without being molested. But the mob then attacked the locked doors, with Markgraf police either helping or giving encouragement from the sidelines. As they did so a Russian liaison officer inside suddenly found pressing reasons to leave and asked for the key to the main door. He was held up while people pretended to look for it. Unable to get in at the front, the mob went round to the back. Here they forced an entrance, surged through and raised their banners again in the Assembly chamber. The Markgraf police came with them and arrested two people, one for "shouting," the other for the crime of "ostentatiously reading" a newspaper at the window. The demonstrators held the building for an hour or more while Litke inside and other SED speakers outside called for "spontaneous activity" to drive out the Magistrat and Assembly. At noon the crowd was led away.[93] No one doubted they would be back.

All three democratic parties were agreed that the City Assembly must not be broken by intimidation. There was, however, argument about whether they could carry on using the defenceless Stadthaus or should move to a safer position under western protection. For some city politicians the priority was to meet soon, never mind where. For others it was essential to hold on to the seat of the lawful city government until the SMA and SED were seen to eject them illegally.[94]

Dr. Suhr, never a dashing figure to the public at large, but a man of quiet courage and principle none the less, made one last attempt to get guarantees of safety for Assembly meetings in the Stadthaus. There was obviously no point in approaching the police. Instead, on the afternoon of 27 August, he wrote to Kotikov appealing for

223

the creation of a neutral area round the Stadthaus within which no demonstration could take place during an Assembly meeting. He was summoned just before midnight to receive a disdainful and evasive reply: Did he want demonstrations banned throughout the city? Kotikov enquired. What kind of protection did he think necessary? And who was to provide it?[95]

In Moscow Frank Roberts protested to Molotov on 30 August about the SMA's failure to protect the City Assembly.[96] It is unlikely that his protest produced the lull in the violence which lasted for the first week in September. It is more probable that there was truth in the stories which began to circulate that the SED was licking the wounds of its failure to break the Assembly, while the SMA packed the east sector police with communist stalwarts from their zone.[97] Events were to prove that the SMA was not holding its fire just because the four Military Governors were holding meetings in Berlin as agreed in Moscow.

The Military Governors opened their formal discussions on 1 September. The three western allies assumed they would proceed on the basis of their directive and that their job was merely to settle details of agreements reached in principle in Moscow. From the very first day Sokolovsky behaved as if no directive existed and no criteria had been discussed or laid down in advance. There were seven main meetings; few lasted more than a couple of hours, only the last extended to six.[98] Their brevity was no sign of quick disposal of business: the Russians refused to start early or stay late which, as Clay noted, was "not characteristic" and could "only result from the desire to stall."[99] The mood was never openly hostile, but it was never relaxed either. Sokolovsky set the Russian style which Robertson described as "a polite and reasonable attempt to make impolite and unreasonable proposals."[100] Clay was perfectly co-operative in public though he kept saying to Robertson in private that he saw no future in the talks but was "not going to make himself responsible for crashing them."[101] Diplomatic incidents were avoided by abandoning diplomatic niceties; Robertson reported: "We have now given up handshaking altogether, which is perhaps no bad thing," and at the first sticky session Koenig, as chairman, did not invite anyone to enjoy the refreshments prepared for them until the Russians had left, which, as Clay said, they made "very easy by rising from the table immediately after the meeting adjourned without wasting time in saying farewells."[102]

The finance, trade and transport sub-committees laboured like mules in a treadmill without generating the driving force of a properly harnessed animal. The Military Governors themselves toiled in similar circles without benefit of blindfolds to conceal their futility. The fundamental problem of the powers of the Finance Commission was treated by Sokolovsky as if it had just been invented by his western colleagues; by the end of any meeting he had usually forgotten all about it. Russians in the financial sub-committee took a more sophisticated line and argued that the Commission was purely intended to control issue and circulation of currency and that no quadripartite supervision could be applied to credit for industry, individuals or municipal institutions – thereby trying to hamstring Berlin's economy and administration. Profiting from a comment in the directive that the east zone economy must not be disrupted, they made clear what no one had so far acknowledged openly: that the Commission would function subject to constant Russian veto.[103] Only the transport talks gave a short-lived illusion of progress. The Soviet representatives soon discarded their claim that the blockade began on 18 June and agreed to lift all restrictions on road and rail traffic imposed since 30 March and to permit sixteen allied trains a day to and from the western zones, though they insisted that the three military trains must carry no Germans and be open to full inspection. Waterways, they conceded, could reopen for interzonal traffic, but they wanted to negotiate a separate agreement for the carriage of coal and food to Berlin.

As if all these provisos for transport were not unacceptable enough, Sokolovsky then dragged air communications on to the agenda. He alleged that existing agreements had been nullified by western violations, and maintained (without any documentary proof) that civil and commercial air traffic was not permitted to fly to Berlin and that the corridors were provided only for the needs of western troops. (Soviet zeal at this stage for redefining air agreements is a useful reminder that for every conversation in a western capital in the last year beginning "What fool let the Russians nobble road, rail and water transport?" there had probably been another in Moscow starting "Which idiot gave the western Powers free run of the air corridors?")

Since Sokolovsky could not shake the West's stand on the air-traffic agreement of November 1945, he tried to jar their airlift. On 4 September he nonchalantly announced that the Soviet air force would hold its "usual exercises" between 6 and 15 September in the region of Berlin and the corridors. As Clay pointed out to the Department of the Army: "This was amusing since in the four summers we have been in Berlin we have never heard or seen these manoeuvres."[104] What he found much less amusing was his understanding that Sokolovsky was actually threatening to use the corridors themselves, not just the airspace around. He sharply reminded the Russian of the safety of American airmen and the psychological impact on the Germans of any interference with the airlift; the State Department decided to complain to the Kremlin.[105] Robertson and Koenig had both taken it that the Soviet air force would steer clear of the actual corridors and try to scare rather than meet head on allied aircraft; London decided against a formal complaint.[106] As it turned out, Soviet officials treated the manoeuvres as if they were an exercise in allied co-operation and air-traffic control – every movement was notified in ample time and with punctilious detail. Although there was a tendency for some Soviet aircraft to infringe the Gatow control zone, the British did not get into a huff; they assumed the Russians were merely failing to find Dalgow and cheerfully admitted to infringing "the Dalgow zone up to 70 times a day" themselves[107] (but only to Whitehall, not to the SMA).

This was the only bit of live and let live among the four Powers for the first week in September. For the rest it was depressingly obvious that the Military Governors' talks were not going to reach agreement on a single point. Bevin and Marshall, however, both felt that the West should not press for a breakdown; this should come in Moscow not Berlin.[108] So the western Governors trundled on until 7 September, the time limit set for their discussions, hoping at best for clarification of the issues which would have to be taken up in Moscow – issues they had imagined already settled there. They told Sokolovsky on the last day that they would report to their governments and ask for fresh instructions, then the talks would resume. They never did. The will-o'-the-wisps of a Financial Commission, quadripartite controls and a unified Berlin had anyway been swept away before their talks ended by a tempest on 6 September.

Faced with the obnoxious scenes in the Stadthaus on 26 and 27 August and the impossibility of getting protection, the Council of Elders of the City Assembly had decided to postpone any meeting. There were, however, pressing arguments for convening from members who wanted to demonstrate they were not afraid or who wished to provoke the Russians to an act of violence which would saddle them with responsibility for breaking the Assembly. So a meeting was announced for noon on 6 September and, in spite of CDU and LPD anxiety, the SPD won its case for making a final attempt to hold it in the Stadthaus.[109]

By 11 o'clock that morning there was a dense crowd outside the building – up to 3,000 on some counts. The demonstrators had arrived in long processions or packed into lorries; they were noticeably rowdier and tougher than the August mobs. They stood by the main entrance, controlled by east sector police, while Assembly members went inside. But at noon, on what observers agreed was a prearranged signal, they rushed forward, smashed the plateglass inner doors with some very active police help, and surged into the chamber and public gallery. Several journalists were beaten up and a RIAS microphone was ripped out. Some Assemblymen got out of the building through side doors; others went to their offices while SED speakers denounced the democratic parties and called for the overthrow of the city government to the cheers of the audience. Meanwhile, Markgraf officers roaming the corridors spied enemies – forty-six west sector police in plain clothes, who, unbeknown to the western authorities, had been invited by Friedensburg to come and give protection. The Markgraf men pounced. They arrested any Stumm officers they could lay their hands on and a couple of bystanders for good measure and hauled them off to their headquarters. About thirty other west sector police sought refuge in Friedensburg's office and that of the Ecclesiastical Adviser; some of them then slipped along to the rooms of the allied liaison officers. At 3 o'clock the Stadthaus was quiet: the crowd had dispersed, the Markgraf police had withdrawn. But there was a tight police cordon round the building and everyone inside was trapped. For eight hours they lurked behind locked doors, wondering if they could sneak out once it was dark. Then, at 11 p.m. east sector police with Russian officers swarmed in, found Friedensburg and ordered him to unlock his office. He refused – unless those sheltering there were given free passage. The police moved on, trying doors along the corridors until finally they broke into the American liaison officer's room and dragged off in handcuffs every German they found there.[110]

Next morning the ring of police round the Stadthaus was braced with troops. Any Magistrat employee who wanted to come and do a day's work was thoroughly searched. No one stuck inside had a hope of escaping. In the afternoon Dr. May, Friedensburg's chief assistant, came to the liaison officers' rooms with a plan to smuggle everyone out between 5 and 6 o'clock when the staff went home.

The strategem failed: police checks were too tight. The British liaison officer instinctively reached for the ultimate weapon of his nation in a crisis: he sent an urgent signal for milk, sugar and tea for twenty.[111] The non-English undoubtedly would have liked something stronger.

And, in the nick of time, enter the French liaison officer – Captain Ziegelmeyer by name but Musketeer d'Artagnan by nature. Having perhaps found life under siege in the Stadthaus undramatic, he had been to the theatre. At 9 o'clock he wanted to return to his office, but the Markgraf police refused to let him in. Ziegelmeyer, however, was a man with a mission. He thrust the police aside and, pausing only to shout over his shoulder "This is the French way in," leapt through the shattered glass doors. Behind him followed companions (three, of course) bearing champagne. Inside the hall, he reported later, "I came up against a second group of Schupos [Schutzpolizei, Protection Police] who dashed to overpower me ... Levering myself off the ground with one hand I kicked one of the Schupos, then getting up I punched the second Schupo on the jaw. Taken by surprise my attackers let me go and I found myself free." "What could we do?" grumbled his assailants. "We were only four."[112] Ziegelmeyer's progress thereafter was not so suitable for gasconade. He got upstairs right enough but found too many police round his office for even his martial arts. All he could do was go back to the hall and unromantically phone his room and General Ganeval, the French Commandant. At 1 a.m. he let off accumulated steam in a row with the Russian liaison officer and at last got into his office.

His champagne must have been welcome to all those who had survived thus far on British cuppas, even though they had been fortified with Marie biscuits. Better still was the news at 4 a.m. that Ganeval had extracted a promise from Kotikov that all those trapped in the Stadthaus would be given free passage out. The allied liaison officers went along the now deserted corridors to rouse everyone in hiding. At 5 o'clock nineteen Stumm police were loaded into one French lorry and a small handful of German and American journalists into another; then with great gasps of relief they drove off.

A few minutes later an armed Russian jeep which had been following them shot ahead, swerved across the road and brought the two lorries to a halt inside an arc of east sector police. The whole lot was taken into custody.[113] At least two of the Stumm men spent a month in Russian jails before coming to trial without legal representation or much understanding of the charges, and serving six-month terms in, of all places, the old Nazi concentration camp at Sachsenhausen. "The clubs in the hands of the Russian and German camp personnel," said one of the police officers, "ruled day and night."[114]

What could the western Powers do faced with such violence, flagrantly directed by the SMA and east Berlin authorities, and an arrant lie by the Soviet Commandant disguised as an offer of pacification? Not threaten violence in return: they did not have the men or arms, and they themselves were surrounded in the city by 300,000 troops and were the only hope for two-and-a-half million or more Berliners. Yet they yearned to hit out. "Pride is a cheap commodity, thank God," wrote Clay, "or I could never hold my head up."[115] The only puny, discredited resort left to the allies was official protest, with a vocabulary already exhausted and never adequate for such outrage. When Howley stormed in to see Kotikov his own remonstrance was drowned by the Soviet Commandant, with a prepared speech lasting one and a half hours condemning American "nonsensical and unfounded allegations" and "attacks on peaceful workers" petitioning the city government by western troops and German "black guards" with firearms and knuckle-dusters.[116] The Soviet response to Herbert's written condemnation of 6 September summed up more concisely the reality of the situation. It was addressed to the "Commander of the British Garrison" and signed "Military Commander of the City of Berlin."[117]

The question that Berlin's city government now faced was no longer whether it should move to the western sectors, but when. On the evening of 6 September, while Markgraf's men held the Stadthaus, the Assembly had held its adjourned meeting in the Tabernica Academica, a students' room in the Technical University in the British sector. The SED did not attend. The other parties unanimously voted to hold city elections in November. Yet in the three weeks that followed there was reluctance to make the final break from the Stadthaus and a strong feeling that the SED should not be given the pleasure of seeing it vacated and putting in their own Magistrat.[118] Assembly members and Magistrat officials still went to their old offices and tried to do their jobs as if they were running a unified city. But all the while Russian liaison officers with SED assistants took over east sector Bezirke town halls with the excuse that the German authorities were incapable of carrying on. This was increasingly true since the same interlopers were sacking local government employees (500 of them by 15 September) and a breakdown of administration seemed inevitable. The Magistrat and Assembly were torn: should they themselves sack SED employees to create jobs for those thrown out in the east, or stand by their liberal belief that no man should be sacked for his political views?[119] The Elders finally promised to find jobs for anyone dismissed by the SED, even if it meant retaliatory dismissals, and they called on east sector Bürgermeisters who had threatened to resign en bloc to stay at their posts – any replacements would surely be worse.[120]

Through the anxiety and confusion of September there was one solid certainty – the resolve of Berliners. On the evening of 9 September, the people of Berlin went to the Platz der Republik in front of the Reichstag to show their confidence and their pride, and to assert their dignity in spite of all violation. Their demonstration had been carefully planned for two days: RIAS broadcast regular information on the best routes to get there, the trades unions called for all work to stop early in the afternoon so that people had plenty of time to travel, the transport authorities for once ran buses and trains after 6 p.m. to make sure everyone could get home. Constant Radio Berlin announcements that the meeting had been cancelled had no effect; a counter-demonstration in the Russian sector drew few. By 5 o'clock there were over 250,000 Berliners in the square – a quarter of a million people, some seventh of the entire population of the city. They stood in response to Franz Neumann's request for one minute's silence in honour of the victims of Nazi persecution and those who had been oppressed since the war. They heard his appeal: "Let us all fight for Berlin's democratic rights and freedoms ... Listen here in the Platz der Republik, listen in Germany and listen in all countries ... Berlin calls the world." They welcomed Suhr's denunciation of the Soviet theft of freedom. They approved Reuter's appeal to the western Powers: do not barter Berlin away or compromise with the Soviet Union at the expense of the city's brave people, but help Berlin not just with the thunder of aircraft but with lasting common ideals. Finally they backed a motion to be presented to the Military Governors recording the suppression of liberties in the Russian sector.[121]

Then at 7 o'clock a few thousand marched with the party leaders to the Allied Control Council building to hand in their petition while the rest dispersed. Many drifted to the Brandenburg Gate. For some it was the most convenient way home, for others a symbol of everything they opposed. The Gate was the historic opening to the East, the monumental entry to the Soviet sector; from its bronze triumphal chariot at the peak fluttered the Red Flag. That flag was an object of loathing and an irresistible prize. A lad shinned up the Gate, grabbed it and heaved; others scrambled up to help. It fluttered down on to the western side and was ripped to pieces by the crowd. Soviet troops opened fire. At the same time a Russian jeep carrying the new guard for the Red Army war memorial tried to force a way through the crush. The crowd hurled stones and tried to overturn it, lashing out at east sector police who ran to the rescue. Bullets spattered round until British military police and Stumm officers drove the people off, shoved the Soviet jeep back into its own sector where other groups were stoning police vehicles, and called on the Russian soldiers to cease fire.

When order was finally restored twelve people were taken to hospital, ten of them with bullet wounds. A boy of sixteen, shot in the stomach, bled to death on the way. It had to be admitted that given the press of people and their pent-up rage the toll could have been much worse. Five Berliners arrested by Markgraf men during the riot were brought to trial with unusual speed. On 14 September a Russian military tribunal sitting in camera sentenced them each to twenty-five years' hard labour. There was such an outcry, not just from Berliners but internationally, that Kotikov actually ordered a re-examination of the sentences and they were ultimately cut on the grounds that the men's behaviour had been caused by "fascistic provocative" speeches in the Platz der Republik. The SMA gained no credit for its clemency, only blame for the initial severity and the cynicism with which it interfered with the legal system. The western authorities dreaded to think how many more would die, be wounded or receive swingeing sentences if there was a repetition of 9 September.

All the allies were revolted by the events in Berlin since late August. Once the Military Governors' talks ended and it was decided to make a new approach to the Kremlin, Marshall, but not Bedell Smith, wanted to deliver an aide-mémoire to Molotov stipulating that Sokolovsky must uphold law and order in Berlin. Bevin, though anguished by the plight of the city, believed that the Russians would welcome the distraction of security matters from the main issues of a general settlement. He saw it as a separate issue and one inappropriate for wrecking the negotiations.[122] He was, furthermore, deeply dissatisfied with the whole approach the Americans wanted to take in the resumed negotiations. Marshall was determined to "face squarely up to the fundamental question" of western rights; to tell Molotov that unless these were agreed and put into writing there was no use in further discussion and no basis for any settlement in the city.[123] For Bevin, this was empty legalism. The only point he could see in talking to the Kremlin (which he had never wanted to do in the first place) was to get the blockade lifted: a row about western rights of presence and access would delay or abort this, and would certainly not impress the international community as a valid reason for failing to settle all the other questions. Marshall did not think he was indulging in legal hairsplitting but calling for recognition of the basic issue on which all else depended. The argument between Washington and London grew heated. Each party accused the other of weakness. The French sided with Bevin. So too did Bedell Smith, who reckoned there could never be a watertight agreement on rights and that they must find a modus vivendi with the Russians after which wider issues could be gone into. He raised the question of what his government intended to do when they failed to get guarantees of their rights and the talks broke down: "I do not know what this decision is," he complained, "but it certainly would help my digestion if I knew that it had been taken."[124]

Underlying all the bad temper there was no dispute over essentials: all three western governments wanted the blockade up, their presence in Berlin secure and a working agreement with the Soviet Union which did not cost them their principles. The real problem, surely, was that everyone was very weary. Marshall pointed out to the American cabinet on 10 September that they had been handling a tense crisis for seventy-nine days – not for the first time he and his officials had ended a teleconference with Douglas in London at 2 a.m. that morning and had started it again at 8:30.[125] (No wonder Bevin noticed that day that Douglas looked "tired and ill."[126]) Bevin himself had collapsed from exhaustion during the Military Governors' talks and gone off for a week's holiday – which, to judge from the tetchiness of some of his comments on return, had not done him much good. Bedell Smith's ulcers seemed to be feeling the strain too. After a week of wrangling and a complaint by Bevin that the Americans were "trying to boss us" which he was ready to make public,[127] Washington reluctantly opted for allied unity rather than the unilateral approach to Moscow they had been considering.[128] It was agreed that the three western envoys would give Molotov an aide-mémoire which dealt only with the Berlin issues of finance, transport and trade, and ask for an interview with Stalin.

The new round of Moscow talks started as did the last with a touch of farce: this time it was Stalin who was said to be away, undergoing "treatment" which could not be interrupted. The negotiations then settled into unrelieved gloom. On 14 September Molotov dismissed the allied note as "one-sided," told Bedell Smith, Roberts and Chataigneau that Sokolovsky had conformed strictly with the directive, and demanded a joint report from all four Military Governors on the areas of disagreement – a process which, incomprehensibly for his visitors, he called time-saving.[129] When he handed the westerners a written reply on 18 September, it mentioned Soviet wishes for new arrangements for air traffic and restriction of the Financial Commission to the issue and circulation of currency, allowing no control over credit or trade. Molotov "seemed disconcerted" when no one made a comment, and he asked them "at least to let him know what impression the Soviet reply had made on them personally."[130] He might as well have said: "Say something, even if it's only goodbye."

For it was clear to everyone that this was the last meeting. No agreement to lift the blockade could be negotiated. No restoration of quadripartite government was feasible. No joint settlement of German problems was imaginable. The Americans would now press for the western case to go to the United Nations. But that was expected to be a lengthy and barren procedure too. The only practical western answer to the Berlin problem now seemed to be the airlift. On 18 September, the very day the Moscow talks collapsed, 6,988 tons were carried to Berlin.[131] Did that mean that the airlift had become a very good answer?

10

Miracles Take Time

It was all too easy to look at the tonnage figures for 18 September and assume that if 6,988 tons could be flown in on one day, then they could be flown in every day. It was so tempting to extrapolate from that particular result and calculate that, given the extra forty C-54s promised in September plus an increased British civil contribution and a couple of squadrons of capacious Hastings, the airlift could achieve 8,000, 9,000, even 10,000 tons a day. Such assumptions and calculations were, indeed, made. Marshall announced on 21 September that once the new C-54s went into action the airlift would be able to deliver 8,000 tons daily and was already carrying almost as much as had been brought to Berlin by road and rail before the blockade.[1] Bevin told the House of Commons that, on present progress, the city could be adequately supplied throughout the winter.[2] Both men gave a totally misleading impression. Perhaps they were whistling to keep up their own spirits and dampen those of the Russians, but it also seems likely that they had not understood the 18 September figures. For these recorded a special event, US Air Force Day, which the airmen had celebrated with a special effort – 144 British and a staggering 651 American sorties to Berlin.[3] Their record was worthy of the occasion. But, as was grimly noted, it had required "extraordinary measures which resulted in a falling off in figures for subsequent days"[4] – and not just a drop from 6,988 tons, but from the average.

Those average figures made profoundly depressing reading. In June when the British "Operation Plainfare" and American "Operation Vittles" were launched, the allies had lifted 1,404 tons to Berlin. For July, the first full month, the total was 69,000 tons (nearly 40,000 by the Americans and over 29,000 by the British), that is to say an average of 2,225.9 tons a day. Throughout August 119,002.6 tons were carried (73,658.1 American and 45,344.5 British). During September the figure rose to 139,622.3 (101,846.1 American and 37,776.2 British), giving a daily average of 4,641 tons. This was a figure no one would have dared hope for at the start of the operation. It was enough, certainly, to provide temporary subsistence for Berlin's western sectors. It was, however, short of the 5,500 tons the city would need in winter for basic food, light and warmth. And the figure was, of course, far below the 12,000 tons a day imported before the blockade to maintain the low economic existence and poor standard of comfort of the allied sectors.

The unpleasant truth was that by September the airlift was supplying barely 40 per cent of what had once been brought to Berlin by land and water. Clay was flattering it when he said in the middle of the month, "We are not quite holding our own."[5] Stocks in the city were actually falling; the airlift was not keeping up with summer needs and was not building up any reserves at all for the winter. Recent flying weather had been good, but winter seemed to be closing in early: it was the coldest September in Berlin for thirty years and there was already snow in the Harz mountains.[6] Inevitably fog would soon clamp the airfields, then snow and ice would close them. Expert assessments of the loss of lift to be expected in winter ranged from 30 per cent to 40 per cent.[7] Berliners were in a parlous state to withstand the rigours of winter on diminishing supplies: they were already some 8.5 lbs underweight, and nutritionists feared that on the present average ration of 1,600 calories a day they would soon be suffering from malnutrition.[8] They were living in leaky, draughty, bomb-damaged homes, yet the allies would be hardpushed to give them 3 cwt of coal for the worst months of the year. The chances were that Berliners would have to endure hunger, cold and fear in the pitch dark. Against such a giant supply problem even the record of 18 September looked a pygmy achievement.

The obvious way to raise the airlift's performance was to increase the number of flights. But aircraft and crews were already working flat out. They had to be reinforced. The British had more or less scraped their barrel of military transport; they could only call on civilian contractors. From 4 August the civil companies poured into

235

Wunstorf and Fassberg. Their names were redolent of the panoply of Walter Scott; their aircraft a ragbag of superannuated wartime machines bought at little over scrap prices and not always converted for haulage. Air Contractors, Air Transport (Jersey) Ltd, Westminster Airways, Kearsley Airways, Scottish Aviation, Trent Valley Aviation and Ciros Aviation contributed between them ten Dakotas. Aquila Airways brought two Hythe flying boats, Scottish Aviation added a Liberator, Silver City threw in two Wayfarers, Transworld Charter a couple of Vikings. Bond Air Services, Eagle Aviation and Skyflight jumbled the gallimaufry still further with Haltons – an adaptation of the RAF Halifax with a mind of its own. (A Polish instructor used to tell pilots who trained on it: "She is like ze cow, always trying to move sideways onto ze grass.")[9]

Mr. Edwin Whitfield, the British European Airways Area Manager for Germany, was given the formidable job of liaising between this motley assortment of companies and had only two days' notice of their arrival. His new bed of nails first pricked him with the realisation that civilians used different radio frequencies from the military. Whitfield had to borrow dispatch riders to rush all over the British zone on 4 August and muster enough crystals to convert the sets. His next jab was that civilian operators were licensed to carry only up to 6,000 lbs; the standard RAF cargo which determined bagging, crating, size of lorry load and number in a loading team was 7,480 lbs. Whitfield had to pester the Air Registration Board for nearly two weeks until the civilian aircraft were cleared for a higher payload. A long-term pain resulted from his charges coming with little or no navigational equipment: they were handicapped now and would be useless for winter operations. He immediately started to badger the RAF, the Ministry of Defence and the Air Ministry for Rebecca sets and instructors for them; the bureaucrats made no response.

The civil aircraft allocated to the coal and food lift were mainly Dakotas: small and uneconomical, with holds of various shapes which had to be stripped and standardised before the loaders could work in them effectively. The wetlift carriers, unlike Flight Refuelling who had been on the job since July, arrived without standard cocks and hose fittings; warehouses were scoured for them and skilled RAF craftsmen diverted to do the adaptations. This was the least of the problems created for the RAF by the civilians. Much worse was trying to integrate them into the airlift operation without having the authority to impose service disciplines. The civil contractors flew when they wanted and, as room had to be found for them in the military cycle, everyone else was thrown out of phase. They tended to fly where they wanted, too – yoyoing in the corridors to avoid cloud or turbulence and scaring the living daylights out of RAF pilots trying to keep to a steady altitude.[10]

The civilian kaleidoscope became yet more complex late in September with the introduction of more Dakotas by Horaton Airways and British Netherland Air Services, and two Tudors by British South American Airways. Glamour had been added by the arrival on 3 September of Air Vice-Marshal Don Bennett in the first of his own Airflight Company's Tudors. Bennett was a legendary character, loved or loathed but always admired even if reluctantly. In the 1930s he had been an airline pilot who had pioneered many Commonwealth routes and he had written a standard work on navigation which was still the primer for many of the airlift pilots. During the war he ferried American and Canadian warplanes to Britain, was shot down in an early attack on the *Tirpitz* but escaped through occupied Norway, and then formed and commanded the Pathfinder Force which led Bomber Command's mass raids on German cities. In 1945 Bennett became an executive with British South American Airways and the champion of Tudor airliners – a role which cost him his job when he launched a diatribe against the Minister of Civil Aviation for grounding them all after one mysteriously disappeared between the Azores and Bermuda. On his first airlift trip to Berlin in September his outer starboard engine caught fire, terrifying his Royal Army Service Corps passenger. "The wind will blow it out," said the Air Vice-Marshal, confidently – and it did. After unloading at Gatow Bennett, in defiance of all flying orders, flew his passenger round Berlin, pointing out the landmarks which he had left standing as markers for saturation bombing.[11] Bennett soon added another chapter to his legend. He took off one day before the locks had been removed from his flaps, which left him with nothing but the turning tabs which had to be operated with his right hand while he held the aircraft with his left. By sending the crew into the tail he gained some height, then painfully edged round in a wide circle before landing at horrific speed. Not many people would have come out of that scrape alive. As one highly skilled pilot was to explain: Bennett needed brilliant airmanship to get out of such a mess, but "bloody awful airmanship" to get into it in the first place.[12] He was always a navigator rather than a pilot; he would always push on regardless, never mind if the chocks were still on.

There was another civilian Bennett on the airlift – Captain Jack

Bennett of Pan Am, whose fleet of nine DC-4s had gradually come into commission since the evening of 23 June when he thought the USAF was pulling his leg by phoning and asking him to carry coal. He put in a regular 128 hours of flying a month in spite of Federal Aviation Administration rules limiting airline pilots to eighty-five, and he claimed to have flown more sorties than any man on the airlift.[13] No other civilian companies were used in the American operation, which saved the military many a headache. The USAF would have been spared even more had they been able to make full use of their enormous Globemaster, capable of carrying 17.7 tons. One did land at Gatow on 18 August with a load of 20 tons of flour, and the aircraft was occasionally pressed into service thereafter to carry exceptionally cumbersome cargo such as construction machinery. But there were too few of them to become a regular feature and only Gatow's runway could accommodate them – at a very tight squeeze. The Globemaster's main job was, therefore, the weekly delivery of supplies across the Atlantic from Westover Field, Massachusetts.

Deprived of bigger aircraft, the Americans made the best of their infinitely smaller C-47s and C-54s. The C-47 was weary, its servicing problems growing with age, its payload uneconomical. The ideal workhorse was the C-54: steady, reliable and able to carry nearly 10 tons. By the beginning of September, Clay had acquired nearly a hundred of them. Even so he did not have enough. On 10 September he begged for sixty-nine more to bring up the potential winter lift to 4,500 tons a day, which he warned "is the absolute minimum and provides no coal for space heating"; to keep Berliners warm he would need at least a further forty-seven. Some days later he was promised a mere fifty in all, less than half of what he really wanted.[14] Worse, Washington thought that even these were unlikely to arrive in Germany before early October.[15] Days and weeks of clear flying weather would be lost, there would be dangerous delays in building up Berlin's food reserves, and less and less chance that even minimal coal stocks could be created. Whatever the force of such arguments, the Joint Chiefs were, in fact, hesitant about sending any of the C-54s Clay had asked for: Marshall told Bevin that they wanted to allocate no more than 30 per cent of their military transport to this one theatre.[16] If Clay was to get enough C-54s political decisiveness, as on 22 July, must override military caution.

*   *   *

Shortage of aircraft might be the obvious impediment to the airlift up to September; but there were plenty of others. Supplying the western sectors would have been difficult enough, no matter how many aircraft had been available.

Feeding Berlin meant balancing a basic equation: quantity and quality of food against weight of cargo. The best way to provide calories was in the form of carbohydrate. Bread is a good source. Berliners preferred rye bread, but wheat was cheap and more plentiful in the west so that is what they had to eat. At first glance it seemed sensible to bake it in the zones and save lifting coal. A second look showed that bread contained at least 15 per cent of water (useless weight) and was relatively bulky but light (taking up undue space). The decision was taken to fly in flour and coal so that bread could be baked in the city – giving people the little luxury of fresh loaves. Yeast was needed too, of course, and in September a furious official discovered that it was being sent in fresh: three times heavier than dried.[17] Dehydrated yeast was substituted, though some consignments in October had low fermentation and gave "cloddy" bread into the bad bargain.[18] For several months it was assumed that Berlin bread was highly nutritious. Then it was realised that it was not being made of traditional German flour but Canadian wheat, which was lower in Vitamin C. Tablets would have to be flown in, which meant extra weight.[19]

Other forms of cereal gave variety, but trouble as well. Noodles and macaroni were light but bulky: they had to be matched with dense, heavy cargo to make full use of the holds. They were too often packed by manufacturers in paper bags: 40 per cent of them broke in September. Forty tons of wheat cereal were flown into Berlin in August, but not often thereafter – it was so much more expensive than flour. Sixty tons of oatmeal transported at the same time were not only over-priced but musty as well.[20] Nutritionists recommended biscuits instead of a certain amount of bread to give a little fat. They were bulkier than flour and arrived as crumbs.[21]

Potatoes are an excellent source of carbohydrate and loved by Berliners, but they were much too heavy to fly in fresh. Dehydration saved bulk and up to 40 per cent of weight. Unfortunately there are ways and ways of drying a potato. When 600 tons of American pre-cooked potato flour arrived in Berlin in August it was so unpalatable that the occupation authorities confessed, "We did not dare to issue it to the population."[22] Another American consignment of potato powder, 3,835 tons of it, was equally inedible (though small quantities were disguised by baking it in bread); 600

tons of French strip dried potato came with enormous lengths of skin and tasted disgusting. British "Pom," dried mash, was actually quite popular ("voted an excellent product," said a proud Foreign Office official – which is more than it would have been at home), but once 4,000 tons had been sent in August UK stocks were emptied. A further 340 tons were found in Army stores in Egypt but would take up to a month to deliver, as would orders put with British manufacturers. By 7 September the British and American Commandants were warning that reserves of dehydrated potato (DHP) were "dangerously" low, down to four days' supply. Hurried contracts were put out: with Hungary (showing interesting economic independence from the Soviet bloc), resulting in the ludicrous need to transport it across or round Berlin so that it could be flown in from the west; and in Holland, where the price was so high that only the desperate would pay it. In late September the US Army agreed to loan a million pounds of DHP from its stores, but on the hardnosed condition of repayment in spring with fresh potatoes.[23]

Meanwhile, something had to be found to fill Berliners' flapping stomachs. Dried pea soup was offered, but it took two hours to cook so used up plane-loads of coal. Forty-three tons of tomato soup powder turned out to be foul, very expensive and needing double the suggested quantities to make it seem anything more than coloured water. A soup of nameless pulses smelled stale and tasted soapy. The reasonable conclusion was drawn that "certain Germans in the Bizone are trying to make capital out of Berlin's difficulties by sending their otherwise unsaleable products to the city."[24]

These space-consuming culinary disasters would have been avoided if Berlin could have been supplied with German dried potato. But up to mid-September factories in the Bizone were only producing 50 tons a day (barely a quarter of what the western sectors required), and local DHP cost twice as much as the best imports – consumers could not afford it and the Magistrat did not have the funds to subsidise it.[25] Berlin, Bizone and occupation officials haggled with the manufacturers over price and tried to persuade them to pack in standard sacks – the variation between 35 lbs and 90 lbs maddened planners and loaders.[26] German DHP output went up a little once guarantees were given to buy all production, but by late October it was only meeting a half of Berlin's needs. Teams of experts were sent round to improve production methods; the Magistrat advanced the cost of ninety days' supply of fresh potatoes to encourage manufacturers to build up adequate stocks.[27] Just as output began to improve in November and reached

65 per cent of the requirement, men described as "people posing as Magistrat inspectors" told manufacturers that dehydrated vegetables should take priority over potatoes. They may, indeed, have been muddled officials, though there was some suspicion that vegetable wholesalers had been looking for quick sales.[28] (No one suggested they were Russian agents, but making a mess of the DHP orders would have been an effective way of sabotaging the Berlin food programme.) As if all this were not enough, a DHP factory in Brunswick then burned down.[29]

Just as man cannot live by bread alone, he cannot keep going for long on dried potato – it lacks vitamins. That is true of any dried vegetable, and given the weight and storage problems Berlin could not be supplied with fresh. So vitamin supplements had to be provided, which meant more room taken up on the airlift, more expense for consumers (until the Magistrat took it on in November and issued them free) and the need for an intensive publicity campaign to persuade people to swallow tablets and cod-liver oil.[30] Berlin itself could grow some fresh vegetables, in gardens and courtyards and in the city's numerous market-gardens and allotments. But was precious airlift space better used for dried vegetables and vitamin pills than for seeds, fertilisers and insecticides? The Americans and French certainly thought so and claimed that dehydrated vegetables took only 75 per cent of the aircraft space needed for fertilisers. The British, who believed they had beaten Hitler by digging up their rose beds for cabbages, argued that fresh produce would do wonders for health and morale and that there was no point in trying to grow crops on the light local soil without fertilisation. General Herbert ordered a survey of all land available to British military government for vegetable growing and his staff set about Digging for Victory.[31]

Manure, of course, grows much better vegetables than chemical fertilisers. There were 3,250 cows in the western sectors. Their milk yield was a paltry five litres each a day and could not be raised unless 200 tons of fodder were flown in daily. Their manure production, however, was more impressive, and it justified not slaughtering them, though did not assuage the ache for fresh meat after months of tinned. The manure argument was less convincing as an excuse to preserve allied horses in Berlin. All three western Powers kept them for sport and exercise; the British alone had eighty-one, only thirty of which worked on farms. The horses at least made use of those horrible oats unfit for human consumption and gave their owners the occasional altruistic glow by dying and providing meat for police dogs and guide dogs for the blind. But they encouraged the allies to torture logic over whether they should be given sawdust as bedding which might otherwise go into briquettes for heating. In the end, their lives were probably saved because horse meat was judged to be totally unacceptable to even the hungriest Berliner and a propaganda gift to the Russians.[32] By October the British could cut enough Havel grass for 40 tons of fodder for the winter – a source which they had the nerve to tell Berlin Zoo was "unsuitable" for its animals because of the "scouring properties." (Had the British been less keen on their own horses, they might have preached the need to increase the output of elephant droppings.) The Zoo was frantic for supplies. Before the blockade it consumed every month 8,000 lbs of hay and 6,000 lbs of meat. By August it could only feed its lions and bears on alternate days.[33] In November the Zoo was promised cereals, meat, 66 kgs of carrots and 74 kgs of other vegetables, though no one knew where to find the tons of sunflower seeds which were required. An official commented tartly on the amount of Zoo land "constantly used for flowers" which should be turned over to food production[34] – he should have used his time in recommending sunflower production.

No one recommended Berliners to follow the example of besieged Parisians in 1871 and eat ostrich steaks or giraffe stew; the blockade was endured on more conventional fare. But for months on end the meat was all tinned: space and weight saving, easy to load and durable without cold storage. There was not always enough of it: a third or more of the "meat" ration often came in the form of dried egg, which was at least a source of vitamin A and had a high calorific value for its bulk and weight. Some of what posed as meat was revolting: tinned blood sausage in September was so unpleasant that customers had to be bribed to take it by being given double what the ration coupon permitted; a liver sausage was not only repellent, but came in underweight tins.[35] A much better use of cargo space would have been fats, giving 800 calories for every 100 grammes flown, but they were in short supply in the west. At least Berliners did not feel deprived of cheese by the blockade: they had had none in their ration since the war.

While the authorities battled to feed Berlin they had to ask themselves how much of their limited airlift capacity should be given over to coal. By late autumn it was estimated that whereas Berliners needed nearly 1,500 tons of food a day, public services had to have 2,534 tons of coal at the very least to meet minimal needs. Once the cold weather set in, a further 550 tons of fuel would have to be carried if there was to be any domestic heating. In theory, there was a choice between eating while freezing in the dark or starving with a bit of warmth and light. In practice, there might be no choice: neither food nor fuel would be available.[36]

The coal lift so far had been bedevilled by every kind of hitch. Shortage of aircraft was the most intractable problem and would never be overcome unless C-47s and Dakotas were replaced with bigger load carriers. But in the earliest days of the airlift there was almost space to spare: the coal simply did not arrive at the dispatch airfields[37] – production and transport had not been organised and co-ordinated. Once coal was available new difficulties had to be faced: German Railways might deliver three trainloads one day but none the next; it came unlabelled and no one knew if it was the grade for power stations or domestic use; the Wunstorf spur was only a single track so one train had to shunt back before another could come through; as Fassberg opened up, its lines were choked with engineering equipment and stores; aircraft and crews moved to new bases but their coal lagged behind. Until the middle of August coal supplies were held up by the slowness of bagging: only 1,330 tons could be put in sacks each day at Hannover and Hildesheim and most of the Ruhr had not begun packing at all. Bags from Duisburg came in all sizes and weights despite the fact that the firm concerned was repeatedly instructed to use the standard 50 lbs sack, and the consignments had to be left in a hangar until there was time and manpower to repack them. One firm in Hildesheim supplied underweight sacks so habitually and found so many excuses not to work at weekends that it was suspected of "having communistic tendencies" and its contract was cancelled.[38] In the long periods of bad weather in July and August the limited flying time had to be given over to food, and coal was left standing in the open or under skimpy tarpaulins until it was wet and heavy. It took time to work out that a 50 lbs sack could put on 7 lbs in a rainstorm, and until then many honest bagging firms had been accused of short weight.[39]

All these mishaps were as nothing compared with the interminable Coal Sack Crisis. Sacks were supposed to be emptied in Berlin, bundled up and sent back to the zones for refilling. By 29 July 112,000 supplied by German wholesalers had gone to Berlin; only 60,000 had come back. Of the 47,000 British Army kitbags sent, a mere 8,000 had returned.[40] Loaders at Fassberg began with 160,000 sacks; by late August they were rustling up potato and flour bags, rummaging in Wehrmacht stores for rucksacks and in warehouses for mattress ticking, and experimenting with plywood

243

containers and old aluminium fuel tanks. By late October the British had supplied 1,300,000 coal sacks at a cost of £125,000, had run out of reserves at home and could not track down further jute supplies. By December the Americans had contributed a million – a high proportion of which had also disappeared as if into a coal black hole.

Coal sacks were not just scarce and expensive, they were fragile. Even dry coal soon wrecked them and wet coal (including that intentionally washed for power stations) rotted them within three trips – since each sack cost 2 shillings, an extra 8 pence was added to every 50 lbs load. American duffle bags were much more durable: they cost $1.60 but could do forty round trips before disintegrating. They were heavy, though, and even a normal jute sack weighed 2 lbs. To save weight three-ply paper bags were tried in October: they were very light but hopelessly flimsy.[41]

By October most of the organisational difficulties in the coal lift had been ironed out – but just in time for delivery targets to be hit by the first fog and the grim news that ice had formed on the Rhine near Wiesbaden. How could Berlin conceivably be kept warm in winter, or given even a few hours of electric light? The airlift had barely kept up with summer demand for fuel; it had proved incapable of building up winter stocks. During the bitter cold of 1946–7 Berliners had been rationed to 4 cwt of brown coal and 3.5 cwt of wood; several hundred people had frozen to death. Next year the coal ration had risen to 5 cwt and Berliners shivered though the weather was unusually mild. For the winter of 1948–9 Hamburg (warmer than Berlin) was promised 17.5 cwt of fuel per household. Southern Britain (very much warmer) would get 34 cwt. The most optimistic British estimate suggested that the western sectors could only be supplied with a mere tenth of that – 3 cwt a family – and the Americans feared that no domestic fuel could be provided at all.[42] And coal supply was not just a matter of health and comfort. It had political consequences too: it could sustain morale which was already vulnerable to the lure of superior Russian rations and would limit the fear which was bound to grow in the dark.

People could, of course, burn wood. It was rationed, though scavenging for fallen branches and twigs might help to kindle a few brief fires. On 7 October the occupation authorities recommended the Magistrat to cut 200,000 cubic metres of wood from the city's forests and another 150,000 from the streets, parks and gardens. According to British forestry experts this proposal would reduce Berlin's woodland by two-thirds and the rest of its timber by a half.

Magistrat officials were appalled and the population outraged. Berliners had always loved their trees, been agonised to see so many destroyed during the war and in the battle for survival which followed; the trees which remained were particularly cherished. Everyone preferred to freeze rather than fell. The Magistrat beat down the target: they would agree to cut 125,000 cubic metres of timber but no more.[43] The western allies accepted the decision: it was not worth arguing when they well knew that even if every tree and shrub were chopped down, the heat provided would be little enough and no electricity or gas could be made. Coal was the irreplaceable commodity. And unless the airlift got more planes Berlin would get no coal. As Washington delayed sending the extra C-54s, weeks of flying weather were wasted and the coal depots stayed empty.

Then, as hopes of Berlin surviving the winter tottered, the situation was transformed more or less overnight. On 14 October the National Security Council advised President Truman that sixty-six more C-54s should be sent to Germany.[44] Clay went to Washington a few days later and told the Council how vital they would be, that the airlift was no longer an experiment, that even bad weather would not prevent the supply of Berlin as long as there were enough aircraft. Truman authorised the increase of C-54s on 22 October,[45] and as a first step two naval squadrons, twenty-four aircraft in all, were ordered to prepare to leave. Clay, on his return to Germany, triumphantly announced: "The airlift will be continued until the blockade is lifted"; winter supply was guaranteed.[46] Even a less euphoric RAF report estimated that the extra C-54s would boost the lift from the previously expected 3,000 tons a day to something nearer 5,000. That was dangerously little, in all conscience, and the report warned: "At least until January the airlift will be unable to fulfil the hopes placed in it."[47] But at least it was now possible to have hopes. There had been very few recently.

In the early days of the blockade there would have been little point in throwing more aircraft into the sky: the organisation could not make effective use of them. By fortunate coincidence, the airlift was ready in October to exploit its new capacity properly. It had evolved from an improvised expedient running on luck and nervous energy into a sophisticated transport operation for unprecedented volume and complexity of traffic over a limitless period.

Sheer experience over three months had, of course, polished flying and navigation skills. Practice had made air-traffic control more efficient and given everyone greater confidence in bad weather flying. The number of controllers had increased, cutting the strain of the work and the risk of mistakes from tiredness, and their burdens had been eased in mid-September by the loan of eighteen experienced men from the American Civil Aeronautics Administration. Everyone engaged in the airlift now had regular shifts and periods of leave in requisitioned hotels for proper rest and real nights' sleep from time to time. New crews from Britain were better briefed than their predecessors who had had to learn on the job. In October the USAF opened a school in Great Falls, Montana, to teach up to 100 crews a month instrument flying along a "Little Corridor." There was even a trained team of RAF falcons at Gatow to keep the local bird population in order.

A much greater hazard to the airlift than the feathered kind had been eradicated, thanks to a frightening experience on, of all days, Friday 13 August. During those twenty-four hours Berlin had its worst storms for thirty years; there were sheets of rain and cloud down to 200 feet, and in eight hours of daylight only eight aircraft managed to land at Gatow.[48] General Tunner had left Wiesbaden that morning in reasonable weather, but he flew to Berlin in conditions of which he remembered Bob Hope once saying, "Soup I can take but this stuff's got noodles in it." He reached Tempelhof in a cloudburst. Radar had been washed out. One C-54 had tried to land, overshot the runway and caught fire in a ditch (the crew had mercifully escaped); another had braked hard to avoid the blaze, blown out its tyres and blocked more of the runway; a third could not find any runway at all in the murk and had touched down on a construction site for a new one. While everyone struggled to sort out the mess on the ground, air-traffic control stacked incoming aircraft from 3,000 to 12,000 feet. The air was packed with machines milling about in dense cloud, and radio traffic was jammed with pilots trying to find out what on earth (in both senses) was going on. No one dared take off into the chaos. Tunner exploded: "This is no way to run a railroad." He grabbed the radio: "This is Tunner talking and you listen. Send every plane in the stack back to its home base." There was silence from the tower, then an aghast "Please repeat." Tunner repeated, in no uncertain terms. Everyone else was sent home, Tunner landed and told his two co-pilots: "Stay in Berlin until you've figured out a way to eliminate any possibility of this mess ever happening again – ever."[49]

One thing was immediately apparent: stacking had to be abolished. From now on, if the weather closed unexpectedly and ground control could not cope, aircraft had to turn round and take their cargoes back. Furthermore, any aircraft having trouble over Tempelhof or Gatow was asked to go and have it somewhere else: there was no time for complicated landings or room for pranged machines. Overshooting then circling round to have another go at landing was prohibited too: airspace could not be wasted on second attempts. As traffic built up in the zones, landing disciplines were tightened there as well. Tunner issued a threat: "I would reduce to co-pilot status any pilot who failed to land with ceiling and visibility greater than 400 feet and a mile"; and if conditions were worse, "I would court martial any pilot who did land." Fortunately, he never had to do either: "I never had any intention of doing so in the first place."[50] In bad weather aircraft were shunted to the nearest runway with clear sky; on occasion USAF pilots were diverted as far as Marseilles. The RAF sanction to get pilots to land first time was to make them fill in a form if they overshot. It was a detested chore. One Canadian coming into Wunstorf too close to the man in front was inspired to begin his descent with his wheels up so as to switch on the warning horn in the cockpit. He then took off his headset, held it to the horn, pressed his transmit button and gave the pilot ahead the full blast. The poor startled fellow assumed it was his own, opened throttles and went round while the exultant Canadian landed in his place.[51]

It was not enough to keep the airspace tidy at either end of the lift. The whole pattern of dispatch, flight, landing and turn round had to be regular and clear. After the dreadful Friday the 13th Tunner incarcerated his two co-pilots in one room, gave them a navigator and artist, and told them to stay put until they had devised a proper traffic system. They looped cat's cradles of string from the ceiling, dangled model planes from them on coat hangers and played until they and their toys were practically worn out, but they found a tight and rhythmic system. Within it each airlift station was allocated a block of time for its aircraft to be over the Frohnau beacon at the end of the corridors: six blocks a day for each dispatching airfield into which as many flights as possible could be crammed. Each pilot had to arrive at Frohnau with a thirty-second margin of accuracy. There was a safety gap of six minutes between the last aircraft of one block and the first of the next, and a separation of three minutes between the planes in each wave when flying by VFR (Visible Flight Rules) and five minutes under IFR (Instrument Flying Rules). One-way traffic was introduced. Aircraft from the British zone flew into Berlin by the northern corridor, those from the American zone by the southern, then both sets went home along the central corridor. Aircraft from each base were given their own operating heights and maintained vertical separation of 500 feet in the northern and central corridors and 1,000 in the Southern.

The system was easily introduced and soon settled to a steady routine. It offered some degree of flexibility. When it started there were not enough aircraft to fill each block, but the blocks had been determined for the happy day when more were available. If one airfield was closed by bad weather, its block could be assigned to another. Within each wave priority could be given to the biggest load carriers or the first aircraft with cargo on board. The pattern did create alternate periods of idleness and rush, and if aircraft were not ready on the dot they missed four hours of flying. The RAF never really liked the system: it was designed for the natural cycle of the C-54 and did not suit the non-standard loads the British often carried or accommodate the different cruising speeds of British aircraft and the various lengths of journey from British bases. The RAF had to lump it: it was clearly the best way to get the best use out of the best load carrier, and it simplified the integration of USAF aircraft into northern airfields. In time the block system was adjusted. A two-hour block was introduced for British airfields in January, which smoothed out the periods of tedium and scurry and allowed planes unprepared for one block to take off sooner. The following April Fassberg, Wunstorf and Celle tried hourly dispatch – all three sent a wave in succession within the sixty minutes.

No method was without drawbacks; all of them were a distinct improvement on "grab and go." Thanks to their navigational equipment the British could get to Frohnau with the necessary split-second timing; American problems were eased by installing more beacons for their radio compasses. Within the general framework, smooth running and safety were improved by tougher flying discipline. The RAF's Examining Unit flew up and down the route making sure British pilots stuck to their course and altitude. The Americans set up a Standardisation Board with their best-qualified pilots to publish recommendations on techniques, and check pilots supervised crews at least once every thirty days and kept them up to scratch.[52]

For all the precision of the air-traffic pattern and the care with which it was maintained, accidents happened. Some of them were fatal. After the two American crashes in July there was a third on 24 August, when two C-47s collided in mid-air over their zone and four men were killed. The first RAF disaster came on the night of 19 September, when a York crashed at Wunstorf after engine failure and all five crew members died. In October a C-54, three minutes from Rhein Main, hit a tree in low cloud and rain and burst into flames killing three aircrew. Next month an RAF Dakota crashed on approach to Lübeck in bad weather. A survivor was rushed to the nearest hospital, which was in the Russian zone, but died some days later; one of those already dead was reported to have been an army sergeant hitching a lift to see his wife who was expecting a baby. To an outsider these tragedies may seem inevitable, given the volume of traffic and the unavoidable dangers of engine failure and weather. Indeed, it would be easy for a civilian to argue that flying in the airlift was a relatively safe occupation: in the week of October when the three men were killed in their C-54, nine other USAF personnel had died in Germany, six of them in car crashes.[53] From a professional's point of view, however, any accident, fatal or not, is intolerable; each crash drove everyone to find ways to prevent another. For other airmen the deaths of crews were heart-rending. They were distressed at the time and forty years later still remembered every name and characteristic of the dead, every detail of the wrecked aircraft, its load and the circumstances in which it perished. The respect and unfading memory of their comrades made fine memorials for those who died.

Whatever the allies did to improve flying safety, the Russians did something else to threaten it. In September their air force staged mock battles over Berlin and held three and a half hours of anti-aircraft practice in the northern corridor, announcing the exercise an hour after it started. At the same time they demanded that the Air Safety Centre be given an hour's notice of each allied flight, with exact detail of the route, altitude and radio frequency, the type, number and load of the aircraft, and the pilot's name.[54] The airlift authorities were already supplying information on time, type and altitude and had no intention of giving more, not least because they themselves often did not have further details until aircraft were ready to take off. Russian anti-aircraft firing went on through October, one day so heavily that all the windows at Gatow were rattled by the shelling. There were mock attacks on allied planes, large scale manoeuvres and aerial target practices in the corridors.[55] Western protests were met by Soviet accusations of "mass violations" of air-safety rules and the claim that the air agreements were no longer valid thanks to western infringements.[56] In the meantime, though many allied pilots never ran into any trouble, a few came to regard buzzing, towed drogues and exploding shells as all in a day's work.

Air Vice-Marshal Bennett, indeed, was pleased to be swooped on by a Russian fighter and thought: "Mine was probably the first Tudor the Russian pilot had ever seen; he came closer for a better look."[57] Bennett no doubt believed that the Russian would be deeply impressed by what he saw. Tudor fliers were a proud and missionary race. One of them was so anxious to convince others of the matchless quality of his machine that on return to Wunstorf he would pick on a C-54 about to turn out of the central corridor towards his base, put on all power, dive until he was level with the C-54, then feather both the engines the American could see and roar past with a cheerful smile and insouciant wave.[58]

To supervise the new traffic flow, co-ordinate the increasing number and variety of aircraft and maximise their deployment, there had to be an overall system of command. This was a necessity which the Americans understood from an early stage, but to which the British turned a blind eye for as long as they could – the RAF would inevitably have to cede authority to the USAF which was providing the overwhelming proportion of aircraft. At first there was ad hoc liaison between the two forces. In August a joint CALTF (Combined Airlift Task Force) headquarters was set up under Tunner with Air-Commodore J. W. F. Merer as his British deputy. Within its loose structure there was at least agreement to implement the new block system of dispatch and the other modifications to flying discipline. For the rest, the two national component parts muddled along fairly independently.

Each had its own command problems. The British airmen steered between the Scylla of Transport Command (a two-headed hazard since the Yorks belonged to 47 Group and the Dakotas to 46 Group) and the Charybdis of BAFO which had its own, often opposed, instructions. At the same time they had to dodge obstructions thrown up by Wunstorf, which as a fighter station had its own separate flying orders. For the entire duration of the airlift Transport Command fought a rearguard action against dis-establishment faced with the expanding authority of Air Officer Commanding-in-Chief and BAFO.[59]

Power struggles within the USAF were just as intense. General Curtis LeMay as Commander of the US Air Forces in Europe had been prepared to tolerate the independence of Tunner's specialised airlift team and his introduction of hand-picked cronies to run it.

When LeMay went to take over Strategic Air Command in the autumn, his successor, Lieutenant-General John H. Cannon, was not so tolerant and he immediately clashed with Tunner. Cannon, in the words of General Ross Milton who was Tunner's Chief of Staff, had a "love of detail, even trivia, and a desire to know everything that was going on"; Tunner had "a proprietary attitude toward the airlift" and having built up his own empire intended to keep running it. Conflict between two such forceful men was unavoidable: Cannon was supposed to be in charge, but his subordinate had grown used to freedom of action; Cannon was a former instructor at Kelly Field, Tunner his quondam pupil; Cannon was a combat officer and Tunner a transport expert. The heat between them only lessened when they could keep out of each other's way.[60]

Some of this command confusion was bypassed in October when the Americans at last got their sensible way and a fully Combined Air Lift HQ was formed with Tunner in charge. It began with a purely American staff – Merer paid only formal visits once a month because he could not be spared from 46 Group, and weeks went by before any other RAF officer was appointed because the RAF had such a manpower shortage. Combined HQ never had more than five British representatives, but Group-Captain Noel Hyde as chief planner became a permanent and welcome fixture, putting up with a great deal of affectionate teasing and giving as good as he got. CALTF HQ, like so many other features of the airlift, succeeded because of goodwill and common sense not because its institutions were perfect.

The official document which established it on 15 October contained a significant phrase: CALTF was ordered to "effect delivery to Berlin in a safe and efficient manner of the maximum tonnage possible." Up until then there had been a fixed, if unattainable, target of 4,500 tons a day. Now there was no limit to ambition even if there were still constraints on performance. In this, as in other areas, October was a major turning-point in the airlift.

The airlift had begun in June 1948 with three supplying airfields: Rhein Main and Wiesbaden in the American zone, and Wunstorf in the British. By the end of the year there were nine. The six new bases were all in the British zone to cut the length of the journey to Berlin. In the intervening months the burden of carrying cargo had increasingly been taken by the USAF, who had the greater number and size of aircraft: in October the RAF and civil lift handled 31,788.6 tons compared with 115,792.2 transported by the Americans. A major British contribution was now in the form of construction, expansion and maintenance of airfields for the combined allied operation.

Finkenwerde, the first new base to open, was also the first to close -- on 15 December. A total of fifteen RAF Sunderland flying boats had been stationed there and they had been joined by three others from Aquila Airways. Jolly though flying boats seemed to Berliners, they had not always been such fun to operate. The Elbe remained clogged below water level with wrecks and on the surface with floating debris; there were no adequate charts to show obstructions or shallows. The RAF had done its best to mark permanent hazards with buoys, but it was still too dangerous to fly at night; during the day a Sunderland was at constant risk of hitting an obstacle and losing a float on take-off (at which the crew had to sit on a wing to stop the craft overturning), or it was in danger of damage to its thin skin by tenders in choppy water. On shore men led damp but surprisingly cheerful lives wading through thick mud from the tents where they lived to the tents or huts where they worked. Finkenwerde's total lift of 6,205 tons does not look impressive but it was mainly of salt, which was essential to Berlin and could not be flown in conventional holds. By November, however, there were Halifaxes available with panniers slung in their bomb bays to cope with corrosive loads, the Sunderlands' crews were exhausted, and ice was threatening to stop landings on the Havel.[61] It was with some relief that the flying-boat operation was finally brought to an end.

Fassberg, which opened on 19 July, was a miracle of speedy adaptation from an old German airfield to a major airlift station. In fourteen days RAF construction units, Royal Engineers and German Railways put down 5,000 tons of PSP for a 2,000-yard runway and marshalling areas, laid five and a half miles of railway, provided power lines and approach roads, and built accommodation for personnel who soon numbered 8,000 including 4,000 German labourers. The station was designed for combined RAF and USAF operations before anyone had worked out how to combine them – that came through painful experience. The Americans arrived during July and August and hated the place on sight. It was isolated, the spartan RAF living conditions shocked transatlantic cousins (the rock-hard hospital beds were a source of constant aches and moans), officers were squashed into a mess intended for only a hundred, NCOs into another for forty, and other ranks were scattered in hangars or an old school. The Americans were expected to live on British rations, which they did not think adequate for a mouse, and on British cooking, which seemed to consist of nothing but overcooked beef and eternally boiled sprouts. They were told they could not drink or gamble in their own quarters because of RAF rules, that the NAAFI would not provide them whisky because it was bonded and only legally saleable to British personnel (and merely half a bottle a month at that), and they had to sit in cinema seats the ushers thought suitable to their rank. The Americans decided that Fassberg was the hell you were sent to as punishment for sins committed in Wiesbaden or Rhein Main.

Gradually it improved to a kind of purgatory. US-issue bunks replaced the hospital beds; whisky was found from American sources and ladled out in three bottles a month (though the NAAFI fastidiously put dollars into a separate till and grumbled that they ought not to accept them); the PX opened and goodies from home compensated a little for mess cooking. Initial rows over who was in charge were resolved: three American commanders left in quick succession (the last of them had only communicated with the RAF's Wing-Commander Biggar by letter until both men announced that one or the other of them must go). Finally Colonel John Coulter took over. He established reasonable allied working relations, persuaded the British to give him virtual control of the station, and raised dangerously low morale by reorganising his men into squadrons with clear responsibilities and plenty of team spirit. Perhaps his greatest gift to Fassberg was his wife: Constance Bennett was a famous film star, who cheered everyone with her glamour and high spirits and kept RAF wives gossiping happily for days by using the service issue earthenware slop basin as a suddenly chic salad bowl. She attracted old Hollywood friends to come and entertain the troops, and won tribute from General Milton as "one of the most formidable scroungers in any service" – getting new furniture, better food and the latest films. Under the Coulters, as Milton explained, "Fassberg, very nearly a Berlin airlift disaster, became a showpiece" – never quite heaven, but efficient and successful.[62]

To make room at Fassberg for the C-54s, RAF Dakotas moved out in August to a new base at Lübeck. This was a pre-war Luftwaffe station with living and working areas on a hill set with firs and oaks and jumping with red squirrels. It had been occupied since 1945 by RAF fighter squadrons and already had adequate hard-standing and PSP runways. A new parking apron and rail spur were added and extra hutting put up to supplement the usual excellent Luftwaffe buildings. Twenty more RAF Dakotas arrived in September; civil Dakotas left in October and were replaced by ten Australian, three New Zealand and eleven South African aircraft and crews.[63] The British had dithered about the legality of engaging Commonwealth contingents. The agreement on the use of the air corridors spoke of "aircraft of the nations governing Germany." This was taken to prohibit acceptance of a Dutch offer of help, but encouraged a great deal of point-stretching over whether Commonwealth aircraft could be put on "British charter," deemed to be "under the British commander-in-chief" or answerable to "the Chief of the Imperial General Staff," or lumped together as "forces of the Crown." Foreign Office lawyers at last convinced themselves that they could act within the letter of the law and did not enquire if the Russians thought they were observing its spirit. The first South Africans arrived in the UK in late September for training in the mysteries of the Rebecca-Eureka system and flying in European weather.[64] Lübeck improved the accuracy of everyone's navigation because it was only two miles from the border of the Soviet zone.

Fuhlsbüttel began operations on 5 October with an assortment of civil aircraft previously based at Lübeck. Schleswigland opened a week later for more of them and for RAF Hastings – brand new shiny aircraft to be immediately battered and besmirched with loads of coal. The Hastings was the first big British carrier – able to take 8 tons – and had a hold which could take girders for Berlin West power station, though each might take three hours to load. It had, however, a design problem: the cargo door was built to meet an Army requirement for height to match the tail gate of a 15-cwt lorry. This had meant fitting her with a tail wheel – a brute which needed great muscle power to control and which bounced the aircraft back into the air if a landing was misjudged. The tail wheel together with a wide side area made the Hastings tricky to handle in even slight crosswinds and impossible to take off or land in anything more than 15-knot gusts. One blowy day when Attlee tried to pay a ceremonial visit to Berlin, he had to transfer from a Hastings to an American aircraft and travel on a load of coal, bewilderedly asking why the British plane did not have a nose wheel. The Army could have told him. The first Hastings to land at Gatow was met by a reception party of military brass and German dignitaries, but its door jammed and the crew took their photocalls with stuck smiles from the cockpit. Thereafter, the untried aircraft proved highly serviceable and showed none of the expected teething troubles. Its crews, who had been hurriedly converted from Halifaxes, came to terms with its peculiarities and soon got used to living in Schleswigland's prefabs. Ground crews, on the other hand, had a miserable time because the existing hangar on the base was 20 feet too low to take a Hastings: they had to work outdoors in rain and cold until a new hangar was borrowed for them from Sylt. Meanwhile, the civil contractors benefited from the old one and from four new 11,000-gallon tanks for the wet lift.[65]

All the lessons learned from the extension and use of these new airfields were put into effect when the last of them was built at Celle on the site of an old Junker base. Construction began in October and, since the ground was unstable and the old PSP runway decrepit, it involved clearing 60,000 tons of earth and laying an 1,800-yard runway on ballast stone delivered along a railway which was extended as the runway grew; 115,482 sheets of PSP provided the surface and covered taxi track and hard-standing. Buildings were expanded into quarters for 2,610 and were constantly stretched as personnel increased; Nissen huts and tents were put up for German labourers. By the start of December the base was ready for the advance party of its mixed Anglo-American personnel. Celle was a model for supply operations: good access roads, production-line layout and methods.[66]

Each new station was provided from the beginning with the best lighting possible; old airfields had to undergo radical alteration. Poor light in the early stages of the airlift had made night work impossible and better visibility was essential if all twenty-four hours were to be used for flying as the long nights drew in. It was a help simply to mark clean white lines down tracks and taxi lines. It was not possible, however, to scatter the usual 30-foot poles with floods on top over a marshalling area or loading bay because they got in the way; lights had to be carefully positioned for safety and convenience. At Wunstorf there were experiments with artificial moonlight: three searchlights were coned to form an apex and diffuse light downwards, but the result was too soft for accurate work; even the two 60-foot towers put up at Celle with clusters of twelve wide-beam 500-watt lamps were still not bright enough for loading. On runways flare paths were replaced by Centre Bar fittings. But when American Horizontal Bar approach lights were first introduced at Gatow and Wunstorf they were too good: pilots could not adjust from their dazzle to the comparative gloom of the runway. The sodium lamps of the approach system were finally replaced with dimmer filament lamps. The installation of Horizontal Bar lighting at Tempelhof meant asking for municipal permission to set posts in the nearby cemetery. This was willingly given, but the Russian-controlled press took great delight in making accusations of desecration of graves.

While new airfields were built old ones had to be repaired: terrible damage had been inflicted by the incessant landings of laden aircraft on runways meant for traffic light in every sense. The runways at Tempelhof and Gatow began to crack up in August thanks to heavy loads and heavy rain; repairs were carried out in patches and slotted in between blocks of arrivals so that most of the track could be kept in use. The surface at Tempelhof was strengthened and waterproofed with coarse sand, grit, hot tar and asphalt. Construction machinery was hacked into transportable chunks in the zone and welded together on site. A new parallel runway was planned. At Gatow (now the busiest airfield in the world, handling three times the traffic of La Guardia, the old record holder), extra hard-standing and administrative offices were built in August. To make sure the runway would be serviceable in winter, aircraft were diverted on to the extended PSP track while it was reconstructed with Berlin brick rubble and ballast from railways which had helpfully been torn up by the Russians. A surface was made from old tarmacadam ripped from local streets and boiled up with 5 per cent of flown-in tar and bitumen to give it body. Legend has it that the work was greatly helped when a man trundled over from the Soviet sector with his steamroller and that the occasional barrel of tar toppled across in the night.[67]

Gatow had a heart-stopping reminder of how precarious its existence was when its electricity supply was suddenly threatened. Startlingly, the airfield's electricity came from a power station in the Russian sector. Providentially, there had been intermittent faults in the supply (which is hardly surprising if one considers the over-loading) and the cables had been modified to allow the system to be switched to a western source if need be. At 2 a.m. on 2 October the chief load distributor at the Soviet-controlled power station telephoned to say that supply would be discontinued, probably "permanently." Four minutes later, all the electricity went off; ten minutes after that a rather flickery current arrived from the western sector by cables known to be incapable of sustaining the load for long. Gatow officials had one trick up their sleeve: they pointed out to the SMA that British-controlled power stations supplied the Russian airfield at Staaken as well as the Radio Berlin building and some of its transmitters. By noon the regular Gatow supply had resumed.[68] The Russians never pulled out the Gatow plugs again.

With the expansion of dispatch from the zones and the vast increase in traffic, Gatow and Tempelhof could not continue to function adequately unless some of the congestion in Berlin were eased. Thanks to the go-ahead given to Clay in Washington on 21 July a completely new airfield was laid out at Tegel in the French sector and construction work began in August. The site was difficult and had originally been thought suitable only for a parachute dropping zone. At its core was an old parade-ground, which had to be opened up for a 5,500-foot runway, 120,000 square feet of aprons and 6,020 feet of taxiway by removing four huge sandhills weighing several million tons. Four bulldozers had to be flown in; a swarm of 19,000 labourers spread a 22-inch layer of rubble, crushed rock and asphalt. The French provided the land and a bit of finance. (They had been unable to contribute aircraft – indeed, there is a rumour that a British pilot paid a lorry driver to back into their one garrison supply plane because it was such a nuisance.) The Americans gave more of the money, all of the construction expertise and eventually took over flying operations. The British were responsible for unloading and emergency servicing, which meant that in November they sent small teams to live at Tegel in tents, sleeping on the hard cold ground and making endless cups of tea on an old coke stove. The new airfield was just about ready to receive its first ceremonial flight on 6 November and a C-54 delivered a celebratory load of cheese with the biggest of all cheeses, Generals Cannon and Tunner. It became fully operational on 18 November when the first Dakota brought in coal and took out twenty-six undernourished children.[69] Tegel had one outstanding, all-too-upstanding drawback: two transmitter masts belonging to Radio Berlin, one over 390 feet tall and the other more than 260 feet high, which endangered the approach. The French Commandant, General Ganeval, politely asked the Radio's director and the SMA to remove them, but they took no notice. They lived to regret it.

New airfields, sophisticated traffic control and all the aircraft in the world would have been wasted if they had been unable to respond to the complex needs of the two-and-a-half million people in the western sectors of Berlin. The airlift had to cater for a variety of everyday needs but also fit in one-off essentials; change cargoes when demand altered; compensate for shortages and foresee future requirements. All this involved alert assessment, intricate planning and continual sensitive adjustment.

The balance of basic supplies was easily upset. By November, for instance, there was such anxiety about providing winter fuel for the city that the airlift authorities conscientiously piled in coal until there was a panic in the city because food stocks had dropped alarmingly.[70] Even when the exact requirement for a particular commodity was known it could not always be met: for a week in October only 6 tons of sugar arrived in Berlin each day whereas the order was for a steady 86[71] – refiners had failed to supply enough. Some needs took time to discover. Only in November did anyone realise that Berlin's remnant Jewish population could not eat the tinned meat being flown in whereas there was no great problem in lifting Kosher meat.[72] Planners never seemed to bring themselves to make the relatively simple calculation of how many sanitary towels Berlin women required. Other needs had to be insisted on: many people wanted or, if diabetic, needed saccharine rather than sugar (which was a light, convenient cargo), but they had to plead for three months before the zonal authorities would send it.[73] Everyone knew that a low, monotonous ration sustained life but did little for morale; providing variety and the occasional treat caused problems, however. Suppliers of smoked fish were hard to come by and worked slowly; the fish itself was a smelly and unpopular payload, and the day a Hastings crew flew in a consignment and forgot to turn off the hold heating the Russians must have thought the allies were starting gas warfare. Honey sounded delicious but was packed in containers which oozed all over Lübeck. It took nearly four months of scrounging ingredients and negotiating with manufacturers before anyone could be certain that Berlin children would get a little chocolate for Christmas.[74]

Some necessities would never have occurred to the male bureaucrats and military men: how, for example, Berliners could "Make do and Mend." An Air-Commodore suddenly had the bright but very masculine idea that "It would help to keep German women occupied during the winter if they can be given facilities for making clothes," and then the airlift planners went mad and put in a monthly order for endless cotton thread, 40,000 packets of machine needles, 30,000 sewing and darning needles, 400 kgs of steel pins and 150,000 gross of safety pins. It all sounds excessively enthusiastic, but who knows off the cuff exactly how many pins and needles are needed every month by two-and-a-half million people?[75] These were light, easily obtained items. Even so they involved a policy decision: priorities, like cargoes, always had to be weighed. It was simple common sense to allocate 9 tons of wholewheat flour for use by rat exterminators in November.[76] It was much more complicated to decide to fly in everything for the renovation of Berlin West power station – each girder had to be justified in terms of a couple of loads of food or coal lost. It was either humane, silly or neither here nor there to satisfy the pining 1st Battalion Welsh Fusiliers by bringing them a new mascot goat.

All the decisions on what should be airlifted to Berlin were made in the city by the Commandants acting on advice from the Magistrat. Each month their Air Staff Committee received a forecast of airlift capacity from the Plans Division of HQ CALTF. This was based on probable numbers of aircraft and personnel available together with the assumed serviceability and weather conditions, and was broken down into daily estimates of tonnage. On this information and with facts and figures drawn up by the city authorities, the Air Staff Committee then planned how the transport should be used. Its detailed requests went to BICO, the Bipartite Control Office in Frankfurt, who organised import, German production and zonal transport, and to BEALCOM, the Berlin Airlift Co-ordination Committee, with representatives from BICO, CALTF, the British Army and US Airlift Support Command who were responsible for sorting out the air transport. The whole business of finding the supplies and getting them flowing at the right rate to the correct base was fiendish. Flour, for example, came from thirteen different mills in the Bizone and two ports. Dried vegetables were supplied by eleven German firms as well as foreign processors. Butter could not be kept waiting for long because of the absence of cold storage. Dried milk was in terribly short supply on the world market.[77] Every commodity had to be distributed among nine dispatching airfields. Someone with a tidy mind once suggested that all the food lift should be concentrated at one base, overlooking the fact that transport costs from some sources would be considerable and that any one airfield might be closed by bad weather for weeks on end.[78]

Deliveries to the zonal airfields were made by German Railways on trains which had track priority. At the railhead the consignments became the responsibility of the allied military. In the American zone they were handled by specialised Field Traffic Sections and in the British by the Royal Army Service Corps' RASO (Rear Airfield Supply Organisation). These units transported goods to their stores where they assembled cargoes of the proper weight for each type of aircraft and, when necessary, married light and bulky commodities with something denser and heavier so as to make full use of the space in the hold. The air forces notified the ground forces of instantly available or returning serviceable aircraft, then the loads were driven out to a specified parking bay at the same time as the fuel bowsers and fitters congregated. As each aircraft arrived the cargo manifest was ready and a team of German loaders leaped to work. At the bases in the American zone tractors towed trailers with the standard loads for C-47s and C-54s. In the British zone 3-ton lorries were suitable for Dakotas; two of them filled a York easily since it had a good low door. But 10-tonners were necessary for bigger aircraft, and on occasion carried loads for two normal holds at a time. This may account for the grisly day when Squadron-Leader Best had trouble taking off at Wunstorf but struggled through to Gatow, where he discovered that his York had carried its own load and a Dakota's.[79]

Most cargoes were loaded manually – there was too little room inside a hold for machinery and using hoists or conveyor belts on hard-standing already littered with aircraft, motor vehicles and fuel tankers would merely have increased the risk of damage to wings and fuselages. Human loaders were actually amazingly quick: their average time for a standard load such as coal or flour was fifteen minutes from the hold door opening to the emptied truck pulling away. During a spot check at Fassberg one team was seen to load 10 tons of coal in less than six minutes. The secret was to organise the men into permanent gangs, give them the same regular military supervisors and gang leaders, then create team spirit with published competition results and prizes of cigarettes or coffee. German labourers often lived in the special cantonments built for them at the airfields; Displaced Persons were bussed in from depressing local camps. The men were weak from undernourishment at the start of the airlift; a free hot meal every day and a high category ration card soon put some vim into them. During the driving rain in July and August they were soaked to the skin day in day out. When Major Crisp Jones of the RASO at Wunstorf used his initiative and signed for 3,000 gas capes for them he had to face a Court of Enquiry to account for his unauthorised use of Army property. Fortunately, he was a dab hand at such ordeals, having already had RASC men and drivers sent out on his own authority and escaped with no more than a warning not to do it again.

For really heavy or awkward loads forklift trucks or cranes did have to be used, and very abnormal cargoes, carried in C-82s, were eased in by a mobile crane which lowered its boom and floated them across the hold floor so that it was not wrecked. Some cumbersome machinery could be dismantled – a steamroller or a fire tender, for instance – but one generator which arrived at Wunstorf could not because it had been built into a truck with all its wiring. A particular BABS wagon went into the hold easily enough but could not be got out when it reached Berlin until someone worked out that its tyres had been let down to fit it in but pumped up once inside. Even a relatively familiar cargo such as newsprint presented difficulty: if its edges got creased or torn it would not run through the presses.

Any cargo had to be loaded with care, however. Each aircraft had its own centre of gravity and items had to be distributed with precision to get the right balance for flying. A standard form was issued with details of what weight could be supported in which compartment of the hold of each type of aircraft and diagrams helped loaders to make stable piles of the various commodities. Once inside, every section of cargo had to be tied down securely to stop it shifting and endangering the aircraft. USAF holds came fitted with standard Evans tie-down equipment. This was fine for the normal work it had been designed for, but not for the unexpected wear and tear it suffered on the airlift. The rods lasted only 100 trips, adding $9,345 to the cost of a month's deliveries. Ropes frayed, and even binding them or dipping them in aircraft dope did not lengthen their working lives by much. Webbing was better, but meant installing new buckle attachments. British link chains were durable but unwieldy and often damaged goods. The tapes which were substituted got hacked off in Berlin and wasted; netting was only efficient on even heaps.

At the Berlin end of the airlift, unloading was again the job of German civilians, under American military supervision at Tempelhof and the FASO (Forward Airfield Supply Organisation) at Gatow. Each aircraft radioed its cargo before arrival. As it touched down and ran to the end of the runway, it was given taxiing instructions by Airfield Control and guided into position on the apron by a team of marshallers. Once the engines were turned off a lorry backed up, chocks were jammed in, and six labourers jumped inside to undo the lashings and manhandle the cargo or slide it down a chute. When the hold was clear the sweepers shot in to clean it. The sackloads of coal-dust they collected were taken every few hours to a dump; spilt flour was bagged for animal feed. From Tempelhof goods were forwarded to central Berlin by road. At Gatow much of the food was driven to a jetty on the Havel and slid along rollers into a barge: coal was discharged from trailers on a wharf built over the water. Liquid fuel was at first driven by tankers from the underground storage to the lake, but at the turn of the year a direct pipeline was laid: the Army discovered it had carried lengths of old P[ipeline] U[nder] T[he] O[cean] pipeline into Germany at the end of the war (which goes to show there is more in the Quartermaster's Store than the old song allows for).[80]

With such hoards of treasure accumulated every day at the Berlin airfields it is not surprising that security was taken seriously. Yet seemingly the biggest problem the police faced was very petty pilfering – pitiable rather than criminal. A search of one civilian shift at Gatow (of perhaps a thousand people) uncovered 36 kgs of sugar, 28 of butter, 4.6 of milk powder, 5.5 of coal and some tins of meat, a few hundred grammes of cake, coffee and tea, three radio sets and three slabs of chocolate.[81] The low rate of crime at the airlift bases tells a lot about Berliners' honesty and is a significant indication of the spirit of group responsibility and selflessness which the blockade had created. It contrasts unpleasantly with the large-scale black-marketeering and customs-evasion rackets of a tiny proportion of airlift crews.

Once unloaded, most aircraft went straight back to base for reloading or servicing. Some, mainly British, turned round more slowly because they took on cargo in Berlin. Dakotas, Yorks and Hastings flew better with ballast anyway, so it was convenient to use them to transport empty sacks or mail. People make good ballast: Yorks or Hastings took about forty minutes to convert for passengers, Dakotas rather less. The main tonnage of the backlift, however, was made up of exports from the city. Arguments between the Americans and British about the value of backloading were never settled. The Americans stuck to their point that the real job of the airlift was to pack goods into Berlin, not use time taking them out; the British doggedly maintained that delays could be cut by using the last aircraft in a wave or specialised load carriers. (Their own aircraft were, in fact, more likely to be grounded for maintenance at base than the USAF's, so might just as well spend a little more time at Gatow.) As far as the RAF was concerned the real American objection to backloading sprang from pride in Tempelhof's turn-round times which, as one RAF officer said, were "very good indeed (ever since we told them our Yorks were hauling in more per aircraft than their C-54s) and they hate to spoil their performance."[82] It could have been argued that the C-54s were perfect standard load carriers and best employed on regular shuttles, whereas the eccentric variety of British aircraft could not compete over tonnage but was well-suited to the multifarious shapes and sizes of Berlin exports.

The British kept close contact with industrial firms in the city and were all too aware of their perilous condition as well as the economic and political benefits of encouraging industrial production. They wanted, as one official put it, to show the Berliner "he is not merely an object of charity but ... performing a useful task and playing his part in the struggle."[83] They appreciated the view of Dr. Klingelhöfer, the head of the Magistrat Economics Department: unemployment was profoundly demoralising, especially for a "population whose burdens have already reached the utmost limit through the continuous political tension, the dis-organization of currency conditions and the lack of light and heating."[84] During the early months of the blockade three Berlin industrial committees advised the occupation authorities on the city's economic needs. These had been criticised for giving voice only to the owners of firms, so in October a new *"Notgemeinschaft"* was set up with representatives from the Magistrat, political parties and unions in addition to industrialists. It had a central body to liaise with the western Commandants and sub-committees to collect and evaluate information.[85]. The British benefited most from this new structure since the Americans had pulled out most of their expert staff to deal with industrial problems in the Bizone.

But it was one thing to be made aware of Berlin's industrial needs, quite another to meet the diverse demands of manufacturers. The incessant want of coal posed terrible dilemmas: should Siemens, who employed a third of the labour force in the British sector and produced a half of all goods sent to the west, be denied coal they asked for and forced to sack 11,500 employees in October?[86] Should they get more than their fair share of the coal allocated to industry at the risk of 60 per cent of the rest of the workforce becoming idle by the end of 1948?[87] It was easy to quote statistics and opinion polls at the Americans to justify the backlift, but very difficult to run it properly. In early August barely 18.5 tons a day were flown out from Gatow; 170 tons of industrial freight were stuck on the airfield and still more in warehouses in the city.[88] Next month easily loaded cargo was regularly cleared, but there were 300 tons of items too bulky to go into available aircraft; stripping them down for loading caused work at either end of the lift and a stream of complaints from customers about missing parts.[89] That particular backlog was eventually shifted by a few nose-loading Bristol Freighters (known as "Frighteners" to pilots, but a reassuring sight to exporters). In October the British laid another rod to their backs by taking over responsibility for most of the export freight usually sent to Tempelhof where 419,931 kgs were already lying about and staff said they would only increase backloading if specifically ordered to do so.[90] Backlift tonnage dropped that month: a disastrous 5 tons only was flown out on 22 October. The crisis was partly caused by the unavailability of an RAF crane for loading and the difficulties of night work, but mainly by priority being given to mail, empty sacks (the umpteenth act of the Coal Sack drama) and passengers. Finally an order was issued on 1 November: all British aircraft, civil as well as military, must spend fifty minutes at Gatow and "be loaded to the fullest extent possible with any load within this time limitation."[91] For a while this new policy had no noticeable effect, thanks to continued lack of loading machinery and, above all, fog. But on 29 December an astounding memo recorded that the entire backlog of cargo had been cleared and, breathtakingly, that outgoing freight was "urgently needed."[92]

There was seldom a shortage of passengers. Once all the west Germans who had been trapped in Berlin by the full blockade had been ferried out, space was made available on the backlift to volunteers for the Ruhr mines, businessmen and politicians, and then to anyone who wished to take up residence in the Bizone for at least six months or could prove they needed to attend an educational course or receive special medical treatment. Each of these categories paid 16 marks, the equivalent of a second-class rail fare to Hannover.[93] There were long waiting-lists for the trip. One old lady had clearly grown impatient at the delay and, when the York she boarded was blown off the runway at Gatow and she had to disembark, she laid about the Canadian pilot with her umbrella as a paying customer's complaint.[94] Sick and undernourished children had priority on all outward flights – 1,317 of them were carried by the RAF in four weeks from 20 September. They travelled free to relatives, hospitals or special homes in the zones. They definitely came under the heading of "awkward cargo": getting lost in spite of careful labelling, wriggling when loaded, shifting whatever tying down method was applied; if there was turbulence they all vomited, if one decided to go to the lavatory they all wanted to go, and at once.

In August the British seriously discussed with Reuter and Friedensburg a proposal to fly out all Berlin schoolchildren for the winter. The advantages were clear: warmer conditions and better food for growing creatures, a considerable saving on fuel and food deliveries, and a comfort to parents who might find it easier to withstand the siege if they knew their children were safe. On the reckoning that there were 248,420 elementary and secondary school-children and 6,625 teachers in the western sectors, it was thought that 500 sorties by a mixed fleet of C-54s and Dakotas could carry them all out in twenty days. Any decision was delayed while the Moscow talks lasted. When the question was revived, it became part of a general plan for a mass evacuation should the Russians try to take over the city. In such a crisis, children would be moved first. But lists were drawn up of prominent democratic politicians, staff of the Magistrat and City Assembly, officials of UGO, (the western trades union) journalists and broadcasters, policemen and teachers, and Germans employed by the British military government to whom a strong obligation was felt and who would be in serious danger under the Russians – as Robertson said, to leave them would be a "stain which we should never wipe out."[95] Tantalisingly these lists have not been released to the Public Records Office in London. It would be interesting to know which names were on them and even more fascinating to see who had been left off.

The horrible thought that Berlin might soon fall to the Russians or that the western allies would be forced to withdraw throbbed more and more painfully as winter approached. In a US Military Government poll in October nine out of ten Berliners staunchly declared that they preferred blockade conditions to communist rule.[96] The airlift and occupation authorities were prepared to do everything they could to back the Berliners' stand, but they knew how conditions would deteriorate once the weather worsened, how it would probably be impossible to supply any coal for domestic heating. And as Robertson explained: "Berlin winters are cold and the houses are bad. To ask people to go through the winter without any heating is clearly to put an inhuman strain upon them."[97] Would the western sectors' resolve shrivel in the cold? Might it be kinder to hand them over to Russian rations and fuel? The same OMGUS opinion poll suggested that 85 per cent of Germans were confident that the airlift could keep Berlin alive in winter. No one concerned in its operation could have such faith.

They had to take into account how cold and wet would reduce the serviceability of aircraft, how fog would prevent flying and frost break up the runways and hard-standing. When, in September, the British looked at the potential performance of the aircraft and studied recent meteorological records, they could not avoid the conclusion that average winter tonnage would drop to 33 per cent below that of August – which meant not just failure to supply winter comforts but the reduction of Berlin to starvation. However hard everyone worked during the remaining clear flying weather, the chances were that all stocks would be exhausted by the second or third week in January. It was possible to make good some of the shortfall by taking risks: increasing payloads past the usual safety limits and reducing flight separation.[98] And the RAF urged that all USAF units should move to the British zone since routes from Rhein Main and Wiesbaden were a third or more longer and lost up to 676 tons a day. The Americans resisted the suggestion, and as day after November day Berlin's airfields were closed by fog and barely half the targets were met, it did indeed look as if the obstacle of weather could not be overcome simply by making adjustments at one end of the airlift.

The safest and most effective way to use whatever good weather occurred was, of course, to deploy the maximum number of big load carriers. Only the Americans could supply them, but how long before they did so? The first of the C-54s promised in October touched down at Rhein Main in mid-November – or, rather, "splashed down," because they arrived in the heaviest of rain on flooded runways. "We ordered this just for you," Tunner told them: they were the advance party of two naval squadrons.[99] Since they were airmen rather than seamen, they were flying again within four hours of arrival on their first sorties to Berlin. As the other C-54s at last flowed in during the rest of the month, not only was it possible to predict that average tonnage would now rise from the previous best estimate of 3,000 tons a day to 5,000, but the USAF announced that C-47s would be phased out. Not least, Berlin had thirty days of food and coal in store by the end of November.[100] This was not much of a safety margin. There was still a fear that the big push had come too late. Everyone was investing all their hope in those C-54s being able to compensate for past failures; there were serious implications in the joking question put to Tunner by a young pilot: "General, do you think the C-54 will ever replace sex?" The airlift had struggled against the odds and achieved miracles. It would go on fighting. But no amount of determination and effort could do anything about the winter weather – that would take the biggest miracle of all. It had to be remembered that historically some of the greatest Russian victories had been won by General Winter.

11

Berlin Splits

A journalist visiting Berlin in November 1948 did what so many of his trade do when looking for a quick, easy story: he interviewed his taxi-driver on the way into the city. He asked the man if the Russian blockade had destroyed Berliners' hopes for a life of their own choosing or, indeed, any form of survival. "We lost all our faith at first," said the driver. "We thought the West would pull out. Now we have it back again. There. You hear? There is another plane. And there another. Our faith doesn't come from our hearts or our brains any more. It comes through the ears."[1]

The noise of allied aircraft, taking off and landing every three minutes for twenty-fours hours a day at airfields right in the middle of Berlin, was not a disturbance; it was a comfort. No one complained at the din of engines just above the rooftops. But if the racket suddenly stopped by day they looked up anxiously; if silence fell in the middle of the night they woke up and were afraid. The noise meant that food and fuel were coming, that the western Powers were keeping their promise to stand by Berlin, that the city had contact with the outside and the world cared.

"The airbridge," Berliners called it, or "our airlift." Not only did their lives depend on it, they worked for it. Between 10,000 and 30,000 local people were employed at the Berlin airfields – building, loading, doing clerical jobs; thousands more drove the lorries, sailed the barges and ran the warehouses to supply the city. They were proud of the airlift's achievements and delighted by newspaper accounts of new aircraft, strange cargoes or record loading times.

Their children were taken to watch the aircraft being juggled up and down, collected plane numbers and went home to "play airlifts" with paper models on rubble runways. And Berliners were grateful. They gave presents to the fliers who had brought them so much: bunches of flowers, home-made lighters or ashtrays of scrap-metal. They wrote letters, posted to the base commanders or slipped into cockpits, struggling to explain how the crews gave them not just food and warmth but a link with life beyond the ring of besieging forces.

The crews seldom, if ever, really understood. They spent less than half an hour each sortie at a Berlin airfield – stretching their legs, swallowing a cup of tea or coffee – then went back to the zones. Hardly any of them got an opportunity to go into the city and see the harshness of life there. (One young man who did visit a Berlin family was staggered by the coldness of their flat: after flying three C-54 loads of coal every day he had imagined the place would have been warm.)[2] The allied airmen were absorbed in their job; thrilled to be flying and fully stretched. If they were old enough to have fought in the war they valued the chance to do something positive not destructive, to save life rather than kill. Personnel on the ground as well as in the air enjoyed the excitement, the absence of bull and boredom which usually afflict military life in peacetime. Only a few planners at CALTF headquarters or in Berlin appreciated the complexities of the airlift and knew what a touch-and-go business it was. Practically no one concerned in it had any interest in the political context of their work. They all tried to do a good job, but they defined that job in their own professional terms: they did not think of it from a Berliner's point of view.

Occasionally, though, sympathy for those in the city was directly engaged. One day in autumn 1948 a twenty-seven-year-old pilot from Utah, Gail Halvorsen, wandered off the station at Tempelhof and met some children. He stopped for a pidgin and mime chat. They were nice, cheerful children, but there was something odd about them which puzzled Halvorsen. Then it struck him: every other child the world over asked for chocolate or gum, but these little Berliners did not seem to imagine such a treat. This, thought Halvorsen, was wrong. He told them to wait that evening at the end of the runway, look up and see what happened. Back at base he went to work with some handkerchiefs. Next time he was about to touch down at Tempelhof he gave a signal to his crew chief and a sprinkling of candy parachuted to the ground. He could hardly stop there: the children would be waiting. So every trip the "Sweet

Bomber," the "*Schokoladen Flieger*," did another parachute drop. He soon ran out of hankies and old shirts; friends joined in with cloth and cargo. News spread; chocolate, sweets and gum appeared from other bases and the United States. By October Halvorsen had a staff of six to deal with the supplies and thank-you letters, the German Youth Activities group was engaged in mass production of parachutes, and the USAF was running "Operation Little Vittles," dropping 6,000 consignments of goodies a day.[3]

The public imagination was seized by treats for children. The American CARE organisation dropped twenty-five dolls, "Schmoos," which were based on a popular cartoon creature which multiplied happiness, and 100 Schmoo balloons. The dolls were to be auctioned for charity, the balloons bore a label: "Hello, I am a Schmoo. Perhaps you never heard of me but I am quite famous in America as a legendary character who is dedicated to doing good turns for everyone I meet. Just to prove it bring me to the CARE office in Berlin ... where I will turn into a CARE package. ..." The balloons were fun for the children who caught them; the package was 10 lbs of lard, which was a very big treat indeed for mother.[4] To make Christmas happier for the young and needy, 86 Fighter Group at Neubiberg enrolled Clarence. Clarence was a camel, bought for $50 in Tripoli, whose service life so far had passed only relatively quietly as a football mascot. But he was destined for higher things. In October he was sent round the American zone to collect money for food and toys. His tour was a triumph: 5,000 lbs of sweets were bought and children came by the busload to Wiesbaden with presents for him to take to others. Next he was posted to Berlin duties: he would lend his strength and saddlebags to unloading at Tempelhof and delivering the gifts. But first he had to undergo a test flight. Then disaster struck: in the hold, the worthy Air Force camel was kicked by a spiteful Army mule and his leg was broken. A new Clarence had to be found. A top priority, secret mission was flown to North Africa to get one. The crew must have been in a hurry and were probably town-bred, because they came back with a Clarissa. Never mind: she took on the name and role of Clarence and bore them laudably; the children cared more about food and toys than the sex of camels.[5]

By comparison the British notion of fun was staid indeed: an Elizabethan Festival for Berlin from 21 August to 5 September. It may seem very peculiar now that in a besieged city on the verge of starvation and conquest there should have been performances of Purcell's "Music for Circe," lectures on sixteenth-century English

269

literature and poetry readings. It is strange to think of an opening party on a lake with guests arriving by barge to be met by a guard of honour of Tommies dressed as Beefeaters (Robertson would only let them take part if they were turned out and drilled to highest Prussian standards); odd to realise that Marshal Sokolovsky was asked to come (until a high-ranking spoilsport insisted he be dis-invited). One wonders whether the obvious need of Berliners at this juncture was the Cambridge Madrigal Society, with a lot of jolly elderly ladies trilling "Fa la la" and "Hey nonny no." Eyebrows might be raised at the choice of plays by the Cambridge Marlowe Society: Shakespeare's *Measure for Measure* and Webster's *The White Devil* seem rather lugubrious. In fact, however, the Festival was a tremendous success. All post-war Germans were starved of cultural activity and hungry Berliners lapped everything up. The sheer irrelevance of most of the programme to their daily existence was a blessed relief; the darkness and violence of *The White Devil*, on the other hand, struck chords. Berliners and occupation officials had seldom shared a pleasure before; this was the first time Germans had been British guests on public, social occasions. The performers asked themselves if they were as useful as a sack of dried potatoes; the audiences thought they were – and felt better for knowing that outsiders were not afraid to visit them.[6]

For the most part, however, living in Berlin was cheerless. People were fully occupied and exhausted by the difficulties of maintaining any simple, ordinary life in such abnormal circumstances.

Getting from place to place was a problem in itself. There were virtually no private cars; public transport was rare during the day, thanks to electricity and petrol shortages, and it closed down completely from six in the evening to six next morning. With small businesses and factories often obliged to operate at night when their four hours of electricity were available, many employees had to walk to and from work in the dark – a long trudge for those who worked at the airfields. Only the Soviet-controlled S-bahn (local electric railway) ran at all regularly. The SMA claimed this as a generous gesture; others said it was to make sure Russians could get from their political and military headquarters out at Potsdam and Karlshorst to their offices in the centre of Berlin.

Rations were assured but meagre; imagination and energy were needed to eke them out. Berliners dug up their courtyards to grow vegetables, wandered the streets offering household items or ciga-rettes as barter for food, and struggled to the Russian zone to trade or pay for eggs or a little cabbage. Few people could afford to use the black market often, especially as they had to pay in western Deutschmarks. If they had money to spare it went on kerosene at 4 marks a litre, or candles at 60–70 pfennigs, because it was worse to sit in the dark than go hungry. Cigarettes were a good investment: for swopping, quietening a rumbling tummy or passing the long night.

Cooking required planning and ingenuity. Electricity came in one four-hour block or separate two-hour periods. Meals might have to be eaten at midnight, or cooked in batches to be eaten cold over several days. A thermos flask was a treasure: the only way to get a hot drink for hours on end. The 90 per cent of homes with gas stoves suffered cuts and wavering pressure, though after December supply was increased to three-quarters of the normal. Berliners with long memories returned to tradition: food was heated, the pot put in a box packed with feathers or cotton-wool, wrapped in blankets and left for many hours so that workers came home to a hot meal even if they had to eat it in the dark and wearing overcoats. Many old stoves had a solid fuel oven which heated the kitchen. People spent their spare time chopping up old tree stumps and furniture, pushing carts into the city's woods to look for twigs and fallen branches or, if they could afford it, crossing to the east to buy handfuls of coal and kindling. Warmth was a treat to share with friends and neighbours. Families made communal meals too, turn and turn about. The blockade had opened doors and hearts.[7]

In November a British official recorded the day of a west sector family. They may not have been typical, but they showed how people tackled some common problems.

Otto Schmidt (perhaps it was his real name) was a skilled metal worker. He and his wife had two children of eleven and seven and were expecting another. Otto earned about 62 marks a week; after tax and social insurance his take-home pay was 50 marks, twelve of which were Deutschmarks. Rent for their three-room flat was 73 marks a month, so they sublet one room. Herr and Frau Schmidt got up in the dark at 5:30 a.m., and while his wife made breakfast by the light of a small paraffin lamp (black-market paraffin but cheaper than candles) Otto washed and shaved in cold water with as little soap as possible (the family was rationed to one small block for ten days and a black-market extra would cost 3 western marks). Breakfast for the parents was two or three slices of dry bread and a cup of ersatz coffee. The children started the day with something more substantial: a kind of porridge made from cereals and a cup of dried skimmed milk (the younger child had a special milk ration, the elder got most of his pregnant mother's allocation). The meal was lukewarm: the Schmidts were nervous about using much gas ever since their neighbour had had her supply cut for three weeks after going over her limit.

Otto walked to work (it was only twenty minutes away) feeling uncomfortable in new wooden shoes, wishing he had had a hinge in the sole and wondering how soon his socks would be in holes. During the mid-morning break he ate four slices of dry bread and at lunch yet more, but this time with a little margarine and a black-market apple. If he had been employed at one of the airfields or by an occupying Power, he would have had a free hot meal and probably tea and a bun for elevenses and in the afternoon. Meanwhile, his wife had taken the children to school, where they would be given more cereal for lunch. She then toured the shops, glad there were never the queues her mother battled with in the Russian sector. Today she had some luck – there were fresh carrots and she bought 6 lbs. They cost 3 precious Deutschmarks, but they would make a special meal tomorrow (her husband's allotment never produced enough vegetables). She seldom shopped on the black market: perhaps a little extra flour for 2.5 marks a pound, but never butter because it cost 17 marks. She stopped at the shoemender hoping he might do a repair, but he had no leather and no nails either. The day before she had tried to exchange some soap coupons for clothing for the new baby, but discovered she would have to pay half the price in Deutschmarks. Once back at home Frau Schmidt ate two slices of bread smeared with sweetened flour paste. Then the electricity came on for two hours and she could do some ironing and listen to the radio. The rest of the afternoon was spent as it always was – patching and darning. Today she had two pairs of worn socks to unravel for knitting up into a good pair. She had seen no wool in official shops for three years.

Once the family reassembled at 4 o'clock they had the main meal of the day: cabbage soup with a stock cube for flavour and a thickening of dried potato. No meat today – it came only twice a week – but plenty of bread with enough left over to wipe the plates and save on soap and hot water. Then a chat round a candle for an hour or so before the children went to bed. The parents were tired, but they did not want to miss the electricity when it came on again at 10 o'clock. So they went out on to the street corner to listen to the evening RIAS news over a local loudspeaker, standing with nearly two hundred other people in the dark and cold to be told there had been no political breakthrough, no glimmer of a chance that the blockade would be lifted.[8]

These sessions round the loudspeaker or touring broadcasting van were vital to Berliners. RIAS gave people a chance to talk to each other: in interviews they could grumble, make practical suggestions, tell personal stories. It made the authorities talk to the people: answer complaints, explain hold-ups and shortages. The very fact of standing in a crowd to listen to the radio created a sense of solidarity. And solidarity kept Berliners going.[9]

So did humour. Many popular jokes were about daily hardships: coffee called "Blumenkaffee" because it was so thin you could see the flower at the bottom of the cup; the promise of a warm, bright Christmas because the allies were airlifting it to 24 July. Dehydration was the running gag. The ultimate dry joke was a cartoon showing a bewildered couple looking at a tiny, flat baby just delivered by the stork and with a label attached: "Dehydrated. Soak in warm water for twenty minutes." The mordant one-liner appealed to sardonic Berliners: "We are heroes because we are afraid of the Russians and we happen to live in Berlin"; "Don't get the jitters, allies, we are in front of you." Much humour was black: "Aren't we lucky. Think what things would be like if the Americans were blockading us and the Russians were running the airlift."[10] Inevitably it often had a political edge. When the Soviet media bruited the achievements of Adolf Hennecke, a Saxon coal miner who increased his output three-fold thanks to devotion to the revolutionary traditions of the German labour movement, the west Berlin newspaper *Der Abend* created a Stakhanovite barber, Oswald Schaumslager (Latherbeater), who exceeded his daily norm by 690 per cent, cut the hair of every local SED official, and with the 2.4 cubic metres of hair obtained stuffed seventeen mattresses for the Party Advanced School.[11] It was as well to have an ersatz Hennecke to laugh at: jokes about the real Hero of Labour were made illegal in the Soviet zone.

Since humour and accurate, up-to-date news were so important to Berlin resistance, the Russians tried to cut one vital source: newspapers, of which more sold during the blockade than for years past. In late September the SMA set up an agency in their sector to vet and distribute every Berlin paper. Markgraf police seized western newspapers from rail and S-bahn passengers; vendors responded by folding offending papers in acceptable east zone journals. Then from 24 September Russian-controlled railway police moved on to stations in the west of the city and began

273

confiscations there. It took a week before Howley could be persuaded to join Herbert and Ganeval and deploy west sector police in several stations to protect newspaper sellers and customers. On 2 October the railway police finally slunk away.[12] What a pity that in return Howley could not coax Herbert to apply similar measures against the Russians in Radio Berlin's Rundfunkhaus – that would have done wonders for Berlin morale, not to mention the British reputation.

Such events highlighted the anomalies of four-Power occupation of the city which the blockade had made even more bizarre. The Allied Control Council and Kommandatura had collapsed, but the fiction of quadripartite government was upheld. The western and Russian authorities were at daggers drawn politically, but they worked side by side at the Air Safety Centre with the Russians doing something to help the airlift which was undermining their blockade. The four Powers changed guard once a month and gave each other heavy lunches at Spandau gaol, where they shared responsibility for the imprisonment of seven leading Nazis sentenced by the International Military Tribunal in Nuremberg in 1946. Two currencies circulated in the city; both were legal tender in the western sectors and the Deutschmark could be exchanged unofficially for the East mark in the Soviet zone at quadruple its value.

The SMA with one hand tried to starve west Berliners by stopping food deliveries from the west and even banning Red Cross parcels; with the other it tempted them to Russian zone rations. The offer was not taken up with much enthusiasm. By the first week in September only 53,000 western residents had registered with Soviet sector shops; in October the total went up to 75,000; by early November it had crept to 78,000. A high proportion of these people either lived near the east sector boundary or worked on the other side and found it easier to shop there. Some of them were known to have registered on both sides to get double rations, but there were plenty of eastern residents who had falsely obtained western ration cards, SED officials among them.[13] Until the western ration increase on 1 November the Soviet sector ration was marginally higher, but it was erratic and heavy in bread and potatoes. After November the western sectors got fats, including cheese. People there were confident that their rations would be maintained whereas they knew Soviet increases had been made possible by stripping stocks and taking in the harvest early: instant gratification at the expense of future nourishment.[14] Many west Berliners who had registered in the Russian sector began to drift back with excuses that they had misplaced their western ration cards. Their neighbours called them "defectors" and "traitors," but the Magistrat decreed they must be forgiven and fed.[15]

Though Berlin was divided into four occupation sectors and by different currency and political systems, it was still one city, and movement across administrative boundaries was not hindered. In the early months of the blockade many west Berliners found it well-worth their while to travel to the Soviet sector and zone to look for food; 110,000 western residents worked in the eastern sector and 106,000 crossed in the other direction every day. There were some eighty roads linking the two sides of the city as well as surface and underground railways. On 18 October the SMA curbed free movement for the first time by bringing in new regulations to prevent "the looting of the Soviet zone." East German food lorries were forbidden to cross Berlin to get from one side of the Russian zone to another (clearly too much food had "fallen off the back of a lorry" on to western black-marketeers' stalls). More worryingly, the east German authorities would now search passengers on what were unpleasantly called in English "food-scrounging" trains but known charmingly in German as *"hamsterer Züge."* Four days later the restrictions were tightened: seventy-one roadblocks were set up on the Soviet boundaries; everyone crossing would now be stopped and searched.[16] The erection of physical barriers in Berlin marked a significant and depressing stage in the division of the city.

Another split was already showing. A second university was growing in the west of the city. The old, great Berlin University in the Russian sector had been founded in 1809 after Prussian defeat and during Napoleonic occupation. It had expressed the vision of Wilhelm von Humboldt, humanist and political philosopher, of a system of Prussian education for the expansion of the human mind and harmonious development of human powers rather than political or vocational training. The idea of a new Free University was born when Germany was conquered and occupied by the four Powers in 1945. Academics who had endured the Nazi educational system and often the concentration camps, young men who had survived the fighting and prisoner-of-war camps dreamed of a new and better world and of a university free to speculate and explore, free from intellectual and pedagogical rigidities.[17]

In January 1946 the SMA reopened Berlin University, but fought off western attempts to bring it under quadripartite control. The western Powers, in the name of quadripartite unity, resisted the pleas of Professor Eduard Spranger and others to create a new university in their part of the city. Thereafter, the Soviet zone authorities carried out a programme of "democratisation" in education. Some of it seemed praiseworthy: old Nazi Party teachers were replaced, the proportion of children of peasants and workers in secondary education went up from 19 per cent at the end of the war to 36.2 per cent by 1949. There was, however, a dark side to the achievement. The curriculum far too often resembled indoctrination. Positive discrimination in favour of the working classes came not from extra resources but from denial of opportunities to the middle classes. At Berlin University political and class background became a more important qualification for admission than educational attainment or potential; liberal teachers were sacked and "politically unreliable" students were denounced by informers and expelled; courses in Marxism and dialectics were compulsory. To the dream of a university free from intellectual constraints was added the wish to escape from a political straitjacket.

The western Powers still refused to make any move which might rock the quadripartite boat. Students struggled to preserve freedom of thought and pursuit of learning in an increasingly cramped scholarly atmosphere. They founded a monthly magazine, *Colloquium*, which was critical and often openly hostile to the educational and political authorities in the Russian zone. In April 1948 three founder members of *Colloquium* – Otto Stoltz and Otto Hess, its editors, and Joachim Schwarz, a regular contributor – printed an attack on Soviet handling of student unrest in Leipzig. They were expelled from the university, not by its governing body as was proper but by the zonal Ministry of Education, and without their statutory public hearing. Their expulsion provoked revolt. On 23 April students flocked to a meeting in the Hotel Esplanade just inside the British sector, defying a notice issued that morning that anyone "who takes part in such a demonstration must expect to lose his right to attend the university." Up to 2,000 young people crammed into the hotel's hall and spilled out into the courtyard or clung to the three floors of its ruined side while RIAS relayed the speeches. They applauded calls for the Magistrat to take over the Berlin University and for the foundation of a Free University in the western sectors. Above all they appreciated the fundamental theme of the meeting: the expulsion of the three students violated the principle of personal freedom – the issue at stake in the whole Berlin struggle. The general public took that point too: what was happening in Berlin University was of more than academic interest.

On 10 May the Magistrat took up the cause of a Free University and petitioned the SMA to hand over the Berlin University to their charge. Once the request was refused, as it inevitably was, the Magistrat gave what support it could for a new foundation, but had only moral support to offer: there were no funds or facilities in their gift and no certainty that a new university could be legally set up without the approval of the full Allied Kommandatura. The students were not prepared to sit about and wait. In June they called a meeting of anyone interested in their project and set up a committee of academics and representatives of the Magistrat under the chairmanship of Reuter to plan the faculties. They themselves took over an empty little house in Dahlem in the American sector, found a table, some chairs and a telephone, and started to build a university from scratch and with no resources to hand. An appeal to the world was launched for help to start an institution "dedicated to the pursuit of truth for truth's sake," where students could "grow in the spirit of democratic enquiry" and teachers work "in freedom from fear"; it would be the "spiritual centre of a free Berlin and a source of strength in the intellectual restoration of Germany." Students contacted academics in Germany and in exile and begged them to come and teach them. They ransacked the city for sticks of furniture, tracked down empty rooms, cadged books and filled the gaps in the growing libraries with plunder from the Berlin University brought out in the pockets of capacious overcoats. Within days of opening the office in Dahlem hundreds of young people had poured in, saying, "I want to study here." Professors and lecturers from Russian zone universities decided to move west; teachers working abroad volunteered to return. The Technical University and various colleges of higher education in the western sectors offered accommodation, equipment and courses; hospitals promised to open their wards for medical students. The public imagination was fired. The western Powers could hardly ignore such a demonstration of independence and courage.

Had it been left to the British, however, the Free University would have been suffocated at birth. British officials responsible for educational affairs were described in August as "rather chary" of the idea and critical that "obvious difficulties" in starting a university had hardly been considered.[18] It would have been reasonable to call them "positively hostile"; they saw only the "obvious difficulties" and had no wish to see them overcome. Underlying British opposition one senses a paternalistic compound of the victor and the middle-aged faced with eager young Germans. There was undoubtedly also a strong measure of academic snobbery: a new university would be "quite incapable of standing comparison with the great Humboldt foundation" and would necessarily be "a very poor affair," as Robert Birley, the British Educational Adviser, sniffed.[19] Souring the mixture of motives was an acid tinge of anti-American feeling. Many officials in US Military Government, especially those who came from an academic background, were excited by the scheme and the energy and resourcefulness it generated. So, indeed, were some British, but there were few of them in the Education Department. Here the view prevailed that brash Americans were making a vulgar attempt to win cheap popularity by praising a naive and amateurish scheme. Birley could claim that American education experts opposed the new university[20] and Dr. Alonzo G. Grace, the Chief of the American Cultural Affairs Division, certainly preached some very British-sounding cautions about the need for "a solid foundation" and avoiding any cause of "disillusion."[21]

Such coolness did not chill others. In August General Clay allocated DM2 million, the profit from the sale of periodicals in his zone, to fund basic running costs for the first year of the Free University and expressed interest in the preparatory committee ("another example of precipitate American action," sneered the Foreign Office).[22] He then appointed Kendall Foss ("a journalist," as the British were pained to point out) to keep an eye on developments ("over the heads of and without consulting any of his educational authorities").[23] Foss wrote a glowing report on the university's progress and prospects ("Woolly," commented Birley; "one of the most dishonest documents I have ever read").[24] Constant American encouragement came from Professor Karl Friedrich, Clay's adviser on government affairs ("A Harvard professor," gasped the British, "a man of considerable calibre whom it is rather surprising to find associated with Kendall Foss").[25] The British pushed a counter-proposal to expand the Technical University in their own sector, hoped to convince Reuter of "our 'educational' reasons for not supporting the project"[26] and did the best they could to get their American counterparts to bring pressure on Clay – though Robertson would not risk a personal clash over the matter.[27]

Meanwhile, the Free University grew and grew. By September 5,000 would-be students had applied for admission – 20 per cent of them from the old Berlin University and another 20 per cent from elsewhere in the Soviet zone; thirty professors and seventy junior staff had volunteered to teach; 400,000 books had been collected and the Americans had promised to bring in the old Reich library, at present in store in Marburg, once the blockade was lifted. The Magistrat approved the foundation on 22 September – without seeking any Kommandatura permission – and issued ration books to those who would teach and study there. As the British noted with regret, the Free University "whether we like it or not has come into being."[28] They would offer it no comforts of any kind: "No statement should be made which gives the impression that we approve the project as a joint undertaking," said a memo; it was important too that it should get no better heating or amenity than any supplied to the Technical University.[29]

Lectures for 2,000 students began on 15 November in medicine, law and economics and philosophy. Money and facilities were still desperately short, but energy and idealism were boundless. The official opening took place on 4 December. The new rector, the eminent historian Friedrich Meinicke, was over eighty and a cold prevented him from attending. His deputy, Professor Redslob, a member of the preparatory committee, took his place. The university's godparents from the Magistrat, Ernst Reuter and Louise Schroeder, made speeches; so too did Howley and the visiting playwright Thornton Wilder on behalf of American admirers. It was a ceremony to celebrate a vision of the free spirit born under blockade. It was not an occasion to mourn a symbol of the painful tearing apart of Berlin.

Until December Berlin's political and administrative unity was maintained, however tenuously, by its municipal authorities – the Magistrat and the City Assembly. Some Magistrat departments had moved to the western sectors and been duplicated in the east, but they still claimed total jurisdiction. The City Assembly had been driven from the Stadthaus in the Russian sector, but continued to meet in the Taberna Academica as the sole elected body for the city and it still contained SED members from east Berlin.

Pressure on the Magistrat and Assembly slackened somewhat after the incursions into the Food Department and the arrest of Dr. Mückenberger in the Coal Office, and the assaults on the Stadthaus in August and 6 September. Even so, coercion continued, if less spectacularly. In late September the second Deputy Speaker of the Assembly, Geschke of the SED, called for a full session in the Stadthaus. The members refused to budge from the west and quickly pointed out that constitutionally only the Speaker, Dr. Suhr, could convene a session – they were all too aware of the dangers of the Stadthaus. Throughout September the SMA had ignored Suhr's request for a neutral, demonstration-free area around the building; at the beginning of October Kotikov, the Russian Commandant, turned it down flat. The suggestion, he said, was "undemocratic"; police protection contradicted practice in every democratic country. All he would promise was that the police would inform Suhr "when representatives of the people of Berlin wish to address themselves to officials."[30] There seemed little point in the City Assembly returning to its proper home if its sole guarantee amounted to advance police notification of a riot.

The Magistrat, meanwhile, clung to its right to stay in the Stadthaus and officials continued to use their offices in the building. Privately, however, they debated whether it would be better to move out. Suhr and Reuter, among others, were ready to go: Reuter believed that free expression was choked there and democratic government endangered. Friedensburg, Neumann and Kaiser wanted to wait until they were driven out.[31] Suhr made the cynical point that Friedensburg's reluctance to go to the west was largely inspired by the knowledge that once there his role as acting Oberbürgermeister would cease and that Reuter would at last take up the office from which he had been barred by Russian veto since 1946.[32]

While the Magistrat waited to be forced out of the Russian sector, the SED tried to scare them away. In October a committee was set up in east Berlin of party leaders, Front organisation officials and journalists from Russian-licensed papers. Its object was said to be "anti-warmongering." Its job consisted of compiling and publishing a blacklist. Names such as Reuter, Suhr, Neumann and Friedensburg came at the top; editors of most western-licensed journals were prominent. The committee invited citizens to send information about the undesirable activities of those listed, especially their "Nazi" pasts. The *Tägliche Rundschau* promised "the day will come when they will be put on trial." Interestingly it then defined a "warmonger" as anyone who criticised conditions in the Soviet Union or raised doubts about the "high purposes" of its policies.[33] The committee was undeterred by the huge numbers it would have to deal with under this definition and by the vast increase in the popularity of those it denounced.

Though the leaders of the Magistrat were not harmed by being called names, their work was damaged by the intimidation of their staffs. Many employees had drifted to the west when their departments moved; by 12 November a further 1,087 had been dismissed by the east sector authorities.[34] Furthermore, the Magistrat's claim to authority over all Berlin and the right to keep its headquarters in the Stadthaus wore thinner and thinner. In mid-October it tried to sack Waldemar Schmidt, the communist head of the Labour Department, for consistently failing to carry out wage agreements made with UGO, the west sector trades union organisation. Schmidt not only refused to leave his post, but insisted on attending all interdepartmental meetings. His nine former Magistrat colleagues chose to avoid his presence by holding their liaison sessions in the British sector. Friedensburg called this a "temporary" arrangement, but it set into permanence.[35] Reuter began to move his Transport Department files to the western sectors; on 15 November the SMA demanded he be dismissed on grounds of "incompetence" and "indolence" and made the charge that he had not turned up at his office for three months.[36] Dr. Klingelhöfer in the Economics Department was also sending his records out of the Russian sector and, while he was at it, a lot of office furniture as well (very much needed because three-quarters of his staff had already moved west).[37] In November the Markgraf police formed a cordon round the Magistrat building to stop any more equipment melting away, and one day Klingelhöfer walked through it, down the Unter den Linden, through the Brandenburg Gate and into the British sector – usually a pleasant fifteen-minute stroll but under these circumstances an experience to make the back of the neck tingle. Dr. Haas, the City Treasurer, would soon follow him to the west: in late November he was denounced by the SMA for his "anti-democratic and anti-social" financial policies.[38] By then it was all too obvious that the Magistrat could not for long straddle the widening gap between east Berlin and the rest of the city.

The rift between Berlin and the western zones was increasingly noticeable too. The blockade had not only emphasised the city's geographical isolation, but it had cut Berliners off from all the benefits to the Trizone which followed the London agreements. Since allied currency reforms and German abolition of price controls in June, west Germany had been economically transfigured. There were plenty of goods in the shops – at high prices, admittedly, but in quantity and variety unknown since the end of the war. There was food available at last: the average ration in the Bizone went up to 1,800 calories a day in August and in October potatoes actually came off ration. Unlike Berliners, west Germans could get fresh vegetables, fruit and eggs. By the end of November industrial production had risen to three-quarters of its 1936 totals. Such achievements had not come as a blessing to everyone. For one thing they had involved a shake-out of labour and it took time before the unemployed found the vacancies which existed or were absorbed by expansion. Berlin's labour problems, however, were infinitely worse: by December 110,000 people were either unemployed or on short time, and the full gravity of the situation was concealed by the Magistrat's rubble clearance jobs and by employers who kept workers busy in repairing or decorating the factories whilst waiting for electricity and raw materials for real production. In the western zones currency reform had hit those with savings or pensions, but at least the money they had was of real value – more than could be said of the East marks in west Berlin wage packets. In west Germany, there was justified hope for the future; in Berlin only dogged perseverance to stop things getting worse.

To Berliners' detachment from confidence and comfort there was added a fear of being cut off from constitutional developments in the west. In August the eleven legislatures of the western Länder had chosen a total of sixty-five delegates to attend the Parliamentary Council which would draw up the Basic Law. All of them, on principle, believed that Berliners should take part in their debates, as spokesmen for the sundered Soviet zone and the capital of the united country. The SPD, as a matter of practical politics, wanted the five-man delegation from Berlin to tip the even balance of twenty-seven SPD and twenty-seven CDU (the rest being unaligned). The western Powers, however, would permit Berliners only a limited role. The French had tried to prevent them taking part at all, arguing that even observers from the city would aggravate the Russians. Clay had insisted that Berliners must take part in the debates: "Western Germans do need some assurance that we are men not mice."[39] Even so, he and Robertson would only concede attendance at meetings, not voting rights. Furthermore, they expressed the hope that the Berlin crisis would not figure in the Council's discussions – they neither wanted the quadripartite status of the city challenged nor the delegates' attention distracted from constitutional business.

These were vain hopes. When the Parliamentary Council opened on 1 September in the Pedagogische Akademie in Bonn, both the SPD and the CDU arrived with prepared tributes to Berlin and motions to seat the city's representatives. At the third session the Council, with only one SED dissenting vote, carried a declaration of unity with the people of Berlin and the Russian zone in their fight for "freedom and justice" – ignoring hefty hints from the Military Governors that such questions were outside their competence.[40] Murphy had to dissuade Clay from publicly condemning the resolution.[41]

Thereafter, the Parliamentary Council settled down to debating the nature of its draft constitution in full sessions chaired by the CDU leader Adenauer, and it divided into committees on principles, organisation, distribution of powers, finance, and a federal court and judiciary. Ernst Reuter made sure Berlin's voice was heard throughout. His passion for west German constitutional development overcame doubters, nervous about betraying the cause of a united Germany; his conviction that the whole nation would gain sooner or later from fuller German involvement in government quelled fears in the Länder of widening the divide with the east. Berlin's influence at Bonn scared the French. On 4 November General Koenig complained to fellow Military Governors in Frankfurt about the complete integration envisaged for Berlin in government and the west German financial system. Berlin, in Koenig's opinion, was the symbol of German nationalism and militarism – everything most hateful and frightening to Germany's neighbours. He got no sympathy: Clay bluntly asked if Koenig wanted to hand the city to east Germany; Robertson said that any belief that Berlin would not be the future capital of a united country was tilting at windmills. When Koenig blustered that he doubted he could ever approve the Basic Law, he was ignored.[42]

However ready the Bonn politician's ear for Berlin's plight, the German public at large was apathetic. If asked for money for the city it became resentful. Berlin's finances were in a parlous state. The credits from the western Länder and the Bizone agencies could not keep pace with the galloping debts. In the autumn of 1948 the Economic Council in Frankfurt introduced a Law for the Collection of a Special Contribution to Relieve Distress in Berlin: an extra 2-pfennig stamp on all domestic letters, a small graduated income tax on individuals, and a compulsory donation from company profits with a maximum payment of 20 marks a month. The levy was eventually expected to raise DM25 million a month; it immediately raised a howl of protest. An American report summarised the initial public attitude as "I told you so: we the Germans always knew what kind the Russians were and if you had only helped us then...." A survey of public opinion in late November suggested that no one wanted to pay a "Berlin tax" to subsidise a conflict seen as "not

Germany's quarrel."[43] A letter from an engineer in Frankfurt sent to Clay and Robertson expressed common views: "We decline this dictated assistance imposed on us because we do not want any revival of Hitler methods"; forcing west Germans to pay for the Berlin conflict was making them take sides in a dispute between the allies.[44] This engineer, like fellow citizens in the west, had probably been doing very well in the recent boom, but his generosity had not expanded with the economy. Those who had not prospered had greater sympathy for the privations of others. Latvian, Estonian, Lithuanian and Rumanian Displaced Persons in a camp at Hallendorf, people who had virtually nothing and some excuse for hating Germans who had reduced them to their misery, actually offered a day's ration to help Berliners. No wonder an official letter of thanks praised their "magnanimous spirit" and "friendly and generous gesture."[45] They had shown qualities which were depressingly rare.

West Germans' self-absorption was perhaps only to be expected in people who had for so long been struggling to keep body and soul together and feared losing recent gains in renewed conflict. It was difficult for them in 1948 to have a sense of civic responsibility when their affairs were mainly directed by foreign occupation forces, hard to see their conquerors as allies in a struggle for German self-determination, and bewildering to change from living with punitive policies to being treated as partners and offered self-rule.

The awkwardness of such intense psychological adjustment was felt in Berlin too. People had no illusions about Russian intentions, but remained ambivalent to the western Powers. They acknowledged that the western presence in the city was a shield against Soviet advance and that the airlift kept them and their freedoms alive. Even so, they seldom felt that Berliners and allies shared in the same struggle. Whatever reassurances were given, people still thought the allies would leave if the going got really rough. Berliners conceded that allied troops and bureaucrats were taking risks and making sacrifices to defend them, but they bitterly criticised the lights blazing at all hours in official buildings, the half-empty staff cars, the luxury of the NAAFI and PX. They preferred not to be told that Britain was experiencing bread rationing for the first time because of a decision to divert grain ships to supply Berlin.

Symptomatic of the gulf between the western Powers and Berliners was the misconception about who was paying for the airlift. When the operation began there was no time to think what it would cost and who would pay. By July the British reckoned that their part of the operation was costing £30,000 a day, £40 for every ton.[46] In late October they estimated they had spent £2,300,000 – an average of £185,000 a week.[47] At about the same time the Americans calculated that they themselves had carried 320,000 tons at an expense of $17,992,735 – which covered the costs of flying personnel, fuel and lubricants, maintenance, administration, depreciation and a percentage of base overheads.[48] Neither the British nor the American figures included the capital cost of extending old airfields or building new ones. The allies had more or less reconciled themselves to footing all the transport and construction bills, but they had not made that clear to the Magistrat whose members were dreading a whacking bill. Nor had they discussed with them who would cover the costs of food which had risen alarmingly as a result of dehydration and special packing. For the time being the Magistrat was providing a subsidy from the Bizone, Länder and Military Government credits and loans.[49] Herbert argued angrily that it was "thoroughly unreasonable that the population of the western sectors of Berlin who dislike dehydrated potatoes exceedingly should be called on to pay twice as much for them," and that expecting Berliners "to bear the cost of the East–West struggle as well as the discomforts is against all democratic principle." He wanted the Military Governors to declare publicly that "the cost of the blockade is not to be passed on to the Berlin Magistrat or Berliners."[50] No such policy was ever clearly drawn up – it gradually evolved and was never announced. The Magistrat and population in Berlin remained in the dark about who would cover the enormous costs of keeping the city going and no one allayed their worries. Typically the occupation authorities did not involve Germans in the decisions taken on their behalf and Germans assumed the worst.

Both sides acted true to form over the crucial question of whether or when the Deutschmark should be made sole tender in the western sectors. The Magistrat had pleaded for the western Deutschmark since June: it would simplify their bookkeeping, put Berlin's finances on a sounder foundation, and tie the city to the burgeoning west German economy rather than allowing it to be sucked into the east zone. They saw the allied Powers' failure to act as weakness and folly; they were not made aware of the reasons for delay.

London and Washington long clung to the belief that Berlin's currency should remain under quadripartite control and could be an instrument to restore four-Power co-operation. Even as late as the autumn of 1948, when one might have thought nothing could get worse, Lovett urged restraint "from action which might be considered provocative"[51] and Bevin was reported to be apprehensive that the introduction of the western mark would "aggravate the situation."[52] Before the Moscow talks opened in August it had been inappropriate to introduce the Deutschmark; while they lasted there seemed a chance of getting a quadripartite currency agreement; as long as the Military Governors were talking no one wanted to imperil the last chance of getting the blockade lifted. Once all four-Power negotiation had failed, however, the western governments were more ready to listen to the arguments of Clay and Robertson that the Deutschmark must be established to check the rapid financial and economic deterioration in Berlin. Yet no sooner were the Military Governors authorised at the end of September to discuss methods and timing than a new obstacle was thrown up. The Berlin case was going to the United Nations. The hearing in the Security Council must not be jeopardised by any challenging move.

Bevin had always disliked the idea of referral to the United Nations: at best a waste of time, but more likely to produce pressure for compromise which would sap the western position. His officials had criticised it sharply. Sir Alexander Cadogan, the head of the British delegation, put the view that "if the four Powers cannot agree among themselves in any conference ... they will not agree any more in the framework of the UN. There is ... no magic in the UN." Nor, in his opinion, would international debate influence Soviet policy: given the absence of an opposition or a free press in the Soviet Union, the Russian government could "go on their way unashamed and unembarrassed."[53] For the Americans it was first and foremost a member's duty to bring the Berlin conflict before the United Nations. The advantages of doing so, as explained by Charles Bohlen, lay in getting world approval for the western case and debating the conflict before it intensified into an armed clash.[54] Yet, privately, American officials were uneasy about the way their referral was being handled. They wanted specific analysis of the line they would take, the points they must hold to, the areas where concessions could be made. Marshall remained enigmatic, even vague. Lewis Douglas put the blunt question to the Secretary of State: In the last resort were they trying to get UN backing for any western action including the use of force or were they submitting themselves to arbitration and willing to accept whatever solution was suggested? Marshall was trapped into admitting that in the highly unlikely case of the UN calling on the western allies to leave

Berlin, the United States would be bound by the decision.[55] As far as Bevin was concerned this was exactly the sort of undesirable settlement he expected the UN to propose, and it was not one he was ready to accept.

Though dragged to the United Nations, Bevin sensed dangers everywhere. He kept rumbling that withdrawal from Berlin should not be discussed, even thought about, since the slightest whiff of it would encourage the Russians to push. He trumpeted, "Hold on resolutely to the Berlin salient" whatever the call to let go.[56] He sniffed worriedly at the prospect that the Security Council might recommend resumption of the Military Governors' talks on the basis of Moscow's tainted 30 August directive. He snorted at the possibility that western representatives might be asked to have discussions with Molotov and be corralled into a Council of Foreign Ministers before the blockade was lifted.[57] The Americans remained confident that good would triumph and that the nations would recognise the West's just cause. Bevin hated forcing issues; Marshall argued that the airlift was buying time, but at a high cost and the time gained must be used to get a quick diplomatic settlement. Bevin saw time as a valuable commodity and was wary of hidden pitfalls in negotiated settlements. (He had been reading a lot about Yalta and Poland recently.)[58]

If nothing else, the submission of the western case on Berlin to the United Nations gave the allies a chance to discuss such differences frankly, at length and in person. The General Assembly met that year from September to November in Paris (there was as yet no permanent home in New York), and as the delegates went through the preliminaries the western leaders held an intensive round of private talks from 20 September to 5 October, often with their Military Governors and the envoys who had conducted the Moscow talks. Marshall and Bevin were meeting for the first time since the miseries of the Moscow Foreign Ministers' meeting in spring 1947. They were never soul mates and recent disagreements on such matters as Palestine had strained their relationship. The long stay in Paris did a lot to restore their mutual respect. The new French Foreign Minister was a pleasure after the stubborn but indecisive Bidault. Robert Schuman was quiet and courteous with a sly sense of humour and the logic and lucidity of a Frenchman trained as a lawyer. He was a patriot, but as a man born in Luxembourg and bred in Lorraine he spoke fluent German and had sympathies which crossed frontiers; he longed for a united Europe in which France and Germany would be reconciled. On the Berlin issue Schuman was flexible over method but unyielding on fundamentals. He did not believe that withdrawal from the city was desirable or inevitable and he was totally opposed to any talks with the Russians until they raised the blockade. General Marshall was delighted to find him so firm; "in striking contrast," as he observed, "to what he had heard about some of the Quai d'Orsay officials."[59] Indeed, Schuman was often at odds with the French Foreign Ministry: its Secretary-General, Jean Chauvel, told the British Ambassador in Paris that by the New Year the West could leave Berlin and extract a price from the Russians such as an Austrian treaty and the evacuation of any Germans at risk;[60] Alexandre Parodi, the French representative on the Security Council, constantly preached appeasement of the Soviet Union as the only way to avoid war.

The western leaders had to learn to deal with a new Russian adversary, Andrei Vyshinsky, who would soon replace Molotov as Foreign Minister. Opinion was divided on which of the two was the more obnoxious. Vyshinsky's neat figure, sharp features, intelligent expression and occasional flashes of humour or even charm gave some people a good first impression. But his truculent negotiating manner and abusive public oratory soon wiped it out. His lengthy responses in any debate were fertile in argument but sterile in result and often brutalised by remorseless jabbing at an opponent's weakness. Unlike Molotov he had no standing with Stalin, no influence in the Party. Guilt at his Menshevik past and exclusion from the Politburo made him the more anxious to please, the more ruthless in carrying out his master's wishes. Vyshinsky opened the bidding for world approval at the United Nations by calling on members of the Security Council to cut their armed forces by a third and ban the offensive use of atomic weapons. Bevin hit back with attacks on the Russians for keeping their satellites out of the Marshall Plan, abuse of their veto in the UN, and a call for renunciation of Stalin's doctrine that peaceful coexistence between the Soviet Union and bourgeois states was impossible. Vyshinsky was not drawn.

Instead, he launched guerrilla warfare against a hearing of the western case on Berlin. It had been brought to the Security Council as a "threat to peace" as defined in the UN Charter. The Russians denied there was any threat, argued that the Council was not competent to deal with the crisis which must be settled by the governments concerned, and on 5 October voted with the Ukrainian member against putting Berlin on the agenda. Overruled by the votes of the other members, he refused to take part in the talks.

The President of the Security Council, Dr. Bramuglia of Argentina, then set up a mediating committee with Council members from Belgium, Canada, China, Colombia and Syria under his chairmanship. Since none of these countries was party to the Berlin dispute the body could be called the Neutrals' Committee, but the records show that the Canadians could hardly wait to get out of meetings and tell the British what had gone on; and Dr. Bramuglia once told Bevin that he had every sympathy with the western Powers, having himself fought communism for a generation. Vyshinsky first avoided contact with the Neutrals by saying he had to wait for fresh instructions from Moscow, next claimed they could only discuss Berlin once it had been removed from the Security Council agenda, and finally maintained that any discussion must be on the basis of Moscow's 30 August directive. On 22 October Bramuglia introduced a Neutrals' resolution calling for an immediate end to the blockade followed by a meeting of the four Military Governors to arrange for a single currency in the city based on the East mark. Vyshinsky rejected the proposal on the grounds that lifting the blockade and introducing the East mark must be simultaneous.[61]

Bohlen had warned Marshall in a prescient memo on 8 October that the Security Council had an unfortunate tendency to "regard as a solution of the problem a formula which can be got through the Security Council – in other words to divorce the actual discussions and manoeuvrings in the Council from the realities of the problem itself."[62] Here was a perfect example of what he meant. The Neutrals had ignored the fact that the four Powers had proved incapable of settling their disputes at Military Governor or any other level, and they had shown no awareness that currency might be a symptom and not the cause of the Berlin dispute.

To make matters worse, their initiative was not only rejected outright by all four Powers, it bogged the whole question down in "manoeuvrings" between the Security Council and the rest of the UN. The Secretary-General, Trygve Lie, himself wanted to play the role of peacemaker and the western allies feared he would press for any solution regardless of suitability.[63] The President of the General Assembly, Herbert Evatt of Australia, pushed for his body to take over the matter – less, it was thought, because of his belief in its efficacy than because he wanted to get his own oar in.[64] Lie and Evatt pooled their ambitions in a letter to the four Powers on 14 November calling for immediate conversations and "all other necessary steps towards a solution of the Berlin question." Their letter offered no suggestions at all for a fruitful basis for such conversations, forgot that the UN itself had been asked to find a solution of the Berlin question, and recommended talks while the duress of blockade continued, something the West had always rejected. Since the Secretary-General and President patently had no understanding of the crisis, the two sides retreated to prepared positions. The Soviet Union suggested the 30 August directive as the basis for talks and called for a Council of Foreign Ministers' meeting on Germany; the West insisted on staying before the Security Council and refused to negotiate until the blockade was lifted.

Firm though the western leaders might sound, they were in a shaky position: they could hardly reject yet another proposal, this time from Bramuglia, that the Neutrals appoint a committee of financial experts to study the Berlin currency problem and report within thirty days. At least this idea committed them to nothing and gave a chance to show willing. Yet it was patently a waste of effort and grotesquely unrelated to Berlin's real problems. Already the procedural manoeuvrings at the UN had given time for the city's condition to deteriorate alarmingly; now another thirty days must elapse without positive action. And by the time the experts started work, the Berlin crisis had outstripped pious calls for negotiated settlement. The city was about to crack asunder.

The final political and administrative disintegration of Berlin came with the decision to hold an election for a new City Assembly. Constitutionally the old Assembly and Magistrat reached the end of their terms on 20 October; notice of an election should be given six weeks in advance. In some trepidation about the consequences, the Magistrat delayed submitting the required election ordinance which had been passed by the Assembly on 6 September. The western Commandants only received it on 2 October; five days later they approved 14 November as polling day. The SMA forbade its Bezirke Mayors to make any preparations. More dangerously they then sabotaged the election elsewhere by taking over the municipal printing works which was in their sector and preventing the issue of electoral lists.[65] So voting had to be be postponed until 5 December. Kotikov next laid down conditions which made sure it would not take place in his sector. In a letter to Friedensburg on 20 October he welcomed an election in view of western policies of "undermining democracy," "splitting the city" and spreading "warmongering propaganda," but insisted that "elementary liberties must be restored" before it was held: various SED-sponsored organisations should be allowed to operate freely in the western sectors, all "fascist and militaristic" groups in the west must be banned, "warmongers" denied the ballot, and Berlin's administration and economy "re-united." Friedensburg replied that the biggest threat to the city's unity would be an SMA refusal to let 1.1 million Berliners vote.[66] The campaign went on in the western sectors alone.

Bevin was a little unhappy about the timing – coinciding with the UN General Assembly and the investigations by the Neutrals' experts. Even so, he put it to the Cabinet that voting must go ahead on the date chosen by the city authorities: "If we lose the confidence and support of the Berlin population which we now enjoy, our presence in Berlin will become intolerable and also pointless."[67] The State and Army Departments, on the other hand, wanted to postpone the election. Marshall wrote anxiously to Murphy on 24 November about the risks of splitting the city, causing friction between the democratic parties and being accused of a sham poll.[68] Murphy replied forcibly that "it would be far better to announce our withdrawal" than to interfere in this matter, and he refused to tell Clay of the State Department's views for fear of "some explosive reaction" and "justified criticism ... of lack of courage."[69] Marshall fell silent, though his officials continued to fret over a possible Neutrals' wish for postponement.[70] They need have had no fears on that score. Dr Bramuglia read a letter of protest against the election sent by Sokolovsky on 29 November to the other Military Governors, then declared that if the western Powers did not make sure it was held on 5 December the Russians would "kick them out."[71]

The election campaign was run in parallel with a campaign of chicanery by the SED and SMA. Posters in the western sectors were torn down or pasted over – in some districts with a picture of the scene after an air-raid and the caption: "Whoever elects the warmongers votes for the return of nights of bombing." SED rowdies tried to break up meetings, but soon learned that SPD guardians of free speech had particularly thick skulls and strong right arms. When a rally was announced for 3 December to be addressed by Reuter and Louise Schroeder, the S-bahn was instructed not to stop at any nearby station. None the less 7,000 people turned up, some having pulled the communication cords at a convenient stopping-point, and they hounded out barrackers, several of whom, it was reported, "subsequently had to have first-aid treatment." As polling day drew nearer SED activists went from house to house in the Neukölln Bezirk to warn residents that the Russians would soon be occupying it. Rumours were carefully fed: Koenig was about to resign, Clay would soon be sacked, Marshall was ill, all the western allies would leave the city in January and many west sector politicians had booked seats on planes out. Most unnerving was the story that the Russians were about to cut the S-bahn. As bullying proved ineffective the east sector authorities tried bribery. On 2 December they announced a miraculous extra ration of 18 cwt of coal per household and the gift of 250 grammes of sweets for schoolchildren. Next day they promised the western sectors unlimited electricity and food and cut their own workers' income tax by nearly a third. They did their best to make sure that west sector residents who worked in the east could not go to the polls: 5 December was declared a "day of reconstruction" when everyone would do an extra shift. The western Commandants immediately said that those involved could vote at any convenient polling station, but UGO came up with a brighter idea – a transport strike until 10 a.m. on polling day which would give everyone plenty of time to mark their ballot papers before setting off for "reconstruction."[72]

While the Soviet-licensed press pumped out accusations that the western Powers and Magistrat were trying to split Berlin with the election, the SMA did some effective fracturing of its own. On 10 November Markgraf ordered all motor vehicles in east Berlin to be re-registered and to carry Greater Berlin number plates. This was much more than an attempt to vex west sector drivers by stopping them to argue about their vehicle papers. It was an open challenge to the Magistrat, who did not recognise Markgraf's authority but who did run all sorts of motor vehicles across sector boundaries. Since the Magistrat refused relicensing, fire brigade engines stationed in the west could no longer go to fires in the east; rubbish and sewage collection ceased to be city-wide services.[73]

Most well-informed observers now reckoned that the SMA was actually preparing for a complete takeover. As one of them put it: "It would certainly conform with Communist practice elsewhere if the Russians and their SED friends were to stage a coup in Berlin before the elections."[74] Intelligence reports lent weight to speculation. In September news leaked through that Bereitschaften, special alert squads, were being formed in the Russian zone: paramilitary groups of thirty-five to fifty men recruited from SED members and the Free German Youth movement, stationed in large towns and strategic areas, armed with rifles, machine pistols and guns, and trained by at least three former German generals recently released from Soviet prisoner-of-war camps.[75] During October the east zone police underwent a particularly thorough purge: key posts were given to SED and old Free German National Committee adherents, and there was a big recruiting drive to increase numbers. The SED itself was given a major shake-up: members suspected of half-heartedness were expelled and on 21 October Litke and Mattern, the Berlin chairman and his deputy (both old SPD members), were replaced by Moscow-trained Jendretzky and by Hoffmann, previously responsible for the Party's youth.[76] The People's Council met in the Russian sector on 22 October to receive a draft constitution for all Germany – thought to have been written in Moscow and given local colour by Grotewohl. All these moves looked like details in the plan for a coup. Would it be ready before 5 December?

In November the east sector authorities actually appeared to be advertising a putsch. The Soviet-licensed papers came out with such headlines as "The Magistrat exists no longer" and articles on "administrative chaos" in Berlin.[77] SED resolutions called for the restoration of a unified city administration and denounced those who had "fled from their posts" in the Stadthaus and left the people "in the lurch at the beginning of winter." During the weekend of 26–27 November workers' deputations went to Ottomar Geschke, the SED deputy chairman of the Assembly, asking for the removal of "saboteurs" from administrative posts and the creation of a "genuinely democratic" city government; Jendretzky demanded a new administration based on the "democratic bloc"; the east Berlin police expressed a desire to arrest Friedensburg, Stumm and others; and Dratvin alleged in a newspaper interview that there was a "state of emergency" in the western sectors. On 29 November Geschke broadcast to the city on Radio Berlin: "The hour is grave. There have been enough fine speeches and promises. There must be action now if Berlin is not to perish."[78]

The very next day Geschke summoned a meeting at the Staatsoper, the Opera House in the Russian sector. All factories in the area closed at noon and workers stood passively outside while representatives of the SED, FDGB, works councils, the Free German Youth and the Victims of Nazi Persecution approved by a show of hands the deposition of the old Magistrat and the names of a new one. The delegates witnessed the swearing in of an Oberbürgermeister, Fritz Ebert, who was the president of the Brandenburg Land Assembly and son of a former President of the Weimar Republic. They applauded his declarations that an immediate Emergency Winter Programme would ensure fuel for every Berlin household and electricity for every factory, that each worker would receive a pay rise of 30 per cent, that Berlin's economy would be integrated with the SED Two-Year Plan and the city would be assimilated into the Soviet zone.[79]

The new "Opera House" Magistrat, or possibly "Berlin Soviet," then went to present itself to the crowd – a necessary ceremony since, as an American intelligence report observed, fifteen out of the eighteen were virtually unknown to the public;[80] only Ebert, Maron and Waldemar Schmidt were familiar. The old elected Magistrat met that evening at Frau Schroeder's house and decided to battle on in the western sectors. Next morning at 8:30 Friedensburg staunchly arrived at the Stadthaus as usual and tried to get into his office. He was refused admission by the police acting, they said, on orders from Ebert. Had he got into the building he would have found workmen removing name plates from every office door.[81] In the days that followed other officials took what papers and equipment they could manage and slipped to the west. Their numbers were swelled by staff sacked for refusing allegiance to the self-styled new Magistrat. They moved to homes in the west which would be particularly miserable since the SMA had ordered that no personal property could be taken from the Russian sector without permission from a local commandant.

Whatever its other consequences the 30 November coup ensured a good poll five days later: 86.2 per cent of those eligible to vote did so. Election officials were given a special ration of coffee to keep them on their toes; west Berlin police and allied troops guarded the polling stations and had little difficulty shooing away three armed Russians who appeared in Reinickendorff and the occasional SED enthusiast who tried to note the names of voters. Seventy-four people were arrested on charges of intimidation, but most of them were released as soon as booths closed. Twelve allied inspection teams had been formed to supervise the proceedings (the Russians had not replied to an invitation to take part) and six British MPs turned up to witness fair play. The vote for the SPD rose (from 51.5 per cent in 1946 to 64.8 per cent); that for the CDU went down (from 24.1 per cent to 19.4 per cent) – in part, it was thought, because Friedensburg's policy of staying on in the Russian sector had been misunderstood. The overall result meant that the SPD could claim nearly all the posts in the Magistrat and it was feared that the CDU would move into opposition. However, the move of the city government to the western sectors had opened an opportunity long denied: Ernst Reuter, free from Russian veto, could at last become Oberbürgermeister. He cherished what unity could be salvaged and succeeded in forming a coalition of all parties.[82]

Nevertheless it was a city government whose writ ran only in the western sectors. Nor was it any longer technically answerable to quadripartite authority. The Kommandatura had died long ago; its ghost was exorcised on 20 December when the western Commandants met in their old headquarters in a room where a photograph of Kotikov still hung on the wall, and agreed to resume work as a tripartite body.[83] The western Powers, like the western Magistrat and City Assembly, had had to acknowledge a sad reality: Berlin was a divided city.

12

Cracks of Light

The division of Berlin had long been feared. To avoid provoking it the western Powers had appeased the Russians to the extent of giving themselves headaches and seeming contemptible in the eyes of Berliners; to stave it off the city government had endured intimidation and frustration. Now at last the division had come – and, as so often, the reality was much less unpleasant than the nightmare. The paralysis of fear gave way to vigour in dealing with problems which were suddenly clarified. The split was, in fact, the lesser of two dreaded evils. The greater – that Berlin would be seized and swallowed whole by the Soviet zone – had not come to pass. Perhaps the SMA and the SED had been wrong-footed by the decision to hold an election in the western sectors regardless of the risks. Perhaps they had not been ready for a coup: their police and paramilitary forces were unprepared, they were still uncertain of the grip of the Party and the submissiveness of the population of the Soviet zone. Probably they had been shocked by the election result: it showed the limitations of their coercion and the opposition they would face if they took over the western sectors. Whatever the reasons might be, the SMA and SED had not staged the anticipated assault. Nor were they expected to do so in the near future. For a while Berliners might have a chance to build up the tattered remnant of their city. For the moment, the Russians who had always been so threatening gave the impression of being on the defensive.

For a start, they had gone very quiet. After all the hectoring and drum-beating of the period before the election there were several weeks of political silence: no more menaces from SMA officials, no more brickbats from Russian-licensed media. The SED was muffled too. They made no attempt to assert city-wide authority for the Opera House Magistrat or to follow up Ebert's promises of an election, fuel and electricity for all, and the absorption of the four sectors into the Soviet zone economy. To some extent this lull could be seen as stunned silence – a reaction to December failure. It might also be a sign that the Russians and the SED could not make up their minds about future policy. There were rumours of a serious difference of opinion between Sokolovsky, the Military Governor, who was thought to favour autonomous development of the Soviet zone, and Colonel Tulpanov, the head of his Information Department, who was pushing for integration with the east European satellites.[1] There was suspicion too that the SED was in ideological disarray. In a newspaper interview on 30 December Pieck, the joint chairman of the party and praesidium, denied that the SED wanted to introduce a Soviet state and implied that the previously smothered notion of a German rather than Kremlin road to socialism was being revived.[2] If so, the comrades would be bewildered and some of them improperly bolshy. Speculation that the SED was in a state of confusion was strengthened by repeated postponements of a scheduled party rally.

When it finally took place between 25 and 28 January observers noted the "comparative mildness of its tone" and the lack of emphasis on the Berlin situation. (Throughout the proceedings there was only one suggestion, made by Pieck, that the western allies should leave the city.) The theme was nationalism and German unity, expressed in airy-fairy language and with no hint of urgency. Ulbricht described Berlin as a national not a Soviet zone capital. No one deduced from all this that the SED had given up the fight for Berlin, just that they were in no mood or state to do battle at the moment.[3]

What particularly titillated analysts of the rally was the SMA handling of a speech made by Tulpanov on the opening day. It was broadcast live on Radio Berlin, but not published in the press where, indeed, the Colonel's presence was not even referred to. Tulpanov had given the conference its only fighting words: old 1948-style West bashing. Was this the Kremlin view (he was just back from a long stay in Moscow) and intended to bring SED revisionists back into line? Would Sokolovsky have dared suppress it if it were? Had Tulpanov overstepped the mark and put his own opinions as if they were official? (Many people thought so and waited to see how soon he would be sacked.) Had he been set up: given a strong case which the Soviet authorities could disclaim? (If so, censoring him out of the newspapers was not a good way to do it.) Was he playing a double game: cheering up the SED with the thought that tough measures had received only a temporary setback and suggesting to everyone else that the Russians dealt severely with those who preached aggression? (His absence from the press was backing for this theory, his promotion to Major-General in May was not.) It is perfectly likely that the speech and its ban reflected muddle over policy and crossed wires in the administration. There seemed to be plenty of both in the Soviet zone at the time.

Not that the authorities there had lost their grip altogether. They might have no idea where they were going next, but they could at least tighten the nuts and bolts on the political machine. By the first week in January 1949 all eight east Berlin Bezirke had new heads of administration: five from the SED and one each from the formerly democratic parties (these three being given SED deputies to keep them on the straight and narrow). Seven of the personnel departments were handed to SED members, six of the Economics offices to FDGB trades union luminaries, all eight Education departments to representatives of the Party-controlled Kulturbund. Municipal employees in the sector were expected to sign a declaration of loyalty to the Opera House Magistrat; 1,500 who refused were sacked. Many more should have been fired, but the east Magistrat could not be entirely denuded of staff; Ebert himself was busy wooing SPD officials because he was so short of expertise.[4]

There was still a flicker of old expansionist ambition. On 7 January an SED meeting in Kreuzberg in the west was broken up by Stumm police while it was electing a "Democratic Bloc" government for the Bezirk; the following week the SED had a spurt of activity in Reinickendorf and the FDGB tried recruiting in Neukölln and Friedenau.[5] For the most part, however, the east Berlin authorities concentrated on sealing off their sector. From the end of December Markgraf police checks on U-bahn and S-bahn trains were rigorous; passengers were searched and packages confiscated. Soon it became necessary to get official permission to move nearly all goods from east to west Berlin.[6] At an east sector police conference on 28 December it was announced that every street connecting with the west of the city would be blocked and 1,100 extra officers would patrol the boundary.[7] The first obviously permanent barrier went up on the Treptow edge of the American sector on 15 February; police fired at people who tried to wriggle through to the west as it was built and killed one man.[8] By late April fifty-three streets from the Russian sector were closed.[9] As many more, of course, were still open, but even so there was a sense of claustrophobia for eastern residents and a real deterrent for westerners who wanted to travel to the Soviet sector or zone.

While the Opera House Magistrat focused on developing its own sector, the west Berlin elected administration settled into the peeling 1900s "Ancient Egyptian" splendours of the Rathaus Schöneberg and rapidly came to terms with the enforced separation of the western sectors. The split of the city had in many ways made their job much easier. They were free from incessant interference and bullying by the SMA and SED and answerable to the single authority of the three-Power Kommandatura. They already had the pick of municipal staff and got more able people thanks to east sector sackings. They felt justified in doing a little purging of their own and dismissed SED troublemakers in several departments. Once the Kammergericht (the High Court and Court of Appeals) and the Berlin Insurance Institute were driven out of the Russian sector, the western administration was almost consolidated; only the gas and water headquarters clung on in the Soviet sector and tried to operate on a city-wide basis. There was no longer any reason to pussyfoot with the SED, so in early February the Magistrat forbade party meetings in schools or public buildings and then prohibited its advertisements on public hoardings.[10] Since the SMA's protégé Magistrat claimed full powers in the Soviet sector, it could be made to accept fuller responsibilities: western prisons would no longer take criminals sentenced by east Berlin courts and would send back 1,300 prisoners who had been eating airlifted food.[11]

As the western Magistrat grew in self-assurance and gave ample demonstration of its energy and efficiency, it won respect from the western Powers and the acknowledgment that it was outgrowing the need for nannying by the Kommandatura. It was trusted to get on with the day-to-day running of the western sectors and the three Commandants considered adjusting the city's constitution along the lines of the proposed settlement of west Germany: freedom of action subject to a few reserved allied powers.[12]

Even so the western Powers stalled on a key policy which could have enabled the Magistrat to make a real go of things, reassured Berliners of allied commitment to the city and given confidence in its survival in a prospering west German context. They would not make the western mark, the Deutschmark, the sole currency in their sectors.

The need for it was pressing: the Magistrat's finances were in a shambles, the average wage earner only got a quarter of his pay in Deutschmarks so found it difficult to make ends meet, and the unemployed on 90 per cent benefit in East marks let alone pensioners with nothing but East marks were virtually destitute. Manufacturers were better off: they could meet their overheads such as rent, insurance, fuel bills and most of the wages in East marks. But even so they appreciated the advantages of tying Berlin's industry to the expanding west German economy and being able to pay for imported raw materials and equipment with a more acceptable means of exchange. The political logic of making the Deutschmark the single legal currency was self-evident: in a divided city there was no need to compromise with a dual system, the western mark would buoy up morale and indicate allied firmness to the west Germans. No one, except in the Security Council, any longer believed that currency problems alone had caused the blockade or that solving them would of itself get the siege lifted.

The American and British governments accepted the force of all these arguments. At the beginning of December they were willing to put them into action. In response to Marshall's insistence on a speedy decision, Bevin got Cabinet approval on 9 December for the Military Governors to work out timing and procedures for establishing the Deutschmark.[13] In theory, the whole process could be completed within three weeks.

But the western Powers were in a snare of their own devising. Having taken their case on Berlin to the United Nations they now had to wait politely until the end of the month for the report of the financial experts appointed by the Neutrals' Committee. They could guess what it would say: their own financial advisers had been frequently consulted and the Neutrals handled a secret as a treat to share. They had known from the start they were unlikely to consent to the report's recommendations since it was based on the assumption that a single, Russian mark could be transmogrified by technical hocus-pocus into a valid means of exchange for a split city and two incompatible economic systems.

When a draft of the report became available on 22 December its proposals turned out to be as objectionable as its hypothesis: a Soviet mark as the sole currency for Berlin, to be issued and controlled by the German Bank of Emission whose city board would have five of its eight members nominated by the SMA and whose decisions would be taken on a majority vote; and the exchange of all existing Deutschmarks in the city for East marks at a rate of one for one, which was roughly a quarter of their present value. Marshall fired off eleven paragraphs of blistering criticism on every aspect of the scheme, adding that this was "not an exhaustive list of objections" and that most of the defects did not seem "remediable by appropriate amendment."[14] Much British reaction was equally damning. The Bank of England called the proposals "highly dubious," thought Berliners would find the rate of exchange "a poor reward for the trust they put in us at the recent elections," and warned that the scheme meant a financial retreat from the city which would shake west German confidence and must be seen as the first step to total withdrawal.[15] A Treasury official praised the report as an academic piece of work: a "most ingenious and capable production." Then he cut it to ribbons: "in practice, however, it would not work"; it merely confirmed his opinion, and that of the Bank, that "no technical solution of the problem was in fact possible."[16]

At that point one might have expected the British and Americans to reject the proposals, abandon the Security Council involvement and introduce their own currency at the earliest opportunity. Not a bit of it. That is what the Americans would have done if they had had their way.[17] But Bevin dug in his heels. Rejection of the experts' proposals, he claimed, would be insulting to the United Nations and playing into the Soviet Union's hands; the western allies must see the whole Security Council business through to the bitter end; a few adjustments to the plan might make it workable for a short time while a proper solution was found; the Deutschmark would freeze the split of Berlin; a way must be left open to allow the Russians to consider restoring quadripartite government; dual currency on a 50–50 basis could solve a lot of the practical financial difficulties and put some limit on Soviet interference in the western sectors.[18] When putting his case to Attlee or Washington Bevin referred to support for it from "our experts." Given the initial reaction of the Bank of England and the Treasury, someone might have asked him, "experts in what?" or suggested that if a senior minister absolutely insists on a policy good civil servants try to make it work, however barmy they think it is. He made barefaced claims about French backing, though he was usually ready to ignore French views when they were motivated by the wish to hobble German development. None of Bevin's arguments was convincing, especially from a man who had been opposed to the intervention of the Security Council in the first place and all in favour of the Deutschmark in December. Put together they suggested, and created, total confusion.

Behind his jumble and incoherence, Bevin's instincts must have been troubling him. Perhaps he feared that a sudden move might shake the delicate structuring of European unity (significantly he once mumbled that timing was all-important and Berlin currency must be considered in the context of west Germany and the Atlantic Pact).[19] Perhaps in the early days of January he sensed a possibility which became more palpable later in the month: he suggested to Robertson in a long, ruminating cable on 24 January that he was not "entirely unconvinced that the Russians are not prepared to raise the blockade, possibly fairly soon" (in mid-March if the city got through the winter) and that everyone should avoid any action which would make it more difficult for them to step down.[20] Certainly Bevin was in no hurry. Before making any decisions he wanted a thorough appraisal of the effect of the East mark on Berlin's morale (as if there had not been plenty already) and an assessment of the future needs and prospects of the airlift.[21] Meanwhile, he was prepared to mark time and go back to the Security Council to discuss the experts' report and any counter-proposals "on a technical basis and without any commitment."[22]

Regardless of his capricious change of policy and inarticulate arguments, Bevin got what he wanted. The introduction of the Deutschmark to west Berlin was postponed and the western Powers returned to the Neutrals. And ironically, the Americans, so anxious to settle Berlin's finances and reject the experts' plan out of hand, were made the fall guys in the new round of negotiations. The British and French delivered replies to the experts which made only mild criticisms, implied that a little alteration to the report was all that was needed and generally suggested a supportive frame of mind. The Americans prepared their own response: honest, well-argued but leaving the impression that they alone were the stumbling-block to a settlement. Thereafter, the technical committee, which had reconvened in Geneva on 14 January, held forty-two meetings in less than a month and barely kept afloat in the cross tides of proposals and counter-proposals from the United States and the Soviet Union, while the British and French sat quietly as if distancing themselves from unreasonable behaviour by their American ally. The committee became increasingly irritated by the American delegation, which was well-versed in the technical details, put its points clearly on the political and economic consequences

302

of each financial proposal, and stuck to the fundamental principles always upheld by the West. It was charmed by Malietin, the leader of the Russian team, who seemed "concise, helpful and reasonable," but who did not budge from the basis of the 30 August Kremlin directive and whose suggested modifications to the experts' scheme merely made it suit Russian interests still better.[23] As the meetings began to grind to a halt in mid-February, largely thanks to Malietin's intransigence, he made a moving plea for further efforts which, as the Canadian chairman put it, left not "a dry eye in the house" and dazzlingly rounded off a skilful propaganda performance.[24] By then the British and French had finally come off the fence and openly sided with the Americans, filling the committee, said an observer, "with a gentle sorrow" at the thought that they had been browbeaten by their ally.[25]

In truth they had let the Americans do their dirty work for them and take all the blame for defending western interests. And Bevin had needed no pressure to drop his complaints and caution about the Deutschmark. He told the Cabinet on 7 February that it should be established as the sole currency in the western sectors on 10 March.[26] What was more he joined the Americans in shoving the reluctant French into accepting the decision. Schuman overrode Koenig on the principle of a single currency even though his Military Governor played several more acts of French farce in the coming weeks over dates and details.[27] (Schuman once commented with a smile, "If Koenig says No on Monday there is no reason why I can't say Yes on Tuesday," but he forgot to add that Koenig thought it reasonable to say "No" again on Wednesday.)[28]

It could be argued that the western Powers had gained some diplomatic advantage from going back to the Neutrals: shown deference to the international community while disabusing it of the idea that the Berlin problem was a simple matter of currency and showing how far apart the West and the Soviet Union really were. Very likely too, the whole United Nations procedure had persuaded the Russians that the western allies would not succumb even when Soviet duress of blockade was intensified by international pressure for compromise and settlement. By February the four and a half months spent at the Security Council might well be regarded not as a waste of time but an investment: when the Neutrals announced on 11 February that they were giving up their efforts, the whole Berlin crisis had taken on a dramatically new aspect. During the diplomatic holding operation at the United Nations the western sectors of Berlin had survived the coldest and darkest days. Winter had not won the city for the Russians – and spring was coming.

Credit for sustaining the western sectors throughout the winter must, of course, be given first and foremost to the airlift. It had kept up the supply of food and fuel without which Berliners would have died or been driven into the arms of the Russians. But in all honesty it has to be said that until the turn of the year the airlift was perilously close to failure. After all, the estimate for the minimum winter requirement for bare, miserable subsistence in the city was 5,500 tons a day. The actual figures of tonnage flown in during the early months of the season were frighteningly short of the need: in October an average of 4,760.5 tons a day, in November a disastrous 3,786.1, in December a still dangerously inadequate 4,563.4.[29] Faced with the shortfall, the airlift authorities had been forced to concentrate on carrying food: over the six months from July they had met 96 per cent of the requirement and by the end of the year there was thirty-eight days' stock in the city. But that had been built up by neglecting the fuel lift: reserves of coal were down to nineteen days, and all of it was earmarked for gas and electricity; there could only be a token offering to industry and there was nothing at all to spare for domestic heating.[30] The margin of safety was flimsy indeed – and Berlin was only halfway through the winter.

The city had kept going so far partly thanks to the sheer fortitude of Berliners. They had put up with insipid rations and shivered in the dark, but somehow remained cheerful and defiant. They were comforted a little by municipal provision of communal warming-rooms, where they huddled together round a stove or radiator and had begun to feel the benefit of the new rations with their scraps of cheese, a smear of fat and even occasional sprinklings of real coffee or tea. Fresh meat, the first since June, had come in at the end of December. There was very little of it, nothing to get the teeth into, but it was welcomed as a token of better days. Until they came, people coped with the dark days by laughing at them. At Christmas RIAS had launched a new regular programme, *Der Insulaner*, in which Günther Neumann and a cast of half a dozen played the population of a Berlin entirely surrounded by water: two chatty ladies from the Kurfürstendamm, a bossy and pompous Party official with a Russian minder, a luckless and bewildered average consumer, and so on. The characters were instantly recognisable and soon became loved; the situations were familiar and were lifted from the depressing to the comic; the types, the accents, the happenings were Berlin through and through: and as Neumann was often still scribbling the scripts as the theme music played, the show was bang up to the minute. *Der Insulaner* made Berlin's frightening isolation something to smile or chortle at; friends as well as enemies became jokes; anxiety and hardship were magically funny.

It was a more serious help for Berliners that they had little or no idea of how near to disaster they were. They were never told how much was flown in daily, never learned the sombre forecasts for future tonnage. They only got news of remarkable cargoes or cheery official pronouncements, and assumed that everything was going smoothly. Yet in early December the airlift authorities well knew they could not meet their desolate target for that month and were equally gloomy about the chances for January.[31] Occupation officials were discussing harsher economies in fuel for transport, hospitals and schools, considering cutting electricity supply to two hours a day and, even so, doubting that they could provide enough food for much longer. Such appalling prospects were not discussed with the Magistrat, nor even with many occupation officials. It was decided to postpone any new stringencies for as long as possible for the sake of morale; if the airlift could struggle through to February when the days got longer people might bear the hardship more easily.[32]

In the meanwhile, Berliners did get one huge boost for their spirits and the airlift was assured of greater safety for its operations. The French made their major contribution to beating the blockade and set about it with a bang. At 10:45 on the morning of 16 December General Ganeval, the French Commandant, gave the order to blow up the two Radio Berlin transmitter towers on the edge of Tegel. He did it without a qualm. After all, he pointed out, he had more than once asked the Russians to be so good as to remove these irksome protuberances; indeed, in his last letter on the subject he had specifically told them that the towers "would not be available after 15 December." He had not felt obliged to consult the British or Americans: he was the French Commandant acting on French territory. He remained unrepentant: "In my opinion it is no longer possible to accept responsibility for accidents." When an enraged Kotikov spluttered "How could you do such a thing?" Ganeval is said to have replied, "With the help of dynamite and French sappers."

The explosion was only the start of the fun. Radio Berlin went off the air for ten hours. It resumed rather quavering transmission in the evening from a 20-kwt long-wave transmitter near Potsdam and its director could just be heard denouncing the destruction of his towers as "an act of brutality against a cultural wireless station." The demolition had, in fact, levelled him from head of a regional broadcasting service to a less prestigious position at a somewhat inaudible local radio station. Berliners were in raptures. Their merrymaking came to a sad end, however. A few days later the Russians moved into the small village of Stolpe, occupied by the French since October 1945 when the Soviet authorities ceded it to them as a possible site for an airfield. Now that the French had an airfield at Tegel – and one relieved of SMA radio towers – the Russians felt justified in taking Stolpe back. The French did not demur: they expected the move and had no troops in the village when the Russians arrived. They had already given help to anyone who chose to leave. Many small farmers could not bear to desert their land, but most of the population, 93 per cent of which had voted in the election, feared reprisals and cleared out, in particular, policemen, firemen and municipal employees. The manager of a municipal farm in the village had had time to evacuate seventeen horses, fifty cows and his equipment. The Russians, said Ganeval, would find the estate in the condition they had left it in 1945.[33]

Even villagers themselves thought the loss of Stolpe was a price worth paying for the chance to hit at the Russians and ease the passage of aircraft into Berlin. The destruction of the towers, however, was not decisive in the survival of the city. Nor was the airlift, however essential, nor yet the morale of Berliners, however admirable. What really saved Berlin at the end of 1948 was the weather – sheer meteorological freak. All records showed that a winter of prolonged cold must be expected: bitter winds from Russia and Poland would freeze Berlin and the supply airfields. The average date for the first snow at Gatow (according to statistics collected between 1881 and 1932) was 14 November, though it had been known to fall in early October and keep coming as late as April. In some respects a normal German winter might provide good flying weather: open skies and clear visibility for landing. On the other hand, frost would tear up runway surfaces, engines would ice up (and there was a known world shortage of de-icing fluid), road and rail transport be brought to a standstill, and motor vehicles on the airfields become a menace as they skidded on frosted track. Most seriously of all, cold weather would burn up Berlin's fuel stocks faster than the airlift could replenish them.[34] From the moment the blockade began, everyone had known they would need even more luck than good management to keep the airlift and the city going through winter.

They got more luck than they had ever dreamed of. The typical numbing cold never settled in. There were days of raw wind or hard frost, but never more than the maintenance teams and de-icing gangs could cope with. For the most part there was relatively mild, moist air. This brought fog, of course: poor flying conditions and frequent closures of airfields. (Fassberg lost 23 per cent of landings from 14 November to 10 December; Gatow 18 per cent.) This fog explains the terrible tonnage figures in November. But thanks to instruments and determined men in the cockpits, aircraft still flew in horrible murk throughout November and December and, thanks to technology and skill on the ground, could land in all but the worst visibility: for a month from mid-November, 22.6 per cent of landings at Tempelhof were by GCA; 49.8 per cent at Rhein Main; 27.7 per cent at Fassberg.[35] Most crucial, Berlin could just about get by on what fuel it had. A few more degrees of cold at the end of 1948, with extended periods of sharp frost to bind aircraft to the ground, and surely the western sectors would have perished.

The meteorological miracle became truly prodigious in January. It was always a hard month and in 1947 there had been ninety-seven hours of severe frost, 281 of very severe frosting. In January 1949 no bad frost was recorded, none whatsoever. Berlin's coal reserves were not drained at the forecast rate – to the contrary, by some extraordinary fluke 7,000 tons of coal which no one had noticed before were spotted in January, and a further 4,863 turned up in February.[36] And the skies were clear: there were short periods of fog in the first week, only one bad day the second, winds and storms the third but no misting, and not enough poor visibility at the end of the month to disrupt targets.[37] To cap it all, Rhein Main and Wiesbaden, where the worst weather had been forecast, had the best: both airfields operated at more or less summer intensity.[38] (If British arguments had prevailed the big C-54s would have been moved to the shorter routes from the British zone and been hit by the poorer weather.) At last the airlift tonnage began to meet Berlin's needs. An average of 5,546.4 tons was delivered every day throughout January.

The February lift was almost as successful: 5,436.2 tons a day in spite of long periods of low cloud and poor landing visibility, and the arrival of the millionth ton on 18 February in a York which could hardly put down thanks to foul murk on the ground and a lorry blocking the radar signal. The month's operation was so successful indeed that there was the confidence to let food reserves drop to twenty-eight days' supply while coal was packed in; an increase of fuel for industry, from 237 to 400 tons per month, could be announced.[39]

The airlift's achievements bore a grim cost. On 5 and 11 December, 7, 12 and 18 January C-54s crashed: in all, thirteen young Americans died. On 15 January the port inner propeller of a Hastings taxiing at night hit a vehicle and killed the German driver and three civilian personnel of Lancashire Aircraft Corporation. Most tragically of all, on 24 January a Dakota coming in to land in bad weather at Lübeck with a crew of three, nineteen German adult passengers and five sick children crashed into the Russian zone. The wireless operator and seven of the passengers, including two of the children, were killed; seventeen people were injured. It was hard to stomach the claim by the *Berliner Zeitung* that no children would have died if the western allies had not started their "corrupt, useless and redundant political and commercial undertaking," the airlift, and set about "politically inspired murder" by evacuating the young.[40] The only consolation was to remember that the death rate was phenomenally low, given the amount of traffic and the appalling flying conditions.

It was some relief, too, that Soviet interference with allied aircraft had been surprisingly limited. There was an unpleasant scare in early January when the Soviet military announced that they would force down any aircraft operating at under 3,000 feet. They clearly had the fighters to do it, or could put up enough balloons to make use of the air corridors impossible. The airlift headquarters had to gamble on Russian unwillingness to commit an act of war: a reminder of the legal status of the corridors was sent to the Soviet authorities together with a curt suggestion that they were exceeding their powers. The gamble paid off; traffic continued without hindrance.[41]

And because the airlift and the fine weather continued, the western sectors of Berlin not only survived the winter and the worst crisis of the blockade, but remarkably (or perhaps "shockingly") were actually better fed than at any time since the war. The new rations were dependably provided and were of higher quality than of recent years. If only they had contained fresh vegetables, potatoes in particular, everyone would have been delighted. As it was, however, production of troublesome, loathed dehydrated potato had at last shown signs of catching up with demand: in the last week of January 1,117 tons were manufactured (the full requirement being 1,260) and a fortnight later 1,302.[42] There was even a chance of fresh locally grown vegetables next season: airlift space had been allocated for 400 tons of seed and the first consignments arrived in the third week of January.[43] Already it was reckoned that the regular supply of adequately nutritious food had cut the tuberculosis rate in half and clearly accounted for a small overall increase in the weight of Berliners (the biggest, in males over sixty, was 6.2 lbs; the smallest was 1.3 lbs for women up to the age of fifty-nine – presumably their rations went into other mouths).[44] By early February even black-market prices for food were dropping noticeably: an indication that food was more plentiful and satisfying rather than that money was short.[45]

Yet survival, even a marginal improvement in the quality of living, could not be taken as an excuse for congratulation or complacency. Berlin was still only receiving about a third of what it had consumed before the blockade. Furthermore, the airlift was not fulfilling its potential. It now had effective organisation and flying discipline, adequately equipped airfields, experienced ground and aircrews and even enough aircraft – the USAF had 225 C-54s by the end of January, the British 131 assorted RAF and civil types. In theory, the Americans should have been lifting 6,487 tons a day and the British 1,481. In practice, both forces were struggling to reach the minimum target of 5,500 tons. Their cargo capacity was on paper, not in the air. Their aircraft were stuck on the ground because no one had managed to solve the critical problem of maintenance.

An aircraft supplying Berlin could be flown by a crew of three. It needed at least a further seven men to keep it fit to fly and ideally each aircraft would have had a maintenance team of fifteen. Servicing and repair of the huge numbers of machines employed in Operations "Vittles" and "Plainfare" meant a major investment of planning and manpower. The conditions of the airlift made the task of maintenance Herculean. Some of the aircraft, like the C-47s and their British cousins the Dakotas, were obsolete, the Hastings was so new that its needs could not be foreseen; neither the old nor the new had adequate reserves of spare parts. Virtually all the planes were doing a job they were not designed for: non-stop flying with maximum loads on short trips. Their engines, built for long periods of cruising, were pounded by constant high-manifold pressure and heavy revving. Their airframes were strained by the weight of cargo and repeated landings fully laden which also overtaxed hydraulics, brake discs and cables. Hold floors were wrecked by hasty loading of bulky freight. Dirty consignments like coal clogged and corroded electrical parts and controls. PSP ripped tyres. Continual running of engines on the ground wore out seals, gaskets and ignition wiring. Flying in dry weather meant windscreens pitted with grit; rain caused electrical faults and used up a normal year's supply of windscreen wipers in two weeks; cold brought starting problems and tattered de-icing equipment.[46]

At Gatow and Tegel nothing more than a minor rectification was ever handled – aircraft were pushed out almost regardless of their condition so as to clear space for incoming traffic. At Tempelhof, where the high surrounding buildings made take-off dangerous, aircraft were often cleared to fly back to Celle or Fassberg on only three engines, but over a period of twelve months sixty-five engine changes had to be carried out and seven collapsed nosewheel sections were replaced.[47] Nearly all maintenance and repair was done at the home airfield. On the return journey a pilot informed his base from thirty miles out of his serviceability. Up to 80 per cent of all aircraft came back from a sortie with some defect, though such was the aircrews' anxiety to keep flying that in November it was discovered that only 10–20 per cent of them admitted when their aircraft were in poor condition.[48] With luck, the ground crew could carry out a quick rectification – change plugs, block an oil leak, put in new bulbs for instrument panels or wing tips, fit a fresh tyre – and get the aircraft ready for the next flying block. All too often, though, the job took longer: brake cables, axle dowel pins and exhaust stubs had to be replaced every 5–8 sorties; there were never-ending boost and carburation troubles, breakdowns in flying controls, and damage to flaps and wing tips from loading accidents.

Repair work was dragged out by a chronic shortage of skilled men. The Americans calculated that they had 160 C-54s before they had reasonable back-up for fifty and once they got 225 they could only really cope with 100. The British tried but failed to overcome their shortage of mechanics by calling up reservists and delaying demobs. The RAF in Germany fought a running battle with Transport Command in Britain to keep what men it could get. The Commander-in-Chief at BAFO complained bitterly in January 1949 that Transport Command's insistence on a quarterly rotation of technical personnel between home and airlift stations was "not only grossly wasteful in manpower ... but means there is complete lack of continuity in the maintenance organisation," and a "greater number of aircraft being held here or en route to and from the UK than should really be necessary to meet our operational requirement."[49] It was spring before Transport Command introduced

standard overseas tours for maintenance staff. By British interpretation of the Potsdam agreement, German labour could only be used
in semi-labouring jobs such as cleaning, defrosting or giving a hand
to change wheels or power plants. The Americans became so hard-
pressed for skilled labour that they read Potsdam differently and
finally broke their own non-fraternisation rules. They took on up
to eighty-five German mechanics, mainly Luftwaffe trained, for
each squadron's routine maintenance. German-speaking officers
were found to superintend them, manuals were translated and the
result was high-class work and the release of USAF men for other
jobs.

Repairs were further complicated and delayed by a dearth of
spare parts and tools. One British analysis calculated that bad
equipment put two hours on to each straightforward rectification.[50]
In the early days of the airlift the USAF was short of wrenches and
screwdrivers; the RAF never got enough for its Dakotas because
they had to be paid for in dollars. Only the two American naval
squadrons could boast sufficient spares. They had arrived in
Germany with enough for half a year of flying and for months
resisted all blandishments and browbeating to pool them. When
they finally had to hand over their store it was booby-trapped:
catalogued in a naval system incomprehensible to the USAF. In
the meantime, Tunner had been gnashing his teeth because first he
could not get access to warehouses full of parts near Munich and,
when at last he did, there was no proper inventory.[51]

Gradually the weekly Globemaster trips from the United States
and Transport Command's "Operation Plumber" Dakotas from
the UK built up better reserves of spares, but they never quite came
to terms with the complexity of so many varieties of aircraft. The
RAF's problem with machines built by Handley Page, A. V. Roe
and Douglas was easy to grasp if not to solve. USAF aircraft,
however, were not as straightforward as they might seem. The C-
54 had gone through eleven series since it was first designed in 1933;
there were several different types on the airlift and not even their
windscreen wipers let alone their flying instruments were trans-
posable. Worse: engine specifications varied and several hundred
engines had to be replaced at one time or another by those of an
earlier version with lower horsepower. (At least, said Tunner
blithely, it "gave the pilot something to think about when he had
both models on one plane.")

Though the USAF and the RAF shared many similar maintenance problems, the Americans tackled theirs infinitely more

311

efficiently. Their utilisation rate per aircraft was three times that of the British. In part, but only small part, this superiority can be explained in terms of the solidity of the C-54, the block system of sorties favouring the bigger load carrier, and the time spent by the RAF in backloading in Berlin. Yet in the end the USAF flew more trips for the simplest of reasons: its aircraft were not so often stuck on the ground. To a large extent money kept them in the air. The Americans could employ more ground staff, afford to keep more spares and, above all, they did not have to spend time fiddling about with elaborate repairs: they could strip out a damaged part and replace it with a brand-new one. Such lavish expenditure was way beyond the means of the indigent British. It was also psychologically alien. The Americans came from an economic culture of mass production and expendability; the British nurtured manual skills rather than technology, regarded throwing things away as a crime and had been forced in recent years to use time and ingenuity because they had nothing else to spend. American machines were relatively simple in design and tough in action; British were minor engineering marvels but temperamental and in need of more adept servicing.

The Americans did not sit back and rest on their financial and design advantages. They worked hard on the management of maintenance. Whereas the RAF had a navigator in each cockpit the USAF had an engineer, monitoring the machine's health and able to direct the ground crew to specific faults and supervise their work until he was satisfied with it. From October the USAF had standardised maintenance control: regular reports on the state of each aircraft, colour coding to indicate its condition, and a form with its complete record. They kept their squadron organisation as far as possible: air and ground crews worked as a team with the same aircraft; they built up trust in each other and pride in their work. The RAF began with maintenance on a station basis: the first mechanics available were sent to an aircraft needing attention. They had probably never seen it before and blundered about, often in the dark, to find it along a line up to 1,000 yards long. Once they found it, they might have the wrong tools and have to grope around for others in all the chaos of men, machines and motor transport; they then had to diagnose the fault with only a vague description from the pilot to help. They worked without much skilled supervision because the NCOs and officers stayed at a central point trying to work out where the next aircraft to be repaired was parked and which team could be sent to it. Eventually the RAF learned to save

312

some time and trouble: servicing was split into three flights, one for about a dozen aircraft, and common faults were identified on a card issued to all personnel which described the symptoms, the number of men and types of tool for the repair, and the time needed for the job. The result of these reforms was striking: British rectification times were cut by half.[52]

Their maintenance times never matched the Americans'. A York took three hours of servicing after every two-hour sortie, a C-54 only one or one and a half. Bigger USAF technical teams and replacement rather than repair accounted for some of the discrepancy. But there was also a very important difference of attitude. The RAF, as one report spotted, "over-inspected."[53] And, indeed, over-repaired. The USAF was permitted to fly with lower standards of serviceability, and all the facts and figures on major breakdowns and accidents proved they were perfectly able to do so. They tolerated 350 minor problems before handing in an aircraft for maintenance; the RAF allowed only thirty-six. The Americans knew their C-54 was sturdy enough to put up with the odd rattle and their flight engineer was capable of judging when a nuisance became a danger. (The very fact that he was prepared to risk his neck in a machine with 349 faults was a comfort to the rest of the crew.) The British, by contrast, made themselves martyrs to perfection; the best became the enemy of the good enough.

The same fastidious approach afflicted the RAF's regular servicing. Initially they insisted on a service after every fifty hours of flying, sandwiched between alternate terminal and base overhauls. Then the flying time between inspections was extended to seventy-five hours, and in November terminal servicing was dropped altogether and base servicing in the UK took place every 100 hours. Aircraft suffered no ill effects from this neglect – indeed, as the final report admitted, the "deletion of terminal servicing improved the serviceability of the York."[54] (As every car owner knows, messing about under the bonnet often breaks more than it mends.) Even so, the reduced amount of servicing took longer than it should and grounded aircraft for an intolerable time. Flying aircraft home was said to be necessary because of lack of hangar space and accommodation for mechanics in Germany, to save the cost of sending equipment to the airlift bases, and to provide a convenient ferry service for personnel and spares. But there is a suspicion that Transport Command saw it as a means of keeping some control over its aircraft, which in other respects had slipped into the hands of BAFO. If so it not only hampered airlift operations by a time-consuming exercise but nobbled itself: as the Commander-in-Chief BAFO put it in an angry letter in January: "if I had the entire running of this show I could make do with less TC aircraft by reorganising the maintenance."[55] As it was, Transport Command had to curtail many of its worldwide operations because more aircraft were assigned to the airlift to compensate for the fact that routine UK services were insisted on at short intervals and took four and a half days – a job the USAF did in less than half the time in Germany.

The Americans did not believe in finicky upkeep, but their aircraft flew just as well when they were only inspected after every 200 hours of flying and given the odd oil change, spark plug replacement or brake check in between. At first they concentrated all their regular servicing in one depot at Oberfallenhofen. By November its facilities were overstretched and Tunner was champing at the bit to transfer the work to Burtonwood in Lancashire, an old American base which in wartime had assembled aircraft shipped in sections across the Atlantic and then kept them in repair. Burtonwood, however, was scarcely able to cope with two aircraft a day and when Tunner went to find out why he was not surprised: it was "dingy, dirty and depressing-looking," he said; the living quarters were cold and dark, the chow was "greasy and tasteless" and the weather was lousy.[56] He could not do much about the climate of north-west England, but he could fight red tape and bureaucratic inertia until the place was brightened up, the food improved, the staff enthused and equipment brought up to scratch. In March, by which time the serviceability of the USAF fleet had dropped alarmingly, Burtonwood was at last able to do six inspections a day; by mid-April it was carrying out all the work required of it.[57] Only the Navy spurned the attentions of Burtonwood; they tried the place, were not impressed by the standards so did their own inspections – and in a mere twenty-four hours too.[58] All USAF aircraft were kept flying for 1,000 hours before being sent back to the United States for a thorough overhaul – the greatest of bonuses for a pilot lucky enough to do the trip since it was the only time he caught a glimpse of home in a six-month tour of duty.

The RAF had quite enough maintenance problems of its own, but one more was added: responsibility for keeping the civil lift in repair. Most of the civil contractors had brought out to Germany decrepit old aircraft but no servicing platforms or battery-charging equipment, not even a ladder. They cadged them from the RAF.

They had few if any spares and little or no capital to buy them, so the RAF stumped up if it had them, but some aircraft were so old that parts were no longer stocked. Tudors were a breed of their own: BSAA had plenty of spares but hated Bennett, who had none, and would not sell him any; he had to persuade Field Aircraft Services to buy them and pass them over on the sly.[59] The civilians did not have enough maintenance personnel either. (Bennett had only six men for two Tudors,[60] but was fortunately no mean practitioner with a spanner and oily rag himself.) The contractors were fierce individualists and pooling maintenance was against their grain; scrounging RAF workshop facilities and fitters was not. Their servicing was done in Britain, and even more slowly than the RAF's. Most Halifax/Halton work was concentrated at Bovington until Bond Air Services lost patience with waiting three months for four of its aircraft and set up its own company in Southend.

The companies engaged for the civil lift proliferated in the last months of 1948: World Air Freight, Lancashire Aircraft Corporation, Airwork, Sivewright Airways, BOAC, Skyways and British American Air Services brought Halton freighters and tankers, Yorks and Dakotas. More did not always mean better. An exasperated cable from Berlin described the tanker which landed at Gatow with 2,000 gallons of diesel: it "carried no hose and gave no previous notification that its requirements for decanting would differ from the Lancastrian arrangement"; there had been a delay of fifty minutes before a suitable hose could be botched together and it then took thirty-four minutes to drain the tank.[61] This was just one example from a saga of inadequate equipment and sheer slapdashery. There was civil sharp practice too. The companies were paid by the flying hour not the load: if they took short weight they cut their operating costs and the time on the ground at either end; if a tanker pilot grabbed a cargo manifest and took off fast, he could fly almost empty, and until proper meters were fitted in Berlin no one realised they were pumping air not fuel into the storage tanks.

All too often, thought the civil contractors could not be persuaded to fly at all. One sorrowful report suggested: "It cannot be said that the operating companies, with certain honourable exceptions, have over-exerted themselves."[62] To be fair, many had, and because they were short of aircrews (they had an average of 1.3 per plane and one company had only nine teams for ten aircraft) they were exhausted. Men who were overworked felt no urge to fill a night-flying slot and they were well-enough paid to afford a day in bed from

315

time to time. Their companies got a flat rate minimum anyway and the management tended to be friendly and weak. Bennett, as in so many ways, was exceptional: when his chief pilot, Captain Utting, was knocked down and killed by a lorry at Gatow in early December, the Air-Marshal himself flew two or three sorties a night for nearly two months, an epic which Mr. Whitfield thought had "few parallels in the history of aviation."[63] It was noticed that there was more keenness to get on with the job among companies based at RAF stations; they were not subject to military discipline, but found it infectious.[64]

The civilians were not always welcome guests there, however. Some of them were old squadron friends or admired as first-rate airmen doing a good job with lousy equipment. Others were regarded as cocky or idle, envied for their pay and written off as mercenaries. Integrating them into station life was no easy business. The commanding officer at Schleswigland recommended that in future the "civilian liaison officer between the RAF and the civil firms should always be a man of mature age and standing with a good background of both service and civil life," someone who carried weight with the "civil element who are inclined to stand on their dignity and call on union rules whenever it suits." The worst social clashes he had noticed were when civilian ground crews did not "acclimatise themselves to the conduct of the Sergeants' Mess and were in general looked on with disfavour by the service members" (and there can be few things more awesome than the disfavour of an affronted sergeant). The civilians had seldom been senior NCOs (whereas most of the pilots had been officers) and "did not know the usages and customs of SNCO mess and apparently did not care." The CO thought it better than they should be "messed and accommodated separately."[65]

The RAF grumbled non-stop about incorporating civil operations with their own, and with some justification. As a BAFO memo complained: "Their serviceability varies from day to day, the number of sorties which they are ready and able to undertake also varies, and their total daily effort is unpredictable for planning purposes."[66] The service chiefs toyed with plans to convert their own aircraft into tankers to replace civilians, to requisition the civil aircraft and fly them themselves, to call up any civil pilot still on the reserve and slap him under military authority.[67] Meanwhile, officials in Berlin cried in despair for an increase in the wetlift's deliveries of liquid fuel. In October 75.7 metric tons of motor fuel a day were needed for the occupation forces and the local economy, but only 34.9 tons were being supplied: the rest had to be brought by the Americans who should have been carrying equally vital coal.[68] In addition the city had to have 58 metric tons of diesel, which it was not getting. In fact, if Soviet reserves of liquid fuel which happened to be stored in the western sectors had not been purloined, the tanks would have been dry in November.[69] More tanker aircraft were hurriedly engaged, old freighters converted. Still the wetlift could not keep up with demand: civil serviceability was 69 per cent, the weather loss was 42 per cent – and to make matters worse in December several Berlin power stations began to run on diesel rather than coal. It was predicted that in January the civilians would be able to supply 120 tons of liquid fuel a day – but 221 metric tons would be needed.[70] On 4 January the situation in Berlin was reported to be "daily approaching a critical state" – drought.[71]

The civilians, however, were taking much more of the blame for the shortcomings of the wetlift than they deserved. Whatever their own faults they were obliged to operate a system with gross defects. Everyone in Whitehall had a finger in the civil-lift pie: the Foreign Office which did the chartering, the Treasury which objected to the cost, the Air Ministry which wanted full powers and could not get them, and the Ministry of Civil Aviation which might have been expected to take responsibility but which was found to show "little interest."[72] Each company had been hired on a mere month's contract, which included a fourteen-day cancellation clause; there was no inducement whatsoever to invest in improvements to aircraft or staffing. When a sensible suggestion was made in October that the contract be extended to three months, the Treasury turned it down flat (following their usual policy of refusing a stitch at the right time and then grudgingly putting in six once nine are overdue). Treasury myopia gave an excuse for civil obduracy: the companies in return would not agree to work to standards of minimum performance.[73] Only one advance was made in October: Edwin Whitfield, the BEA manager in Germany, who had so far had a restricted liaison role, was now given fuller managerial powers (and by February had complete authority over the civil lift).

How the companies loathed Mr. Whitfield ("interfering busybody," "fussy old woman," "jumped-up bureaucrat"). What a thorough, well-deserved shake-up he gave them. Contracts with unsatisfactory firms ended abruptly; those for uneconomical Dakotas and Vikings were not renewed; some contractors were given the option of converting freighters to tankers or being replaced by new firms. No one ever succeeded in shepherding the civilians into flocks of the same aircraft (which would have eased operational planning), but Whitfield and the RAF between them at least tidied up some of the confusion. Wunstorf became an Avro base with Tudors, Yorks and Lancastrians; old Haltons and various freighters were cleared out to Fuhlsbüttel; many new tankers went to Schleswigland. Whitfield even managed to sort out who flew when: on 4 December it was decreed that each base would allocate a separate block time for civil-lift aircraft to get to Frohnau. It was their tough luck if they missed their slot and they would then have to wait for the next (no popping in and making a mess of an RAF block). Every station got a BEA Operations Controller with one administration and four operations officers to share out times in the blocks between the companies and to chase them up.

The companies were furious: BEA was "nationalised," "feather-bedded," but they had "a living to make"; BEA staff were "wet behind the ears," but the civilian fliers were hardened old veterans with "real business experience." There were rows for two months until Whitfield wore everyone down by sheer persistence and scrupulous fairness. Slowly the civil operators learned that he not only understood their difficulties, he sympathised with them. He put pressure on the military in Germany and got better accommodation than the usual outlying, damp hotels and better messing arrangements at the airfields. He nagged company headquarters until they introduced rotas, increased staff and sent out competent managers. Largely thanks to Whitfield's pestering Flight Refuelling, which in January 1949 had the second worst utilisation record of all the companies, appointed Wing-Commander Johnson, who sacked the lazy, drew up proper rosters, revolutionised living, working and repair conditions, and by March had achieved a better utilisation record than the RAF.

Yet even the efficacious Mr. Whitfield was unable to clear the main impediment which hampered civil efficiency and nearly wrecked the winter fuel lift: the lack of Rebecca-Eureka navigational equipment. Way back on 13 August he had warned that Rebecca sets must be supplied and fitted by the RAF if the civilian companies were to fly in bad weather. Nothing was done. A conference in London on 14 October was told that unless immediate action was taken the civil lift would come to a halt within the next two months. The RAF and Foreign Office finally took the point. But they could not find enough Rebecca sets. When sixteen were at last tracked down in a warehouse in Carlisle, nearly all of them were out of order. While

318

more delving took place and bits and pieces were assembled, the fog closed in, civil aircraft were stuck on the ground and Berlin's liquid fuel stocks drained away. The tankers worst affected were those stationed at Schleswigland: the airfield, on the Baltic coast, was constantly wrapped in low cloud and sea mist, never mind fog. Even in clear weather, flying from the base was dangerous for civil aircraft: their operating height was 6,000 feet, icing was harsh and most of them did not have the equipment to deal with it. One captain iced so heavily while climbing to his cruising altitude that he dropped 3,000 feet before he could regain control. On 17 December the RAF decided that no aircraft without a Rebecca set would be allowed to fly except in VFR conditions. It was only by 13 January that every Halton had been properly fitted out.[74]

The delay had not only blocked fuel supply in the months it was most desperately needed, but held back the conversion of many freighters to tankers – until they got their navigational equipment they simply hung about. A tanker fleet of thirty-one had been planned for the beginning of January; only eleven were ready and it took to the end of the month to bring the force up to strength. Fortunately its new size and flying capability coincided with the rerouting of aircraft from Fuhlsbüttel and Schleswigland to Tegel rather than Gatow: they now used the northern corridor in both directions, which cut the journey time, and they operated at 1,000 feet to Berlin and 1,500 on return so avoided the worst of the freezing. By February the civil lift was flying an average of fifty-four sorties every twenty-four hours (and only 3 per cent more by day than night) and was pouring in a daily average of 262.2 tons of liquid fuel. Next month the combined wet- and drylifts did seventy trips a day and delivered a total of 479.8 tons. And their totals kept rising. There were even signs that the tangled web of authority in London was straightening out. A working party with members from all government departments concerned first met on 14 February and began to consider bringing the civil lift under unified control. ("This is the first time we have got any sense out of the Ministry of Civil Aviation," said a startled Foreign Office official.) Proper contract arrangements were discussed and plans made to put the civilian contribution on a long-term basis of anything up to two years.[75]

By February everyone – service chief, politician, diplomat – was thinking in terms of a prolonged and expanded airlift. General Cannon and Air-Marshal Williams submitted a joint report to their governments on 14 February, which estimated that even with present forces they could supply a daily average of 7,824 tons from July 1949 to the end of the year. If they could replace the RAF's fifty-four little Dakotas with C-54s or something similar, the volume would go up to 8,685. Basing more American aircraft in the British zone, building new airfields there together with a second runway at Tegel, and the introduction of more new American CPS-5 radar units would push the total over 9,000 tons. Throw in seventy-five 10-tonners as well and it would be easy to supply 11,000 tons a day. Once C-74s or C-97s were available (not for another eighteen months) the possible increase was almost beyond intellectual grasp.[76] In the long term Berlin could actually be sustained by air as fully as it was once supplied by land and water. Meanwhile, planning was no longer concerned with mere subsistence but with realistic schemes to raise the standard of living: providing more varied food, making sure that at least a third of the potato ration would be fresh, ensuring enough coal for domestic heating and six hours of electricity a day, boosting industry with more fuel, raw materials and replacement machinery, meeting the need for medical and agricultural supplies, and brightening lives with more consumer goods.[77]

What an astounding transformation from June when everything had been cobbled together in such haste and everyone assumed that the airlift would be over, for good or ill, in a matter of weeks. What a wondrous change of attitude from the early days of winter when Berlin's survival had seemed so dubious and the failure of the airlift inexorable. For months the airlift had been seen as a desperate means of staving off disaster while a more or less humiliating agreement was found with the Russians; now it was viewed as an operation which could go on indefinitely, at a much lower price than war or withdrawal, until the Soviet Union raised its siege on allied terms. Analysis and planning from February onwards were based not on fear but confidence. The question was not how long the western sectors would hold out but when the Russians would give way. They had missed their chance to take Berlin in the winter when food was scarce, the lights were out and the airlift was so very infirm. There were eight months or more of good flying weather coming: stocks could be built up, the city would never again be so vulnerable. Never mind that west Berlin had been saved more by the weather than man, that the airlift had only kept going by the skin of its fuselages. The city and its allies lived to fight more effectively another day.

The Russians perhaps guessed what a close-run thing the Berlin winter had been. They had calculated on the climate winning the city for them, but had got it wrong. They could hear the ceaseless drone of engines in the sky, knew that western rations and coal supplies had increased, and understood that short of risking war there was nothing more they could do to increase their pressure. And at the same time, as they assessed the impotence of their blockade to crush the western sectors, they could see that it was failing to curb west European or west German developments either. In fact, the blockade was probably spurring those developments on.

The states of west Europe had seen the blockade of Berlin from the beginning as a possible threat to their own security. Bevin had played on their fears to promote his plans for Western Union and an American alliance. On 25 and 26 October, when the prospects for Berlin looked doleful indeed, the Consultative Council of the Brussels Treaty nations had approved proposals to negotiate a North Atlantic defence pact with the United States and Canada. No one expected these negotiations to be quick or easy. There were so many varieties of national pride to be ruffled and smoothed, questions of which areas to include, complications over the duration of any agreement and doubts about whether it should commit all signatories to automatic response in case of an attack on one. Above all, American reluctance to reverse its historical tradition of non-involvement would have to be overcome and Congress assured that it would not lose its constitutional power to declare war.

Contrary to all expectations, however, once the Ambassadors' Committee of all interested states convened on 10 December, it made rapid headway. The catalyst in its progress was the sudden enthusiasm of the Americans for the scheme. President Truman, giving the lie to every opinion poll, had been re-elected to office on 2 November and now felt he could press on with matters previously politically risky or which he did not have confirmed authority to tackle. His Democratic Party had control of both houses of Congress and public opinion had recently hardened against the Soviet Union, partly as a result of the Berlin blockade. Given the driving force of Under Secretary of State Lovett, the Ambassadors' Committee had a draft text for a North Atlantic treaty on 24 December. This was only a beginning: invitations had to be sent to potential members of an alliance (Iceland, Norway, Denmark, Ireland, Portugal); the geographical conundrum had to be answered on whether Italy was in the North Atlantic (or, indeed, whether North Africa was, as the French contended); Congress had to be won over. But it was a solid start. Already the western Europeans were encouraged by the amount of accord they had discovered among themselves and by the chance that American strength would shield them. For the French above all this new-found sense of solidarity and security began to offset dread of German revival. Conversely, the speed and nature of the western agreement was surely a painful jolt to the Soviet Union. As harmony and drafting success continued through January and early February, the Russians must have been jarred even more. A schoolroom map in Moscow, marked with the possible members of a North Atlantic Treaty Organisation, would have been a chastening sight: the Soviet Union, which only a year ago could have planned expansion in any direction, was likely to be encircled.

Furthermore, it was being shut out of west Germany. An agreement to set up an international Ruhr Authority had been thrashed out in November 1948 and January 1949. The intention was to allocate the riches of coal and steel between western Germany and its neighbours – and the USSR would get nothing, while west European industrial renewal was fuelled by German resources.

Over the same period, the Parliamentary Council in Bonn had made impressive strides towards creating a Basic Law, a quasi constitution for west Germany. It had actually completed its first draft at the beginning of January. No matter that the SPD still argued for centralised government and the CDU for a looser federal state, that there were unsettled questions about how revenue would be raised, the status of Berlin, the nature of the presidency, and the controls over the civil service and judiciary. No matter either that the Military Governors had still not agreed on criteria for judging the draft or on their reserved powers for the Occupation Statute. The fact was that by the beginning of 1949 the Russians could see that all their threats against constitutional evolution had been ignored, that the bait of lifting the blockade in return for western suspension of political unification and German self-rule had not been swallowed. Seemingly the west Germans and the allies were going to settle their own affairs no matter if the Soviet Union refused a settlement of the Berlin crisis.

And it was perfectly clear that Berlin itself was willing to withstand a long siege if need be. The city had endured the worst the Russians and the winter could do; it had emerged stalwart and proud. Berliners did not believe they were fighting for mere survival nor for themselves alone. Ernst Reuter put what they felt in a speech to the City Assembly on 1 February: "We must never forget that we are involved in disputes of much greater magnitude than we would like them to be, and particularly we must not forget our obligation which we owe to the whole of Germany which is to defend in the midst of the Soviet Zone of Occupation the high values on which our whole material and cultural existence depends."[78] The people of Berlin shared the ideas Reuter expressed to Foreign Office officials during a visit to London later in the month: the western sectors offered east Berlin and the Soviet zone their only hope of freedom; the city must be fully incorporated as a Land in the new west German state; only firmness, never compromise, would bring the Russians to seek an agreement.[79] If Berliners had to wait for a solution of their city's crisis, if they had to suffer to play the role they had chosen, then so be it. They had proved to themselves and the world that they could live and grow under blockade. They had won total adherence from the western allies – even France: Schuman told Bevin in mid-January that the French would never withdraw from the city and he repeated his guarantee to Reuter the following month.[80] In early 1949 Berliners and western Powers alike were speaking with confidence and would act from strength.

At the same time as the Russians were losing the political and diplomatic upper hand, they were feeling economically tender. Their own total blockade of Berlin had failed to kill finance and industry in the western sectors whereas the allies' half-hearted, tentative counter-blockade of trade sanctions was having a noticeably debilitating effect on the Soviet zone.

The zone's economy was sickly anyway. Land reform, increasing concentration of agricultural credit and sales in state-run co-operatives, the monopoly of state equipment pools over procurement and repair of farm machinery and the provision of seed had all impeded rather than encouraged food production. The competitive rations introduced to the Russian sector of Berlin and offered to the whole city had stripped shops and storehouses, required expensive buying in other east European states, and meant that the 1948 harvest was taken in long before crops were fully grown. By the end of 1947 probably 65 per cent of the total industrial capacity of the Soviet zone had been moved to the Soviet Union. Stocks of raw materials and manufactured goods had been pillaged too, and current production was constantly milked (in some industries anything up to nine-tenths of output was taken). Over a third of the productive capacity left in the zone was controlled by SAGs (Soviet Companies), a further 40 per cent was nationalised. Both

323

these forms of state enterprise got priority over private companies in raw materials and machinery; both were geared primarily to Russian needs. They were managed by men qualified by political devotion rather than business expertise. They were unproductive and the remnant of private companies was too small and short of resources to make up for their inefficiency.

For 1948 it was thought that the Soviet zone had just about met its targets for coal and oil production, been more than 25 per cent short in manufacture of sulphuric acid (needed for fertilisers and synthetic yarns), even shorter in pig-iron output, and had only managed to produce about half the textiles for which it had the capacity.[81] And Soviet targets had been low, even if they were too high for attainment. No one believed the east German Economic Commission when it boasted that its 1949 plan would raise zonal production to 75 per cent of 1936 totals – and west Germany had already passed that figure. East Germans queued outside empty shops, then went home to listen to the radio from the Bizone and talked about the "Golden West."[82] By the middle of 1949, 398,000 of them were reckoned to be out of work, in spite of compulsory employment in the uranium mines, state direction to undesirable jobs or the USSR, and the imprisonment of at least 230,000 in concentration camps. When, at the beginning of the year, tens of thousands of east zone residents a month fled to the west, economic even more than political motives drove them from home.

Such an unhealthy economy did not have the resilience to put up with the strains of the allied counter-blockade. It was particularly hard-hit by being deprived of Ruhr coal and steel from July. Russian zone industrial furnaces and rail locomotives were built for high quality hard coal; the brown coal they were now forced to burn cut their efficiency and choked them with dust. Brown coal probably caused the repeated breakdowns at electricity generating stations too. Lack of steel held up heavy industry of all kinds, and led to a cut in the railway extension and maintenance programme for 1949 from 1,150 kms of track to 250. Want of steel cables restricted mining. From September 1948 the western allies had prohibited sales of some manufactured items and introduced export licences for others. The east zone economy soon ran short of boiler tubes, electrical motors, conveyor belts, ballbearings, ignition and transmission systems, diamond drills, optical goods, lubricants, cellulose for textiles, anti-oxidants and vulcanisers for synthetic rubber, and every manner of spare part and machine-tool for every kind of equipment.[83] The "A" list of banned exports and "B" list of goods needing permits grew each month: in February zinc coffins, tin-foil bottle caps and Lametta strips for decorating Christmas trees were added to the "B" list because they were all sources of raw materials which the West was reluctant to supply to the East.[84]

Neither list was ever comprehensive: there was fear of political and economic damage to west Germany if trade was stopped completely. Nor were the export bans ever applied rigorously: the allies simply did not have the resources or manpower to make their counter-blockade watertight. The borders between the Trizone and the Russian zone were long and criss-crossed by innumerable small roads and tracks. No extra troops were available for patrolling them and the German police were not only thin on the ground but liable to look the other way when contraband goods went through. Many a consignment went across a checkpoint with a false declaration, a forged licence or a reused manifest. A crossing place like Heiligenstadt was known to have "a lively interzonal traffic"; in October some 70,000 Deutschmarks' worth of goods slipped into Treptow and although the names of the illegal exporter, his paying agent, haulage firm and drivers were all known, the cargo had not been intercepted.[85] One Erfurt firm had regular contracts with west German lorry owners, who plied back and forth with permitted goods but packed illegal items in sealed-off compartments in their petrol tanks.[86] Sometimes spot checks or passing patrols hit lucky. One British report gleefully recorded successes in October and November: the dispatch of an entire steel-rolling mill had been prevented, 2 million marks' worth of chemicals impounded, metal deliveries to a Leipzig manufacturer of Red Army tanks stopped. But the report then ruined the triumphal effect by admitting that in the same period up to 25 million marks of goods had probably dodged through.[87]

Illegal trade was not just carried on by enterprising individuals. Some time in September the SMA was known to have set up a department to buy goods and materials in west Germany. Its agents were provided with textiles and silk stockings which were in short supply in the Trizone. (The stockings cost 1.15 East marks to produce, the agent paid 2 Deutschmarks for them, and he got between DM 14 and 16 a pair from a wholesaler.) By the end of 1948 it was calculated that the SMA had sold fifteen million pairs of stockings and made as much money or more from its textiles.[88] Organisation and finance on this scale were way beyond the means of the western Powers to control.

The easiest place for illegal trade was Berlin. A watch repairer with shops on both sides of the city had spare parts from west Germany or Switzerland airlifted to his western branch and then used them in his eastern premises. The owner of a radio firm in the Russian zone had consignments delivered to his private address in the British sector. Not all Berliners who contravened the trade regulations operated at the minor level of the scrap-metal merchant who protested with vehement innocence that a Russian car had "broken down in his warehouse." There was a thriving manufacturer of special glass in the British sector who sold everything he made to the Soviet zone, using false invoices and bribing officials. It was well worth his while: the Russians supplied all his raw materials (without all the red tape with which western authorities garlanded them), they were ready to accept a small proportion of the cost in East marks, then bought the finished goods for Deutschmarks (with which his old Bizone customers could only pay a quarter), and on one occasion even offered dollars. To add to the man's profits it was suspected that his factory ran for twenty-four hours a day on "black current," electricity siphoned off from the nearby Zoo railway station (though that was one aspect of his business acumen he was not prepared to be candid about when he opened his heart to an American official).[89]

Busting the counter-blockade was lucrative, the risks of getting caught were low and the chance of punishment negligible. Given shortage of troops and police, the western authorities left most of the enforcement to their intelligence agencies. These departments had excellent sources of information (there were plenty of honest men about as well as paid informers and envious businessmen happy to denounce rivals). They had well-established techniques: signed-up friends in the Soviet zone and the run of telephone exchanges and postal sorting offices. But the evidence they collected had little or no legal standing: courts would not be impressed by "an anonymous tip-off" or information from "a reliable source," and ought not to be told of "an intercepted letter" or phone call nor shown the memos of Soviet zone export-import figures which seem to have been regularly produced by an Economic Commission photocopier working overtime for western democracy.[90] British and American economic and financial officials begged for a Bizonal department to be created with full powers and staff to investigate illegal trade, arrest smugglers, dispose of impounded goods, and prepare charges and cases for prosecution.[91] They did not get it.

Nor was effective action taken to stop the Soviet zone trading with other countries. From 27 July 1948 its transit rail traffic across the Bizone was banned, hampering its access to Switzerland, Scandinavia and the Benelux countries.[92] Even so, goods to and from those areas could still be shipped through Stettin and Rostock, and the British did not clamp down hard on barge traffic. Other countries could not be persuaded to give up remunerative contracts with east Germany, especially as the counter-blockade had induced customers to offer high prices. (There was nothing unusual about the Leipzig firm with a warehouse stuffed with machine-tools from Belgium and Holland; like other companies it waited longer and paid more for them.)[93] The western allies did not take up the cunning idea of a German official that they buy up the year's supply of Norwegian pyrites destined for the Soviet zone which would only cost the equivalent of two days of airlift.[94] It was legally uncertain whether the Soviet zone border could or should be declared a national frontier and subjected to standard customs controls.[95] Virtually nothing could be done to stop the Czechs buying 500 Ford trucks in France, then sending some to east Berlin and others to Krupps in Magdeburg; getting machine-tools in the Bizone and diverting them to Wartburg; or purchasing nickel in Denmark for several firms throughout east Germany.[96]

Allied officials, grinding their teeth about lack of counter-blockade enforcement, got standard replies from their military and national governments: economic sanctions never really work, they bring the law into disrepute and merely make money for the rogues. It is probably fair to say that the counter-blockade was introduced and allowed to run not because people in high places thought it would have any real impact on the Russians, but because they accepted the psychological need for it among their own people – occupation staff and Germans would have thought it totally ridiculous to supply the Soviet zone with what it wanted when the Russians were doing all they could to deprive Berlin of everything. Even the keenest proponents of economic sanctions admitted that ultimately a counter-blockade would drive the Russians to find alternative sources of materials and goods, re-tool their factories, even overhaul their management. It would be counter-productive. In the short-term the enforcement agencies eagerly collected straws to build up their belief in the effectiveness of their campaign: news of difficulties in a synthetic oil plant, retorts for chemical production out of action in Bremnitz, power stations broken down and with no parts to carry out repairs, half the production of radio valves in Erfurt lost and rail locomotives cannibalised for spares. They knew they had damaged the Two Year Economic Plan in which there was heavy political as well as financial investment. They guffawed when they heard that some east German industrial plant stripped at the end of the war had had to be returned from the Soviet Union.[97] They realised that for the moment the effect of their trade restrictions was felt only by factory managers and planners, that once the public at large began to suffer the Russians would think economic difficulties and popular discontent supportable as long as they could still expect a major political success from their blockade of Berlin.

But how optimistic were the Russians by February 1949? They had seen what the airlift could do in winter, they had witnessed the strengthening of west Berlin's resolve and allied commitment to the city, they had huffed and they had puffed but the west German house had not blown down, they could foresee west European economic prosperity founded on the Marshall Plan and the Ruhr, and western security fortified by a North Atlantic buttress.

The Soviet Union made no obvious move to suggest loss of confidence in its siege of Berlin. But on 31 January Stalin himself made a statement through the western press. He had been contacted a few days earlier by Kingsbury Smith, the European manager of the International News Service, with a cable containing four broad questions on general policy. Such approaches were often made by western correspondents mooching about the office with nothing to do, and they were ignored. On this occasion the Soviet leader actually honoured a try-on with a reply. Yes, he confirmed, the Russians "did not intend to resort to war." Yes, they would consider gradual disarmament. Yes, Stalin was willing to meet President Truman, but in Poland or Czechoslovakia because his doctors forbade him to make the long journey to the United States. Yes, he would raise the blockade of Berlin, but only if the western Powers agreed to postpone a west German state pending a meeting of the Council of Foreign Ministers on all German problems and on condition that allied transport and trade restrictions were lifted at the same time. At first glance there was nothing startling in any of this: some traditional hot air in response to the first three questions and the customary string of unacceptable conditions for the last. Yet possibly, just possibly, Stalin had opened a chink – not by what he said, but by what he left out. There was one aspect of the Berlin crisis which the Soviet Union had always laboured – and Stalin had not mentioned it. Had he overlooked it? Or had Stalin sent a coded signal?

13

Prodigies of Agreement

What Stalin had missed out of his answers to Kingsbury Smith was, of course, any mention of Berlin's currency. Perhaps there was nothing odd in the omission. Conceivably the Russians thought the issue was too obvious to refer to; or for once they were dropping the claim that their blockade was purely in response to western currency reform and concentrating on their wider aim: stopping all the London proposals, especially west German government. Those were the conclusions Bevin drew. In a memorandum for his colleagues he suggested that Stalin's shift was "almost certainly one of emphasis and not of substance."[1]

The State Department thought otherwise. Charles Bohlen, its Soviet expert, had sensed recently that the Russians were ill at ease and he had been on the lookout for a signal. This might be it. He pointed out the possible significance of Stalin's omission to the new Secretary of State Dean Acheson (who had taken over when General Marshall retired in January) and recommended that they make soundings to see if Stalin intended what he had implied.[2] Acheson was intrigued. He was cautious though: Stalin might be tempting the West into rash negotiation. He was ready to let the Russians know that if they had sent a message, it had been received and understood. But he was determined to avoid looking eager, to play down the Soviet initiative and make the Kremlin do all the pushing. Above all he wanted any further communication to be absolutely private so that both sides could explore their positions without any political commitment, any playing to the public gallery. President

329

Truman approved his strategy: they would probe to see what Moscow was ready to do, turn down flat any offer to raise the Berlin blockade in return for postponing west German developments and keep the whole affair secret. If nothing came of it, nothing was lost – but softly, softly.[3]

Acheson chose to reply to Stalin in kind – a coded message in the newspapers. He sent it through the regular weekly State Department press conference on 2 February. The Kingsbury Smith interview was bound to be the main topic, and any comment he made would seem a natural response to journalists rather than an excited grab at a Soviet offer. The answers he gave to the inevitable questions were all predictable repetitions of American foreign policy. He had, however, thought out the wording and rehearsed the tone carefully to give an impression of being dismissive of a journalistic "stunt built up out of all proportion to its intrinsic importance." His key phrase could be read as nothing more than disparagement of the whole story: "If I, for my part, were seeking to give an assurance of my seriousness of purpose I would choose some other channel than a press interview." Yet that phrase was his message: if Stalin had, indeed, a serious purpose he must find a private way of expressing it.[4] Acheson had responded to the Kremlin without showing anxiety or avidity, and at the same time given a deft display of how to use the public prints to blinker the public eye.

Though working hard to appear offhand, Acheson did not let matters drift. A few days after his press conference he called to Washington the deputy US representative at the Security Council, Dr. Philip Jessup, for a confidential discussion with himself and Bohlen. It seemed sensible to all of them to keep any further contact with the Russians as casual as possible: communication by letter would pin everyone down too soon, meetings through embassies would involve too many people and look like the start of negotiations for which no one was ready. An informal chat, however, between Jessup and Yakov Malik, the Soviet representative to the United Nations, would arouse no public comment but suggest a private channel if the Russians wanted one.[5] Jessup was the ideal man for this delicate manoeuvre. He was modest, pleasant, had a mind like a razor and plenty of diplomatic experience; he was judicious (and actually a judge in later years at the International Court) and was never thrown off balance or rushed into ill-considered moves. Malik was an opponent worthy of him: well-mannered, smiling and controlled. He handled whatever brief he was given with competence and never lost his temper or his head. To maintain the air of American indifference, it was decided that Jessup would issue no invitation and make no appointment with Malik. He would wait until they "just happened" to bump into each other.

That opportunity came on 15 February at the temporary home of the UN at Lake Success. Jessup was loitering with intent in the delegates' lounge across the hallway from the Security Council chamber and was hailed by Malik. They exchanged a few remarks about the weather – a subject, as Jessup put it, "on which we could usually agree." Malik commented on Jessup's recent appointment as an Ambassador at Large and cheerily suggested he might like to rove to Moscow one day. There was a little more of this social tattle until Jessup carelessly popped the question: was Stalin's failure to mention currency accidental? He recorded that Malik replied "rather seriously that he had no information on that point." He himself commented that he would be quite interested to hear if Malik got any. They gave each other a few digs about who was the cause of the trouble in Berlin, all in a very bantering manner, then wandered into the Security Council meeting as if a debate on Korea's application for UN membership was the only thought-provoking event of the afternoon.[6]

When Jessup sent three copies of a memo on this conversation to Washington and circulated another five among his UN colleagues, Bohlen gave him a thorough ticking-off and the New York memos were called in and destroyed. Only a handful of officials in the State Department must know what was going on. In Bohlen's opinion it could "almost be stated as a principle that when the Soviets are serious about something they do it in secrecy and when they are not they indulge in propaganda." In this affair, secrecy might ensure seriousness. But when a whole month went by without a word from Malik, Bohlen and others began to think they had misread the signs and that Stalin had never intended a signal.[7] Jessup left the UN and took up his ambassadorial duties in Washington. It was here that he at last received a phone call from Malik on 14 March and an invitation to meet next day in New York at the Soviet UN mission offices on Park Avenue.

This time their conversation began with an even more engrossing subject than the weather: personal health. Jessup explained that his hand was bandaged because he had burnt it putting out a fire in a pan on the stove. Malik reciprocated with the information that he had just spent a week in bed with lumbago. When he had once suffered from it in Tokyo an American nurse had given him an injection which had really made him yell – his first time in the hands of an American woman. Was it the last? Jessup enquired with interest.[8] Then they got down to business. Malik read a formal statement relaying the message from Moscow that the lack of reference by Stalin to currency was "not accidental"; the matter could be discussed at a meeting of the Council of Foreign Ministers where all Berlin and German questions were covered. He read his piece in Russian and the interpreter had a translation typed out ready for Jessup. He continued to speak Russian, though his English was totally proficient, which meant long interruptions to the flow of both men while the interpreter did his work, but which at least gave Jessup time and excuse to scribble detailed notes. For the most part the two men stalled. Jessup tried to prod Malik into a little movement: Would the Berlin blockade, he asked, continue during a CFM? Malik had no answer: he had only put one question to Moscow, he explained, and had no directive on any other matter, though he was willing to transmit further questions. Jessup did not show more of his hand by asking any. It was now Malik's turn to probe: what did Jessup think of Stalin's other answers? Jessup gave him a couple of thoughts: there was no need to postpone a west German government during a CFM meeting because such a government did not yet exist; there were blockade measures imposed by both sides, and they should be lifted simultaneously. Malik suggested that all Soviet steps in Berlin had been in response to western policies; Jessup thought it possible to argue the opposite. They laughed and left it at that. As he stood up to go Jessup commented that he came to New York from time to time and should Malik ever have anything to discuss they could meet. Malik replied that there might be some new information from Moscow in a week or so.[9] Both remained casual to the last.

But they had been very serious. In spite of the light manner of the conversation and the skirting round the issues, Jessup and Malik had established that both sides were willing to talk and that the informal, private method suited them. Malik's next invitation came more quickly than the first. Jessup saw him again on 21 March. Their conversation moved more easily than before – a new interpreter seemed to speak so little English that Malik had to do so. His main points had been typed out. Though Jessup often intervened to ask for expansion or clarification, Malik soon returned to reading his precisely worded but deliberately ill-defined statements. Vyshinsky, he announced, believed that if there was an agreement to hold a CFM, there could be reciprocal lifting of restrictions on transport and trade. Both at the same time? asked Jessup; or perhaps lifting in April then a meeting later? Malik would give no specific reply. When pressed he supposed that Vyshinsky would like a CFM in the near future: how soon could one be arranged? Jessup responded like a Russian: he had no instructions, he must report to his government. He then enquired how Vyshinsky would like future discussions to be conducted. Perhaps, thought Malik, the two of them might talk a little more before turning the matter into more regular channels. Jessup gave a reminder that two other governments were involved; Malik ignored it. He went back to his notes to explain that the Soviet government still considered currency important but would discuss it at the CFM, and that Vyshinsky attached importance to Jessup's statement at the previous meeting that a west German government did not yet exist. At this moment the interpreter cut in and showed either his poor command of language or diplomatic ambitions. He said that Vyshinsky understood that the United States would "call off" a west German government if there were a CFM. Jessup disabused him of that idea. He went through exactly what had been said: the government would not yet be in existence if a CFM took place soon; there was no promise that it would not be established in the near future; it might even come into being while the Foreign Ministers were meeting. As he recorded in his notes, he "dwelt on this point at some length" – it was, after all, vital – and he decided it must be spelled out with care at any further meeting.[10]

Until 21 March only Acheson, Bohlen and a very few others had known about the Jessup-Malik talks. At the time of the first contact in the UN it was uncertain that there was going to be anything to tell the British and the French; after the 15 March meeting there still seemed good reason to stay quiet rather than upset the sensitive one-to-one balance or reveal the secret contact to the notoriously leaky French. But the discussions became so much of common concern that the allies must be informed.[11] A few hours before going to see Malik on 21 March Jessup had put the British and French UN representatives in the picture. When the news reached London Foreign Office noses were put painfully out of joint: indignant minutes called the Jessup approach "a decidedly amateur way of doing business with the Russians." Bevin, however, was not a professional diplomat but a skilled negotiator, so saw things differently. He was not usually given to writing. If he had to do it he used an enormous silver fountain pen (known as "the Caber" to his staff), which he jabbed down with his first and second fingers to scratch "Yes" or "See me."[12] On this occasion he read the cable from New York, then along the left-hand side of its full A4 length he incised in huge splattered letters: "Watch this. Stalin may now raise the blockade."[13]

Obviously everyone wanted Stalin's blockade to be lifted. Some observers, unaware of the Jessup-Malik talks, thought there was hope in new Soviet appointments in March: Molotov was to be replaced by Vyshinsky, Sokolovsky was going to leave Germany to become First Deputy Minister for the Soviet Armed Forces and his role as Military Governor would be taken by General Chuikov, who was judged to have no political interests. Did these staff changes presage policy changes? Many believed they did not: they saw little to choose between Vyshinsky and Molotov and even thought Vyshinsky's promotion showed that Stalin did not expect negotiations in the near future which would need Molotov's skills; Chuikov, they reckoned, had been put in to hold the fort not surrender it. Why, they argued, read such significance in a few staff adjustments? After all, Acheson had succeeded Marshall, Herbert's job as British Commandant of Berlin had been taken over in January by General Bourne, but western policy was not altered. And these arguments seemed increasingly valid in the coming days and weeks as no news seeped from New York and no shifts in SMA attitudes were discernible in Berlin. The siege of the city continued and there was little public expectation that it would be raised in the near future. It had, however, ceased to terrify; Berliners, Germans and allies had learned to live with it and it in no way deterred them from pressing on with what they wanted to do.

The damage which the blockade was inflicting on Berlin was, however, grievous. In March there were 67,028 people unemployed in the western sectors and 59,258 others on short time. The Russians had not entirely lost their power to frighten: at the end of the month the gas and water administrations were finally driven out of the Soviet sector by the bullying of their staffs and threats to arrest leading officials.[14] Yet the mood was buoyant. In January, Friedensburg, making much play on his training as a mining engineer, had announced substantial deposits of brown coal in western parts of the city, which were lying near the surface, easily exploited and likely, he promised, to produce "several hundred tons of fuel a day." Trial borings were made, but by March it was clear that more coal would be needed to get the fuel out than could ever be mined in the Bezirke of Berlin.[15] This could have been a great disappointment to Berliners. In the event, it simply caused huge hilarity – a municipal addition to already high spirits.

They had just had a tremendous boost from the introduction of the Deutschmark as the official currency in the western sectors. The western Powers, emboldened by Stalin's failure to mention currency in his newspaper interview on 2 February and relieved of the trammels of the United Nations, had at long last established the western mark on 20 March. All wages and salaries were to be paid fully in Deutschmarks; even people working in the eastern sector and drawing rations there were entitled to change 30 per cent of their earnings into western currency. The East mark could still circulate and it was legal to hold it. The first allocation of Deutschmarks was small: only fifteen were issued per person, just enough to cover the cost of rations for the first twenty days in April. The exchange rate – 5 east marks for 1 west – hit savers, but trades unionists were pleased ("you can buy more on the black market") and west Berliners could afford to go to lawyers, doctors, tailors and hairdressers in the Russian sector. The use of the Deutschmark caused some inconvenience: since it was illegal in the east, trams had to stop on the sector boundary and drop off their conductors with the fares collected. More seriously, the Soviet-controlled railways refused to pay Deutschmarks to those of their employees who lived in the western sectors. In addition, Russian sector residents who worked in the west, as did so many Magistrat staff, got only 10 per cent of their wages in Deutschmarks. But even if the financial effects of currency reform were not enjoyed by everyone, enormous political advantages were felt. Berliners had been given the assurance they had always asked for: they were part of the West. Economic gains were expected too: links with the prosperity of the Trizone and a chance to apply for Marshall Aid.[16]

Berlin's future seemed rosier than for a year or more, blockade or no blockade. And, at last, the airlift could guarantee it. Having flown in 5,436.2 tons a day in February, the combined allied operation delivered 6,327.5 in March. The month had begun badly: there was snow the first day, hurricane-force winds to follow, then a cold snap when 12 degrees of frost were recorded.[17] It is tempting to wonder if the long delay before the Kremlin replied to Jessup's first contact with Malik had been encouraged by the weather: even at this late date it might have seemed that winter was coming to aid the Soviet Union. But spring arrived suddenly. There was perfect flying weather and a good supply of serviceable aircraft; record

335

after record for tonnage was broken. To celebrate – and show that the allies were capable of yet more – Tunner decided in April to give Berliners an Easter present. There were already plans to fly in 34 kgs of chocolate, 13 kgs of real coffee and 400 tons of frozen pork.[18] Tunner was going to supply something bigger. From midday on Easter Saturday to noon on Sunday he staged the Parade: 1,398 flights carried 12,941 tons. All the cargoes were coal – heavy standard loads used less time and space – and to get them to Berlin everyone from general to cook's assistant slaved round the clock. It was wonderful razzamatazz, a thrill for Berliners and a daunting exhibition to the Russians of allied air strength. This was not a repetition of the 18 September record, not an effort which overtaxed the system. The airlift was resilient now. In April it achieved an average of 7,845.4 tons a day. There was every reason to believe that it could go on improving.

Even the former ugly duckling, the civil lift, had come out in finer feathers. On 5 March the operators finally got proper government contracts – three months long and with bonus payments for higher than average performance. Immediately several companies uprated their aircraft and increased their aircrews and ground staff. Their sorties went up from fifty-four to seventy a day in March; that month the wetlift carried 353 tons of liquid fuel, in April, 423.[19] The civilian firms knew they could do even better if Haltons, which were weary and suffering from undercarriage trouble, were phased out and replaced by Tudors. On 14 April the interdepartmental working party concerned with the civil lift instructed Avro to convert six Tudor Is and IIIs for liquid fuel and eight Tudor IVs for dry freight. The Treasury found out and refused to pay.[20]

The fresh triumphs of the airlift had not been achieved without tragedy. A civilian York crashed on approach to Gatow on 15 March and its crew of three died. A Halton belonging to Lancashire Aircraft Corporation came down near Schleswigland a week later and three more men were killed; another from World Air Freight crashed north of Tegel at the end of April and four civilians died. One man was lost in a C-54 accident on 4 March; three others when a Dakota crash-landed in the Russian zone near Lübeck on 22 March.

There were fears that the death rate would go up: aircraft and crews were noticeably exhausted by the months of intensive flying. Even the C-54, that most robust of machines, was wearing out. Spares for it were in short supply; thirty-six of the aircraft would soon need total replacement, but the design was obsolete and out

336

of production and there was, as yet, no obvious alternative in service. Too few Hastings were being made to succeed the RAF's Dakotas. Flight Refuelling, who had already bought fifty new engines for its Lancastrians, did not expect many more to be made.[21]

The men were tired but, for the British especially, it was no easier to find fresh crews than new aircraft. The Americans had a reasonably steady supply from their training base at Great Falls; they kept them flying hard for six months, then sent them home. The RAF was constantly short of aircrew. In March they warned that they were "hard-put to get the maximum use out of all available Hastings and Yorks,"[22] telegrams from HQ BAFO showered to Transport Command throughout April and May begging to be brought up to strength,[23] but it had to be admitted that virtually "the whole of the resources of Transport Command have been committed to the operation" to the point where scheduled services and training had stopped, and "barrel scraping for crews" had reached the very bottom.[24] British airmen were luckier than Americans in being able to go home for a short leave every month. These leaves were too short, though, to be refreshing; they were spoilt by official stinginess with travel warrants (there was not even any transport to take the men who arrived at RAF Oakington into Cambridge to get a train). And no limit had been set to the time RAF crews would stay in Germany – for all they knew they might be flying flat out for years. Flying, in fact, did not worry most of them. When 121 Dakota crews were questioned about tiredness and problems which lessened their efficiency only 8 per cent grumbled about the hours in the air. Most complaints (85 per cent) were about the irregular hours, which meant irregular meals and poor sleep in crowded rooms with crews on different shifts. Under these conditions it was not safe to make men fly more than eighty hours a month. The other major problem mentioned by those questioned was domestic worry – a few civilian firms were setting up married quarters, but servicemen were cut off from their families. Miserable though the British felt about this, the Americans suffered even more from separation and homesickness.[25]

All these mechanical and mental strains could be cured in time, of course. And time was now on the allies' side: they had beaten the winter, could build up ample provisions for the next with the resources they had and devise an operation for total supply of Berlin – for ever and a day if need be. The long-range plan was for bigger and better aircraft: more tonnage lifted in fewer flights by fewer crews. CALTF was thinking of phasing out the C-54 in favour

337

of the DC-6 – tried, reliable and able to carry 15 tons. They wanted to speed up production of the C-124 (so far only expected to be ready for trial in mid-1950). That aircraft could lift an amazing 125 tons. There would have to be a huge construction programme to match the size of the new machines – extension and strengthening of the runways at Tegel and Rhein Main for a start. There was every confidence that it could be carried out and a new-style operation run effectively. A glimpse of future possibilities was given the public on 4 May when a C-97 "Stratocruiser" landed at Tempelhof. No matter that it was only carrying a fifth of its potential load (the fear was that a heavily laden aircraft of that size would run into Poland before the brakes worked), nor that the airlift authorities had already decided it was thoroughly unsafe for regular use in Berlin.[26] This aircraft was in regular production and could carry 25 tons – and the word was put out that it was being tested for thirty days before deciding whether to bring it into service.[27] Its arrival in Berlin must certainly have given the Russian representative at the Air Safety Centre something to tell his friends.

By then the Russians had more than enough troubles on their plate, mainly political troubles. In January and early February the Parliamentary Council in Bonn had streaked ahead with preparation of a Basic Law for the west German state. On 5 February a revised draft was ready; the next week it was approved by a large majority of the delegates. (Was the timing of Stalin's reply to the Kingsbury Smith questions purely coincidental?) The agreement in Bonn had been painfully achieved and the draft was an awkward compromise between opposing views. The SPD had pushed for strong federal government and, in particular, for central control over taxation and expenditure, the right of the federal government to redistribute revenue between poorer and richer Länder and to legislate on social policy. The CDU had pressed for relative independence for the Länder. Its Bavarian ally, the CSU, was especially clamorous and influential in demands for freedom of action for each Land; the eleven Christian Democrats from the British zone, on the other hand, were more willing to accept some degree of central direction. There had been long arguments over whether to have a President and if his role should be decorative or functional; further wrangles about the nature of a second chamber and the Bundesrat (should it play a full part in the legislative process or simply advise and check, should it have equal representation from each Land or members in proportion to population?).

338

Given the complexity of the questions the Parliamentary Council had to answer and the range of opinion it had to take into account, it might be thought that the delegates had prepared their draft Basic Law with commendable speed. That was not the view of the allies. The Military Governors were impatient for a settlement, irritated by time consumed in Bonn which they felt the western allies were purchasing at the high price of defending Berlin. The allied liaison officers with the Council grumbled continually about the verbosity of the debates and criticised the delegates for not sinking their party differences in the civic interest. Most western grumbles came from people who were relatively ignorant of political processes and above all of the particular stresses of constitution making. The allies, in fact, seem to have misunderstood what was going on at Bonn. The Parliamentary Council had begun in September with the intention of making provisional arrangements for a temporary and disappointing second-best: an enforced west German combination rather than a restored national state. As they warmed to their work, however, the delegates' mood had changed. There was soon nothing makeshift about their construction: they were founding it on the lessons of the Bismarck and Weimar states and building to grow and last. That took time.

No member of the Parliamentary Council knew when or how their Basic Law could be applied to a united Germany, but that was what they were designing it for. The capital of a reunified nation must be Berlin. All German politicians of whatever hue wanted full representation for the city in the Council and as a twelfth Land in the west German federation. The British were willing to back them, though they saw political and legal problems in making a divided city in the middle of the Soviet zone a full member of a western state.[28] American officials in Germany sympathised with the Council's wishes. Murphy argued that exclusion of Berlin would play into Russian hands, encourage dangerous irredentism and deprive the new federation of men of outstanding calibre such as Reuter.[29] Clay thought it unpardonable to reject the unanimous will of the Council and pointed out that the western Länder had taken on some of the financial burdens of the city and would bear them more readily if Berlin were a partner.[30] Washington was chary: thought Berlin should not have a vote at Bonn, that its inclusion as a Land would break four-Power agreements and complicate solution of the blockade, and that west Germany should not be lumbered with even more problems.[31] The French, as ever, argued that any status for Berlin would be a revival of hated

Prussianism; they threatened to reject the Basic Law.[32]

But then the French seemed to have an inexhaustible mine of objections to any proposal from the Parliamentary Council. Nothing but a loose confederation with a weak government and ineffective administration would satisfy them. Furthermore, they were determined that the allies' Occupation Statute should keep west Germany on the tightest of reins. They wanted a long list of reserved powers with the Germans obliged to seek prior approval for much legislation and the right of any Military Governor to appeal to all three governments the moment there was disagreement. If France got its way, Clay lamented in February, it was doubtful that "the new government will have as much freedom of action as the present Economic Council";[33] the right of appeal would be almost as obstructive as the use of the veto in the Allied Control Council.[34] In fact, all the discussions between the Military Governors in the first three months of 1949 were very reminiscent of the ACC: Clay described their rows as a "duplicate of quadripartite meetings with Koenig taking the place of Sokolovsky."[35]

There was something positively laughable about the Military Governors' criticisms of the Parliamentary Council when the sixty-five men at Bonn had shown remarkable willingness to compromise whereas the three who met in Frankfurt had non-stop disputes and failed to get even the haziest sketch of a draft Occupation Statute or a set of principles for judging the Basic Law. The French should not take all the blame for the deadlocks. The British and Americans were frequently at odds, but at least were ready to keep talking. They both agreed that most powers must be devolved to the Germans, though the British stipulated that an independent judiciary and civil service must be assured. Clay was alarmed, however, by British enthusiasm for strong central government. Old Southerner and Republican that he was, he fought for states' rights and suspected (correctly) that British zeal for centralism sprang from devotion to two dogmas both anathema to Americans: nationalisation and a welfare state.

Enough temporary agreement was finally patched together by the Military Governors to present the Parliamentary Council with a memo on 2 March laying out objections to the draft Basic Law. Contrary to British views, this expressed disapproval of the strong powers envisaged for federal government. A vague statement was made about the role of Berlin in the Council, which served to blur the sharp differences between the Military Governors but did not clarify what part the city should play. It expressed understanding of the Council's "solicitude" for Berlin and made no objection to "responsible authorities" in the city designating "a small number of representatives to attend the meetings" – but what constituted "responsible" or a "small number" and what the nature of the "attendance" should be was not defined. With that much accomplished, the Military Governors lapsed back into futile squabbling.

Their fleeting moment of accord simply disrupted the harmony in the Parliamentary Council. The CDU was prepared to amend the Basic Law to meet the allies' criticisms – many of them, after all, pushed the constitution in the decentralised direction the party had always wanted to go. The SPD felt it had already been dragged too far down that road. Though both sides managed to produce a new draft by 17 March neither was happy with it, and they well knew it still retained too many fiscal and legislative powers for central government to be acceptable to the Military Governors. By mid-March, party had been set against party, the allies were at daggers drawn, and a major clash between the occupation Powers and the Parliamentary Council seemed unavoidable. How much simpler things appeared in east Germany. On 20 March, after "consulting the broad masses," the People's Council unanimously approved a constitution for a united Democratic German Republic.

Emotions in west Germany were running too high for anyone there to see that with a little magnanimity and a few adjustments they could have what at heart they all wanted – an immediate constitutional settlement. It would not be ideal, certainly, nor to everyone's taste in every detail. But it could be workable, encourage rapid growth in the new state and enable Germans to take a part in west European life. Calm outsiders were needed to see all this and to hack through the tangles which had been knotted. By a stroke of good fortune, one of those uncanny coincidences which intersect the Berlin crisis, the Foreign Ministers of the three western Powers were due to meet. The final draft for a North Atlantic treaty was ready in mid-March. Representatives of the twelve future member states of the Atlantic Pact were going to assemble in Washington, put the finishing touches and then sign the treaty on 4 April. It was the perfect opportunity for Acheson, Bevin and Schuman to sort out all their interconnecting problems: a western alliance, the west German state and the tactics for responding to Soviet willingness to discuss Berlin. They could talk in an atmosphere of new confidence: their successful airlift saved them from unpalatable concessions over Berlin and their new pact would give them the strength to stand up to the Russians on European controversies. In a single week in Washington the three men were going to achieve what Acheson later called "prodigies of agreement." They paved the way for even more.

It was just as well that when so many decisions had to be made the three key personalities all hit it off so well. Acheson and Schuman, lawyers both, shared an ability to analyse incisively, to grasp fundamentals and stay flexible over individual items. They not only spoke the same professional language, Schuman even understood Acheson's English – slow and precise – whereas Bevin's West Country burr flummoxed him. They remained on the formal terms Schuman set – "Mr. Acheson," "Monsieur Schuman" – but appreciated each other's ability and enjoyed each other's wit – Schuman's quiet and ironic, Acheson's quick and often caustic. Bevin and Acheson made an odd but devoted couple: the American tall, elegant, debonair and very much a man of the world; the Englishman short, stout and rumpled with the motto coined by Peter Ustinov: "When in Rome do as Taunton does." Acheson was an intellectual, highly educated and articulate; Bevin was instinctive, self-taught; and either came straight to the point with a frankness Acheson respected or wandered through metaphors which were collectors' pieces: "Don't open that Pandora's box, you never know what Trojan horse will get out." The relationship between the two was warmed by fun. Acheson could be woundingly sarcastic or arrogant with those he thought fools; with Bevin he was relaxed and amusing. Bevin had never broken through Marshall's reserve and the General probably thought him brash and uncouth; but his broad humour and rollicking disregard for the niceties appealed to Acheson, who in American company too often appeared affected and a snob.[36]

When the two men first talked in Washington on 31 March Bevin pleaded for caution in the coming weeks. He had laboured for so long on the grand design, the four-legged table of European economic recovery, Western Union, American military support and a prosperous, co-operative west Germany. The final components were almost ready but, as he explained to Acheson, he now "sensed the possibility of a very dangerous situation arising." He feared that the Soviet moves through Malik were intended to jolt the table. An offer to lift the Berlin blockade might persuade waverers not to ratify the Atlantic Pact; if a CFM were exacted in return, it would be used to delay west German government and to demand a Russian part in the Ruhr, withdrawal of troops from Germany and the establishment of Berlin as the capital of a united country with the Red Army only forty miles away. Bevin wanted his table finished and sound before talking to the Russians; "We did not want to rush ahead too fast," he told Acheson. The Secretary of State, however, felt that the final stages of the grand design were progressing splendidly: the North Atlantic treaty would be signed within a week, and there was every hope that agreements on Germany could be reached while Bevin and Schuman were in Washington. Seize the initiative from the Russians, Acheson urged; get the blockade up by early April and arrange a CFM for the end of the month. A Foreign Ministers' meeting was unlikely to solve all German problems, he admitted, but it might create a modus vivendi; if it failed, the western Powers would have lost nothing and would have denied the Soviet Union a chance to accuse them of rejecting a peace offering. Bevin was not convinced: if the Russians really wanted to get out of the Berlin situation then leave them in it; if they genuinely wanted to talk, make them talk about matters they usually avoided such as Austria, Greece, Eastern Europe. He certainly did not want to give Stalin the tiniest diplomatic victory by taking even a single step to meet him.[37]

Privately Acheson had a hunch that the sense of urgency and pressure which Bevin was trying to avoid was just what was needed to get decisive action on the Atlantic Pact and west German government.[38] Schuman proved his point. On 2 April the French Foreign Minister recommended continuing the Jessup-Malik talks, but making sure of agreement on west German government before they came to a head. The French Ambassador in London revealed that his Cabinet was so concerned at the damage the Soviet Union might do in a CFM that it was encouraging Schuman to make any number of concessions on German matters to secure agreement as quickly as possible.[39] Bevin was not going to niggle over perfect tempo when the prospects of a settlement suddenly looked so good.

The three men went to work on it with a will. They tore up the immensely long and complicated preparatory documents drawn up by their diplomats in London – as Acheson wrote later, "The chances of the ministers even understanding to say nothing of disentangling this mess seemed small." They adopted Schuman's idea of following the precedent set in Austria: making a short and simple list of allied reserved rights and leaving it to the Germans to decide how to use the powers handed over to them. Given that principle it took only four meetings to agree on an Occupation Statute, Tripartite Controls and the criteria for judging the Basic Law.[40] Schuman made no more than token resistance to centralised government and a majority vote among the occupation Powers. Bevin must have paralysed his colleagues from opposing strong federal powers by the sheer tedium of his ponderous explanations of how federal taxes were needed for a vigorous social policy to defend the new state against communism, and his sentimental details about the British house-building programme.[41] Discussions were cordial, trust grew and everything was ready for signature on 8 April.

The three Ministers were anxious that the momentum they had created should be kept up in Germany. They wanted to restore tolerance between the combatants and an understanding that common sense must prevail over prejudice. So they composed a message for the Parliamentary Council to explain that they would give "sympathetic consideration" to "any provisions" in the financial field which gave "independence and adequate strength" to both the Länder and the federal governments. They promised approval for any proposals which made the Länder "vigorous governmental bodies" whilst assuring central government "sufficient powers" when the interests of more than one Land were involved; they were "ready to contemplate" the right of the state to supplement local revenues with grants for "education, health and welfare purposes" as long as the Bundesrat agreed. In other words, the western Powers would not make a fuss about a gentle tilt to or from central power; what was important was a settlement which was practicable and received maximum support. This message was to be communicated by the Military Governors, the three Ministers decided, "before opinion in the Parliamentary Council has crystallised" and in time for the views to be "reflected in the Basic Law."[42] It was left to the Military Governors to choose the appropriate moment for delivery.[43] That had been Acheson's suggestion: as a self-respecting man himself he did not want to pre-empt the expert judgment of the responsible authorities on the spot. He and his colleagues would rue the day they had not risked hurt feelings and issued a firm instruction.

Given the intensity of work on the west German settlement it must have come almost as a half-term holiday to Acheson, Bevin and Schuman to break off their talks on 4 April and attend the ceremonial signing of the North Atlantic Treaty. Its final draft allayed the fears of the US Congress by stipulating that the partners would act in accordance with their respective constitutional processes. It appealed to national pride by allowing each member state to maintain its own "capacity to resist armed attack," and respected internationalist feelings by affirming faith in the principles of the United Nations and the hope of settling disputes by peaceful means through the Security Council. At the core of the treaty was the statement that an armed attack on any party to it was an attack against them all, and the following paragraph made clear that this included aggression against allied occupation forces in Europe. Germany, and Berlin in particular, were tightly wrapped in the blanket of western security.

The treaty was signed by twelve Foreign Ministers in the presence of President Truman and 1,500 diplomats, officials and congressmen. The proceedings were broadcast on radio and television. The ceremony celebrated a previously unimaginable alliance and marked a turning-point in the post-war world. In historians' cliché it was "a solemn moment." In strict historical accuracy it was a hilarious few hours. Everyone was in party mood after the labours of getting an acceptable text. Just before the ritual began Bevin, well knowing the worst ordeal on such occasions, prudently stumped off to the lavatory and swept along with him his Dutch counterpart, Dirk Stikkers, with the socialist battle cry: "Let us take the means of production into our own hands." As the signatures were recorded on multiple copies of the treaty, giggles spread through the hall: a Marine band was trying to while away the time pleasantly with a Gershwin selection and was giving more entertainment than it intended. "Bess, You Is My Woman Now" sounded rather different with Mrs. Truman sitting in a place of honour; "I've Got Plenty of Nothing" reduced penurious Europeans to hysterics; "It Ain't Necessarily So" produced gales of relieved laughter.[44]

Then it was back to serious business. In addition to all their other duties, Acheson, Bevin and Schuman must supervise the next round of Jessup–Malik talks. The two visiting Foreign Ministers had been thoroughly briefed by Jessup; it was clear to them that he had handled matters with skill and circumspection. Bevin suggested it was now time to pin the Russians down on paper. By no accident, Acheson had ready a written statement which might elicit one from Malik. Bevin did not like the draft: it was too polite and looked as if the West was asking for favours. Make the Russians do all the asking, he insisted; be firm that west German developments would

345

take their own course and a CFM would be held only when it suited the allies. A much tougher statement was written.[45]

This was read by Jessup to Malik on the morning of 5 April. Malik wriggled to find room for manoeuvre over west German government: quoted Stalin's reply to Kingsbury Smith, sent out for a newspaper clipping so that he could do it again in Russian, and read extracts from his own notes on what Jessup had said and what Vyshinsky said Jessup had said – all struggling to get a postponement of preparations until a Council of Foreign Ministers opened. Jessup would not slacken the western position. Nor would he let Malik fix any date or agenda for the CFM. There might be a meeting in six weeks' time, he suggested; as to what it would discuss, the US government had an "open mind." This phrase caused something of a linguistic flurry. Malik and his new, competent interpreter could not find a Russian equivalent (which raises interesting psychological as well as philological questions). Finally they decided that they could more or less guess what it meant. Jessup pointed out that British and French representatives must soon join these discussions. Malik enquired rather flirtatiously if this meant that the two of them would have no more talks alone. Then, cool as ever, Jessup announced he was returning to Washington; should Malik ever want to get in touch with him he could leave a message.[46]

A message came nearly a week later that new instructions had come from Moscow. The two men met again in Malik's office on 11 April. Their discussion went round and round over the same old points. Jessup sensed that Malik realised the western allies would not budge from their stand but that Vyshinsky was still hoping to jostle them. The conversation kept coming back to the Russian "understanding" that a west German government would not be set up before or during the CFM. Jessup, patiently but firmly, had to repeat that west German developments would move at their own pace and that if a CFM began within six weeks there would be no government in existence. He would not play a question-and-answer game with Malik: would the government be set up the day after the conference began "as a surprise for the Ministers," or the next day, or the day after that? But he noted with some satisfaction that the quizzing indicated willingness to negotiate from a position short of Vyshinsky's wish for postponement throughout the conference. He spotted, too, something he believed Malik had genuinely not noticed: Vyshinsky had produced a formula for reciprocal lifting of transport and trade restrictions, which implied that only those between the western and eastern zones were involved, and made no mention of communications between Berlin and the west. Tempting though it might have been to enquire what sort of fools Vyshinsky thought he was dealing with, Jessup politely requested clarification from Moscow.[47]

This meeting had given adequate grounds to believe that the Soviet Union was nearly ready to raise the Berlin blockade and start negotiations at a CFM. It was time for the Americans to let their allies in on the action. On 13 April Jessup talked to Sir Alexander Cadogan and Jean Chauvel, his former British and French counterparts at the United Nations. He explained the moves so far and recommended that their governments approve a joint aide-mémoire which he had drafted with Acheson for the Russians.[48] Allies can be as difficult to deal with as opponents. There were immediate arguments over the wording of the aide-mémoire, over the desirability of sending one at all and about tactics for proceeding with Malik. One huge source of potential dispute was plugged by the wisdom of Schuman: he said that Cadogan and Chauvel should leave Jessup to talk to Malik alone. The reason he gave was that the presence of three men would give the impression of commitment to full negotiation, but he undoubtedly knew that three points of view at the talks would weaken the one western case and that the delicate relationship which Jessup and Malik had built up was better undisturbed.[49]

By mid-April the possibility of the Soviet Union raising the siege of Berlin was exciting but not to be counted on. All those in the secret of the Jessup-Malik talks were too hardened by recent experience to trust hints, promises or even statements on paper. There was some unease too about timing: whatever the wish to see the blockade up, no one wanted a Berlin agreement to disrupt a west German settlement. It is ironic that whilst the western politicians strained to catch a whiff of last-minute trickery by the Soviet Union, their plans for west Germany were nearly wrecked by someone nearer and dearer than Vyshinsky.

Whilst the Foreign Ministers in Washington reconciled so many differences, the delegates to the Parliamentary Council in Bonn had drifted further and further apart. When a note came from the Foreign Ministers in Washington on 5 April expressing the hope that agreement on a draft constitution would be reached within a few days, it came too late. Discussions between the two main parties had broken down. The SPD refused to make any more concessions.

They met at Bad Godesberg on 11 April and decided to start from scratch. They wrote a draft of their own which had the virtues of concision and simplicity, but which gave too much power to central government to be tolerated by the CDU. The Christian Democrats would not discuss it; the Social Democrats would not modify it. Instead, they called for a party meeting in Hannover on 20 April to get backing for a campaign of no compromise in the Council. The Foreign Ministers had asked for a speedy decision on the Basic Law. In these circumstances it was improbable they would get one for months; the delay and bitterness would sap the strength of any negotiations with the Russians on Berlin and Germany.

Yet the three Ministers themselves had created the means to ease this political log-jam. Their message to the Parliamentary Council promising sympathetic consideration for any proposals had been deliberately written to prevent intransigence, to persuade the parties to give and take a little in the common interest. Why had the Military Governors not delivered it? Why, oh why, as the situation at Bonn deteriorated, was the remedy not applied?

General Clay had put his foot down. He would not transmit the message. He was convinced he knew best what kind of Basic Law Germany needed, he believed that the leniency of the Ministers would allow the wrong constitution to emerge, and he was determined to hold out until he got the settlement he wanted. Acheson, Bevin and Schuman had left it to the Military Governors to choose a suitable time for communicating their views. As far as Clay was concerned there would never be a right moment to pass on such a misguided statement.

As the mood at Bonn worsened State Department officials were puzzled by the hold-up and were chivvied by anxious British and French diplomats who wanted to know what was going on. Murphy, recently posted back to Washington, admitted on 12 April that Clay would only say he could not get in touch with Robertson to discuss the message.[50] When the three Military Governors met in Frankfurt on 14 April to explain their Occupation Statute to a group from the Parliamentary Council, Robertson begged Clay to deliver the message there and then. Clay argued that this was an inappropriate occasion and they must not distract attention from their Statute; he then let slip that he did not want to give an impression of siding with the SPD. Even Koenig was willing to pass on the Foreign Ministers' views. The most Clay would promise was delivery in ten days time if, and only if, the Germans had agreed on a better draft.[51] Such a gap would be filled with public wrangling and leave the SPD time at their Hannover meeting to reach total obduracy. Robertson was anxious that Kurt Schumacher, the party leader, was adopting "rigid and even fanatical views" (recent amputation of his leg had not improved his notoriously rancorous temper). To spread a little calm before Hannover he did what Americans thought the British spent their entire time doing – had a quiet chat to a couple of SPD members, and made heavy hints about the Foreign Ministers' tolerance.[52]

Washington perfectly understood the need to set the tone before the SPD meeting. More requests were sent to Clay to deliver the message. He rejected them. In a teleconference on 20 April he seethed: "I am not trying to run this show.... If you want to judge the German political situation here, please simply give me instructions and take away my discretionary power.... My real suggestion is you let me come home tomorrow."[53] In the British view Clay was, indeed, running the show while playing, as one Foreign Office official put it, the big role of "the one Saint who can save the Germans" and gambling he could keep it because the State Department was not ready to take over German affairs from the Army.[54] London had a new cause to worry: Schuman was arguing against delivery of the Ministers' message on the grounds that the allies should not show their full hand.[55] On 20 April Bevin sent a stern cable to Washington: he was "profoundly disturbed," he said, at the threat "to wreck all our plans for the establishment of a west German government and so play into the hands of the Russians"; the message must be passed on in plenty of time to have effect before the Military Governors and Parliamentary Council next met on 25 April.[56] Murphy did his best to spur Clay to action in a teleconference on 21 April. The General complained angrily at being asked to "bow to the arrogance and defiance of Schumacher and make him the top hero in Germany." "If you want that," he said, "go ahead. Don't ask me to do it." Murphy touched both Clay's prejudices and his loyalty. The Ministers' message, he explained, was a compromise Acheson had wrested from Bevin, who had wanted to go much further in the SPD direction; the Secretary of State's good faith was now being impugned by the British and he wanted delivery straightaway. Clay accepted Acheson's right to decide. But he demanded to be relieved of his post and added plangently: "I see four years' work being destroyed ... it is most unfair to ask me to take on an act which is entirely inconsistent with my deep conviction...."[57]

On the very day this exchange took place, the SPD in Hannover voted by a large majority to support its group's draft and stance at Bonn, and heard a swingeing attack by Schumacher on allied interference in the work of the Parliamentary Council. The party's fighting mood would clearly provoke similar belligerence in the CDU. Even now, however, disaster might be averted if both sides realised how well-disposed the allies felt. Even Schuman admitted the time was ripe for delivery of the Foreign Ministers' message.[58]

Still Clay would not pass it on. State Department requests having failed, Army Department orders were tried. General Bradley, Chief of Staff, pulled rank and tugged Clay's military heart-strings. He told Clay on 22 April he understood that the message did not meet with his approval. "However," he pointed out, "we as soldiers in our long careers have often had to carry out orders with which we did not entirely agree." Clay was unmoved. He did not accept, he replied, that the "duties of a Military Governor are strictly those of a soldier"; he had a right to resign when political decisions were taken against his country's interests and he claimed that right now. He would not deliver the message himself (the allied liaison officers would have to do it), he would not preside at the meeting with the Council on 25 April ("I am not a good negotiator when conviction is lacking"), and the moment the Foreign Ministers' views had been put he would leave Germany (he could be packed and out in three or four days). Lest Bradley be in any doubt as to his feelings, he added for good measure that these last "few days in the Army are proving to be the unhappiest and least satisfactory of my service."[59] The Army Department had lived through dozens of resignation threats from Clay, though few so uncomfortably timed; they knew that in the end he showed his allegiance. To make sure he did so now, Bradley came back later in the day to wring a promise from the General to stay at his post until mid-May, and Murphy flew out to Germany to exploit every ounce of diplomatic skill and personal affection in getting Clay's toes back on the line of duty.[60]

The Parliamentary Council finally received its message from the Foreign Ministers seventeen days after it was written, on 23 April. The reaction was as if it read "Abracadabra": tightly shut minds sprang open, goodwill and co-operation were magically released. Within twenty-four hours both parties had found bases for discussion and were fruitfully redrafting. A new proposed Basic Law was brought for discussion at the conference with the Military Governors on 25 April. Clay, having swallowed the pill of loyalty, was restored to top form. At this Frankfurt meeting, held in his headquarters, he presided with efficiency and charm and displayed all the concern for Germany's interests which had so endeared him to its people and won him the trust which his colleagues had never inspired. The Military Governors heard the delegates' proposals and explanations. They offered criticisms and then withdrew so that the politicians could talk privately and decide if they were willing to adjust to them. The Germans stuck by their draft. There was more discussion and some amendments were made which came part way towards satisfying the Military Governors' requirements. There was another recess while the politicians tried to reconcile their own differences over education and the role of the Churches. These were issues on which the allies did not wish to interfere, but which they did want settled without further delay. An hour and a half later Adenauer, the leader of the delegation, was able to announce that their work was complete and that approval of the Basic Law by a sound majority of the Parliamentary Council could be expected before 15 May. Clay replied that this was a happy occasion for the Military Governors and for the German people. He thanked the delegates for the "sacrifices in viewpoint" they had all made.[61] In fact, he himself had made major ones.

For a week or so before this Frankfurt meeting there had been rumours that the Berlin blockade was about to be lifted. Clay, on 17 April, denied the stories: "There have been no signs of any Russian approach here and if it had happened at government level I am absolutely sure I should have heard about it."[62] He spoke in all honesty: the State Department had kept the total secrecy it wanted for the Jessup-Malik talks, not even their Military Governor had been told. Once he found out (from the newspapers and Robertson) he was, he wrote, "somewhat chagrined"[63] – and that was putting it mildly. The rumours continued to grow in Berlin, fed by stories from the Russian sector: the railway summer timetable restored a Berlin to Cologne train; there had been numerous consultations with SED politicians at the SMA headquarters in Karlshorst; Heinrich Rau, the president of the eastern Economic Commission, had described the economy of his zone as in "a state of stagnation which is to be attributed to the cutting off of west Germany" and had called for "the reopening of traffic and the exchange of goods."[64] In Paris Le Figaro carried an Associated Press story on 19 April that the Soviet Union had offered to raise the blockade and four-Power talks on Germany would be held. A few days later the Dutch Ambassador in London said his colleague in France had been told by the Quai d'Orsay of overtures from Malik.[65]

Washington wanted to move quickly to a tight agreement between Jessup and Malik before the whole affair flooded out. Bevin put on the brakes, afraid of giving too much to the Russians in a rush of eagerness, suspicious that the Soviet Union was trying to stave off west German government and ratification of the North Atlantic Treaty.[66] He was under strong pressure from the Americans, however, and once the French accepted the Basic Law on 23 April he had lost a major argument for delay. On 26 April Tass released a communique giving a brief account of the Jessup-Malik talks and the news that if a date were fixed for a CFM the blockade would be lifted. With the whole situation public Bevin could no longer resist. He agreed that Jessup should now make an approach to Malik.

There was a crowd of reporters and photographers outside Malik's office when Jessup arrived there on 27 April. Inside the talk was as private and intimate as ever. Jessup read a statement of the allies' understanding of agreement so far. Malik passed on Vyshinsky's assurance that all restrictions, including those between Berlin and the west, would be lifted. He tried a little sleight of hand by casually referring to 30 March as the start to those restrictions. Jessup was not deceived, nor rude. He said his "memory was not exact," he could not remember whether any restrictions existed before 30 March, but recalled the Americans having mentioned 1 March. He then came slowly but deliberately to a request that the Russians would lift each and every one. The two men had a ritual exchange of questions and answers about preparations for west German government. They dodged away from details about the date of a CFM and the length of time between the raising of the blockade and the start of a meeting. Finally Jessup suggested that if Vyshinsky approved what had been decided so far, Cadogan and Chauvel might come to the next meeting. Malik coquetted: he had "enjoyed our private conversations." So had Jessup, but he explained he was "generous and was glad to share the pleasure with others"; Malik implied that he too was unselfish.[67] Neither man, however, was ready to share anything with the waiting journalists. Their discussions would retain what secrecy they had.

There was little of it left by the time they next met. The Military Governors had been brought up to date, diplomats and politicians in all capitals had either learned officially or in the corridors what had been going on, and the newspapers were announcing details which had not even been settled yet. Clay and Robertson were delighted to see that the possibility of a solution to the Berlin crisis did not put the Parliamentary Council off its stride or cause public alarm about an allied sell-out. They agreed to keep the Germans fully informed.[68] Malik gave the press advance notice of his next talk with Jessup and promised he would have something to say afterwards.[69]

The talk between Jessup and Malik on 29 April satisfied neither of them. Jessup assumed he had been invited purely to hear Vyshinsky's acceptance of the points in the previous discussion and he refused further negotiation without his British and French colleagues. Malik, on the other hand, was equipped with a full text of a communique on final agreement and wanted to push it through immediately with Jessup alone. He proposed that the Council of Foreign Ministers should begin to meet in Paris some time between 10 and 14 June and that all traffic restrictions should be lifted a week before. Jessup asked why the Soviet Union wanted a CFM in June. To give time to prepare, said Malik, and make sure the UN General Assembly was over and the Soviet representative, Andrei Gromyko, was back in Moscow to run the Foreign Ministry while Vyshinsky was in Paris. Why did the Russians leave a week between restoring communications and the start of the CFM, Jessup wondered. To be certain all the restrictions were removed, Malik replied. Jessup was not happy to discuss all this detail without Cadogan and Chauvel, and said so. Malik argued it was quicker for just the two of them to talk, that four people would make everything too official; the others could be informed and he and Jessup could have another private meeting. Jessup was particularly disturbed by Malik's insistence that no traffic restrictions existed before 30 March. He would certainly not be drawn into fixing an agenda for the CFM. So at the end of the meeting there was no statement to the expectant press, let alone the communique Malik had wanted. All the reporters got was the usual bromide about "satisfactory progress."[70]

Some people wondered if there had been any progress at all or whether the Russians had taken two paces back. The Foreign Office was troubled by the suggestion of starting a CFM as late as 20 June when west German elections were due on 15 July and it was desirable to avoid any possibility of Russian threats or bribes to the voters.[71] Clay and Robertson were more optimistic that the German electorate would not be influenced and pointed out there was a good chance that the Basic Law would be ratified before a CFM.[72] Clay warned, however, that a late meeting might disturb the settling in of a new west German government.[73] Everyone was worried by the persistence of Russian attempts to hoodwink them over the starting date of traffic restrictions and foresaw nasty problems in getting them raised. Jessup, Cadogan and Chauvel "recalled with a shudder" the fate of the 30 August directive in Berlin.[74] Acheson and Bevin agreed there must be a set period over which the lifting took place, so that if communications were not fully restored they could refuse to go to a CFM.[75]

All these suspicions and fears were converted into a strong allied note which Jessup sent to Malik on 2 May: 1 March must be seen as the starting date for traffic restrictions, lifting must be on 12 May, the CFM must start on 23 May. Firmness was rewarded. Malik's reply, sent with rare speed the next day, conceded every point.[76] At his suggestion all three western diplomats met him on 4 May in the American UN delegation offices further along Park Avenue to burnish their final agreement. They issued no communique after this meeting, but the beaming smiles on the four faces were proof enough of success.

The details of the bargain over Berlin and a CFM were published next day. Bevin told a cheering House of Commons that he was setting out immediately for Germany to thank everyone engaged in the airlift, and he praised the people of Berlin who had "borne their ordeal with courage and restraint." Clay and Robertson too paid tribute to allied airmen and promised Berliners that their bravery would not be forgotten and their interests would be safeguarded. Berliners themselves were reserved. They would believe in the lifting of the blockade when they saw it, and they were not at all certain that it would last. They knew better than most the danger of false hopes and their sceptical eyes had noticed how much was left out of the 5 May text – whether, for instance, the two currencies in the city would be reconciled, or electricity supplies would be resumed.[77]

It was up to occupation officials on the spot to clear up such problems. They did so without any direct contact between the western Powers and the SMA. This was inconvenient, but in some ways better than the old four-cornered fights round a Kommandatura or ACC table. On the other hand, since no one met the Russians it was impossible to test their mood or get a clue about what they were doing. The final preparations for lifting the siege of Berlin were tense. Anything could still go wrong.

A major fear was allayed on 9 May, however. After a long debate in the Parliamentary Council the Basic Law was approved. The decision was not unanimous – a total of twelve opposition votes was cast (six Bavarian, two each from the German and Centre parties, and two communists). This had been predicted and did not tarnish delight in the unanimity of the two main parties and the size of the mandate to establish a Federal Republic. The new constitution was passed on the fourth anniversary of Germany's capitulation at the end of the war. As soon as it came into force Military Government would give way to supervision by civilian High Commissioners.

There was sadness that Berlin was not permitted to become the twelfth Land. There was surprise when it was announced on 11 May that Bonn would be the new seat of government. Bonn? Germans asked. Such a small, provincial city, with no geographical significance, no historical resonance? Of course the Parliamentary Council would have preferred Berlin, but a united Berlin as the capital of a unified Germany. Some had talked of Frankfurt and its glorious associations with the Holy Roman Empire; the SPD had looked for a site in the British zone (where their support was strongest), but could not find a city undamaged enough to accommodate a government. So Bonn it had to be, but only for a while, just until Berlin was free.

At the very last minute it looked as if Berlin would not even be free from blockade in the near future. On 10 May the Russians published orders for the lifting of their restrictions in two days' time. Most were unexceptionable. But tucked among them was the instruction that there would be only sixteen goods trains and six passenger trains a day, and the unpalatable order that all of them must be drawn by Russian zone engines manned by Russian zone personnel. The western Military Governors were furious: a sharp letter was sent to the SMA and another when the Soviet authorities seemed unwilling to climb down.[78] How many more booby-traps had been set?

In fact, none. The Russians even cleared one obstruction no one had expected them to. On the evening of 11 May the lights came on all over Berlin, for the first time in nearly a year: there was current from the Soviet zone. As the evening drew on a crowd began to gather at Helmstedt, the crossing-point from the British zone and the entry to the Berlin autobahn. The place was sparkling: the military had spent the last twenty-four hours painting fences and buildings, trimming the verges, running up flags, and spitting and polishing. They had inspired the Russians: Marienborn, a couple

355

of hundred yards away in the Soviet zone, was looking just as smart, and drivers coming from Berlin noticed that the Elbe bridge at Hohenwarte was in good repair and had lost its old disconcerting shake.

At a few seconds after midnight a corporal of the Royal Corps of Military Police opened the iron gate at Helmstedt and a procession of cars and lorries moved through. The first car from Berlin, an American, crossed in the other direction two hours later. At 1:23 a.m. a British military train set off from Helmstedt station bound for Berlin, pulled by a west German locomotive, driven by a west German driver. It was laden with occupation officials, soldiers back from leave and a crush of journalists. It chugged east to a rousing chorus of "It's a Long Way to Tipperary." The blockade of Berlin was up.

14

Back to Normal?

There was no mafficking in Berlin to celebrate the lifting of the siege; no uproarious celebration, no singing and dancing in the streets. The first lorries came into the city draped with banners and garlands, and raised the odd cheer; the first trains drew into the stations and were met by small groups, curious rather than jubilant. There were no festivities at the airlift stations to mark the victory. It was business as usual for the air and ground crews who had to fly as many sorties as ever to build up a stockpile of food and fuel in Berlin; the only difference was that they no longer flew dehydrated potato (that had stopped on 6 May) but more real coffee and tea, some fats and ingredients for baking.[1] A few marvels signalled that the blockade had ended. Within hours of the opening of the barriers at Marienborn oranges and lemons, cucumbers and fresh fish reached Berlin; on 12 May seven coal trains and five passenger trains arrived; a consignment of good Rhine wine was said to be on its way; eastern zone farmers returned to their old markets with fresh vegetables and delicious new potatoes.[2] But even such delights did not cause jollification. Berliners were not exultant; they were suspicious and afraid.

After all, what did the lifting of the blockade really amount to? The Russians could cut the access routes any day, or they could slowly choke them with bureaucratic obstructions and "technical difficulties." Had the Soviet authorities really admitted defeat, would they allow the western sectors to flourish? Was it not more likely that they wanted a breathing-space or were just changing

357

tactic? No Berliner would have been surprised by information filtering to American intelligence: Tulpanov had instructed Soviet zone Ministers President on 6 May to take full advantage of the lifting of the counter-blockade to stock up; officials of the Economic Commission were told on 15 May that once bottlenecks in the east German economy had been cleared, the blockade would be reimposed if the western sectors had not fallen by autumn.[3] These two speeches might be interpreted as the best face the SMA could put on the lifting of the siege; Berliners would have assumed that they both meant exactly what they said. People felt no great pleasure in the restoration of communications as they had existed in March 1948: they were at the mercy of arbitrary Soviet controls. They would feel easier if the access routes to the city were increased and neutralised or internationalised, but few believed the Russians would ever allow that. It was some consolation to know that the airlift was still running in top gear and to hear the British Secretary for Air promise on 15 May that the allies would maintain supplies until Berlin "returned to normal."[4] But what was "normal?" Surely not a fixed limit of sixteen freight trains a day, interzonal passes for travellers, a city littered with roadblocks where there were two rival administrations and two competing currencies.

It was all very well to see fresh vegetables again, to be told that clothes would soon be off-ration. Berliners had not endured privation for nearly a year just for lemons and shoes. They had fought for a united city with democratic institutions and a free economy, firm ties to the prosperity and self-rule of west Germany, and the extension of these benefits to the east zone. What had they gained? Praise and promises. They had won a return to the traffic conditions of March 1948 but not to the political situation: Berlin was now divided and the systems of East and West had set into rigid confrontation. No one assumed that the Council of Foreign Ministers would solve fundamental problems in Paris at the end of May. The best Berliners hoped for was quadripartite agreement on a modus vivendi within the present unhappy circumstances. Their worst fear was that the Soviet Union would extort in Paris what the Soviet zone press was already clamouring for: a centralised German government, a peace treaty and the withdrawal of occu- pation troops. As Berliners saw it, this would mean a government permeated by communist Front organisations and vulnerable to communist takeover, the permanent loss of the eastern territories to Poland, the continued drain of reparations payments, and depri- vation of western military protection and economic aid.[5] The people of Berlin preferred what they had. It was just about tolerable though far from normal and nothing to rejoice in.

So the lifting of the Berlin blockade was commemorated in the city with sombre observance. On 12 May shops and factories closed, schoolchildren heard their teachers explain the significance of the day, then went home. The western Military Governors and twelve leading members of the Parliamentary Council attended a meeting of the City Assembly in the Schöneberg Rathaus. Clay's arrival in the hall was warmly applauded; he was respected, even loved, and due to leave Germany soon. Suhr praised him as a soldier who had worked for peace; Reuter vowed that the "memory of General Clay will never fade in Berlin ... we will never forget what he has done for us." The presence of Adenauer was welcomed as a sign of the solidarity of all Germans (a remarkable one since Adenauer was known to detest Berlin and had avoided visits). His pledge that west Germany would maintain ties with the city was much appreciated. The audience stood twice in tribute: once when Reuter gave thanks for the allied pilots who had given their lives for Berlin in the past year, again when Neumann read the names of the fifty-four men – American, British and German – who had died in the airlift. The Assembly passed unanimously a resolution that the square in front of Tempelhof be renamed Platz der Luftbrücke, Airbridge Square.

There was equal solemnity in the demonstration outside the Rathaus that afternoon. Nearly 200,000 Berliners filled the square and neighbouring streets – a crowd almost as impressive as the one which had massed so memorably in front of the Reichstag in September. They listened quietly as Adenauer and Carlo Schmid emphasised Berlin's role in drawing up the Basic Law and called for restoration of civic and national unity on the basis of free elections and institutions. They warmed to Reuter's words: "We have not finally succeeded.... We want self-government. We want to rebuild our city. Our trains must run again to Stettin and Breslau and we shall live again unfettered by interzonal passes."[6] Typically Ernst Reuter had avoided platitudinous compliments and facile optimism. He had put people's aspirations into words and voiced their deep anxiety.

Berliners' fears were confirmed in the next few days. The Russian authorities persisted in making all western transit trains use Soviet-supplied engines and crews. They fixed timetables without consulting west German railway officials, held up military trains so that the journey from Marienborn to the western sectors took up

359

to seven hours, and prohibited the export of 90 per cent of goods from the city. In theory, sixteen freight trains a day should have travelled to Berlin; in practice, many of them were turned back on the grounds of "technical defects." Only about five a day were allowed to return – resulting in a shortage of rolling-stock to add to the debt of 5,000 wagons owed by the Soviet zone since June 1948. Protests from the western Military Governors on 16 May elicited promises of eighteen trains a day, which were not kept and were followed by repeated delays or cancellations of passenger services. German travellers by any means of transport had to carry letters of recommendation from their firms or a permit from the local government at their destination. Barge traffic briefly moved without hindrance, then was held up until crew lists and transit permits were submitted. Lorries were forbidden to use the autobahn at night. On 18 May a queue of 400 food transporters was stuck at Helmstedt because the Russians demanded an Economic Commission stamp on purchase contracts.

Early interference with road traffic had been excused as failure of Russian soldiers to understand their new instructions or spasms of SMA jealousy at the sight of so much fruit and fish. On 18 May, however, the Department of Interzonal Trade of the Economic Commission announced that the Helmstedt autobahn was reserved exclusively for the supply of the allied garrisons unless special and individual permission was granted to German lorries. The Military Governors protested again. Lorries began to move more freely, but no one believed they would keep moving. The bitter reality was expressed by the American Acting Political Adviser on 19 May: Berlin "remains today in a state of semi-blockade."[7]

There was only one answer: supplies must continue to be flown to Berlin. In May the airlift remained the biggest transporter of goods for the city and carried 250,834.5 tons, the highest total yet. In the last ten days of the month, when Soviet restrictions tightened yet further, 70,915 tons got in by rail, 12,484 by water and only 39,831 by road.[8] All mail had to come by air: the Russians had diverted the mail trains to their sector and would not release the contents; they refused transit for a Magistrat lorry which had hoped to go to Hannover to collect post.[9] Yet the airlift itself now seemed to be under challenge by the Soviet authorities. Towards the end of the month there was a noticeable increase in Russian fighter activity over the Berlin airfields and along the air corridors.[10] On 27 May the Russian representative at the Air Safety Centre announced a programme of ground-to-air firing in the Bückeburg corridor in connection with Red Army manoeuvres and proposed narrowing the route to nine miles.[11] The allies protested, naturally, and continued to use the full width of their corridors. Even so, they were worried: Berlin's lifeline had seldom been so roughly threatened.

The new crisis revived thoughts of forcing a way to Berlin by road. The former champion of the armed convoy had, however, retired. Clay now believed it would be met by force and defeated; the airlift, he argued, was "the only acceptable alternative."[12] Acheson, on the other hand, offered a convoy or an allied probe of the access route among a series of proposals for response to the new blockade which he put to the National Security Council on 17 May.[13] All the old objections to using force and provoking armed retaliation were now put more strongly than ever: there seemed less chance that the Russians were bluffing, a greater likelihood that an incident would lead to war.[14] Even so, Truman believed that the risk might have to be taken in the end, though for the moment he was ready to rely on the airlift.[15] Fingers were crossed in London and Washington that the semi-blockade was nothing more than preparatory bullying for the Council of Foreign Ministers and that continued demonstration of air power with diplomatic firmness would get it lifted.

Yet by the time the Ministers began their talks in Paris on 23 May, the clear issue of Russian failure to keep their New York agreement to restore Berlin's communications had been hopelessly blurred. A new blow had been dealt to the revival of normal life in Berlin – a self-inflicted blow. The city's railway workers were on strike.

The strike had been brewing for two months, ever since the March currency reforms had left about 15,000 railwaymen who lived in the western sectors receiving wages in East marks from the Soviet-controlled railway headquarters, the Reichsbahn directorate (RBD). Their pay packets were always thin once changed into Deutschmarks; they shrank as the value of the East mark waned. The west sector trades union, UGO, called for full payment in Deutschmarks; the RBD would only negotiate with the rival communist-run FDGB. In April the Magistrat tried to persuade the RBD to accept fares in Deutschmarks so that they could pay at least a proportion of wages in the desired currency; they even went so far as to exchange the men's wages for western marks at a one for one rate, which cost them DM2 million in a fortnight. The rail

361

authorities refused to adjust their policies or to negotiate with UGO. Instead, they offered extra rations and set up shops on railway premises to sell them for East marks. UGO would not settle for food; it wanted cash in western marks and recognition. On 5 and 6 May it held a ballot. The union had fewer than 3,000 rail members but 12,275 railway workers, 94.6 per cent of all who went to the poll, voted for a strike.

It was staved off for a time. On 9 May the RDB offered the Magistrat all the Deutschmarks it had and began to accept them for S-bahn fares, but there were nowhere near enough to cover the wage bill. Next day UGO decided that in view of the New York agreement to restart Berlin's traffic they would keep working and bring in the longed-for supplies. But the men were not prepared to put up with their conditions for long. At midnight on 20 May they did not down tools (they used them to jam points and lift rails), but 16,000 men refused to operate the rail network. Links with the west, the Soviet zone traffic system and the city's S-bahn all came to a standstill.[16] The railways were in a worse mess than they had been during the Soviet blockade.

The Soviet authorities saw only one way to tackle the strike – and may, indeed, have relished the chance to extend their authority. On 21 May Russian sector and zone police took over most of Berlin's stations, west as well as east; their troops seized Wannsee station. Strikers fought with fists, clubs and iron bars to regain possession; they were fired at. The British public safety officer sent Stumm and military police into Charlottenburg and after scuffling with both sides they took control on 22 May. Next day the Zoo station was recaptured in the same way after several strikers had been wounded and one killed by east police fire. Elsewhere, however, railwaymen fought Markgraf and rail police unchecked and unaided. Berliners thought the western authorities lily-livered and did not change their minds when the Commandants got all the eastern police withdrawn from stations on 24 May and railway police restricted to guarding wagons, goods and technical installations.[17]

The western Commandants were, in fact, in a cleft stick. They had always preached the desirability of democracy in action and were loth to prevent it even when it took the form of industrial action which crippled Berlin's recovery and damaged the allied case in Paris. What flustered the Commandants as well was that they were pledged to renounce their powers and hand over responsibility to German civil authorities – yet here was a situation which the

Magistrat patently could not handle. For as long as they dared the western Commandants bit their tongues and tried to avoid intervening, the British in particular arguing that it was important for the morale of the western sectors that this strike should end successfully: that is to say in defeat of the RBD by unaided west Berlin effort.[18] But it was obviously even more important for west sector morale that people should be fed properly and, as Clay complained, the strike was preventing the build-up of food and fuel reserves, helping the Soviet semi-blockade and allowing the Russians in Paris to shrug off blame.[19] It was, in addition, grievously harming the sickly finances of the western sectors: the Magistrat was paying huge sums in unemployment relief to the railwaymen; it would be cheaper to convert their wages into Deutschmarks, whether or not that was really the RBD's responsibility. So though the western Commandants agreed on 26 May to take no direct action themselves, they suggested that their economic advisers should threaten to stop trade talks with the Russians until all Soviet transport obligations were met and they recommended Reuter to negotiate with the railway authorities.[20] He, like them, was most reluctant to intervene.

The RBD, by contrast, was only too keen to talk. Its officials were described as "in a state of agitation and apprehension" about the effect of the strike on its revenues and the East zone economy and under pressure from the SED to settle the matter before the meeting of the Volksrat on 29 May.[21] On 26 May the RBD offered DM100 to anyone who returned to work; on the 27th they made a major concession and agreed to take Deutschmarks for all rail tickets and pay 60 per cent of wages with them; next day they went further and raised their offer to "at least 60 per cent."[22] UGO was unimpressed. The union wanted full wages in Deutschmarks and recognition; it added new demands for reinstatement of any rail worker sacked for political reasons and a guarantee that no one would be victimised once the strike ended. The railwaymen voted on the RDB offer, but turned it down: they were getting union strike pay as well as Magistrat unemployment relief, both in Deutschmarks, and were better off than they would be under the RBD conditions. In the ballot on 2 June only 398 men voted for a return to work; 13,477 were in favour of continuing the strike – more than had voted for a strike in the first place.

By now western authorities, German as well as allied, had lost patience. Reuter offered himself as a mediator on 30 May and told the head of the Labour Department to begin talks with the RBD

chief, Kriekmeyer. UGO wrecked the talks by demanding Kriekmeyer's dismissal as yet another condition for going back to work.
A clear message came from Bevin: he did not want to sell UGO
down the river, but he did want a quick settlement and did not
approve of the union's "over-ambitious claims."[23] And if that was
the feeling of an old trades union stalwart it was not surprising that
the western Commandants were ready to drop their pose of lofty
indifference. On 3 June they persuaded Kotikov to meet them at
French headquarters. It was the first time the four members of the
old Kommandatura had talked for over a year, and an unpleasant
reminder of why they had stopped. Kotikov turned down every
allied proposal for negotiation and, for good measure, lobbed in
the claim that he was not involved since the strike was taking place
only in the western sectors.[24]

Since the SMA refused to help, the western Powers had to try
to settle the dispute themselves. In the second week in June the
Commandants authorised the Magistrat to top up the RBD offer
of 60 per cent Deutschmarks with a further 15 per cent for three
months until the railways had acquired enough western mark fares
to pay the extra. Howley personally recommended the offer to the
strikers, Reuter appealed for acceptance so that vital supplies could
be brought to Berlin, and the British and American manpower
advisers leaned so heavily on UGO that its executive decided to
settle. Not so the members. They called for another ballot. They
did not trust the Soviet-controlled RBD to honour any agreement
nor would they take Howley's word that the SMA had promised
him on 10 June not to victimise strikers. Their vote on 14 June
rejected the latest offer by 11,922 to 1,973 – reflecting, no doubt,
the effect of a *Tägliche Rundschau* article handed out at the booths
which denied that the SMA had given any guarantee on victim-
isation.[25] It took another week before Kvashnin admitted that such
an undertaking had been given.

In that time the western authorities had been driven to stern
measures to settle the strike. The manpower advisers warned UGO
that the 60 per cent and 15 per cent offer was the best they would
get and that the allies and the Magistrat would not tolerate the
financial and political cost of the strike much longer.[26] Acheson,
with Schuman's approval, recommended that if the union did not
end this "senseless self-imposed blockade," the Commandants
should do so by prohibiting strike pay and relief.[27] Bourne, the
British Commandant, was all in favour; Howley jibbed at the role
of strike-breaker[28] (or perhaps, as some people suspected, still hoped

for the personal glory of settling the strike himself). He again tried to exercise persuasion rather than compulsion; UGO again refused to start work.[29] On 26 June the western Commandants made their final offer: they would provide funds for the Magistrat to make up the wages of west sector railwaymen to a full payment of Deutschmarks for three months; the city government would find alternative employment for anyone unwilling or afraid to work for the RBD; but – and here was the iron hand – all relief payments must stop. That left the railwaymen with no real option. They voted to end the strike.

It had cost the Magistrat DM2 million in unemployment pay, the union DM750,000 in strike funds and the railways DM11 million in fares and freight charges. It had meant that most of the 240,325 tons of supplies flown into Berlin in June had been consumed rather than reserved for future emergencies. The Magistrat was saddled with more debt and new financial commitments, and with the bitterness of other west sector residents who worked in the east but were still paid in East marks. Against these losses UGO had made only a limited financial gain for its railwaymen. It had no guarantee that the RBD would take over payment in western marks once the Magistrat stopped or that the promise on reprisals would be kept.

The rail strike had for a time distracted attention in Paris from the fact that the Russians were still preventing the free flow of traffic through their zone and had embarrassed the western Ministers in their negotiations with Vyshinsky. That said, it is doubtful that the eventual outcome of the Council of Foreign Ministers' meeting would have been any more satisfactory had the strike never taken place.

The western Powers seemed to be in a position of some strength at the Paris Conference. The Soviet Union had suffered a defeat in the blockade of Berlin for all the stridency with which Russian propaganda claimed a triumph in forcing "warmongers" back to obedience to Potsdam principles and quadripartite negotiation on Germany. Whether or not the Russians kept their promise to restore Berlin's communications, the allies knew they could supply the city and even raise its standard of living by air transport alone. In the twelve months of blockade the three western nations had achieved a truly remarkable degree of mutual trust; France had a new sense of security; the United States was fully committed to military and financial assistance for Europe; Britain could hope for safety and revival in a stable and prospering western alliance. NATO would defend west Europe against armed invasion and Marshall Aid would cure the social and economic ills which had made the area susceptible to political incursion.

The final leg was ready for Bevin's table in time for the Paris meeting: a democratic west German state. In the middle of May the Länder had ratified the Basic Law. Bavaria alone rejected it, but had agreed to abide by the decision of the majority. By one of the many coincidences of the period the new Federal German Republic came into existence on 23 May, the very day the CFM held its first formal session in Paris. The Basic Law was signed in Bonn, by all but the two communist members of the Parliamentary Council, by the Ministers President and the Presidents of the Landstage. The signatures of the Berlin representatives were added and cheered, though the city was still refused status as a twelfth Land and was not legally part of the new republic. Before elections were held for the Federal Government in August the new allied High Commissioners were appointed: John McCloy, who had turned down the job in 1945 in favour of a Military Governor; André François-Poncet, a pre-war French Ambassador in Berlin; and Sir Brian Robertson, who would be seconded from the Army but who began practising for civilian status by wearing morning coat rather than uniform on ceremonial occasions.

Whatever the strengths of the western position at Paris, however, the allied Foreign Ministers did not feel it was impregnable. They feared that the Soviet Union had abandoned blockade in favour of an alternative assault on the western sectors. They knew that the meeting could easily turn out to be a western disaster if it gave the Russians a chance to get their fingers back in the west German pie and prod for plums like influence in the Ruhr, resumption of reparations payments and a veto on future development. They were still not sure that Marshall Aid would be effective or NATO firmly established if the Russians menaced western Europe. They were not certain that the infant Federal Republic of Germany could stand up to Russian toughness or to its new sibling, the east German Democratic Republic. (A third People's Congress had been elected on 15 and 16 May to adopt its draft constitution.)

Given these anxieties the western Foreign Ministers went to Paris with little expectation of winning new ground, but reasonably confident about defending their corner. They assumed that Vyshinsky would press for the Warsaw demands and had agreed to fight them. They would not accept unification of Germany on Soviet terms: it offered the superficial attraction of a buffer between East and West but would be cut off from Marshall Aid and unable to contribute to the European Recovery Programme.[30] A centralised government as envisaged by the Kremlin would be open to a communist takeover and would not guarantee the democratic procedures or civil liberties of the Basic Law which the allies wanted extended to the whole country.[31] The British were willing to offer a co-ordinating body between the western and eastern states as a clearing-house for practical problems and as a new justification for allied presence in Berlin.[32] On no account, however, would western Ministers countenance any suggestion that members of the Parliamentary Council and Volksrat should meet to explore ways of harmonising their two states: the allies shared Adenauer's distaste for Soviet-sponsored bodies and his belief that discussions could only be held with freely elected members of genuinely independent institutions.[33] Nor would they adjust the Occupation Statute: the return to civilian government and handover of responsibility to Germans were non-negotiable. The western Powers were open to proposals for restoring some elements of four-Power machinery, but resolutely opposed to revival of the veto.[34] The West's economic programme was as uncompromising as its political policy: German industrial production to be fixed at present Bizonal levels and allowed to rise, economic and customs unity with free interzonal trade, quadripartite controls for any unified currency, no reparations from current production and rapid abolition of all other forms of payment.[35] The British suggested that the Russians should only be allowed any part in the Ruhr (and only three out of eighteen votes at that) if they gave up control of the east German economy, their SAGs in particular – terms patently unacceptable to the Soviet Union.[36]

With the reasonable assumption that the Soviet Union would be just as inflexible as the western Powers, hopes for the Paris CFM were low. Adenauer, Schumacher and Karl Arnold, the Minister President of North Rhine–Westphalia, had all told Bevin that they expected little from the conference and would be satisfied if he kept his promise not to hazard the long-term aim of a fully democratic Germany.[37] Acheson thought there was a good chance of securing a modus vivendi in Berlin which relaxed the tension between West and East but did not risk west German gains.[38]

Only one lone voice called for greater ambition. George Kennan of the State Department Policy Planning Staff equated settling merely for west German development as abandoning the east zone to the Soviet Union, allowing the Berlin problem to fester and hardening the division of Europe. On 15 November 1948 he had presented the State Department with what came to be known as Plan A for any future four-Power talks on Germany. He proposed a new civilian quadripartite body framing policy by majority decision, all-German elections held under international supervision, a provisional government to draw up a constitution for a united Germany, and – the bait for the Soviet Union – withdrawal of all occupation troops: the Americans to Bremen, the British to Hamburg, the French to their own border and the Russians to Stettin. If Plan A were refused by the Soviet Union, then it should be kept on offer while the full London programme was put into effect.[39] Kennan's Plan gathered dust until he drew attention to it during the Jessup-Malik talks when the Russians were so obviously keen on a CFM and everyone was trying to guess what they wanted from it.[40]

When it was explained to Clay on 5 May he vilified it. Drafting a new constitution when there was already a "good" west German one was breaking "faith completely with our assurances to the Bonn Germans"; troop withdrawal would be "suicidal" and turn Germany over to the Soviets; Kennan's ideas would "offset all the gains of the past two years" and came "close to the Cominform proposals." "Thank God," pronounced Clay, "we have British and French allies who will never buy this one." (And Clay seldom gave thanks for the creation of France.)[41] The American military were just as hostile to troop withdrawal: it would make Russian aggressive preparations more difficult to spot, put allied forces in a poor strategic position (the Rhine would be better) and leave the west Germans defenceless.[42] The British Chiefs of Staff added that the proposed deployments would overcrowd their troops, leave them short of airfields and put their front 300 miles from Berlin while the Russians would be in easy striking distance.[43] Acheson decided that allied troop withdrawal was too high a price to pay for easing the Russians back a few miles,[44] though he kept in play the idea of regrouping or reducing forces.[45] His allies were distinctly alarmed, however, when the columnist James Reston gave all the details of Plan A in an article in the *New York Times* on 12 May. On arrival in Paris next day, Jessup and Bohlen had to scamper round ladling out public and private reassurance that this was not official American policy.

The week that followed was spent by western officials at the Quai d'Orsay thrashing out common positions, drafting papers on key topics for their Ministers and trying to foresee Soviet tactics.[46] The Foreign Ministers then put finishing touches to their strategy and the Council held its first full meeting on 23 May. The conference, which lasted for a dreary, sterile month, took place in an incongruously frivolous and cheery setting: the Hôtel Talleyrand-Périgord, the "Palais Rose" of pink marble which Acheson thought suitable for a musical comedy, but which did not engender light-heartedness nor ensure a happy ending. The formal sessions were held in the salon round a circular table covered with green felt, and here Acheson whiled away many an hour in contemplation of the ceiling where satyrs vainly pursued nymphs through clouds. It was an appropriate image for the conference. Bevin reflected before he left London that he had already spent twenty-eight weeks of his life in fruitless chase after four-Power agreement; he was going to waste another four. Perhaps, fortunately, he did not notice the ceiling until Acheson pointed it out at the last session: the satyrs' frustration could only have increased his own and it certainly added some bawdy touches to his last speech.[47]

The meetings of the Ministers fulfilled the most melancholy predictions. They began on a daily basis; as hopes of agreement decreased the number of sessions doubled. Vyshinsky leaped at the idea that many of the talks should be held in private with only an aide and interpreter each, but he said nothing in them he would not have been happy to see verbatim in *Pravda*. The western Ministers gave him full rein for five days. He wanted to restore the Allied Control Council and Kommandatura with their military powers and individual veto and to set up an all-German State Council with delegates from German economic organs which would be subservient to the Military Governors. He did not give an inch under western criticism that he was calling for a return to outmoded or discredited institutions. He was proud to be accused of the slogan of "Back to Potsdam." The western Powers took the initiative on 28 May and put forward their own ideas for a country unified in accordance with the Basic Law and Occupation Statute, freed from reparations demands and severe limits to industrial production, and subject only to light guidance from a civilian High Commission acting on majority decisions. Vyshinsky condemned the Basic Law as a "secret and undemocratic" constitution dictated by the West and designed to dismember Germany, and accused the allies of trying to prolong military occupation indefinitely. As the days went by his vocabulary ripened: the Bonn constitution was "Hitlerite centralism," German industry was permeated by "monopolistic

369

capitalism" and run by "Junkers," majority voting was the impo-
sition of the will of three against the rights and wishes of one.[48]
Acheson tried a private friendly chat with Vyshinsky to see if it
would be more profitable to abandon discussions on Germany and
go on to Berlin problems instead. Vyshinsky averted the switch by
insisting on the need to consult his government first.[49]

Having no doubt done so, he was no more forthcoming when
Berlin at last came on to the agenda on 2 June. For four days he
listened to the allied proposals without putting his own and made
it clear that he would not agree to the western wish for city-wide
elections, full powers for a new Magistrat and Assembly who
would draft a civic constitution, and the establishment of a limited
Kommandatura whose members would have no veto power. Then
gradually Vyshinsky's own demands emerged: the right of "social
organisations" including trades unions to put up candidates for city
elections; Kommandatura control over finances, trade, fuel and
power, transport and communications, the police, appointments
and dismissals; and an individual veto for each member. Acheson
said these proposals meant that everything in Berlin would require
Kommandatura approval except dying. The western Ministers
refrained from pointing out the logical flaws in the Soviet argument
that the Russian sector should have equal representation with the
other three in a unified Assembly because the city was split in two.[50]
Or perhaps they were too weary to notice. It must certainly have
been a relief for Bevin to slip away in the second week in June to
the Labour Party conference (never can two days in Blackpool have
been so welcome) especially since Bevin explained to the King in
courtly third person that Vyshinsky, Acheson and Schuman were
"all lawyers by profession. They consequently tended to embark
with zest on long legalistic arguments that Mr. Bevin was alone in
finding tiresome."[51] One wonders if by this stage Acheson was still
getting quite the same delight from the game he had invented of
waiting until Vyshinsky was in full spate, then having a window
opened so that the Soviet Foreign Minister, who hated draughts,
was paralysed by convulsive sneezes.

The meetings got longer and stormier when they moved on to
the currency question and Vyshinsky demanded withdrawal of
the western mark from Berlin and the 30 August arrangements for
issue and circulation of the East mark. No calm was restored when
Acheson suggested reducing forces in Germany: the only sign that
Vyshinsky had noticed was his accusation next day that the western
Powers had more troops in Germany than the Soviet Union.[52] In

view of the negotiating stalemate and the increasingly acrid mood round the table, the western Ministers were ready to pick up a hint dropped to Murphy and Bohlen by two Russian officials that the Soviet Union would not give way on major issues but was willing to consider small measures of normalisation.[53] Bevin sounded out Vyshinsky informally and wondered if they were all trying to do too much. He then seized Vyshinsky's suggestion that they concentrate on "smaller and more simple" questions in Paris and encourage periodic meetings of the Commandants in Berlin.[54]

On this very restricted agenda the Foreign Ministers began to find some modicum of agreement. From 12 June they talked about Berlin traffic and the resumption of trade.[55] It was depressing but hardly surprising to hear Vyshinsky say that any settlement of these questions would be by a "gentleman's agreement and not a formal legal document." It did, however, rather take the breath away to discover how short-lived a Soviet gentleman's agreement actually was. On 20 June when the Foreign Ministers had held their final plenary session and issued their communique which included details of a possible Austrian treaty, everyone hurried away from the Palais Rose at 6 p.m., delighted to see the back of the place and hoping, as Acheson put it, "not to meet again soon." Two hours later Vyshinsky telephoned to Schuman and insisted that the Council reconvene. Schuman was startled; not so his officials who had been tapping the Soviet embassy phones and had just overheard a long diatribe from Gromyko in Moscow, against a detail of the Austrian treaty and the brutal language in which he instructed the Foreign Minister to renegotiate it. The Ministers converged on the Quai d'Orsay. Acheson and Bevin met at the door, and with arms linked marched to confront Vyshinsky singing, each according to his taste, the "Red Flag" or "Maryland, My Maryland." Suitably inspired, the West fought and won its last defensive battle in Paris; the official statement was not altered.[56]

This communique justified all the low expectations of the meeting. It promised nothing more than continued efforts to produce economic and political unity in Germany, maintenance of the New York agreement on Berlin's traffic, and quadripartite talks in Berlin to seek ways of lessening the ill-effect of disunity on trade. A key phrase could only raise a wry smile in Berlin: it called for "normalising as far as possible the life of the city." What a defeated and defeatist qualification: "as far as possible." What hope of "normalisation" when the traffic situation of March 1948 was restored and might even deteriorate? What chance of "normalising" through four-Power consultation given the dismal history of such talks? Berliners were appalled that the western Powers seemed to have made no attempt to secure guarantees of their rights of access to the city, let alone an increase in their communications. Yet it had been difficult enough in Paris merely to hold on to what existed. In the final analysis the conference had been a negative success: the Soviet Union had not abrogated the New York agreement nor had the West renounced its dedication to liberal and democratic institutions in the western sectors and zones.

If any normality was to return to Berlin as a result of the Paris conference it would come in penny packets and slowly. So for Berliners the biggest improvement to their lives in June was the end of the railway strike. The S-bahn opened on 1 July; most trains were running again by 2 July and one of the first brought back to the city 100 children who had been evacuated during the blockade. After a week, letters, but not parcels, were getting through to the western sectors.[57] But 12 per cent of the railway workforce had been unwilling or afraid to accept the RBD terms and were looking for jobs elsewhere, and the Russians were not honouring all their agreements: they refused to allow 173 former strikers to take up employment again and by the end of August the RBD had sacked 1,372 men who had worked in the western sectors.[58] In addition, about 2,000 west sector residents who worked in the east were not being paid in western marks: since there had been no strike in the Russian zone or sector, explained the SMA, the agreement did not apply there. The western Commandants had to put DM6 million at the disposal of the Magistrat so that these wages could be brought up to full value.[59]

Road traffic took a long time to return even to the irksome conditions of March 1948. Interzonal transport could only use the Helmstedt autobahn, in early July the SMA insisted on signatures rather than stamps on food permits, and checking of documents at Marienborn was infuriatingly slow. (On 13 July there was a twelve-mile queue of Berlin-bound lorries waiting to get through.) Soviet zone vehicles were forbidden to take fruit and vegetables to west Berlin. When east zone residents began to flood over the "Magic" Gleinicke Bridge to the western sectors to buy fats, needles, shoe-laces and soap, the Russians closed it. From the middle of the month, however, lorries began to move more freely – possibly as a result of strong western protests or the Americans' declared intention on 12 July to send a weekly convoy of sixty trucks under military police escort with supplies for their garrison. Even so, when Dratvin informed the western Commandants on 25 July that "the Soviet military authorities never had nor have the intention to impose any 'blockade' big or small," it was welcome news – no one would have guessed.[60]

In spite of all the traffic hold-ups, one aspect of the Paris agreement had been fulfilled: the four Deputy Commandants were meeting, warily and infrequently, and experts from the four Powers were discussing financial and economic problems.[61] These contacts sparked no startling progress, but at least they set up circuits for communication. It was a sign of reduction in quadripartite tension that Russians began to turn up at official functions, though one British participant pointed out that they were only prepared to chat about the weather, their war service and everyone's uniforms.[62] Yet no amount of diplomatic cordiality, tea drinking with Deputy Commandants or even lashings of vodka and caviar from Russian chairmen, convinced the western Powers that the Soviet Union had settled to permanent respect for their agreements: in late September Robertson was still warning London that the Russians could turn nasty at any moment.[63] It was a general belief by autumn that the Soviet Union had abandoned full blockade, but was ready to put all manner of squeeze on Berlin.

Everyone was confident, though, that if a new Berlin crisis blew up they could tackle it more quickly and effectively than last time. Berliners and western authorities were practised in standing up to Russian intimidation and the airlift was a proven counter. Furthermore, if Berlin had to endure siege again it would do so with ample provisions. Even while the rail strike lasted, enough food was flown in to build up stores for sixty-five to seventy days. Such was the scale and efficiency of the air-transport operation that the decision was taken in June to fly the next month's food quotas from Wunstorf or Fuhlsbüttel only; Rhein Main's warehouses would be emptied, then closed.[64] That adjustment apart, there was no urge as yet to scale the airlift down: everyone agreed with Bevin's argument in mid-June that Berlin must have a five-month reserve before the effort slackened.[65] On 27 June, the first anniversary of the airlift, Robertson promised that "the empty cupboard of Berlin must be filled before our pilots return to their normal tasks," and a few days later McCloy extended the pledges: the airlift would continue "as long as it is necessary to cover our commitments in Berlin."[66]

The airlift now had such capacity and proficiency that it was soon obvious the target stockpile would be achieved by the end of August.[67] During July 253,090 tons of supplies were flown in – a record never to be beaten. The only restriction on performance was Berlin's inability to finance or store more provisions.[68] At last the allies could consider winding the operation down. Not, though, abandoning it altogether: the Military Governors recommended that a nucleus be preserved from which to build up again in ninety days if need be. Their suggestion was approved by the British Cabinet on 18 July and by the National Security Council on 27 July.[69] Two troop carrier groups of the USAF and two heavy transport squadrons of the RAF would be kept indefinitely in Germany and basic installations maintained.

Since the process of running down would take time, available aircraft might just as well be kept flying, but in a more relaxed manner: on 12 August the airlift went on to a five-day week and that month delivered an easy, confident 79,310 tons. There were fewer aircraft now. The wetlift was dwindling away and several civil companies had ended their contracts. The final civilian flight – an Eagle Aviation Halton – touched down at Tegel on 16 August. The military farewells followed: the Yorks stopped flying on 26 August, the Hastings on 6 September, the Dakotas on 23 September and the C–54s on the 31st. Those aircraft still flying in September notched up a token 14,898.6 tons.

This was the last contribution to the phenomenal 2,325,808 tons with which the airlift had kept the western sectors of Berlin alive, given west Germany the confidence to found a new state, and western politicians and diplomats the chance to avert war and find a settlement, however precarious, to the Berlin crisis and security for western Europe. It was hard for those engaged in the airlift to realise at the time that they had won a great victory and contributed to major changes in Europe: they had been so absorbed in their jobs and there had been no dramatic moment at which the aircraft stopped flying and everyone could say, "We've done it." The airmen and ground crews went home happily, glad they had worked well but hardly aware of the importance of their achievement. They had triumphed over the morose prognostications of every kind of expert that their task was impossible, they had overcome inexperience and paucity of means to mount a relief programme without precedent or comparable sequel. For the first time, air forces had taken on the traditional roles of armies and navies: they had relieved a siege and been a tool for diplomatic pressure. Air power, created for war, had become an instrument of peace.

374

Recognition by their governments of what the airmen had done was fulsome in words but grudging in deeds. It was only thanks to a campaign by the journalist Walter Winchell that members of the USAF who had laboured so valiantly were awarded a medal. Nothing could persuade the British authorities to give similar commemoration and thanks – medals, they insisted, gave the airlift "a military and perhaps even an aggressive character."[70] Instead, a ceremonial march was arranged for early December. RAF personnel were reviewed by the King in the forecourt of Buckingham Palace and marched with colours flying along the Mall and the Strand to Guildhall, where they enjoyed a hearty lunch. American comrades took part. Bevin's instinct had been to exclude the French, but political cunning rather than generosity prevailed: he crossed out the section in his memo which complained that the French had done nothing useful and replaced it with the decision that it would be best to avoid resentment.[71] Medals and marches were all very well, but long after the ribbons had faded and no one could remember the menu at Guildhall, airmen still treasured scrap-metal lighters inscribed with lucky chimney sweeps, children's paintings, flowers once found in cockpits. It was the tribute of Berliners, former enemies and targets, which gave the greatest and the lasting pleasure and pride.

As the skies above the city finally became silent, Berliners suffered a sense of isolation and depression. They were, of course, exhausted and flat after such a long period of sustained effort. The melancholy deepened as occupation staffs moved out, visitors stopped coming and they felt their struggle had been forgotten. Despondency was not just an emotional reaction to the end of crisis. It came too from awareness that even more effort and endurance were called for. Berlin faced a new, daunting emergency. It was in an alarming financial plight. Over the twelve months from June 1948, the Magistrat had received DM500 million in interest-free credits from the Military Governors' deferred imports account, DM275 million in loans from the Bizone, a further DM20 million in special taxes and DM2 million from the French zone. Most Bizonal funds stopped as soon as the blockade was lifted. The Military Government assistance was to be wound down over four months; the city could only look forward to the proceeds from a west German coffee tax. The Magistrat had been overspending recently at the rate of about DM2 million a month; on 15 June it had been unable to pay its staff's wages and by late September the city budget had a deficit of DM800 million in a total expenditure of DM1,700 million.[72] A new burden

375

was added to existing Magistrat obligations: in early August up to 1,300 refugees a week were coming into the city from the east and had to be housed and fed.

There were few local sources of revenue. The unemployed did not pay income tax – there were 200,000 of them at the beginning of August, the numbers swollen by former Military Government staff, airlift workers, sacked railwaymen – but they did have to be paid relief. Local trade could not create wealth: after a short flurry of consumer spending when the blockade ended, money ran out and what little remained tended to be spent on Russian sector goods and services because a Deutschmark had six times the value of an East mark. Industrial production by late September was stuck at 20 per cent of 1936 figures with no hope of revival: equipment was obsolete, firms were moving west, banks were reluctant to invest, orders from west Germany were few and far between, and those from east Germany, virtually non-existent. Only in December were there glimmers of a possibility that the economy might one day pull out of the trough: Telefunken decided to concentrate its valve production in Berlin, Daimler-Benz to resume manufacture of diesel engines, Siemens, to restore several of its plants. Secure and lasting progress was at last promised with the offer of Marshall Aid: DM95 million for the first instalment, DM60 million for the second.

Investment alone could not cure Berlin's ills. Berliners would need every ounce of the toughness they had shown under blockade to surmount their problems and every resource of courage to tackle them at a time when they felt so very alone. The last Dakota to fly into the city had carried not just a cargo but an inscription: "Positively the last load from Lübeck – 73,705 tons – Psalm 21, verse 11." A King James Bible decoded the message. The verse read: "For they intended evil against thee; they imagined a mischievous device, which they are not able to perform." Berliners would need to keep reminding themselves why that "device" had not been performed, that they had beaten off Soviet assault and survived blockade, and if they could do that they could live through the next crisis and the next. Their struggle had persuaded the allies to mount the airlift and ensured the independence of the western sectors, had built a bridge not only in the air but to the institutions and conscience of west Germany, and won the admiration of the world, transformed hatred and fear of Germans into respect and alliance. History tells of many individual heroes, but has few examples of heroic cities whose valour has wrought such change.

*   *   *

Such achievements could not be celebrated at the time: in 1949 they were too close to be perceived or too uncertain to be relied on, and everyone was too tired for roistering. Yet in the years to come Berliners and the western world would honour the epic fortitude of civilians and the intrepid feats of airmen; it was possible to admire the mastery of administrators and the calm persistence of politicians and diplomats. Their victory had not been total, but it was lasting and it conserved values held dear.

One does not diminish their accomplisment by wondering if the western Powers would have been quite so steadfast if the Soviet Union had made its earliest threats to Berlin less hazy, whether the city would have survived the winter without the help of unseasonable weather, how allies and Berliners would have responded to full-scale assault on the western sectors or an incident, however accidental, in the air. All victories, after all, depend on an element of luck and are in some part triumphs over the weakness of the victors. It by no means reduces the credit due to Berlin and the West to ask to what extent the Soviet Union had contributed to its own defeat. It could surely be argued that the Kremlin overreached itself by trying at one and the same time to take over the western sectors, check west German development and force adherence to its own interpretation of the Potsdam Agreement; and that it fouled its chances by acting with such barbarity and clumsiness. But whatever the scale of Soviet blunder and ineptitude, it can only be discussed with hindsight. In 1948 what was conspicuous was Soviet strength; it had to be combated in spite of awareness of western frailty and against a backdrop of the sickening prospect of war.

The story of the Berlin blockade is rich not only in danger and the courage to meet it, but in irony. The western sectors had withstood siege and retained their independence, but they could not resist geography and they remained an island. Even so, their fight ensured they would never be insular: Berlin's struggles continued to be the world's struggles and its people who had once symbolised hated Prussianism had become the champions of freedom. While the blockade lasted, west Germans who wanted an independent and united country built a separate state and accepted formerly resented occupiers as defenders; the western Powers who had rejected plans for dismemberment were reconciled to the division of Germany and came to regard the zones they had intended to punish as partners. The Soviet Union who preached the necessity for quadripartite government, having wrecked the Allied Control Council and Kommandatura, found themselves without influence in west Germany

377

and deprived of its resources. Before the siege was imposed, west Europe was ruined and helpless; when it was lifted the states were welded in strong military and economic alliance. The United States, who in 1945 wanted the boys back home, had now committed its forces to western Europe; after vowing to stop subsidising its allies, it was giving aid on the most munificent scale. Americans had welcomed Hull's promise that in the post-war world there would be no need for spheres of influence, alliances or a balance of power, but in 1949 they were the linchpin of NATO, and having tried harder and longer than anyone to retain co-operation with the Russians, they now confronted the Soviet bloc on the Continent.

Everyone had talked of Berlin "getting back to normal" once the blockade was up. It never did. The city's story from 1949 is one of painfully slow adjustments to the abnormal. Communications between the western sectors and the outside world remained vulnerable to Soviet interference; then the government of the east German Democratic Republic in May 1952 cut the telephone links and in early 1953 suspended tram and bus traffic with the eastern sector. The split of the city grew more anomalous and distressing with time. The forlorn plight of the eastern Bezirke was demonstrated in June 1953 when a building workers' strike escalated into a popular uprising and was crushed by Russian troops: there was no western airlift to help east Berliners. Yet the western Powers stood firm throughout the 1950s while the Soviet Union tried to challenge their position in the city; they refused Nikita Khrushchev's demand in November 1958 for troop withdrawal and were not intimidated by a threat that the GDR would terminate their rights by an exercise of sovereignty "on land, on water and in the air." A new laceration of Berlin in 1961 was more agonising even than the wounds of 1948 and 1949: on 13 August East German troops and police tore up pavements at eighty sector crossing-points, put up barricades of barbed wire and trenches and cut the U- and S-bahns. The obscene concrete scar of the Wall then mutilated the city: forty-five kilometers along the east sector boundary, 120 kilometers more around the perimeter of the western sectors. Only at the end of 1963 did west Berliners get permission to visit relatives on the other side of the city, and it was not until November 1964 that GDR pensioners were allowed to travel west – and even so, moving a few streets either way meant visas and currency changes as if voyaging to an alien land.

At last in 1969 the first hesitant diplomatic steps were taken to establish, if not "normalisation," at least a degree of alleviation.

Four-Power talks began in March 1970 in the old Allied Control Council building, and meetings were held between representatives of both German states to draw up new transit arrangements. Under the Quadripartite Agreement which came into force on 3 June 1972 the Soviet Union promised not to disrupt civilian traffic to west Berlin; the telephone links were re-established. The four Powers confirmed that the "ties between the western sectors of Berlin and the Federal Republic of Germany will be maintained and developed," but the western allies conceded that their section of the city was not "a constituent part of the Federal Republic." The Agreement served to stabilise a situation which had always threatened to erupt, the German practical arrangements eased many inconveniences; there was no "Berlin crisis" in the 1970s or early 1980s. But the city continued to pay a price for calm and peaceful if separate development: though the eastern and western states moved from military government to civilian supervision and finally to sovereignty, though the West and the Soviet Union agreed to end the state of war with Germany in the mid-1950s, Berlin was to remain under military occupation.

The presence of troops was to be a continual reminder of past and present problems which had not been solved. Forty years after the blockade Berlin is still divided. The city, cut by a wall, makes palpable the division of Europe and the hostility between two Power blocs and two sets of political and economic beliefs. The city can never be reconstituted until there is a German treaty, a united country and a peaceful European settlement. How and when will Berlin become a city like any other?

Sources

Unpublished Papers

It is a sign of the good relations between the American and British governments of the period that so many official papers were exchanged. As a result, the same document often appears in the archives of both nations. References we have given are either to the first we came across or to the fuller version.

Public Records Office, Kew
Foreign Office documents. Those in the reference section prefixed "FO 371" come from the general and political files; those beginning "FO 800" are from the papers of the Foreign Secretary; "FORD" is the Foreign Office Research Department.
"FO" followed by four numbers "/," and a figure denotes a former British Military Government document.
Cabinet papers are prefixed "CAB"; Air Ministry "AIR."

Bundesarchiv, Koblenz
The papers of the US Military Government are available here on microfiche and carry the prefix "OMGUS." The letters "POLAD" show that a document came from the office of the Political Adviser, "FA" from the Food and Agriculture Department, "ODI" from the Office of the Director of Intelligence.

SOURCES

The Harry S. Truman Library, Independence, Missouri
With admirable efficiency and speed, we were sent photostats of
relevant documents from the papers of the former President and
transcripts of oral interviews in the Library's collection.

Private Papers and Personal Communications

We were fortunate to be given access to letters, diaries or manuscripts
in private possession and would like to thank Audrey Beaumont,
Squadron-Leader Eric Best, Major A. K. Crisp Jones, Brigadier
Rupert Crowdy, Air-Commodore N. C. Hyde, Adrian Liddell Hart,
Squadron-Leader Richard Martin, Rev. D. W. A. Quinlan, Evelyn
Smith and John Stroud. We are also most grateful for information
received from Colonel I. le C. Bergh SAAF, Flight-Lieutenant O. V.
Brooks, Lieutenant-Colonel Lawrence Caskey, Edward N.
Dahlberg, Sir Terence Garvey, Group-Captain R. Morris, J.
Pacey, Mrs D. Vergen, Squadron-Leader G. E. Willis and George
Wyatt. We were enormously helped by those who went to such
trouble to tape their memories for us and charmed by a recording
of *Der Insulaner* sent by Curt Flatow.

Interviews

Ruth Anding, Ambassador Lucius D. Battle, Evelyn Beaumont,
Marion Beiber, Captain Jack O. Bennett, Squadron-Leader Eric
Best, Flight-Lieutenant M. G. Blomer, Lieutenant-Colonel Philip
Chernis, Clark Clifford, Professor Hans Coper, Brigadier Rupert
Crowdy, Alan Dawes, Sir Patrick Dean, C. A. Eade, Group-
Captain P. J. S. Finlayson, Curt Flatow, Helga Galler, Dudley
Heesom, Air-Commodore N. C. Hyde, Squadron-Leader P. R.
Jones, Sir John Killick, Captain Robert Kimener, W. W. King, Dr.
Werner Klatt, Hans Christoph Knebusch, Sir Denis Laskey, Adrian
Liddell Hart, Professor Richard Lowenthal, Friedrich Luft, Hugh
Lunghi, Anthony Marreco, Squadron-Leader Richard Martin,
Ambassador Paul Nitze, Sir Frank Roberts, Squadron-Leader L.
Schulkins, John Sherwood, Group-Captain Jack Short, Audrey
Smith, Gretel Spitzer, Air Vice-Marshal Sir Brian Stanbridge,
Shepard Stone, Squadron-Leader Ken Taylor, Major-General
G. R. Turner Cain, Mrs. Wilby, Dr. Gunter Wilitzki.

381

Published Sources from which Facts or Quotations Have Been Taken

Foreign Relations of the United States, 1948 volume II and 1949 volumes II and III (FRUS); edited by the Historical Office, Bureau of Public Affairs of the Department of State, 1973

A Report on "Operation Plainfare" (which includes sections on "Operation Vittles")

Dean Acheson, *Sketches from Life* (Hamish Hamilton 1961)

Dean Acheson, *Present at the Creation* (Hamish Hamilton 1970)

Konrad Adenauer, *Memoirs 1945–53* (Weidenfeld & Nicolson 1966)

Stephen E. Ambrose, *Eisenhower,* vol one, *Soldier, General of the Army, President Elect.* (George Allen & Unwin 1984)

Mark Arnold Forster, *The Siege of Berlin* (Collins 1979)

Vincent Auriol, *Mon Septennat 1947–54* (Editions Gallimard 1970)

John H. Backer, *Winds of History: The German Years of Lucius D. Clay* (Von Nostrand Reinhold Co. 1983)

Walter Bedell Smith, *Moscow Mission 1946–49* (Heinemann 1950)

Charles E. Bohlen, *Witness to History 1929–69* (Weidenfeld & Nicolson 1973)

Willy Brandt (as told to Leo Lania), *My Road to Berlin* (Peter Davies 1960)

Alan Bullock, *Ernest Bevin: Foreign Secretary 1945–51* (Heinemann 1983)

James F. Byrnes, *All in one Lifetime* (Museum Press 1960)

Lucius D. Clay, *Decision in Germany* (Heinemann 1950)

John Colville, *The Fringes of Power: Downing Street Diaries 1939–45* (Hodder & Stoughton, 1985)

Milovan Djilas, *Conversations with Stalin* (Rupert Hart Davies 1962)

Lewis J. Edinger, *Kurt Schumacher, A Study in Personality and Political Behaviour* (Stanford University Press 1965)

John Erickson, *The Road to Berlin* (Weidenfeld & Nicolson 1983)

John Gimbel, *The American Occupation of Germany: Politics and Military, 1945–49* (Stanford University Press 1968)

Lord Gladwyn, *The Memoirs of Lord Gladwyn* (Weidenfeld & Nicolson 1972)

Alfred Grosser, *Germany in Our Time* (Pall Mall Press 1971)

Kenneth Harris, *Attlee* (Weidenfeld & Nicolson 1982)

Sir Nicholas Henderson, *The Birth of NATO* (Weidenfeld & Nicolson 1982)

George F. Kennan, *Memoirs 1925–50* (Pantheon Books 1967)

William D. Leahy, *I Was There* (Gollancz 1950)

Curtis E. LeMay (with MacKinlay Kantor), *Mission with LeMay* (Doubleday & Co. 1965)

Wolfgang Leonhard, *Child of the Revolution* (Collins 1957)

Martin McCauley, *The German Democratic Republic since 1945* (Macmillan in association with the School of Slavonic and East European Studies 1953)

David S. McLennan, *Dean Acheson, The State Department Years* (Dodd, Mead & Co. 1976)

Peter H. Merkl, *The Origin of the West German Republic* (Oxford University Press, New York, 1963)

Robert L. Messer, *The End of an Alliance: James F. Byrnes, Roosevelt, Truman and the Origins of the Cold War* (University of North Carolina Press 1982)

Walter Millis (ed.), *The Forrestal Diaries* (Viking Press 1951)

Robert Murphy, *Diplomat among the Warriors* (Collins 1964)

W. Phillips Davison, *The Berlin Blockade, A Study in Cold War Politics* (Princeton University Press 1958)

Robert Rodrigo, *Berlin Airlift* (Cassell 1960)

Avi Shlaim, *The United States and the Berlin Blockade 1948–49: A Study in Crisis Decision-Making* (University of California Press 1983)

Dirk V. Stikkers, *Men of Responsibility* (John Murray 1966)

Lord Strang, *Home and Abroad* (André Deutsch 1956)

Harry S. Truman, *Memoirs*, vol. II: *Years of Trial and Hope* (Doubleday & Co. 1956)

William H. Tunner, *Over The Hump* (Duell, Sloan & Pearce 1964)

Arthur V. Vandenberg Jnr (ed.) with the collaboration of Joe Alex Morris, *The Private Papers of Senator Vandenberg* (Houghton Mifflin Co. 1952)

F. Roy Willis, *The French in Germany 1945–49* (Stanford University Press 1962)

Edwin Whitfield, *Civil Airlift Operation Plainfare 4 August 1948–15 August 1949: A Final Report of the Manager Civil Airlift Division to the Air Officer Commanding No. 46 Group Royal Air Force* (Control Commission for Germany)

Articles which Have Been Quoted from or Proved Useful

Civil Airlift Flyer, "I Wouldn't Have Missed It," *Flight*, 15 December 1949

Paul Fisher, "The Berlin Airlift," *The Bee Hive* (United Aircraft Corporation), vol. 23, No. 4, Fall 1948

John E. Fricker, "Feeding Berlin by Air," *The Aeroplane*, 23 July 1948

Philip C. Jessup, "Park Avenue Diplomacy," *Political Science Quarterly*, vol. 87, No. 3, September 1972

Philip Kidson, "Avro on the Airlift," A. V. Roe & Co. Ltd, 1948

H. F. King MBE, "BEA to Berlin," *Flight*, 30 September and 7 October 1948

Lieutenant P. L. MacGregor and K. N. Hansen, SAAF, "The Berlin Airlift," *South African Air Force Journal*, July 1949

Lieutenant Colonel Kenneth L. Mall USAF, "The Berlin Airlift," *Air Force Magazine*, July 1968

General T. Ross Milton USAF, "The Berlin Airlift," *Air Force Magazine*, July 1968

Philip E. Moseley, "The Dismemberment of Germany," *Foreign Affairs*, vol. 28, No. 3, April 1950

Philip E. Moseley, "The Occupation of Germany: New Light on How the Zones were Drawn," *Foreign Affairs*, vol. 28, No. 4, July 1950

Captain Laurie Nutton, "The Berlin Airlift," *Propliner*, Summer 1983

Retired Occupation Officer, "Life in Berlin Today," *The World Today*, vol. 14, No. 12, December 1948

Harald Seabrook-Smith, "The Berlin Airlift," *Aeroplane Monthly*, April 1977

Avi Shlaim, "Britain, Berlin and the Cold War," *International Affairs*, Winter 1984

Kenneth J. Slacker USAF, "The Pink Gooney Bird," *Daedalus Flyer*, 1980

J. E. Ward and H. G. L., "The Breakdown of Four Power Rule in Berlin," *The World Today*, vol. 14, No. 8, August 1948

P. R. Wood, "Twenty Years On: The Berlin Airlift – A Reassessment," *RAF Quarterly*, Autumn 1978

"The Navy Lifts its Share," *Naval Aviation News*, November 1948

"Navy Wings over Berlin," *Naval Aviation News*, March 1949

References

1: Fumbling the Peace

1 *The Private Papers of Senator Vandenberg*, 11 February 1943
2 *Ibid.*, 19 May 1943
3 Robert Murphy, *Diplomat among the Warriors*
4 Alan Bullock, *Ernest Bevin: Foreign Secretary 1945–51*
5 Milovan Djilas, *Conversations with Stalin*
6 Murphy, *op. cit.*
7 Djilas, *op. cit.*
8 Lord Gladwyn, *The Memoirs of Lord Gladwyn*
9 Memo from Roosevelt to Hull, 20 October 1944, in Murphy, *op. cit.*
10 John H. Backer, *The Decision to Divide Germany*
11 Gladwyn, *op. cit.*
12 Backer, *op. cit.*
13 *Ibid.*
14 F. Roy Willis, *The French in Germany 1945–49*
15 Lord Strang, *Home and Abroad*
16 John Colville, *The Fringes of Power: Downing Street Diaries 1939–55*
17 Walter Bedell Smith, *Moscow Mission 1946–49*
18 Strang, *op. cit.*
19 *Ibid.*
20 Dean Acheson, *Present at the Creation*
21 Philip E. Moseley, "The Occupation of Germany: New Light on How the Zones were Drawn"
22 George F. Kennan, *Memoirs 1925–50*
23 Moseley, *op. cit.*
24 Kennan, *op. cit.*

25 Moseley, *op. cit.*
26 Kennan, *op. cit.*
27 Strang, *op. cit.*
28 Bedell Smith, *op. cit.*
29 Strang, *op. cit.*
30 *Ibid.*
31 Moseley, *op. cit.*
32 *Ibid.*
33 Murphy, *op. cit.*
34 Strang, *op. cit.*
35 Moseley, *op. cit.*
36 Murphy, *op. cit.*
37 James F. Byrnes, *All in one Lifetime*
38 Gladwyn, *op. cit.*
39 Robert L. Messer, *The End of an Alliance: James F. Byrnes, Roosevelt, Truman and the Origins of the Cold War*
40 William D. Leahy, *I Was There*
41 Charles E. Bohlen, *Witness to History 1929–69*
42 Backer, *op. cit.*
43 Bohlen, *op. cit.*
44 Willis, *op. cit.*

2: Who Is Going To Take Berlin?

1 Brigadier J. Whiteley, quoted by Stephen E. Ambrose, *Eisenhower The Soldier*
2 *Ibid.*
3 Murphy, *op. cit.*
4 Following quotations from Ambrose, *op. cit.*
5 John Erickson, *The Road to Berlin*
6 Ambrose, *op. cit.*
7 Djilas, *op. cit.*
8 Wolfgang Leonhard, BBC TV *Timewatch* programme: "The Fall of Berlin," May 1985
9 Wolfgang Leonhard, *Child of the Revolution*
10 Interview in *Neues Deutschland*, 17 April 1965, quoted by Martin McCauley, *The German Democratic Republic since 1945*
11 Leonhard, *op. cit.*
12 *Ibid.*
13 *Ibid.*
14 Kennan, *op. cit.*
15 Bullock, *op. cit.*
16 Murphy, *op. cit.*
17 Report by General Clay for signature by General Eisenhower, *The*

Papers of General Lucius D. Clay, Germany 1945–49 (hereafter referred to as The Clay Papers)

18 Lucius D. Clay, *Decision in Germany*
19 The Clay Papers
20 Leahy, *op. cit.*
21 Paper by A. R. Walmsley, 12 August 1948: Foreign Office Research Department: FO 371 70508
22 Murphy, *op. cit.*
23 Moseley, *op. cit.*
24 Quoted in Walmsley, *op. cit.*
25 Frank Howley, *Berlin Command*
26 Squadron-Leader G. D. Wilson, *History of Gatow*
27 Details from minutes of 29 June 1945 meeting by Major-General Floyd D. Parker, The Clay Papers
28 Clay, *Decision in Germany*
29 Murphy, *op. cit.*
30 General Clay in oral history interview, 16 July 1974. Harry S. Truman Library
31 The Clay Papers
32 Memo by Field Marshal Montgomery, 7 April 1948, in Walmsley, *op. cit.*
33 Foreign Office minute, 2 July 1948: FO 371 70498
34 Howley, *op. cit.*
35 Clay report on the meeting, The Clay Papers
36 *Ibid.*
37 Clay, *Decision in Germany*
38 Leahy, *op. cit.*
39 Bullock, *op. cit.*
40 Kenneth Harris, *Attlee*
41 Messer, *op. cit.*
42 Leahy, *op. cit.*
43 Bohlen, *op. cit.*

3: Doctors or Heirs?

1 Willis, *op. cit.*
2 Konrad Adenauer, *Memoirs 1945–53*
3 Clay, *Decision in Germany*
4 Howley, *op. cit.*
5 Information from Mrs Beaumont and Mrs Smith
6 British Military Government reply to Foreign Office enquiry, 29 June 1948: FO 371 70498
7 Clay, *Decision in Germany*
8 Report by Air Directorate, 22 November 1948: FO 1012/572
9 Wilson, *op. cit.*

10 John H. Backer, *Winds of History: The German Years of Lucius D. Clay*
11 Clay, *Decision in Germany*
12 Clay to McCloy, 29 June 1948, The Clay Papers
13 *Ibid.*, 4 October 1945
14 Adenauer, *op. cit.*
15 Bullock, *op. cit.*
16 Dean Acheson, *Sketches from Life*
17 Bullock, *op. cit.*
18 Details from Sir Patrick Dean, Sir Denis Laskey and Sir Frank Roberts
19 Murphy, *op. cit.*
20 Byrnes, *op. cit.*
21 McCloy, in foreword to Backer, *op. cit.*
22 Byrnes, *op. cit.*
23 Clay in interview with Jean Smith, February 1971, quoted by Backer, *op. cit.*
24 Murphy, *op. cit.*
25 Clay to McCloy, 26 April 1945, The Clay Papers
26 Clay to McCloy, 29 June 1945, *ibid.*
27 Clay, *Decision in Germany*
28 Leonhard, *op. cit.*
29 McCauley, *op. cit.*
30 Lewis J. Edinger, *Kurt Schumacher: A Study in Personality and Political Belief*
31 Clay, *Decision in Germany*
32 Bullock, *op. cit.*
33 Byrnes, *op. cit.*
34 *Ibid.*

4: The Patient Sinks

1 Clay to Hilldring, 28 January 1946, The Clay Papers
2 Clay to Hilldring, 27 February 1946, *ibid.*
3 Clay to Echols, 24 May 1946, *ibid.*
4 Clay to Echols and Petersen, 27 March 1946, *ibid.*
5 Bullock, *op. cit.*
6 British zone figures from Bullock, *ibid.*; US zone figures from W. Phillips Davison, *The Berlin Blockade: A Study in Cold War Politics*
7 John Gimbel, *The American Occupation of Germany: Politics and the Military, 1945–49*
8 Clay, *Decision in Germany*
9 Press conference, 4 May 1946, quoted by Gimbel, *op. cit.*
10 Clay to Eisenhower and Department of War, 26 May 1946, The Clay Papers

11 Murphy, *op. cit.*
12 Kennan, *op. cit.*
13 Bullock, *op. cit.*
14 Talk to Byrnes, 5 January 1946, Harry S. Truman, *Memoirs*, vol. II
15 Bullock, *op. cit.*
16 Molotov's and Byrnes's speeches in Byrnes, *op. cit.*
17 FO 371 76546
18 Leonhard, *op. cit.*
19 House of Commons debate, reported in *The Times*, 6 February 1946
20 "Review of the Proceedings of the CFM in Moscow" and "Conferences 1947–48": The Private Papers of Mr Ernest Bevin (hereafter referred to as The Bevin Papers), FO 800 477
21 Acheson, *Sketches from Life*
22 Murphy, *op. cit.*
23 Letter from Bevin to Attlee, 16 April 1947, "Conferences 1947–48": The Bevin Papers, *op. cit.*
24 "Review of the Proceedings of the CFM in Moscow": The Bevin Papers, *op. cit.*
25 Bohlen, *op. cit.*
26 Bedell Smith, *op. cit.*
27 Bohlen, *op. cit.*
28 *The Times*, 7 May 1947
29 Teleconference with Petersen, 13 May 1947, The Clay Papers
30 30 August 1947 in ACC, *ibid.*
31 Bullock, *op. cit.*
32 *The Times*, 3 November 1947
33 Clay to Draper, 3 November 1947, The Clay Papers
34 Special Report No 3. Research Branch, Information Control Division, 2 September 1947: OMGUS ODI 13/429-2/35
35 *The Times*, 25 September 1947
36 Political Adviser to Secretary of State, 24 May 1947: FRUS 1947 (11)
37 Clay, *Decision in Germany*
38 *Ibid.*
39 Avi Shlaim, *The United States and the Berlin Blockade 1948–49: A Study in Crisis Decision-Making*
40 Memo for Cabinet, 5 January 1948: CAB 129 vol. 23
41 Memo from Acting Chief of the Division of European Affairs, Lichtner, to Assistant Secretary for Occupied Areas, Satzmann, 26 December 1947: FRUS 1947 (11)
42 Bedell Smith to Secretary of State, 30 December 1947: FRUS 1947 (11)
43 *The Times*, 20 December 1947
44 Weekly Background Notes (FORD) No. 122, 1 January 1948: FO 371 70616
45 Minutes of Commandants' meeting, 30 December 1947: FO 371 70531

5: Putting on the Squeeze

1 US Political Adviser to Secretary of State, 3 March 1948: FRUS 1948 (II)
2 Extract from British Intelligence Staff Monthly Summary, 14 February 1948: OMGUS ODI 3/430-1/2
3 10 January Weekly Intelligence report: OMGUS ODI 3/430-1/1
4 Morale Report, 16–31 January 1948: FO 1049/1391
5 Extract from British Intelligence Staff Monthly Summary, 14 February: *op. cit.*
6 Clay to Draper, 16 January 1948, The Clay Papers
7 US Political Adviser to Secretary of State, 7 January 1948: FRUS 1948 (II)
8 *The Times* 17 January and 5 February 1948
9 Morale Report, *op. cit.*
10 *The Times*, 17 January 1948
11 Details in Murphy to Secretary of State, 1 February 1948; Riddleberger to Secretary, 12 February 1948: FRUS 1948 (II); Clay to Draper, 12 February 1948, The Clay Papers
12 See, for example memo from Frank G. Wisner (Deputy to Assistant Secretary of State for Occupied Areas) to Under-Secretary of State 10 March 1948: Lovett: FRUS 1948 (II)
13 Clay to Draper, 12 February 1948, The Clay Papers
14 US Political Adviser to Secretary of State, 8 January 1948: FRUS 1948 (II)
15 Quotations in Weekly Background Notes (FORD) No. 124, 15 January 1948: FO 371 70616
16 Clay in teleconference with Royall, 12 January 1948, The Clay Papers
17 *The Times* and Riddleberger, Acting US Political Adviser, to Secretary of State, 21 January 1948: FRUS 1948 (II)
18 Extract from British Intelligence Staff Monthly Summary, 14 February: *op. cit.*
19 Details from *The Times*, 26 January 1948, and FO 371 70616
20 Military Government Liaison Section Weekly Report No. 12 for period up to 27 January: FO 371 70481
21 Most notes in FRUS 1948 (II)
22 Clay, *Decision in Germany*
23 Memo from Bevin to Cabinet, "Talks on Germany," 7 March 1948: CAB 129, vol. 25
24 Memo by Montgomery, 30 January 1948: The Bevin Papers, Defence January-June 1948, FO 800/452
25 Record of conversation between Bevin and Douglas, 26 February 1948: FRUS 1948 (II)
26 Gladwyn, *op. cit.*
27 John D. Hickerson, Director of the Office of European Affairs, quoted by Sir Nicholas Henderson, *The Birth of NATO*

REFERENCES

28 Military Government Liaison Section Weekly Report No. 15: FO 371 70481
29 US Political Adviser to Secretary of State, 3 March 1948: FRUS 1948 (II)
30 Military Government Liaison Section Weekly Report No. 13 for period up to 3 February: FO 371 70481
31 Minutes of Commandants' meeting 2 March 1948: FO 371 70533
32 Clay to Chamberlain, 5 March 1948, The Clay Papers
33 Bradley to Clay and MacArthur, 12 March 1948, The Clay Papers
34 Undated Robertson memo, "Berlin Prospects": FO 371 70489
35 Strang to Bevin, "The Future of Berlin," 24 February 1948: FO 371 70489
36 Details from Military Government Liaison Section Weekly Report No. 18 for period up to 8 March: FO 371 70482; and "Pressure on the Parties in the Soviet Sector of Berlin": FO 371 70483
37 Details from The Times; Clay, Decision in Germany; and US Political Adviser to Secretary of State, 20 March 1948: FRUS 1948 (II)
38 Weekly Intelligence Report, Office of Military Government for Germany (US), Office of the Director of Intelligence (hereafter referred to as Weekly Intelligence Report), 30 March 1948: OMGUS ODI 3/430-1/3
39 The Times, 23 March 1948
40 Weekly Background Notes (FORD) No. 133, 1 April 1948: FO 371 70617
41 See, for example, Military Government Liaison Section Weekly Report No. 21 for the period up to 30 March: FO 371 70483
42 The Times, 23 March 1948
43 Details from Weekly Intelligence Report, 27 March 1948: OMGUS ODI 3/430-1/3
44 21 February report. OMGUS ODI 3/430-1/2
45 US Political Adviser to Secretary of State, 1 April 1948: FRUS 1948 (II)
46 Kirkpatrick to Robertson, 24 March 1948: FO 371 70490
47 "US Course of Action in Event Soviets Attempt Force US out of Berlin", quoted by Shlaim, op. cit.
48 Robertson to Herbert, 23 March 1948: FO 1030/60
49 Herbert to Robertson, 30 March 1948: ibid.
50 The Times, 25 March 1948
51 US Political Adviser to Secretary of State, 8 April 1948: OMGUS POLAD 796/1-1
52 Weekly Background Notes (FORD) No. 133, 1 April 1948: op. cit.
53 Dratvin's letter in FO 1030/57
54 31 March 1948: Mil. Gov. to FO: FO 371 70480
55 Clay to Bradley, 31 March 1948: Files of Clark M. Clifford, Papers of Harry S. Truman
56 The Clay Papers

391

57 *The Forrestal Diaries*
58 The Clay Papers
59 *Daily Telegraph*, 1 April 1948
60 Details from the diaries of Mrs Beaumont and Mrs Quinlan
61 Clay to Bradley, 1 April 1948: The Clay Papers
62 3 April 1948: FO 371 70490; and 22 April 1948: FO 371 70491
63 Details from Weekly Background Notes (FORD) No. 134, 15 April 1948: FO 371 70617
64 March press summary Moscow Embassy to Foreign Office: FO 371 70490
65 Weekly Intelligence Report: OMGUS ODI 3/430-1/4
66 *The Times*, 2 April 1948
67 *Ibid.*, 5 April
68 Teleconference with Bradley and Royall, 2 April 1948, The Clay Papers
69 2 April 1948, Mil. Gov. to FO: FO 371 70490
70 Shlaim, *op. cit.*
71 Letter and minute for Bevin, 1 April 1948: FO 371 70490
72 Teleconference, 1 April 1948, The Clay Papers
73 Teleconference with Deputy Chiefs of Staff and Chamberlain, 17 March 1948, The Clay Papers
74 Teleconference, 1 and 2 April, The Clay Papers
75 Clay to Bradley, 2 April 1948, The Clay Papers
76 See, for example, Strang to Bevin, "The Future of Berlin", 24 February 1948: FO 371 70489
77 Robertson to Foreign Office, 2 April 1948: FO 371 70490
78 Shlaim, *op. cit.*
79 *Ibid.*
80 Murphy, *op. cit.*
81 Bohlen, *op. cit.*

6: A War of Pinpricks

1 SMA correspondence with Military Governors, quoted by *The Times*, 5 April 1948
2 Vincent Auriol, *Mon Septennat 1947–54*
3 *The Times*, 5 and 8 May, 1948
4 *The Times*, 21 and 27 April 1948; Weekly Background Notes (FORD) No. 135, 29 April 1948: FO 371 70617
5 Military Government Liaison Section Weekly Report No. 27 for the period up to 11 May: FO 371 70485
6 Summary of Commandants' meeting, 28 May 1948: FO 371 70535
7 Military Government Liaison Section Weekly Report No. 29 for the period up to 25 May: FO 371 70485

8 Report by J. A. N. McEwan, Regional Economic Officer, Economic Group HQ Military Government (Berlin) to Information Services Division CCG (BE), 9 June 1948: FO 1012/193

9 *A Report on "Operation Plainfare"*; and AIR 38/333

10 Details from Murphy to Secretary of State 6 April 1948: FRUS 1948 (II); *The Times* 6 and 7 April; and conversation with General Turner Cain

11 Clay to Bradley, 6 April 1948, The Clay Papers

12 Weekly Intelligence Report, 8 May 1948: OMGUS ODI 3/430–1/5

13 Details from *The Times*, 8 and 20 April 1948; and Clay to Bradley, 9 April 1948, The Clay Papers

14 Clay to Bradley, 6 April, 1948, *ibid.*

15 *Ibid.*, 9 April.

16 *Daily Telegraph*, 12 April, 1948

17 Murphy to Secretary of State, 6 April, 1948: FRUS 1948 (II)

18 Berlin to Foreign Office, 6 May 1948: FO 371 70493

19 Clay to Draper, 7 May 1948, The Clay Papers

20 *Täglische Rundschau*, quoted in Weekly Intelligence Report, 8 May 1948: OMGUS ODI 3/430–1/5

21 Military Government Liaison Section Weekly Report No. 29 for the period up to 25 May: FO 371 70485

22 Weekly Intelligence Report, 15 May 1948: OMGUS ODI 3/430–1/5

23 Military Government Liaison Section Weekly Report No. 29, *op. cit.*

24 Teleconference with Bradley, 10 April, 1948, The Clay Papers

25 Record of lunch at Foreign Office with Strang, Robertson, Clay and Douglas, 28 April 1948: FO 371 70492

26 Quoted by Shlaim, *op. cit.*

27 Aide-mémoire from Bevin to Marshall, 30 April 1948, quoted by Bullock, *op. cit.*

28 Record of lunch on 28 April, *op cit.*

29 Teleconference of 10 April, *op. cit.*

30 FO Washington to CCG(BE), 9 April 1948: FO 1049/1352

31 Letter from Douglas to Lovett, 17 April 1948: FRUS 1948 (II)

32 Douglas to Secretary of State, 28 April: *ibid.*

33 Marshall and Lovett to Douglas, 30 April: *ibid.*

34 Record of talk between Bevin and Douglas for Inverchapel, Washington, 29 April 1948: The Bevin Papers, FO 300/467

35 Memo to Attlee, 5 May: *ibid.*

36 Details from Bullock, Bohlen and Bedell Smith, *op. cit.*

37 Bedell Smith, *op. cit.*

38 Record of meeting in Strang's room, 29 April 1948: FO 371 70493 and FO 1030/60

39 Minute by Sargent, 13 April 1948: FO 371 70491

40 Teleconference with Bradley, 10 April 1948, The Clay Papers

41 Record of meeting in Strang's room and lunch, 28 April, *op. cit.*

42 Robertson to Kirkpatrick, 6 April 1948: FO 371 70491
43 Mil. Gov. to FO, 8 May 1948: FO 371 70493
44 Military Government Liaison Section Weekly Report No. 25 for the period up to 27 April: FO 371 70484
45 *Ibid.*, No. 26 for the period up to 4 May
46 *Ibid.*, No. 23 for the period up to 13 April
47 Liaison Section report, "Pressure on the Parties: Oct. 1946–Dec. 1948": FO 371 76542
48 Weekly Intelligence Report, 8 May: *op cit.*
49 Report of interview with Colonel Whitefoord, 10 June 1948: FO 1012/215
50 Herbert to Robertson, 30 April 1948: FO 1030/60
51 Conversation with General Turner Cain
52 Details from Mil. Gov. to FO 2 May 1948: FO 371 70484; Military Government Liaison Section Weekly Report No. 26, *op. cit.*
53 Whitefoord interview with Dr Suhr: FO 1012/215
54 Military Government Liaison Section Weekly Report No. 28 for the period up to 18 May: FO 371 70485
55 Details from Intelligence Staff Report: FO 371 70485; Weekly Political summary for the period up to 7 June: FO 371 70486; Military Government Liaison Section Weekly Reports 8 and 22 June: *ibid.*, and for the period up to 18 May: *op. cit.*; Weekly Intelligence Report, 5 June 1948: OMGUS ODI 3/430/1–6; Fortnightly Background Notes (FORD) No. 139, 24 June 1948: FO 371 70617
56 Mil. Gov. to FO, 13 April 1948: FO 1049/1352
57 *Ibid.*, 3, 5, 8 and 13 April 1948.
58 Minutes of Deputy Commandants' meeting, 6 April 1948: FO 371 70531
59 Warren M. Chase, 29 April 1948: FRUS 1948 (II)
60 Minutes of Public Safety Commiteee, 14 May 1948: FO 371 70534; minutes of Kommandatura, 28 May 1948: FO 371 70535
61 Information kindly supplied by Mrs Beaumont
62 Murphy to Secretary of State, 29 May 1948: FRUS 1948 (II)
63 *Ibid.* and minutes of Kommandatura, 28 May, *op. cit.*
64 Morale Report, 1–15 May 1948: FO 1049/1391; Weekly Summary for period up to 15 June 1948: FO 371 70485
65 *The Times*, 10 April 1948
66 Report on lunch, Steel to Foreign Office, 10 May 1948: FO 1049/1151
67 Report on SPD party convention, 8–9 May 1948: FO 371 70485
68 Report by Wesley C. Haraldson to Murphy, 23 April 1948: OMGUS POLAD 796/1–1
69 Douglas to Secretary of State, 19 May 1948: FRUS 1948 (II)
70 Caffery to Secretary of State, 21 May 1948: *ibid.*
71 Douglas to Secretary of State, *ibid.*

72 Memo from Lovett on conversation with the French Ambassador, *ibid.*
73 Fortnightly Background Notes (FORD) No. 138, 10 June 1948: FO 371 70617
74 Army to Clay, 28 April 1948: FRUS 1948 (II); Army to Clay, 29 April 1948, The Clay Papers; Clay to Draper, 22 May 1948, *ibid.*
75 Military Government Liaison Section Weekly Report No. 28 for the period up to 18 May: *op cit.*
76 Weekly Intelligence Report, 8 May: *op cit.*
77 Military Government Liaison Section Weekly Report No. 30 for the period up to 1 June: FO 371 70485
78 Weekly Summary, 15 June: *ibid.*
79 Details Military Government Liaison Section Weekly Report No. 31 for the period up to 8 June: FO 371 70486
80 *The Times*, 5 June 1948
81 Mil. Gov. to FO, 7, 8, 10 and 14 June 1948: FO 371 70494
82 *Ibid.*, 14 June
83 *Ibid.*, 7 June
84 Fortnightly Background Notes (FORD) No. 138, 10 June 1948: FO 371 70617
85 Mil. Gov. to FO, 7 June: *op. cit.*
86 *Ibid.*, 10 June
87 *Ibid.*, 14 and 17 June
88 Fortnightly Background Notes (FORD) No. 139, 24 June 1948: FO 371 70617; and *Daily Telegraph* 17 June, 1948
89 Note, 10 June 1948: FO 371 70494
90 *Ibid.*, 12 June
91 Mil. Gov. to FO, 16 June 1948: *op. cit.*
92 Information from the Rev. Dermot Quinlan and General Turner Cain
93 Howley, *op cit.*
94 Bevin to Attlee, 16 June 1948: The Bevin Papers, FO 800 467
95 *The Times*, 18 June 1948
96 Details from Special Report to Chief Liaison and Protocol Section by two members of his department present at the meeting: OMGUS POLAD 804/37
97 *Ibid.* Howley, *op. cit.*, Mil. Gov. to FO, 17 June 1948: FO 371 70636
98 Murphy to Secretary of State, 18 June 1948: FRUS 1948 (II)
99 Howley, *op. cit.*
100 *The Times*, 21 June 1948
101 Fortnightly Background Notes (FORD) No. 139, 24 June 1948: FO 371 70618
102 Murphy to Secretary of State, 19 June 1948: FRUS 1948 (II)
103 *The Times*, 22 June 1948

104 Digest of interview with Herr Heinzelmann (SPD, banking) by US liaison officer, passed on by Colonel Whitefoord, 21 June 1948: FO 1012/215
105 Clay to Draper, 23 June 1948, The Clay Papers; Murphy to Secretary of State, 23 June 1948: FRUS 1948 (II)
106 From Friedensburg's diary, quoted by Davison
107 *The Times*, 26 June 1948
108 Details from Mil. Gov. to FO, 26 June 1948, based on account by Suhr: FO 371 70496; Friedensburg account given to Military Liaison: FO 1012/215; and note by Whitefoord, 24 June 1948: *ibid.*
109 Mil. Gov. to FO, 25 June 1948: FO 371 70496

7: Scramble

1 Clay, *Decision in Germany*
2 Manuscript by Major Crisp Jones kindly lent to the authors
3 *A Report on "Operation Plainfare"*
4 FO 1012/183
5 Report by T. Harker, head of Fuel Branch, Military Government, 2 July 1948: *ibid.*
6 Report from Public Utilities Branch to Secretariat, Military Government, 25 July 1948: *ibid.*
7 Harker to DDMG. *ibid.*
8 *The Times*, 26 June 1948
9 Public Utilities Branch to Secretariat, Military Government, 5 July 1948: FO 1012/183
10 "Berlin Air Lift" issued by the Air Ministry and Central Office of Information
11 Details in this paragraph and the next from *A Report on "Operation Plainfare"*
12 *The Times*, 29 June 1948
13 "Berlin Air Lift"
14 Report by Colonel Whitefoord, 24 June 1948: FO 1012/215
15 Weekly Summary for the period up to 30 June: FO 371 70486
16 Report by American liaison officer enclosed with Colonel Whitefoord's, *op. cit.*
17 Teleconference with Noce (Chief of Civil Affairs Division), 26 June 1948, The Clay Papers
18 Quotations from *Daily Telegraph*, 25 June, 1948
19 Crisp Jones manuscript
20 Résumé of talk between Bevin and Douglas, 26 June 1948: FO 371 70497
21 Diary of Richard Martin, kindly communicated by him to the authors
22 *A Report on "Operation Plainfare"*

23 Clay to Draper, 25 June 1948, The Clay Papers
24 Interview with General Trudeau, 14 August 1978, quoted by Backer, *op. cit.*
25 Interview with Howley, 15 April 1980, *ibid.*
26 Willy Brandt, *My Road to Berlin*
27 Murphy to Secretary of State, 26 June 1948: FRUS 1948 (II)
28 *A Report on "Operation Plainfare"*
29 Fortnightly Background Notes (FORD) No. 140 for period up to 8 July 1948: FO 371 70618
30 FO 371 70498
31 Crisp Jones manuscript
32 Clay to Draper, 27 June 1948, The Clay Papers
33 Both quoted by Shlaim, *op. cit.*
34 Douglas to Secretary of State and Lovett, 28 June 1948: OMGUS POLAD 35/3–32
35 The Bevin Papers, FO 800/467
36 Minutes of Cabinet meeting, 25 June 1948: CAB 182, vol. 13
37 *Ibid.*; note on the meeting by Kirkpatrick to Hollis, 26 June 1948: FO 371 70496
38 Interview with Sir Patrick Dean
39 *The Times*, 2 July 1948
40 Note on meeting, 28 June 1948: The Bevin Papers, *op. cit.*
41 CAB 128, vol. 13
42 Report by Bevin for Franks (Washington), 25 June 1948: FO 371 70497
43 Quoted by Bullock, *op. cit.*
44 Secretary of State to the Embassy in the UK, 27 June 1948: FRUS 1948 (II)
45 Report by Bevin for Franks, *op. cit.*
46 Secretary of State to the Embassy in the UK, *op. cit.*
47 *The Forrestal Diaries*
48 CAB 130, 38 GEN 241
49 Douglas to Secretary of State and Lovett, 2 July 1948: OMGUS POLAD 35/3–32
50 *The Forrestal Diaries*
51 *Ibid.*
52 Record of talk between Bevin and Douglas for Franks, 28 June 1948: FO 800/467
53 Note by Roberts for Strang, 29 June 1948: *ibid.*
54 Conversation with Sir Frank Roberts
55 Truman, *op. cit.*
56 Teleconference with Royall, 25 June 1948, The Clay Papers
57 Secretary of State to the Embassy in the UK, *op. cit.*
58 *The Forrestal Diaries*
59 Murphy to Secretary of State, 26 June 1948: FRUS 1948 (II)
60 Beckett to Dean, 12 July 1948: FO 371 70508

61 *The Forrestal Diaries*
62 *Ibid.*
63 Department of State Bulletin
64 Tedder at second meeting of Committee of Ministers, 29 June 1948: CAB 130, 38 GEN 241
65 *Ibid.*
66 Foreign Office to Robertson, 29 June 1948: FO 371 70496
67 30 June entry in diary of Group-Captain Hyde, generously lent to the authors
68 J. C. Lynn, Assistant Chief Food, Agriculture and Forestry Group to US Army Quartermaster, 8 July 1948: OMGUS FA 12/2
69 Lynn to Economic Adviser (US) BICO, 7 July 1948: *ibid.*
70 Lynn to Frau Hahn, Lurgihaus, 3 July 1948: *ibid.*
71 G. E. Bell, Senior Information Officer, HQ Military Government, 3 July 1948: FO 1012/183
72 Public Health Authority to CONCOMB, Lübbecke. 3 July 1948: *ibid.*
73 Public Utilities Branch to Secretariat, Military Government 5 July: *ibid.*
74 Herbert to DDMG, 1 July 1948: FO 1012/313
75 Clay to Draper, 25 June, 1948, The Clay Papers
76 Marshall to Douglas, Clay and Murphy, 3 July 1948: FRUS 1948 (II)
77 Conversation between Bevin and Attlee, 30 June 1948: FO 371 70498
78 Teleconference with Department of Army, 25 June 1948, in Clay, *Decision in Germany*
79 FO 371 70498
80 Douglas to Secretary of State and Lovett, 30 June 1948: OMGUS POLAD 35/3–32
81 Franks to Foreign Office: 1 July 1948: FO 371 70499
82 Clay to Noce, 1 July 1948, The Clay Papers
83 Mil. Gov. to FO, 30 June 1948: FO 371 70498
84 Teleconference with Douglas, 2 July 1948, The Clay Papers
85 Teleconference, 25 June 1948, *ibid.*
86 Clay to Draper, *ibid.*
87 Clay to Royall, *ibid.*
88 Clay, *Decision in Germany*
89 Clay to Royall, 28 June 1948, The Clay Papers
90 Mil. Gov. to FO, 1 July 1948: FO 371 70536
91 *Ibid.*, 13 August: FO 371 70507
92 Mil. Gov. to FO, 1 and 2 July 1948: FO 371 70500; Clay to Noce, 1 July, *op. cit.*
93 Mil. Gov. to FO, 3 July 1948: FO 371 70499; Clay to Bradley and Royall, 3 July 1948, *ibid.*
94 *Ibid.*

95 New York delegation to Foreign Office: FO 371 70497
96 Record of conversation between Bevin and Douglas, 1 July 1948, The Bevin Papers, *op. cit.*
97 Murphy to Political Branch, "Review of Berlin Situation as of 9 July 1948"; OMGUS POLAD 796/1–3
98 Details from *ibid.* and *The Times*, 9 July 1948
99 Harrison to Foreign Office, 10 July 1948: FO 371 70501
100 Group-Captain Hyde's diary
101 Group-Captain B. C. Yarde, *The Times*, 2 July 1948
102 *A Report on "Operation Plainfare"*
103 Arthur Pearcey, Jnr, *The Dakota*
104 *The Times*, 7 July 1948
105 *Aeroplane*, July 1948
106 FO 1012/183
107 9 July 1948: FO 1012/313

8: A Cushion of Time

1 Quoted in *The Times*, 15 July 1948
2 Franks to Foreign Office, 19 July 1948: FO 371 70502
3 Department of State Bulletin
4 Lovett memo on talk with Franks and Reber, 14 July 1948: FRUS 1948 (II)
5 Secretary of State to Douglas, 20 July 1948: FRUS 1948 (II); and Franks to Foreign Office, 19 July 1948: *op. cit.*
6 Record of meeting between Bevin, Douglas, Bedell Smith, Bohlen, Strang and Peterson, 26 July 1948: FO 800/467
7 Bevin report to Franks on talk with Douglas, 22 July 1948: FO 371 70503
8 E.g., Douglas report to Secretary of State on talk with Bevin, 24 July 1948: FRUS 1948 (II)
9 E.g., Bevin to Franks, 21 and 22 July, *op. cit.*, and 26 July meeting, *op. cit.*
10 Secretary of State to Embassy in the UK, 21 July 1948: FRUS 1948 (II)
11 Teleconference between London and Washington, 22 July 1948: *ibid.*
12 Secretary of State to Embassy in the UK, *op. cit.*
13 Foreign Office to Washington, 13 July 1948: FO 800/467; *The Forrestal Diaries*
14 Douglas to Secretary of State, 13 July 1948: OMGUS POLAD 35/3–24
15 OMGUS POLAD 796/2–1
16 Clay to Bradley, 10 July 1948, The Clay Papers
17 Teleconference, 13 July 1948, *ibid.*

18 Both quoted by Shlaim, *op. cit.*
19 27 July 1948: FO 800/453
20 E.g., Clay to Draper, 19 July 1948, The Clay Papers
21 A. V. Alexander to Attlee, 7 July 1948: FO 800/453
22 Note by Chiefs of Staff, "Preparations for Defence": CAB 131/6
23 27 July, *op. cit.*
24 *The Forrestal Diaries*
25 Murphy, *op. cit.*
26 *The Forrestal Diaries*
27 A. V. Alexander to Attlee, *op. cit.*
28 "Preparations for Defence," *op. cit.*
29 Meeting of Committee of Ministers on Germany, 22 July 1948: CAB 130, 38 GEN 241
30 Report by the Ministry of Defence: CAB 131/6
31 *The Forrestal Diaries*
32 NSC meeting 22 July, 1948: FRUS 1948 (II), and Bohlen and Murphy, *op. cit.*, both of whom say the meeting was on 20 July
33 "A Report to the NSC by the Secretary of Defence: Views of the Joint Chiefs," 28 July 1948: President's Secretary's File, Harry S. Truman Library
34 FO 1012/183
35 *Ibid.*
36 *Ibid.*
37 *The Times*, 19 July 1948
38 McEwan to Air-Commodore Waite, 19 July 1948: FO 1012/313
39 Herbert to Waite, 14 August 1948: *ibid.*
40 Waite to AATO Bückeburg, *ibid.*
41 *Aeroplane*, 23 July 1948
42 Kirkpatrick to Robertson, 24 March 1948, and memo from Brownjohn to Kirkpatrick, 14 April: FO 1030/60
43 Crisp Jones manuscript
44 FO 1077/3; FO 371 70501; *A Report on "Operation Plainfare"*
45 Edwin Whitfield, *A Final Report on the Civil Airlift*
46 31 July 1948: FO 1077/3
47 21 July 1948: *ibid.*
48 William H. Tunner, *Over The Hump*
49 *A Report on "Operation Plainfare"*
50 Mil. Gov. to FO. 28 June 1948: FO 371 70496
51 Clay to Bradley and Royall, 1 July 1948, The Clay Papers
52 Anglo-US military liaison meeting, Washington, 30 June, 1948, quoted by Shlaim, *op. cit.*, Douglas to Secretary of State, 30 June: FRUS 1948 (II)
53 *New York Times*, 7 July 1948, and *The Times*, 8 July 1948
54 *New York Times*, 18 July, 1948
55 Mil. Gov. to FO. 20 July 1948: FO 371 70503; and *The Times*, 24 July 1948

56 Interview with Mr. Eade
57 Tape from Mr. Willis
58 *Daily Telegraph*, 16 July 1948
59 Details in this and previous paragraph mainly from *A Report on "Operation Plainfare"*
60 *Ibid.*; interview with Bob Kimener; Alfred Goldberg (ed.), *History of US Airforce*
61 *A Report on "Operation Plainfare"*; interview with Mr Eade; information from Group-Captain R. Morris
62 *A Report on "Operation Plainfare"*; "Berlin Air Lift"; interview with Peter Jones
63 Details from many of above and a complete performance by Jack Short
64 *The Times*, 26 July 1948
65 Tempelhof Papers
66 Coverage from *Der Tagesspiegel*, quoted by Davison, *op. cit.*
67 Paul Fisher, "The Berlin Airlift," *The Bee Hive*
68 *A Report on "Operation Plainfare"*
69 *Ibid.*
70 Tunner, *op. cit.*
71 Opinion Surveys Branch, No. 130, "Berlin Reactions to the Airlift," 30 July 1948, quoted by Davison, *op. cit.*
72 OMGUS POLAD 796/12
73 Whitefoord report on talk with Suhr, 8 July 1948: FO 1012/215
74 FO 1049/1391
75 Military Government Liaison Section Weekly Report No. 36 for period up to 13 July 1948: FO 371 70487
76 FO 371 70494
77 FO 371 70496
78 E.g., record of 1 July talk between Suhr and Whitefoord, FO 1012/215; and Military Government Liaison Section Weekly Report No. 35 for period up to 6 July 1948: FO 371 70486
79 Military Government Liaison Section Weekly Report No. 36, *op. cit.*
80 John B. Holt to Murphy, 16 July 1948: OMGUS POLAD 796/1-4
81 Suhr talk to Whitefoord, 1 July *op. cit*; and US report on 23 July talk to Schroeder: FO 1012/216
82 Military Government Liaison Section Weekly Report No. 38 for period up to 27 July: FO 371 70487
83 Suhr talk to Whitefoord, 7 July 1948: FO 1012/215
84 *Ibid.*; Fortnightly Background Notes (FORD) No. 141, 22 July 1948: FO 371 70618
85 Davison, *op. cit.*; FO 1030/61; Fortnightly Background Notes, *ibid.*
86 E.g., Suhr talk to US liaison officer, 23 July 1948, *op. cit.*; complaints

by Reuter and leaders of the three political parties to Herbert, 27 July 1948: FO 371 70504

87 E.g., Mil. Gov. to FO, 27 July 1948: *ibid.*

88 Military Government Liaison Section Weekly Report No. 35, *op. cit.*; Weekly Intelligence Report, 10 July 1948: OMGUS ODI 3/430–1/7

89 Whitefoord 2 July report, FO 1012/215

90 Whitefoord note, 13 July 1948: *ibid.*

91 Talk between May and US liaison officer: 6 July 1948; talk between May and Whitefoord, 7 July: *ibid.*

92 Talk between US liaison officer and Schroeder, 23 July 1948: *ibid.*

93 Whitefoord report 24 July 1948: FO 1012/216

94 Weekly Report of Food, Agriculture and Forestry Group (BICO), 23 July 1948: OMGUS FA7/3

95 "Report on German Morale" 16–30 July 1948: FO 1049/1391

96 Fortnightly Background Notes (FORD) No. 142, 5 August 1948: FO 371 70618

97 Military Government Liaison Section Weekly Report No. 37 for period up to 20 July 1948: FO 371 70487

98 *Ibid.*, No. 38, *op. cit.*

99 Whitefoord report, 28 July 1948: FO 1012/216

100 Military Government Liaison Section Weekly Report No. 36, *op. cit.*

101 Herbert to DDMG, 14 July 1948: FO 1012/183

102 Friedensburg talk to Whitefoord, 17 July 1948: FO 1012/215

103 Reuter talk to Whitefoord, 23 July 1948: FO 1012/216

104 Reuter talk to US liaison officer, 27 July 1948: FO 1012/216

105 Herbert to Robertson, 19 July 1948: FO 1030/61

106 Schroeder talk to US liaison officer, 21 July 1948: *op. cit.*

107 Military Government Liaison Section Weekly Report No. 35, *op. cit.*

108 CCG(BE) to Foreign Office, 27 July 1948: FO 1012/216

109 Whitefoord report, 19 July 1948: FO 1012/215

110 FO 1012/216

111 Mil. Gov. to FO, 27 July 1948: FO 371 70504

112 *Daily Telegraph*, 2 August, 1948

113 Mil. Gov. to FO, 4 July 1948: FO 371 70499

114 Schroeder talk to Whitefoord, 23 July 1948: FO 1012/215

115 Military Government Liaison Section Weekly Report No. 39 for period up to 3 August 1948: FO 371 70487

116 Mil. Gov. to FO, 30 July 1948: FO 371 70504

117 Details from various newspaper reports and 20 July Düsseldorf to Berlin: FO 1030/61

118 Political Adviser to Secretary of State, 9 July 1948: FRUS 1948 (II)

119 *Ibid.*

120 Letter from Con O'Neill to Peter Garran, 13 July 1948: FO 1049/1152

121 FRANCOMB to BERCOMB, 23 July 1948: FO 1012/230

122 Record of meeting between Bevin, Douglas, Bedell Smith, Bohlen, Strang and Peterson, 26 July 1948: FO 800/467
123 Douglas to Lovett, 26 July 1948: FRUS 1948 (II)
124 Quoted by Davison, *op. cit.*

9: Amiable Bears

1 Bedell Smith, *op. cit.*
2 Bedell Smith to Secretary of State, 30 July 1948: FRUS 1948 (II)
3 Bedell Smith, *op. cit.*
4 Interview with Sir Frank Roberts
5 Interview with Hugh Lunghi
6 Bedell Smith, *op. cit.*
7 Letter from Roberts to Strang, 10 August 1948: FO 371 70508
8 Bedell Smith to Secretary of State, *op. cit.*
9 Moscow to Foreign Office, 31 July 1948: FO 371 70505
10 Bedell Smith to Secretary of State, 31 July 1948: FRUS 1948 (II)
11 *Ibid.*, and Moscow to Foreign Office, 1 August 1948: FO 371 70505
12 Moscow to Foreign Office, 31 July: *op. cit.*
13 *Ibid.*
14 Bedell Smith to Secretary of State, 31 July: *op. cit.*
15 Djilas, *op. cit.*
16 Details from Bedell Smith to Secretary of State, 3 August 1948: FRUS 1948 (II); Moscow to Foreign Office, 3 August 1948: FO 371 70505; Roberts letter to Strang, 25 August 1948: FO 371 70512; Bedell Smith, *op. cit.*
17 *The Forrestal Diaries*
18 Bevin to Moscow, 3 August 1948: FO 371 70505
19 Douglas to Secretary of State and Lovett, 3 August 1948: OMGUS POLAD 35/3
20 Clay to Department of the Army, 4 August 1948, The Clay Papers
21 Counsellor of Department of State (Bohlen), 4 August 1948: FRUS 1948 (II)
22 Secretary of State to the Embassy in the Soviet Union, 3 August 1948: FRUS 1948 (II)
23 Bedell Smith to Secretary of State, 3 August 1948: FRUS 1948 (II)
24 Summary of Bedell Smith's views by Kennan, minutes of Policy Planning Staff meeting, 28 September 1948: FRUS 1948 (II)
25 Marshall to Bedell Smith, 4 August 1948: OMGUS POLAD 35/3-24
26 *Ibid.*
27 Meeting of Committee of Ministers on Germany, 4 August 1948: CAB 130, 38 GEN 241
28 Bevin to Moscow, 4 August 1948: FO 371 70505
29 Roberts to Strang, 6 August 1948: FO 371 70505

30 Details from reports by Bedell Smith and Roberts on 6 August 1948: FRUS 1948 (II) and FO 371 70506
31 *Ibid.*, and Moscow to Foreign Office, 8 August 1948: FO 371 70506
32 Secretary of State to the Embassy in the Soviet Union, 7 August 1948: FRUS 1948 (II)
33 Douglas to State Department, 7 August 1948: OMGUS POLAD 35/3–21
34 *Ibid.*, 10 August 1948
35 Clay teleconference with Draper, 9 August 1948, The Clay Papers
36 Bevin to Franks, 10 August 1948: FO 371 70506
37 *The Times*, 10 August 1948
38 Robertson to Foreign Office, 10 August 1948: The Bevin Papers, FO 800/467
39 Bevin to Franks, *op. cit.*
40 Bevin to Franks, 11 August 1948: FO 371 70507
41 Quoted in *Manchester Guardian*, 14 August 1948
42 Details from Ambassador in the Soviet Union to Secretary of State, 9 August 1948: FRUS 1948 (II); 9 August résumé, "Moscow Meetings Records": FO 1030/59
43 Ambassador in the Soviet Union to Secretary of State, *ibid.*
44 Bevin to Franks, 11 August, *op. cit.*
45 Ambassador in the Soviet Union to Secretary of State, 12 August 1948: FRUS 1948 (II)
46 Meeting of the Committee of Ministers on Germany, 14 August 1948: CAB 130, 38 GEN 241; Ambassador in the Soviet Union to Secretary of State, 12 August, *op. cit.*; Department of State to Bedell Smith, 13 August 1948: *ibid.*
47 Details from Bedell Smith to Secretary of State, 17 August 1948: FRUS 1948 (II); 16 August résumé: FO 1030/59
48 For example, Bedell Smith to State Department, *ibid.*
49 Bevin to Moscow, 18 August 1948: FO 371 70508
50 Account sent separately from the record of the meeting, 23 August 1948: FO 1030/59
51 *Ibid.*
52 Bedell Smith to Secretary of State, 23 August 1948: FRUS 1948 (II)
53 Mil. Gov. to FO, 24 August 1948: FO 371 70510
54 Teleconference with Byroade, Royall, Draper, etc, 24 August 1948, The Clay Papers
55 Secretary of State to Embassy in the Soviet Union, 24 August 1948: FRUS 1948 (II)
56 *The Forrestal Diaries*
57 Bedell Smith to State Department, 25 August 1948: FRUS 1948 (II)
58 Secretary of State to Embassy in the Soviet Union, 26 August 1948: FRUS 1948 (II)
59 Moscow to Foreign Office, 27 August 1948: FO 371 70510
60 Roberts to Foreign Office: *ibid.*

61 Bedell Smith to Secretary of State, 39 August 1948: FRUS 1948 (II); 30 August record: FO 1030/59
62 FO 1030/57
63 Robertson to Foreign Office, 31 August 1948: FO 371 70512
64 Report on the first two weeks in August: FO 1049/1391
65 Foreign Office to Roberts, 5 August 1948, and cutting from *Le Monde*, 7 August 1948: FO 371 70505
66 Fortnightly Background Notes (FORD) No. 143, 19 August 1948: FO 371 70618
67 Report on Magistrat meeting, 25 August 1948: FO 1012/216
68 US report on meeting with Suhr, 3 August 1948: FO371 70488
69 8 August report: OMGUS POLAD 796/3–2
70 *Ibid.*, and *The Times*, 6 and 13 August 1948
71 *Daily Telegraph* and *The Times*, 7 August 1948; Weekly Summary for period up to 23 August 1948: FO 371 70488
72 FO 371 70488
73 Magistrat Liaison Section Weekly Report, 16 August 1948: FO 1012/216
74 Intelligence report on August, 18 September 1968: OMGUS ODI 3/430–1/9
75 *The Times*, 3 August 1948
76 OMGUS ODI 7/22–3/17
77 *The Times*, 23 August 1948
78 Magistrat Liaison Section Weekly Report, 30 August 1948: FO 1012/216
79 *Daily Telegraph* and *The Times*, 21 August 1948; Mil. Gov. to FO, 21 August 1948: FO 371 70509
80 Military Government Liaison Section Weekly Report No. 4 for the period up to 3 August: FO 371 70487; OMGUS ODI 7/22–3/17
81 Military Government Liaison Section Weekly Report, *op. cit.*
82 US Magistrat Liaison Section Report, 6 August 1948: FO 1012/216
83 British liaison officer's interview with Füllsack, 16 August 1948: FO 1012/213
84 FO 1012/216
85 Sorokin, Chief Economy Dept. SMA to Klingelhöfer. 17 August, FO 1012/213; Weekly Summary, *op. cit.*
86 Magistrat Liaison Section Weekly Report, 21 August 1948: FO 1012/216
87 US liaison officer's interview with Mückenberger, 24 March 1949: FO 1012/218
88 Mil. Gov. to FO, 25 August 1948: FO 371 70509
89 *Ibid.*, 26 August 1948
90 British liaison officer's interview with Friedensburg, 26 August 1948: FO 1012/216

91 Mil. Gov. to FO, 26 August 1948: FO 371 70510
92 Details from *The Times*, 27 August 1948; Friedensburg interview with British liaison officer, *op. cit.*; Military Liaison Section Weekly Report No. 43 for the period up to 31 August 1948: FO 371 70488; Magistrat liaison officer's report, 26 August 1948: FO 1012/216
93 Details from *The Times* and *Daily Telegraph*, 28 August 1948; Magistrat liaison officer's report and interview with Friedensburg, 27 August, FO 1012/216; 27 August Mil. Gov. to FO, 27 August: FO 371 70510
94 Mil. Gov. to FO, 27 August, *ibid.*
95 *Ibid.*, 28 August 1948
96 Moscow to Foreign Office, 30 August 1948: *ibid.*
97 For example, *The Times*, 30 and 31 August 1948
98 Many verbatim reports are in FO 371 70514; summaries in FRUS 1948 (II) and FO 371 70512/3
99 Clay to Draper, 6 September 1948, The Clay Papers
100 Mil. Gov. to FO, 4 September 1948: FO 371 70512
101 Letter from Robertson to Strang, 3 September 1948: FO 371 70513
102 Clay to Draper, 1 September 1948, The Clay Papers
103 Murphy to Bedell Smith, 5 September 1948: FRUS 1948 (II)
104 Clay to Draper, 4 September 1948: The Clay Papers
105 State Department to Embassy in the UK, 4 September 1948: FO 371 70512
106 Mil. Gov. to FO, 5 September 1948 and Strang minute, 6 September 1948: FO 371 70512
107 Berlin to Foreign Office, 9 September 1948: FO 371 70513
108 Ambassador in the UK to Secretary of State, 5 September 1948; Secretary of State to the Embassy in the UK, 5 September 1948: FRUS 1948 (II)
109 Military Government Liaison Section Weekly Report No. 44 for the period up to 7 September 1948: FO 371 70488
110 Details from Mil. Gov. to FO, 6 September 1948: FO 371 70512; Military Government Liaison Section Weekly Report No. 44, *ibid.*; *The Times*, 7 September 1948: Government Structures Branch report to Secretariat, 6 September 1948: FO 1049/1355
111 Whitefoord to DDMS, 7 September 1948: FO 1012/216
112 French Military Government of Greater Berlin Liaison to the Magistrat, 14 September 1948: FO 1012/217
113 *Ibid.*, and Mil. Gov. to FO, 8 September 1948: FO 371 70512
114 Statements of Gerhard Lickert and Ernst Welk, dispatch No. 391 from Berlin, 28 March 1949: OMGUS POLAD 454/6
115 Clay to Draper, 6 September 1948, The Clay Papers
116 *Daily Telegraph* 8 September 1948; Clay to Draper, 8 September 1948, *ibid.*
117 Fortnightly Background Notes (FORD) No. 146, 30 September 1948: FO 371 70619

118 Whitefoord interview with May, 15 September 1948: FO 1012/217; report on meeting of the three western liaison section officers with Suhr, 20 September 1948 and report on British liaison officer's meeting with Friedensburg, 30 September 1948: *ibid.*
119 *Ibid.*
120 *Ibid.*
121 Details for this and the following paragraph from *The Times* and *Daily Telegraph*; Military Government Liaison Section Weekly Report No. 47 for the period up to 29 September 1948: FO 371 70488; Mil. Gov. to FO, 10 September 1948: FO 371 70513; memo from Thomas J. Dunnigan, Political Branch, to Chief of Public Safety Branch, 10 September 1948: OMGUS POLAD 461/52; intelligence report, 18 September 1948: OMGUS ODI 3/430–1/9
122 Moscow to Foreign Office, 11 September 1948: FO 371 70514; Bevin to Franks, 12 September 1948: *ibid.*
123 Secretary of State to Embassy in the Soviet Union, 8 September 1948: FRUS 1948 (II)
124 Ambassador in the Soviet Union to the Secretary of State, 9 September 1948: FRUS 1948 (II)
125 *The Forrestal Diaries*
126 Bevin to Washington, 10 September 1948: FO 371 70513
127 *Ibid.*, 12 September 1948
128 Secretary of State to US Political Adviser for Germany, 11 September 1948: FRUS 1948 (II)
129 Report, 14 September 1948: FO 1030/59; Moscow to Foreign Office, 14 September 1948: FO 371 70515; Ambassador in the Soviet Union to Secretary of State, 14 September 1948: FRUS 1948 (II)
130 Report, 18 September 1948: FO 1030/59; Embassy in the Soviet Union to Secretary of State, 18 September 1948: FRUS 1948 (II)
131 Clay teleconference with Royall and Draper, 19 September 1948, The Clay Papers

10: Miracles Take Time

1 Herbert to Robertson, 27 September 1948: FO 1030/63
2 *The Times*, 23 September 1948
3 Military Liaison Section Weekly Report No. 46 for the period up to 21 September 1948: FO 371 70488
4 Mil. Gov. to FO German Section, 24 September 1948: AIR 38/304
5 Clay to Bradley and LeMay, 10 September 1948, The Clay Papers
6 *The Times*, 23 September 1948
7 Met. officer and Wing-Commander Flying Gatow, 13 September 1948: FO 1012/562; Washington to Foreign Office, 25 September 1948: FO 371 70517

8 Brigadier W. Strelley Martin, Public Health Adviser BAOR, 1 September 1948: OMGUS FA 101/6
9 Letter from Mr J. Pacey
10 Whitfield, *op. cit.*
11 Crisp Jones manuscript
12 Interview with Eric Best
13 Blockade, Airlift and Airlift Gratitude Foundation booklet by Andreas Anderhub and Jack O. Bennett
14 Clay to Bradley and LeMay, 10 September 1948, The Clay Papers
15 Clay to Bradley, 23 September 1948, *ibid.*
16 Record of conversation between Bevin and Marshall, 29 September 1948: The Bevin Papers, FO 800/467
17 L. G. Razzell to GOC, 16 September 1948: FO 1012/190
18 Food Report 6–12 October 1948, Central Food Office, Magistrat: FO 1012/380
19 J. H. Jordan, Principal Health Officer, Public Health Branch to DDMG, 2 September 1948: FO 1012/190
20 Lewis Ansara, Special Feeding Programs Chief, 28 September 1948: FO 1012/380
21 Strelley Martin, *op. cit.*; Razzell, *op. cit.*
22 GOC to BICO, Frankfurt, August draft: FO 1012/190
23 Details from FRANCOMB to Foreign Office, 10 September 1948; FO to Mil. Gov., 4 September 1948; Foreign Office to BERCOMB, 27 September 1948; EUCOM Heidelberg to BICO Frankfurt, 21 September 1948; US/UK Commandants to OMGUS, BICO etc., 7 September 1948; Foreign Office to BERCOMB, 3 September 1948; FRANCOMB to Foreign Office, 10 September 1948: all in FO 1012/190
24 Ansara, *op. cit.*; Razzell, *op. cit.*
25 BICO to Berlin, 1 September 1948; Food and Agriculture memo, 14 September 1948: OMGUS FA 101/5
26 Memo from Berlin Supplies, 24 November 1948: *ibid.*
27 Weekly Report, Food, Agriculture and Forestry Group, BICO, 15 October 1948: OMGUS FA 7/3
28 BICO to BERCOMB, 8 November 1968, and OMGUS, 11 November 1948: FO 1012/190
29 Weekly Report Food, Agriculture and Forestry Group, BICO, 26 November 1948: OMGUS FA 7/3
30 J. C. Lynn to Berlin Food Team, 26 August 1948: OMGUS FA 12/3; Strelley Martin, *op. cit.*; Berlin Public Health Bureau, 5 November 1948: FO 1012/190
31 Various reports and minutes of Berlin Food Committee: FO 1012/190; Brigadier Firth to Gatow, 9 October 1948: FO 1012/192
32 Details from file FO 1012/192 and Razzell to GOC, 1 November 1948: FO 1012/190

33 *The Times*, 1 August 1948
34 FO 1012/192
35 Food Report, 30 September 1948: FO 1012/380; Lynn to Frau Hahn, 27 August 1948: OMGUS FA 12/3; Razzell to GOC, 16 September 1948: FO 1012/190
36 Memo from Major-General George P. Hays to General Cannon, 20 October 1948: AIR 38/304; C.W. Glannister, Principal Control Officer Public Utilities Branch, to GOC, 10 September 1948: FO 1012/318
37 W. Jarman to Hannover, 30 July 1948: FO 1077/1
38 Reports on first two months of coal lift, Jarman to G.F. Anderson, Coal Control Group, *ibid.*
39 Jarman to Littlefair, HQ Essen, 9 and 17 August 1948: E.V. Burrow to Kinnear, 27 August 1948: *ibid.*
40 Jarman to DAQMG, AATO Bückeburg. 29 July 1948: *ibid.*
41 Innumerable reports July to December, *ibid.*
42 Report from Herbert to Mil. Gov., September 1948; unsigned report: FO 1030/63
43 Report by Robert Berry on conversation with Klingelhöfer, 14 October 1948: OMGUS POLAD 776/5
44 FRUS 1948 (II)
45 Truman, *op. cit.*
46 *Stars and Stripes*, 23 October 1948
47 Report 146, November, BAFO: AIR 55/98
48 *The Times*, 14 August 1948
49 Tunner, *op. cit.*
50 *Ibid.*
51 Interview with Jack Short
52 Details from *A Report on "Operation Plainfare"*; Whitfield, *op. cit.*; P.R. Wood, *RAF Quarterly*, autumn 1978
53 Details from Tempelhof Papers: *A Report on "Operation Plainfare"*; *Stars and Stripes*
54 *New York Times* and *New York Herald Tribune*, 11 September 1948; *Daily Telegraph*, 25 September 1948
55 *New York Herald Tribune*, 4 October 1948; *The Times*, 7 and 16 October 1948; *Daily Telegraph*, 8 October, 1948
56 Lt. Gen. Dratvin to Maj. Gen. N.C.D. Brownjohn, and J.L. Avon to Chief of Staff. 2 and 6 October 1948: FO 1012/587; General Lukyanchenko, 10 November 1948: AIR 2/10063
57 *Daily Mail*, 5 October 1968
58 Interview with Jack Short
59 *A Report on "Operation Plainfare"* and account by Eric Best
60 Tunner; *op. cit.*; *A Report on "Operation Plainfare"*; interview with Air-Commodore Hyde; General Ross Milton in *Airforce Magazine*, June 1978

61 American Consul General Hamburg to Secretary of State, 3 August 1948: OMGUS POLAD 804/56; ACAS OPs to DO Ops, 4 December 1948: AIR 2/10063; letter to authors from Colonel le C. Berg; interview with Squadron-Leader Leslie Schulkins

62 Rodrigo, *op. cit.*; paper by Lieutenant-General T. H. Downes lent by Brigadier Crowdy; Milton in *Air Force Magazine*, *op. cit.*

63 *History of Lübeck*: AIR 55/117; P. L. MacGregor and K. N. Hansen, "The Berlin Airlift", *South African Air Force Journal*, July 1949

64 Minute, 10 August 1948: FO 371 70509; various minutes in FO 70521; HQ BAFO to BERCOMB, 4 January: FO 1030/63

65 *History of Schleswigland*, AIR 55/115; *A Report on "Operation Plainfare"*; interviews with Group-Captain Peter Finlayson and Air-Marshal Sir Brian Stanbridge

66 Crisp Jones manuscript; *A Report on "Operation Plainfare"*; *History of Celle*: AIR 55/108

67 *A Report on "Operation Plainfare"*; *Berlin Airlift*; *History of Gatow*

68 Correspondence, 21 September to 15 October 1948: FO 1012/318

69 *A Report on "Operation Plainfare"*; *Stars and Stripes*, 24 October 1948: *The Times*, 6 and 18 November 1948; interviews with Richard Martin and Alan Dawes

70 Herbert to DDMG Food and Agriculture, 20 November 1948: FO 1012/183

71 Razzell to GOC, 26 October 1948: FO 1012/380

72 OMGUS FA 101/5

73 OMGUS FA 101/2

74 FO 1030/380; OMGUS FA 101/2

75 Air-Commodore Waite HQ Airlift to Deputy Commandant, 22 September 1948; McEwan to DDMG 28 September 1948: FO 1012/186

76 Food Committee, 5 October 1948: FO 1012/460

77 G. Garnett, BICO on November shipments: FO 1012/380; 24 August 1948: OMGUS FA 12/3

78 Record of meeting in Wiesbaden, 28 October 1948: FO 1012/190

79 Details for this and the next three paragraphs from *A Report on "Operation Plainfare"*; *History of the US Air Force*; Crisp Jones manuscript; interview with Brigadier Rupert Crowdy and papers he generously lent; interviews with Sir Brian Stanbridge and Eric Best

80 *A Report on "Operation Plainfare"*; *Berlin Airlift*; interview with Brigadier Crowdy, various papers borrowed from him

81 *History of Gatow*

82 Waite to Herbert, 16 August 1948: FO 1012/313

83 J. D. Urquart to McEwan, 25 October 1948: *ibid.*

84 Klingelhöfer to Herbert, 29 November 1948: FO 1012/193

85 Riddelberger to Secretary of State, 21 October 1948: OMGUS POLAD 802/46
86 Siemens to BMG, 19 October 1948: FO 1012/318
87 J. E. I. Gaymer, Senior Industry Officer to Siemens, 23 October 1948: *ibid.*
88 Urquart to Waite, HQ BAFO, 16 August 1948: FO 1012/313
89 Urquart to McEwan, 15 September 1948: *ibid.*
90 Gaymer to McEwan, *ibid.*
91 Waite to REO and Mil. Gov. Secretariat, 1 November 1948: *ibid.*
92 Gaymer to Industrial Section, 29 December 1948: *ibid.*
93 Memo, 27 November 1948: FO 1012/225
94 Interview with Mr Blomer
95 Brownjohn letter to Bevin, 28 August 1948: FO 371 70512; paper, 30 September 1948: FO1012/565; Robertson memo, 23 September 1948: FO 371 70517
96 *Stars and Stripes*, 21 October 1948
97 Robertson to Air-Marshal Williams, AOC-in-C BAFO, November 1948: AIR 38/304
98 GOC winter forecasts, 13 September 1948: FO 1012/562
99 Tunner, *op. cit.*
100 Report 146, RB BAFO: AIR 55/98

11: Berlin Splits

1 *Stars and Stripes*, 8 November 1948
2 Interview with Bob Kimener
3 Interview by Paul Fisher with Halvorsen, *The Bee Hive*, fall 1948; various stories *Stars and Stripes*, October 1948
4 Various stories in *Stars and Stripes*, October 1948
5 *Ibid.*
6 Interviews with Adrian Liddell Hart and Dudley Heesom
7 Details from "The Economic Situation in the Western Sectors of Berlin", report sent by Robert M. Berry to Murphy: OMGUS POLAD 796/6; and interviews with Ruth Anding, Helga Galler and Gretel Spitzer
8 Report forwarded on 9 November by Colonel J. P. C. MacKinley, DDMG, to Admin. Commandant, HQ, CCG(BE): FO 1012/193
9 Interview with Hans Christoph Knebusch
10 Interviews with Curt Flatow and others
11 Air Ministry Intelligence Summary, vol. 4, No. 8, June 1949: AIR 22/87
12 *The Times*, 24, 25, 27, 29 September 1948; Berlin to Foreign Office, 25 September and 4 October 1948: FO 371 70516
13 Military Government Liaison Section Weekly Reports, No. 44 for the period up to 7 September, No. 47 up to 29 September, No. 50 up to

20 October, No. 53 up to 9 November 1948: all in FO 371 70488; Berlin Situation Report No. 16, 11 October 1948: OMGUS ODI 7/29–2/8

14 Intelligence Reports, 4 and 25 September 1948: OMGUS ODI 3/430–1/9

15 Memo by Dr Füllsack, 26 October 1948: FO 1012/380

16 Intelligence Report, 30 October 1948: OMGUS ODI 3/430–1/10; *The Times*, 20 October 1948

17 Details in this and the next three paragraphs from Weekly Intelligence Report, 1 May 1948: OMGUS ODI 3/430–1/5; Weekly Political Summary up to 4 May 1968: FO 371 70484; Military Government Liaison Weekly Report No. 29 up to 25 May 1968; and interviews with Professor Helmut Coper and Adrian Liddell Hart

18 Minute on 4 August letter from British Element CCG: FO 371 70506

19 Birley to Chief Political Division, 30 July 1948: all papers on subject in FO 1050/1241

20 See, for example, Birley to Mil. Gov., 6 August 1948, *ibid.*

21 Grace to Clay, 11 September, *ibid.*

22 4 August minute, *op. cit.*

23 Undated draft, *ibid.*

24 Birley to Steel, 12 August 1948, *ibid.*

25 Undated draft, *op. cit.*, *ibid.*

26 Birley to Chief of Political Divisions, *op. cit.*; Birley memo, *op. cit.*, *ibid.*

27 Draft letter Robertson to Foreign Office, *ibid.*

28 Undated progress report by S. P. Whiteley, *ibid.*

29 Memo GOC 15 November 1948, *ibid.*

30 *The Times*, 2 October 1948

31 Friedensburg interview with Magistrat liaison officer, 30 September 1948: FO 1012/217

32 Suhr interview with Magistrat liaison officer, *ibid.*

33 Fortnightly Background Notes (FORD) No. 149, 14 October 1948: FO 371 70619; *The Times*, 25 and 28 October 1948

34 Report on governmental and political affairs for November: FO 371 70526

35 Suhr interview with Magistrat liaison officer, 5 October 1948: FO 1012/217

36 Order of 15 November 1948: *ibid.*

37 Kressman interview with Whitefoord, 10 November 1948: *ibid.*

38 *The Times*, 22 November 1948

39 US Political Adviser for Germany to Secretary of State, 27 August 1948: FRUS 1948 (II); Clay to Draper, 28 August 1948, The Clay Papers

40 Military Liaison Section Weekly Report No. 46 for the period ending 21 September 1948: FO 371 70488

41 US Political Adviser for Germany to Secretary of State, 16 September 1948: FRUS 1948 (II)
42 Note by US Political Adviser on Frankfurt meeting, 4 November 1948: FRUS 1948 (II); Clay to Department of Army, 5 November 1948, The Clay Papers
43 Weekly Intelligence Report, 11 December 1948: OMGUS ODI 3/430–1/2; Report on German Morale in second half of November: FO 1049/1391
44 Letter from Rud. Hummel to Clay and Robertson: FO 1049/1579
45 Brigadier A. C. Todd, Chief POW and DP Division, to Commander, Hallendorf Camp, 20 September 1948: FO1012/190
46 *Daily Telegraph*, 6 July 1948
47 Answer by Under-Secretary for Foreign Affairs to Parliamentary Question, quoted in *Flight*, 11 November 1948
48 Report from Analysis and Cost Control Section, Office of the Comptroller HQ USAFE, to Political Adviser's Office, 29 October 1948: OMGUS POLAD 819/54
49 See, for example, BICO to BERCOMBE, 20 September 1948: FO 1049/1579
50 Herbert to Chief of Staff CCG(BE), 15 September 1948: *ibid.*
51 Lovett to Bohlen, Paris, 2 October 1948: OMGUS POLAD 3/35–28
52 Report of meeting in Henderson's office, 6 November 1948: FO 371 7052
53 Letter from Cadogan to Strang, 16 August 1948: FO 371 70509
54 Bohlen memo on conversation with Henri Bonnet, 21 August 1948: FRUS 1948 (II)
55 Memo by deputy US representative on Security Council (Philip Jessup) on conversation between Douglas, Rusk and Marshall in Paris, 27 September 1948: FRUS 1948 (II)
56 Record of 4 October meeting between Bevin, Marshall, Schuman and others at Quai d'Orsay: FO 371 70519
57 Record of meeting, 2 October 1948: The Bevin Papers, FO 800 467
58 Record of 4 October meeting, *op. cit.*
59 Record of 4 October meeting between Marshall and Bevin at US Embassy, Paris. The Bevin Papers, *op. cit.*
60 Record of conversation between Harvey and Chauvel, 1 October 1948: FO 371 70517
61 Details from various cables in FRUS 1948 (II) and FO 371 70518, 70519, 70520
62 Memo by the Counsellor to the Department of State to the Secretary of State, 8 October 1948: FRUS 1948 (II)
63 Undated telegram from Cadogan (Paris) to Foreign Office: FO 371 70520; Jessup to Acting Secretary of State, 3 November 1948: FRUS 1948 (II)

64 See, for example, Cabinet meeting, 15 November 1948: CAB 128, vol. 13
65 Details from Political Adviser for Germany to Secretary of State: OMGUS POLAD 802/46
66 Kotikov to Friedensburg, 20 October 1948; Magistrat declaration, 25 October 1948: both in FO 1012/217
67 Cabinet meeting, 11 November 1948: CAB 128, vol. 13; and Bevin memo discussed at it: FO 371 70521
68 Secretary of State to Murphy, 24 November 1948: FRUS 1948 (II)
69 US Political Adviser for Germany to Secretary of State, 26 November 1948: *ibid.*
70 See, for example, Department of State to Jessup and Bohlen, Paris, 28 November 1948: *ibid.*
71 UK delegation, UN to Foreign Office, 30 November 1948: FO 371 70525
72 Details from Military Government Liaison Section Reports, No. 55 up to 23 November, No. 56 up to 2 December and No. 57 up to 9 December 1948: FO 371 70488; Fortnightly Background Notes (FORD) No. 150, 25 November 1948: FO 371 70619; and various reports in *The Times*
73 Military Liaison Section Weekly Report No. 55, *ibid.*; Fortnightly Background Notes No. 150, *ibid.*
74 Military Liaison Section Weekly Report No. 52 up to 3 November 1948: FO 371 70488
75 Report Political Branch Berlin to Chancery, UK High Commission November 1949: FO 1049/1939
76 Military Liaison Section Weekly Report No. 51 up to 27 October 1948: FO 371 70488
77 Fortnightly Background Notes (FORD) No. 150, *op. cit.*
78 Weekly Summary up to 4 December 1948: FO 371 70488; various reports in *The Times*
79 Details from Report on Governmental and Political Affairs for November 1948: FO 371 70526; Military Liaison Section Weekly Report No. 56 up to 2 December 1948: FO 371 70488; Weekly Summary up to 4 December, *ibid.*; Weekly Intelligence Report, 25 December 1948: OMGUS ODI 3/430–1/12
80 Weekly Intelligence Report, *ibid.*
81 American report "Events on 1 December at the City Hall," 1 December 1948: FO 1012/217
82 Weekly Intelligence Report, 25 December, *op. cit.*; Fortnightly Background Notes (FORD) No. 151, 9 December 1948: FO 371 70619; Allied Election Committee Report: FO 371 76537
83 US Political Adviser for Germany to Secretary of State, 21 December 1948: FRUS 1948 (II)

12: Cracks of Light

1 Fortnightly Background Notes (FORD) No. 153, 6 January 1949: FO 371 76690
2 *Neues Deutschland,* 30 December 1948, quoted in Military Government Liaison Section Weekly Report No. 59 for the period up to 5 January 1949: FO 371 76703
3 Military Government Liaison Section Weekly Report No. 63 for the period up to 3 February and No. 65 for the period up to 16 February 1949: FO 371 76703
4 Military Government Liaison Section Weekly Report No. 59, *op. cit.;* Fortnightly Background Notes No. 153, *op cit.*
5 Military Government Liaison Section Weekly Reports No. 60 for the period up to 12 January and No. 61 for the period up to 19 January 1949: FO 371 76703
6 Military Government Liaison Section Weekly Report No. 62 for the period up to 26 January 1949: *ibid.*
7 Weekly Intelligence Report, 29 January 1949: OMGUS ODI 3/430–1/13
8 Military Government Section Weekly Report No. 66 for the period up to 23 February 1949: FO 371 76703
9 *The Times,* 28 April 1949
10 Berlin to Foreign Office, 4 February 1949: FO 371 76544; Military Government Liaison Section Weekly Report No. 59 for the period up to 5 January and No. 64 for the period up to 12 February 1949: FO 371 76703
11 Military Government Liaison Section Weekly Report No. 62: *ibid.*
12 See, for example, Berlin to Foreign Office, 6 January 1949: FO 371 76538
13 McNeil (Paris) to Foreign Office, 4 December 1948; Bevin to Mil. Gov., 10 December 1948: both FO 371 70526
14 Marshall to Douglas, 30 December 1948: OMGUS POLAD 35/3–30
15 Macdonald (Bank) to Serpell (Treasury), 29 December 1948: FO 371 76537
16 Playfair (Treasury) at meeting in Strang's room, 30 December 1948: *ibid.*
17 See, for example, Franks (Washington) to Foreign Office, 31 December 1948: *ibid.*
18 Meeting in Bevin's room, 29 December 1948: *ibid.*. Foreign Office to Franks (Washington), 3 January 1949: *ibid.;* Bevin talk to US Chargé, 10 January 1949: FO 371 76539; Bevin to Attlee, 4 January 1949: FO 371 76538
19 29 December meeting in Bevin's room, *op. cit.*
20 Bevin to Berlin, 24 January 1949: FO 371 76541
21 Foreign Office to Berlin, 18 January 1949: The Bevin Papers, *op. cit.*
22 Bevin to Attlee, 4 January, *op. cit.*

23 Full details in FRUS 1949 (II) and FO 371 76539–42
24 Knapp (Geneva), 5 February 1949: FRUS 1949 (II)
25 Gordon summary of Geneva meetings: FO 371 76544
26 Report on ninth meeting of Berlin Committee, 7 February 1949: FO 371 76543
27 See, for example, Political Adviser for Germany to Secretary of State, 17 February and 2 March 1949: Ambassador in France to Secretary of State, 19 February 1949: FRUS 1949 (II)
28 Ambassador in France to Secretary of State, 6 February 1949: FRUS 1949 (II)
29 *A Report on "Operation Plainfare"*
30 Hays (OMGUS) to Bradley and Wedemeyer, 3 January 1949: OMGUS FA 72/3
31 Berlin to Foreign Office, 13 December 1948: AIR 2/10063; GSO I (Plans) to GOC, 21 December 1948: FO 1012/563
32 Herbert to GSO I (Plans), 8 December 1948; GSO I (Plans) to Herbert, 14 December 1948: *ibid.*
33 Details from Mil Gov to FO, 16 December 1948: FO 371 70526; Mil. Gov. to FO; 21 December 1948; FO 371 70528: Military Government Liaison Section Weekly Report No. 58 for the period up to 22 December 1948: FO 371 70488; Fortnightly Background Notes (FORD) No. 153, *op. cit.; The Times* 17, 18, 20 December 1948
34 Met. Officer, Gatow, Notes on Berlin Weather: AIR 55/100; Science 2, Memo 145, October 1948: AIR 55/101
35 Report from Research Branch, BAFO, 11 May 1949: AIR 55/96
36 Memo P4 "Notes on Progress": AIR 55/100
37 Mil. Gov. weekly reports on airlift to Foreign Secretary: FO 371 76651
38 Reports by Dr A. Charlesby, Research Branch BAFO: AIR 55/96
39 Interview with Eric Best; weekly report from Food, Agriculture and Forestry group, BICO, 4 February 1949: OMGUS FA 7/3; *Daily Telegraph*, 11 February 1949
40 Details from Tempelhof Papers; *A Report on "Operation Plainfare"*; review of Berlin press, 26 January 1949: FO 371 76632
41 See, for example, AOC-in-C to ACAS Ops, 31 January 1949: AIR 2/10063; Bevin to Washington and reply, 4 February 1949: FO 371 76543
42 Weekly reports from Food, Agriculture and Forestry Group, BICO, 4 and 17 February 1949: OMGUS FA 7/3
43 Weekly report, 21 January 1949: *ibid.*
44 Weekly report, 25 February 1949: *ibid*
45 Weekly Intelligence Report, 19 February 1949: OMGUS ODI 3/430–2/1
46 Details mainly from *A Report on "Operation Plainfare"*
47 Historical Airlift Report of Tempelhof Air Base, June 1948–June 1949

48 Draft for 46 Group by Dr. Charlesby: AIR 55/98; Science 2, memo P3, 24 November 1949: AIR 55/102

49 Letter from C-in-C BAFO entered in 5 January Air Ministry minute: AIR 2/10063

50 Details from *A Report on "Operation Plainfare"*; Tunner, *op. cit.*; draft by RB BAFO for *Airclues*, July 1949: AIR 5/98

51 Tunner, *op. cit.*

52 Details from *A Report on "Operation Plainfare"*; interim Science 3 report and *Airlines* article: AIR 55/98

53 Comparison of aircraft utilisation by Dr. Charlesby, CRO BAFO: AIR 55/97

54 *A Report on "Operation Plainfare"*

55 Letter from C-in-C BAFO, *op. cit.*

56 Tunner, *op. cit.*

57 *A Report on "Operation Plainfare"*

58 *Naval Aviation News*, No. 291, March 1949

59 Letter to the authors from Mr J. Pacey

60 "Avro on the Airlift," November 1948

61 BERCOMB, Berlin, 1 October 1948: AIR 38/302

62 "Appreciation of the Civil Air Contribution," 31 January 1949: FO 1030/63

63 Whitfield, *op. cit.*

64 Report by AOC 46 Group to Air Ministry meeting, 18 January 1949: AIR 2/10063

65 Report on Schleswigland by CO, July 1949: AIR 55/115

66 Memo from HQ BAFO to Robertson, 1 October 1948: AIR 38/304

67 Meeting of interdepartmental working party, 14 February 1949: AIR 2/10573

68 BERCOMB to London, 13 October 1948: AIR 38/302

69 BERCOMB to Foreign Office, 20 October 1948: *ibid.*

70 HQ Airlift Berlin to AATO Bückeburg, 13 December 1948; HQ BAFO to HQ Airlift, 14 December 1948: AIR 38/302

71 Merer HQ BAFO to BERCOMB and Air Ministry, 4 January 1949: *ibid.*

72 Note on civil contribution by Group-Captain Rainsford, DDASTO to DCAS, 11 February 1949: AIR 2/10573

73 Paper by Mr Whitfield for Foreign Office, 12 October 1948: Whitfield, *op. cit.*

74 Details from Whitfield, *ibid.;* Stroud manuscript; *A Report on "Operation Plainfare"*

75 Various records of meetings and memos in FO 371 76547; minutes, 14 February 1949: AIR 2/10573

76 Report by Commanding General USAF in Europe, John K. Cannon, and Air Officer Commanding-in-Chief BAFO, T. M. Williams, 14 February 1949: FO 371 76549

77 See, for example, assessment by Robertson at the end of January 1949: FO 371 76542
78 Statement, 1 February 1949: FO 1012/337
79 Record of discussion between Reuter, Kirkpatrick, Robertson and Dean, 7 February 1949; undated minute by P. Ramsbotham: FO 371 76544
80 Record of conversation between Bevin and Schuman at Foreign Office, 13 January 1949: FO 371 76540
81 Details from *The Times,* 28 November 1948; Special Reports Branch article, 21 January 1949: FO 371 76605; Monthly Report Nos 1 and 2 on developments in the Soviet zone: FO 371 76606 and 76607
82 Soviet zone Morale Report, April/May 1949: FO 1049/1903
83 Murphy to Saltzmann, 20 January 1949: OMGUS POLAD 435/69; Monthly Report No. 2 *op. cit.,* and Soviet zone Morale Report, *ibid.*; Holt memo to Washington, 22 January 1949: OMGUS POLAD 453/69
84 "Additions to the B List," 9 February 1949: FO 1012/235
85 Holt to State Department, 5 January 1949: OMGUS POLAD 453/69
86 Political Adviser to State Department, 12 January 1949: *ibid.*
87 Special Reports Branch article, "Interzonal Trade," 4 January 1949: FO 371 76605
88 *Ibid.*
89 Memo from Robert M. Berry to Murphy and Riddleberger, 8 November 1948: OMGUS POLAD 796/6
90 Reports in FO 1012/334; memo 15 March 1949: OMGUS ODI 17/20–1/5
91 Murphy to Saltzmann, 20 January, *op. cit.,* Special Reports Branch, *op. cit.*
92 Fortnightly Background Notes (FORD) No. 142, 5 August 1948: FO 371 70618
93 Holt memo, 11 January 1949: OMGUS POLAD 453/69
94 *Ibid.,* 22 January 1949
95 See, for example, Holt memo, 11 February: *ibid.*; Calhoun to Riddleberger, 24 January 1949: *ibid.*
96 Harris to Gerber, 17 March 1949: OMGUS ODI 7/2–1/5; Holt memos, 11 January and 22 April 1949: OMGUS POLAD 435/69
97 Details from various reports, *op. cit.*; Special Reports Branch article, 15 March 1949: OMGUS ODI 7/20–1/5

13: Prodigies of Agreement

1 Memo for Committee on Germany, 4 February 1949: CAB 130 38 241/4
2 Bohlen, *op. cit.*

3 Acheson, *Present at the Creation*, and Truman, *op. cit.*
4 Acheson, *ibid.*
5 Bohlen, *op. cit.*; Jessup article in *Political Science Quarterly*, vol. LXXXVII, No. 3, September 1972
6 Jessup, *ibid*; Memo by Jessup, 15 February 1949: FRUS 1949 (II)
7 Bohlen, *op. cit.*
8 Jessup, *op. cit.*
9 Memo by Jessup, 15 March 1949: FRUS 1949 (II)
10 Memo by Jessup, 21 March 1949: *ibid.*
11 Record of meeting in Department of State, 17 March 1949: *ibid.*
12 Bullock, *op. cit.*
13 See copy of New York to Foreign Office, 21 March 1949: FO 371 76549
14 Fortnightly Background Notes (FORD) No. 161, 28 April 1949: FO 371 76691; *The Times*, 28 March 1949
15 Fortnightly Background Notes (FORD) No. 154, 20 January 1949: FO 371 76990; No. 160, 13 April 1949: FO 371 76691
16 Details from Military Government Liaison Section Weekly Report No. 70 for the period up to 24 March 1949: FO 371 76703; Fortnightly Background Notes (FORD) No. 159, 31 March 1949: FO 371 76555
17 *A Report on "Operation Plainfare"; History of Gatow;* Magistrat control report: FO 1012/218
18 Gwyn Garnett, Assistant Chief (US) BICO, 7 April 1949: FO 1012/380
19 Whitfield, *op. cit.*
20 Interdepartmental working party meeting, 26 April 1949: AIR 2/10573
21 HQ CALTF paper, 21 April 1949: AIR 2/10064; McEwan to HQ Airlift: FO 1012/298
22 DCAS, Walmesley, 12 March 1949: AIR 2/10064
23 For example, HQ BAFO to TC, 4 May 1949: *ibid.*
24 End of April joint appreciation by working party, signed Walmesley: AIR 2/10573
25 Research Branch BAFO report on questionnaire, 3 April 1949; September analysis by Dr Charlesby: AIR 55/102
26 HQ CALTF paper, 21 April: *op. cit.*
27 *The Times*, 5 May 1949
28 Political Adviser to Secretary of State, 26 January 1949: FRUS 1949 (II)
29 *Ibid.*, 4 February 1949
30 Clay to Voorhees, 7 February 1949, The Clay Papers
31 Secretary of State to Political Adviser, 7 February 1949: FRUS 1949 (II)
32 Acting Political Adviser to Secretary of State, *ibid.*
33 Clay to Department of the Army, 3 February 1949, The Clay Papers

34 Clay, *Decision in Germany*
35 Clay to Voorhees, 17 March 1949, The Clay Papers
36 Details from Bohlen, *op. cit.;* Bullock, *op. cit.*; Acheson, *Sketches from Life*
37 Bevin to Strang, 1 April 1949: FO 371 76577; 31 March 1949: FRUS 1949 (II)
38 Acheson, *Present at the Creation*
39 Kirkpatrick to Bevin, 4 April 1949: FO 371 76578
40 For details see FRUS 1949 (II) and FO 371 76581/3/5
41 For example, transcript of 5 April meeting: FO 371 76581
42 Text in FO 371 76579
43 Record of meeting, 7 April 1949: FO 371 76583
44 Dirk V. Stikkers, *Men of Responsibility*; Acheson, *op. cit.*
45 Reports on 1 April 1949 meeting: FRUS 1949 (II) and FO 371 76577
46 Memo by US Ambassador at Large, 5 April 1949: FRUS 1949 (II) and FO 371 76595
47 Memo by US Ambassador at Large, 11 April 1949: *ibid*
48 Memo by Jessup, 13 April 1949: FRUS 1949 (II); New York to Foreign Office, 13 April 1949: FO 371 76580
49 FRUS II 1949
50 Washington to Foreign Office, 12 April 1949: FO 371 76580
51 Riddleberger to Acheson, 14 April 1949, The Clay Papers
52 Robertson to Foreign Office, 14 April 1949: FO 371 76581
53 Teleconference with Voorhees and Murphy, 20 April 1949, The Clay Papers
54 Marjoribanks minute, 22 April 1949: FO 371 76581
55 Paris to Foreign Office, 20 April 1949: FO 371 76582
56 Aide-mémoire, 20 April 1949: FRUS 1949 (II)
57 Teleconference with Murphy and Voorhees, 21 April 1949, The Clay Papers
58 Paris to Foreign Office, 21 April 1949: FO 371 76582
59 Teleconference with Bradley and Voorhees, 22 April 1949, The Clay Papers
60 FRUS 1949 (II) and Washington to Foreign Office, 22 April 1949: FO 371 76582
61 Clay, *Decision in Germany*
62 *The Times*, 18 April 1949
63 Clay, *Decision in Germany*
64 *The Times*, 20 and 21 April 1949
65 Strang minute, 22 April 1949: FO 371 76550
66 US Ambassador in the UK to Secretary of State: 25 April 1949 FRUS 1949 (II)
67 Memo by US Ambassador at Large, 27 April 1949: FRUS 1949 (II) and FO 371 76595
68 Robertson to Foreign Office, 29 April 1949: FO 371 76587

69 New York to Foreign Office, 29 April 1949: FO 371 76586
70 Memo by US Ambassador at Large, 29 April 1949: FRUS 1949 (II) and FO 371 76595
71 New York to Foreign Office, 30 April 1949: FO 371 76587
72 Robertson to Foreign Office, 2 May 1949: *ibid.*
73 Teleconference with Voorhees, 30 April 1949, The Clay Papers
74 Jessup in *Political Science Quarterly, op. cit.*
75 Secretary of State to Embassy in the UK, 30 April 1949: FRUS 1949 (II); Foreign Office to New York, 1 May 1949: FO 371 76587
76 Texts in FO 371 76588
77 Military Government Liaison Section Weekly Report No. 77 for the period up to 11 May 1949: FO 371 76703
78 Berlin to London, 11 May 1949; Robertson to Chuikov, 12 May 1949: FO 371 76551

14: Back to Normal?

1 Weekly report of the Food, Agriculture and Forestry Group, BICO, 6 May 1949: OMGUS FA 7/3
2 *The Times*, 12 and 14 May 1949; Military Government Liaison Section Weekly Report No. 78 for the period up to 18 May 1949: FO 371 76703
3 Acting US Military Governor to US Military Attaché in France, 8 June 1949: FRUS 1949 (II)
4 *The Times,* 16 May 1949
5 Assessments of Berlin mood in Military Government Liaison Section Weekly Report No. 76 for the period up to 4 May 1949: FO 371 36703; Weekly Political Summary, 10 May 1949: FO 371 76678
6 Details from *The Times*, 12 May 1949, and Berlin to Foreign Office, 13 May 1949: FO 371 76552
7 Details from Military Government Liaison Section Weekly Report No. 78, *op. cit.*; *The Times*, 19, 20 and 21 May 1949; Berlin to Foreign Office, 16 May 1949: FO 371 76553; Acting US Political Adviser to Secretary of State, 19 May 1949: FRUS 1949 (II)
8 Fortnightly Background Notes (FORD) No. 165, 23 June 1949: FO 371 76691
9 Military Government Liaison Section Weekly Report No. 80 for the period up to 2 June 1949: FO 371 76704
10 Chief of Staff Berlin to Foreign Office, 26 May 1949: AIR 2/10064
11 *Ibid.,* 27 May 1949
12 Memo to General Gruenther, 15 May 1949, The Clay Papers
13 US Delegation at CFM to Acting Secretary of State (Webb), 22 May 1949: FRUS 1949 (II)
14 Report to NSC by Acting Secretary of Defence, 1 June 1949: FRUS 1949 (II)

15 Report by Webb on meeting with the President, 31 May 1949: FRUS 1949 (II)
16 Details from Military Government Liaison Section Weekly Reports No. 71 for the period up to 31 March; No. 74 up to 21 April; No. 75 up to 27 April; No. 77 up to 11 May 1949: FO 371 76703; Acting Political Adviser to Secretary of State, 20 May 1949: FRUS 1949 (II)
17 Military Government Liaison Section Weekly Report No. 79 up to 26 May 1949: FO 371 76703
18 Berlin to Foreign Office, 23 May 1949: FO 371 76553
19 Department of the Army to US Military Attaché, Paris, 28 May 1949: FRUS 1949 (II)
20 Berlin to Foreign Office, 26 May 1949: FO 371 76554
21 *Ibid.*, 25 May 1949
22 Military Government Liaison Section Weekly Report No. 88 up to 2 June 1949: FO 371 76704
23 UK Delegation at CFM to Foreign Office, 2 June 1949: FO 371 76555
24 Acting Political Adviser to Secretary of State, 3 June 1949: FRUS 1949 (II)
25 Bourne to Robertson, 14 June 1949: FO 371 76556
26 Berlin to Foreign Office, 21 June 1949: *ibid.*
27 Secretary of State to Embassy in UK, 24 June 1949: FRUS 1949 (II)
28 Berlin to Foreign Office, 23 June 1949: FO 371 76556
29 *Ibid.*, 26 June 1949
30 Kirkpatrick, Parodi and Bruce at Quai d'Orsay meeting, 14 May 1949: FRUS 1949 (III)
31 For example, Foreign Ministers' meeting, 21 May 1949: FO 371 76593
32 Preparatory meeting, 18 May 1949: FO 371 76592
33 British Secretary of State to US Secretary of State, 10 May 1949: FRUS 1949 (III)
34 For example, 18 May preparatory meeting, *op. cit.*
35 For example, Kirkpatrick to Foreign Office, 17 May 1949: FO 371 76775; Secretary of State to Acting Secretary of State, 22 May 1949: FRUS 1949 (III)
36 For example, 14 May preparatory meeting: FRUS 1949 (III)
37 British Secretary of State to US Secretary of State, 10 May: *op. cit.*
38 Secretary of State to Embassy in UK, 11 May 1949: *ibid.*
39 Kennan, *op. cit.*
40 Memo by Ware Adams, 1949; memo by Ambassador at Large, 19 April 1949: FRUS 1949 (III)
41 Teleconference with Voorhees and Dorr, 5 May 1949, The Clay Papers
42 Secretary of Defence to Secretary of State, 14 May 1949: FRUS 1949 (III)
43 British Secretary of State to US Secretary of State, 13 May 1949: *ibid.*
44 Secretary to Embassy in UK, 11 May 1949: *ibid.*

45 Secretary of State to Acting Secretary of State, 22 May 1949: *ibid.*
46 Details in FRUS 1949 (III) and FO 371 76590/1/3
47 Bullock and Acheson, *op. cit.*
48 Details in FRUS 1949 (III) and FO 371 76775
49 Memo on conversation, 31 May 1949: FRUS
50 Details in FRUS 1949 (III) and FO 371 76778 and 76779
51 With report on Paris CFM, 6 June 1949: FO 371 767782
52 11 and 12 June 1949 reports: FO 371 76779 and 76780
53 Memo on talk to Smirnov and Semeonov, 6 June 1949: FRUS 1949 (III)
54 Record, 11 June 1949: FO 371 76780
55 Details in FO 371 76781
56 Acheson, *op. cit.* UK Delegation in Paris to Acting Secretary of State, 20 June 1949: FRUS 1949 (III)
57 Fortnightly Background Notes (FORD) No. 67, 21 July 1949: FO 371 76692
58 Military Government Liaison Section Weekly Report No. 93 up to 30 August 1949: FO 371 76704
59 *Ibid.*, No. 89 up to 3 August 1949
60 Details from *The Times*; Fortnightly Background Notes (FORD) No. 167, *op. cit.*; Military Government Liaison Section Weekly Report No. 85 up to 6 July 1949: FO 371 76704
61 FRUS 1949 (II)
62 Letter from Major-General K. G. McLean to Foreign Office, 9 August 1949: FO 371 76558
63 Robertson to Foreign Office, 25 September 1949: FO 371 76559
64 Weekly report from Food, Agriculture and Forestry, BICO, 24 June 1949: OMGUS FA 7/3
65 Bevin to Acheson, 13 June 1949: FO 371 76558; Acting Military Governor to Paris, 15 June 1949: FRUS 1949 (III)
66 *The Times,* 28 June and 4 July 1949
67 Berlin to Foreign Office, 14 July 1949: FO 371 76558
68 Report to NSC by Secretary of Defence, 25 July 1949: FRUS 1949 (II)
69 CAB 128, vol. 15; FRUS 1949 (II)
70 Minute written on Air Ministry advice, 24 May 1949: FO 371 76555
71 Bevin drafts, 21 and 24 October 1949: FO 371 76560
72 Appendix to Report on Financial Aid to Berlin, 18 June 1949: FO 1032/1628; Military Government Liaison Section Weekly Report No. 85 up to 6 July and No. 86 to 13 July 1949: FO 371 76704; Report by High Commissioners' Committee on Economic, Financial and Administrative Position of Berlin, 27 September 1949: FO 371 76560

Index

425

INDEX

INDEX

United States—*contd.*
draft surrender document, 10
and access to Berlin, 13, 18, 28, 31, 32, 34
dispute over transit to ports, 14
and reparations, 16
at Potsdam, 39
and German economy, 41
and Germany's political future, 42
policy in American zone, 58–9
mistrustful of Britain, 63
and food supply, 65, 66, 77
and Western Union, 97–8
evacuation plans, 111
common purpose with Britain, 119, 121
air transport facilities, 143, 144, 146–7, 150, 157, 165, 177, 211, 234, 238, 245, 266
plan to meet Stalin, 171, 173
pro-UN, 172
and currency, 302–3
and aircraft maintenance, 310, 311–12, 313, 314
and North Atlantic Treaty, 321
and Berlin's part in united Germany, 339
committed to military and financial assistance for Europe, 365–6, 378
military hostile to troop withdrawal, 368
US Air Force, 143, 146, 151, 177, 178, 182, 183, 185, 238, 246–52 *passim*, 261, 262, 266, 269, 309, 311, 313, 314, 374, 375
US Department of Commerce, 110
US Army, 28, 30, 31, 49
US Department of War, 7, 8, 33, 55
Civil Affairs Division (CAD), 8, 9, 12, 14
and JCS 1067, 56
and German economy, 57
US State Department, 55, 120–1
and projected dismemberment of Germany, 5
activities restricted, 7–8
proposed zonal boundaries, 9
and JCS 1067, 56
and General Marshall, 78
and UN, 163–4

and Moscow talks 1948, 215
complains to Kremlin, 226
wants to postpone City Assembly elections, 291
fails to persuade Clay to pass on Foreign Ministers' message, 350
and Jessup–Malik talks, 351
and Plan A, 368
US Treasury, 106
universities, 275–9
Unter den Linden, 180, 281
uprising (1953), 378
Utting, Captain, 316

Vandenberg, Arthur H., 1
Vandenberg, General Hoyt, 211
Vandenberg Resolution, 175
vegetables, 241, 259, 270, 282, 308, 357, 358, 372
Versailles, Treaty of (1919), 3
VFR (Visible Flight Rules), 247, 319
Vichy government, 51
Victims of Nazi Persecution, 293
Vienna, 13, 21
Virginia, University of (School of Military Government), 58
visas, and GDR, 378
vitamin supplements, 241
Voice of America, 188
Volksrat, 363, 367
Vyshinsky, Andrei, 49, 216, 288, 289, 332–3, 334, 346, 347, 352, 353, 365, 366, 369–70, 371

wages, 218–19, 282, 300
increase in, 196
railwaymen's, 361–2, 363, 365
Magistrat unable to pay staff, 375–6
Wagner (head of Protection Police), 141, 222
Wallace, Henry, 120
Warsaw Declaration, 159–60, 170
Wartburg, 327
water supply, 144–5, 299, 334
water transport
in Berlin, 23
Rhine unnavigable, 43
access to Berlin, 48, 49, 134, 139, 147, 168

444

Ann Tusa met **John Tusa** when they were undergraduates at Cambridge University, and they married a year after graduating. She worked briefly in book publishing, and subsequently taught history on the secondary and college levels. John Tusa was born in Czechoslovakia and moved to England in 1939. He joined the BBC in 1960 as a staff producer specializing in international relations, later reported for "Newsnight," the network's nightly news broadcast, and in 1982 successfully started "Timewatch," a history magazine program. Named Journalist of the Year by the Royal Television Society the following year, he is currently managing director of external services for the BBC. The Tusas, who live in London with their two sons, are authors of *The Nuremberg Trial*, winner in 1985 of the American Bar Association's Silver Gavel Award.